RACISM IN THE UNITED STATES

Racism in the United States

Implications for the Helping Professions

Joshua Miller
Smith College School for Social Work

Ann Marie Garran
Smith College School for Social Work

THOMSON
™
BROOKS/COLE

Australia • Brazil • Canada • Mexico • Singapore • Spain
United Kingdom • United States

THOMSON

──── ✳ ────

BROOKS/COLE

Racism in the United States: Implications for the Helping Professions
Joshua Miller and Ann Marie Garran

Social Work Editor: Dan Alpert
Development Editor: Tangelique Williams
Assistant Editor: Ann Richards
Editorial Assistant: Stephanie Rue
Technology Project Manager: Julie Aquilar
Marketing Manager: Meghan McCullough
Marketing Communications Manager:
  Shemika Britt
Signing Representative: Lora Sandhusen
Project Manager, Editorial Production:
  Tanya Nigh
Creative Director: Rob Hugel

Art Director: Vernon Boes
Print Buyer: Nora Massuda
Permissions Editor: Roberta Broyer
Production Service: Sachin Sharma,
  ICC Macmillan Inc.
Copy Editor: Carolyn Acheson
Cover Designer: Lisa Langhoff
Cover Image: Altrendo Panoramic, Getty Images
Cover Printer: West Group
Compositor: ICC Macmillan Inc.
Printer: West Group

Thomson Higher Education
10 Davis Drive
Belmont, CA 94002-3098
USA

For more information about our products,
contact us at:
**Thomson Learning Academic Resource
Center
1-800-423-0563**
For permission to use material from this text
or product, submit a request online at
http://www.thomsonrights.com.
Any additional questions about permissions
can be submitted by e-mail to
thomsonrights@thomson.com.

Library of Congress Control Number:
2006908903

Student Edition:
ISBN-13: 978-0-495-00475-2
ISBN-10: 0-495-00475-8

This book is dedicated to our families, friends, colleagues, students, and all who came before us and will follow us in the struggle against racism.

With gratitude to Davina, Lucy,
Corina, and Sophie for their love and support.
J.M.

For Katherine, Jocelyn, Madison, and Brayden—
with love and hope for their future.
a.m.g.

BRIEF CONTENTS

Contents

CHAPTER 7

Intersectionality: Racism and Other Forms of Social Oppression   134

PREFACE

Racism has evolved as a persistent part of the human condition. Its obstinacy and intractability are frustrating and at times baffling. We live in a world in which most nations have signed United Nations declarations of human rights and claim to be democracies, yet racial and ethnic conflict abound. The United States cherishes its Constitution and Declaration of Independence. Abraham Lincoln is viewed as a great President and the Civil War as an important milestone in the march toward freedom and social justice for all. Surveys find that today the vast majority of Americans believe in civil rights for all citizens and that racial prejudice and discrimination are wrong. As this book amply illustrates, though, racism is profoundly entrenched in United States society, in many ways and forms.

Perhaps the complexity of racism is part of the problem. Racism is manifested and embedded in institutions, the economy, politically, socially and culturally, in social welfare policies, everyday practices, internalized stereotypes, interpersonal and intergroup relations, and public discourse. Despite efforts to eradicate it, racism has demonstrated a remarkable capacity to mutate and evolve, much as bacteria respond to antibiotics. Racism wreaks havoc in many lives—physically, economically, socially, and psychologically—while remaining virtually invisible to those with the privileges of whiteness. And it damages and dishonors those who benefit from racism, though many people are unaware of this. Racism divides and alienates people from one another, leaving emotional, psychological, and spiritual wounds. The magnitude and doggedness of racism can be demoralizing to those committed to ending it.

Many people do want to dismantle racism but do not know how. The helping professions—which include social work, psychology, counseling, nursing, medicine, education, and law—usually have codes of ethics that commit practitioners to cultural competence, nondiscrimination, and, in some instances, social justice. Helping professionals interact with millions of people, work in thousands of agencies and offices, and contribute to policy formation and enactment at many levels of society. They can make a real difference in the struggle against racism. They receive training about how to do their jobs, and anti-oppression and anti-racism material is part of the curriculum.

We have been anti-racism activists and educators for many years, working with individuals, families, organizations, and communities to dismantle racism. We have pursued our anti-racism work as a team, working alone, and in collaboration with many others throughout the United States. In co-teaching an anti-racism course for professional social workers for more than a decade, we were unable to find a text directed toward helping professionals that covered the entire spectrum of racism affecting helping professionals and their clients—which motivated us to produce this book.

Writing this book has posed a number of challenges. One is that racism is so deep and pernicious that we would have to cover many forms of racism. We could not concentrate only on racist stereotypes, or institutional racism, or interpersonal and intergroup racism. Knowledge of all forms of racism is relevant to helping professionals. Therefore, we had to place racism in a historical context and link it to other related forms of oppression, such as classism, sexism, and heterosexism. Thus, this book approaches racism comprehensively, with an emphasis on how helping professionals can respond.

Another challenge is that racism affects people in many different ways, ranging from those who endure it daily to those who do not experience it and often have little awareness of its pervasive and destructive reach. Workers and students in the helping professions have had very different experiences with racism and represent a range of racial and social identities, with very different levels of understanding and awareness about racism. We have attempted to write a book from which all helping professionals can benefit. We hope this book will engage those who are new to an exploration of racism while appealing to those who are engaged in anti-racism work already.

Race and *racism* are complex and disputed notions, with varying meanings that are historically situated. In Chapter 2 we explore different ways of understanding and conceptualizing these concepts and conclude that race is a social construction. All social constructions involve the use of language in ways that reflect social positioning, power, conflict, and contested meanings. These terms shift over time and are interrogated, challenged, and reworked. Thus, in this book we use many words to describe race and ethnicity—white, African American, black, people of color, Anglo, Latino, Hispanic, American Indian, Native American—which in many cases are not literally correct or even logically consistent, but they do reflect idioms and labels commonly used in public conversations about race and racism. We have, however, stayed away from two terms, Caucasian and minority. For us, Caucasian is a remnant of essentialist views of race, in which the world was misleadingly divided into biological races. We critique this position in Chapter 2. Although the term *minority* is used quite frequently in public discourses, for many people of color the term has embedded, or pejorative, meanings that imply "less than." Even when people of color are in the majority, as in a public school, they often are referred to by white teachers and administrators as "minorities."

Another challenge has been to strike the proper balance between understanding racism and sustaining hope. We cannot confront racism effectively without thoroughly appreciating its complexity. Yet we could easily be demoralized if we were to read only about the consequences of racism without addressing how to tackle it. The early chapters explore and map out the contours of racism, and the later chapters place greater emphasis on how to dismantle it.

At the end of each chapter are exercises to help readers explore racism and how it is manifested in their social world, as well as how they have internalized it. Learning about racism and how to challenge it must be experiential and affective, in addition to being cognitive. The exercises are geared toward action, as working against racism is in itself empowering.

We believe in many ways of knowing and understanding, and we value multiple and different perspectives. Still, we have a clear and constant bias: We are against racism in all of its manifestations and conceive of this book as an act of resistance to racism. Although we have tried to understand empathically how people are inducted into a social and psychological racial calculus, we stand firmly against racism, and the ultimate purpose of this text is to help readers further their own anti-racism work.

During our years of anti-racism activism, we have had many mentors, teachers, colleagues, compadres, and students. We have attempted to give credit to anyone who contributed specific ideas used in this book, but much of our own thinking has been forged in collaboration with those with whom we teach, as well as our students; they have evolved collectively. So, although we are listed as the authors of this book, there are many, many people who have participated in constructing its concepts, devising the exercises, and whose voices are woven into the book's narrative fabric. In this spirit we encourage readers to take the ideas that are presented and to revise, rework, and integrate them into their own anti-racism work.

ACKNOWLEDGMENTS

We wish to express our gratitude to a number of people. The course we have taught is located at a school for social work that has made an explicit anti-racism commitment as part of its mission statement. Thus, we thank the entire faculty at the Smith College School for Social Work, as well as the deans present during this commitment: Ann Hartman, Susan Donner, Anita Lightburn, and Carolyn Jacobs. We also acknowledge the work of the chairs of the Human Behavior in the Social Environment sequence where the anti-racism course is lodged: Joan Berzoff, Joan Laird, Kathryn Basham, and Dennis Miehls. We also appreciate the financial support of the Clinical Research Institute of Smith College School for Social Work.

Since we began teaching this course, we have worked alongside many other anti-racism teachers at the Smith College School for Social Work, whose ideas and commitments have been inspirational: Beverly Tatum, Andrea Ayvazian, Elba Carballo, Orlando Isaza, Norma Akamatsu, Arlene Avakian, Frank Robinson, Helen Page, Darius Burton, Deborah Carlin, Alex Deschamps, Cynthia Gallagher, Andrea Canaan, Cheryl Stampley, Camille Hall, Lisa Werkmeister Rozas, Matt Ouellette, Edith Fraser, Johnnie Hamilton-Mason, Mary Gannon, Rani Varghese, Sheri Schmidt, John Orwat, Victor Mealy, Lois Bass, Ximena Zuniga, Mary Hall, Eve Bogdanove, Valerie Richards, Tim Wise, and Sarah Stearns.

While working on this project we submitted drafts of chapters to colleagues who provided us with constructive criticism and helpful advice: Matt Ouellette, Fred Newdom, Rani Varghese, Lisa Werkmeister Rozas, Edith Fraser, Peter Rose, Liz Keenan, Cheryl Stampley, Betty Ruth, Irene Rodriguez Martin, and Kimberlyn Leary. We also thank the hundreds of colleagues we have collaborated with in anti-racism work in agencies and communities throughout the United States.

Any reasonable manuscript requires a good editor, and we were blessed to work with Eileen Dunn. Additional editorial suggestions were made by our student Sandra Hall. We also received much technical and administrative support from Lisa DeCarolis, Irene Rodriguez Martin, and Nicole Kutcher. And we would like to thank our editors at Wadsworth Learning—Lisa Gebo, Alma Dea Michelena, Ann Richards—as well as our anonymous reviewers. Our production manager Sachin Sharma was very helpful, and we are grateful to Carolyn Acheson for her excellent copy editing, David Heath for his immense help with proofreading. Finally, we thank our family and friends for their support and forbearance while we worked on this project.

INTRODUCTION: RACISM IN THE UNITED STATES: IMPLICATIONS FOR THE HELPING PROFESSIONS

In a social service agency that offers clinical services to children and adults, a "multicultural task force" has been formed to ensure that the agency's clients, more than half of whom are people of color, receive "culturally sensitive" services. The task force consists of clinicians, administrators, and top-level managers. Although some people of color work as clinicians and in administrative positions, most of the staff members are white, as are all members of the senior management team.

Many of the people of color on the task force are frustrated because they believe the agency is riddled with racism, which negatively affects the working environment and the quality of services offered to clients. They are concerned that racism often is unconscious within the white staff and that many of those staff members' assumptions and biases result in the agency's being a predominantly white, Eurocentric workplace. Some people of color wonder whether the agency is truly interested in meaningful change.

Many of the white task force participants are frustrated, too. A few share the concerns of their colleagues of color, and others worry that too much emphasis has been placed on race and racism, which divides and categorizes people. Most of the staff members at the agency have liberal political views and are against discrimination of any kind, so even though they understand the importance of cultural sensitivity toward ethnic and racial "minorities," they are apprehensive about the task force's focus on racism. Some white members also question why more emphasis is not placed on other forms of discrimination and oppression, such as sexism, heterosexism, and ableism.

The conversations in the task force are quite strained at times, with heated confrontations, even expressions of rage and anger. Participants have accused each other of being racist. Feelings have been bruised, and a number of people have become mistrustful and wary of those in the group. They are wondering about how much more to invest and risk in this project. Some are concerned that their views may not be considered "politically correct," and they fear being misjudged and attacked. Others are wary of participants' making racist and stereotypical statements in meetings without acknowledgement or self-reflection. One participant says, "I'm a white male, so no matter what I say, I can't win." Another member thinks, "Will he ever get in touch with how much privilege he has every day, which I can never take for granted?"

For many helping professionals, this is an all-too-familiar experience, albeit well-intentioned. In our example here, an agency has at least tried to consider and discuss issues of culture and difference, in an attempt to better serve its clients. Yet the domain of what should be under consideration is contested, the assumptions about what is real and important are under dispute, and the very words used to discuss the topic (such as "racism") carry different meanings for the diverse participants, who have had different experiences of racial oppression, power, and privilege. Although they may share certain professional values and ethics, they do not necessarily agree in their worldviews. And no one stands above the fray. All participants are situated by virtue of their race, ethnicity, social identities, group memberships, and personal experiences.

This example offers a taste of the complexity of racism in human service organizations today, to illustrate how challenging, if not daunting, is the task of understanding, discussing, and working to overcome it. This is not unique to human service organizations. It is true of racism in the United States in general. As Charles Tilley (1998) has described, racism is an example of a "durable inequality"—emulated and adapted by social institutions and organizations, each a synecdoche for society at large.

Tackling racism is compounded by a lack of agreement about what exactly racism is. Racism has been equated with prejudice and bias. By this definition, anyone can be racist or a nonracist. Other definitions limit racism to egregious acts of discrimination and oppression, such as the separate facilities and water fountains of the pre-civil rights era in the southern United States, or acts perpetrated by overt racists, such as the racially motivated savage murder of James Byrd in Texas in 1998. Others view racism as a comprehensive system of privilege and oppression, with rights and privileges for members of some groups but not others.

Even when there is not *de jure* racism, differential access to resources and privileges by virtue of one's skin color, identity, or group membership reflects a racialized calculus. Social psychologists (Dovidio, Gaertner, Kawakami, & Hodson, 2002) have described "aversive racism" or the enacting of "racial micro-aggressions" (Pierce, Carew, Pierce-Gonzalez, & Wills, 1978; Solorzano, Ceja, & Yosso, 2000), both of which are beyond the consciousness of perpetrators, while wounding the targets of such interactions. We will cover these varied definitions of racism the Chapter 2, and we offer our own working definition, but we first wanted to illustrate how confounding it can be to even begin to think about racism.

WHY BOTHER?

Given the complexity and tenacity of racism, and the tremendous resistance (whether this be societal, institutional, group, or individual) to undoing it, why should we even attempt to dismantle it? We can offer many answers—first and foremost, that it is morally wrong and injures everyone, depriving all—perpetrators and beneficiaries alike—of their full humanity. Racism wounds and dehumanizes those who are targeted by it and morally compromises those who benefit from it. It also is illegal in the United States, although this certainly does not prevent it from occurring. Racism divides and alienates people, extracting an emotional cost and a social and economic one as well.

In our increasingly multiracial and multiethnic society, corporations lose hours of productivity and cooperative endeavor because of racism and racial tensions. Many lives are truncated and constrained by racism, reducing the contributions that individuals can make to society while incurring the costs of services or imprisonment. Cities become more dangerous and communities less cohesive as racism exacts its social toll. People voluntarily or involuntarily live in highly segregated neighborhoods, which increases social isolation, perpetuates social inequality, and decreases the capacity of citizens to collaborate and share across racial and ethnic lines. Still, most Americans would agree that racism is morally wrong and violates modern-day visions of fairness and justice.

We have written this book for another reason as well: Racism violates professional codes of ethics and compromises the capacity of human service professionals to help their clients and to uphold their professional ideals, including social justice. The American Psychological Association's (2002) *Ethical Principles of Psychologists and Code of Conduct* states in Principle D, "Justice," that "fairness and justice entitle all persons to access to and benefit from the contributions of psychology and to equal quality in the processes, procedures, and services being conducted by psychologists." Psychologists also are urged to ensure that their biases do not contribute to "unjust practices." The ethical standards further mandate, in paragraph 3.01, that psychologists not engage in discrimination, including by virtue of race.

The American School Counselor Association's (2004) *Ethical Standards for School Counselors* states that each student must have access to a school counseling program that affirms all students, whatever their race or ethnicity. The section on diversity (E.2) includes clauses about how racism affects counselors personally and professionally, including developing an awareness of cultural values and biases. Counselors are expected to achieve "cultural competence."

The most comprehensive professional statement about ethical obligations and social injustices, such as racism, comes from the *National Association of Social Workers Code of Ethics* (1999). In its Preamble, the code of ethics reminds social workers that the

> . . . primary mission of the social work profession is to enhance human well-being and help meet the basic human needs of all people, with particular attention to the needs and empowerment of people who are vulnerable, oppressed, and living in poverty.

This code also emphasizes the profession's commitment to social change and social justice. Social workers are expected to achieve "cultural competence" (1.05) and are expected to understand the nature of "social diversity and oppression" (1.05), with prominent mention of race and ethnicity.

Paradoxically, while belonging to professions dedicated to upholding ethics and values that are inconsistent with racism, human service professionals are part of a society structured by racism, serving clients who are either beneficiaries or targets of racism, working in agencies that reflect society's institutional racism and that employ practitioners who experience conscious, unconscious, and internalized racism when providing services. Practitioners are taught their professional skills in schools that are embedded in a racist society and reflect institutional racism by professors who are racially positioned in that society and who may or may not have explored the meaning of racism in their work.

Professions such as social work, too, are agents of social control and, as a result, unintentionally perpetuate racism despite codes of ethics to the contrary. For example, in working to prevent child abuse and neglect, social workers are participating in child welfare and juvenile justice systems that place children of color disproportionately in substitute care and in juvenile detention centers. When working in health and mental health arenas, social workers are part of a system that allows greater access to white consumers while disproportionately stigmatizing, misdiagnosing, and underserving clients of color.

OUR OBJECTIVE

Our purpose in writing this book is not to indict helping professionals, accuse individuals, or universally condemn society and its institutions. Nor do we want to instill a sense of hopelessness or a feeling that racism is so overwhelming, ubiquitous, and entrenched that nothing can be done about it. We believe that racism can be undermined, dismantled, and eventually overcome. We have witnessed societal gains (such as passage of the Civil Rights Act of 1964), worked with organizations that have made significant progress toward becoming anti-racism institutions, taught students who became more aware of their internalized stereotypes and internalized racism and worked actively to become allies in the struggle against racism. Counselors and clinicians have learned the skills needed to work effectively cross-culturally, and human service workers and social service agencies have contributed to coalitions working to address racism in the community.

Yes, we have ample ground for hope. But we also have learned that it is important not to minimize the complexity, obstinacy, persistence, and power of racism in society; its power to shape lives, create wounds, construct blindspots and rationalizations, and to divide and alienate people from themselves and from one another. We cannot challenge racism effectively while wearing rose-colored glasses, but neither can we succeed in confronting it without hope. As

Primo Levi (1982) described in his novel, *If Not Now, When?*, even when facing the most overwhelming and dismaying odds, to struggle on behalf of oneself and others is in itself the key to hope and survival; the actual act of resistance is an act of liberation.

Therefore, we intend to examine how racism exists outside of us, as well as inside of us, for we believe that health and human service workers must confront racism in both of these sites. We are ethically obligated to work for a society of fairness and social justice and to provide culturally responsive services to all of our clients, ensuring equal access and quality for all. We also recognize, however, the insufficiency of focusing solely on social structures, services, institutional practices, or on changing other people. We must look within and explore our own wounds, biases, and blindspots, as these surely will affect how we view ourselves and those whom we are committed to helping. Thus, in this book we will pursue both themes, analyzing the social and psychological dynamics of racism.

ORGANIZATION

Chapter 1 introduces the notion of social identity and explains how understanding ourselves—whatever our social identity—is essential in examining racism. In Chapter 2 we consider how racism is conceptualized and defined, as this influences perceptions of racism and how it is discussed, and has implications for professional practice, social action, and social welfare policies. This chapter clarifies the terminology, which include consideration of what "race" and "racism" are. We will draw on a body of scholarship known as "critical race theory," which emphasizes the historical, social, and political constructions of race and racism and how the "racial project" (Omi & Winant, 1994) is constantly shifting and evolving.

Chapter 3 places racism in the United States in a historical context. It considers the foundations of racism in this country from its inception and tracks the legal construction of race (Lopez, 1994, 1996) and how this has shaped the nation economically, politically, and socially. We link the treatment of ethnic and racial "minorities"—such as Native Americans, African Americans, Mexican Americans, Chinese Americans, and Japanese Americans—with domestic policies, as well as with the United States' international role, including its forays into colonialism and imperialism. By comparing the experiences of ethnic and racial groups "of color" with those of European-descended immigrants, such as the Irish, Italians, Ashkenazi Jews, and Armenians, we can examine how certain groups "became white" (Guglielmo & Salerno, 2003; Ignatiev, 1995; Sacks, 1996). Last, this chapter considers the historical formation of the helping professions and their relationship to the construction of race and racism in the United States.

Chapter 4 examines the "web of institutional racism" in the United States today—its various forms and how they interact and potentiate one another to form a matrix that allows some people to have access to opportunities and resources while blocking others from these life prospects. The chapter presents data illustrating the scope and incidence of institutional racism in this country and how some social policies sustain and reinforce racism while others challenge it.

Chapter 5 explores why many white people have difficulty recognizing, acknowledging, and responding to racism, despite its historical and contemporary ubiquity. We employ concepts such as "the racial contract" (Mills, 1997), "invisible white privilege" (McIntosh, 1989, 1992), and "the discourse of denigration and the creation of other" (Miller & Schamess, 2000) to examine how racism is masked, obfuscated, and excused, which can present cognitive challenges for those with race privilege.

Chapter 6 continues in this vein, expanding on the discussion begun in Chapter 1 and presenting and comparing theories of racial, ethnic, and social identity development. We link these concepts with theories about group membership and intergroup relationships and conflict. The chapter explores the impact of racial identity and group membership on clients and practitioners and offers a model of racial identity development for human service professionals.

Racism does not exist in a social vacuum. Racial identity is linked to other aspects of social identity, including gender, class, sexual orientation, citizenship status, and immigration experiences. The topics of Chapter 7 are the interaction and relationship between race and racism and other facets of social identity and forms of social oppression.

This leads to a consideration in Chapter 8 of why talking about race and racism is so difficult. We consider the importance of discussions about race and racism, the negative consequences of avoiding these conversations, what impedes them, and how to structure and facilitate racial dialogues. The chapter offers a model for talking about racial reconciliation and reparations (Yamamoto, 1999).

Chapter 9 shifts the focus to the dynamics of racism in communities and how human service professionals can intervene effectively. Chapter 10 continues this theme by examining organizational and agency racial dynamics and how human service workers can strive to create antiracism organizations.

Chapter 11 looks at how race and racism influence clinical work. The chapter begins by considering differential access to clinical services, unequal treatment of consumers, the use and misuse of power, and the mismatch between those who receive services and those who provide them. It covers issues such as client rage and "noncompliance," as well as clinician reactivity and defensiveness. We examine racial assumptions and biases in theories, as well as what is needed to become a culturally responsive clinician. Then we present a model of empowerment-based, culturally responsive clinical practice and offer implications for training and continuing education.

When it comes to understanding race and racism in society and within ourselves, we are all perpetual students and potential teachers. Thus, Chapter 12 offers suggestions for how to teach effectively about race and racism, whether this occurs in classrooms, agencies, or the community. It considers typical teaching problems and challenges and presents helpful pedagogical approaches and teaching techniques.

The final chapter, Chapter 13, is a call to action. We firmly believe that none of us can be neutral in a racialized society and that it is important that citizens—particularly those with race privilege—do not sit on the sidelines (Staub, 2001). Thus, we articulate a professional imperative for challenging racism and review the various ways by which people can work individually and collectively to dismantle racism, ranging from broad strategies to concrete and specific actions. Racism will not end without recognizing it and taking concerted actions to dismantle it. Helping professionals are ethically obligated to work toward this goal—and we have a great deal to contribute.

BACKGROUND: SOCIAL IDENTITY AND SITUATING OURSELVES

CHAPTER CONTENTS

1

Reading a book like this takes effort. It asks us to examine our society and also to examine ourselves in society. Even though racism in the United States affects us all, we will have a variety of individual reactions to this material. Some people of color reading this book may think they already know the content or may feel ambivalent about the pain that the content evokes. Some white people will experience resistance, denial, or powerful feelings of guilt and shame. Even the terms "white" or "people of color" (discussed in Chapter 2) are contested and can evoke varied, and at times powerful, reactions. Racism is not a neutral topic. It stirs up strong reactions and feelings in all of us. Yet, if we are to become competent helping professionals, we must take steps to confront racism as it is manifested in society, in our professions, and within ourselves.

None of us *is a bystander* in a society structured by racism. We either benefit from it or suffer the consequences of it, or, in some instances, we do both. When we say "benefit," we are referring to the unearned privileges that white people have in American society as a result of racism. But ultimately racism hurts and degrades us all, even those with race privilege. It undermines democracy and scapegoats and dehumanizes people, poisons the wells of interpersonal contact, fosters friction between groups, and causes people to doubt or feel badly about themselves or to unfairly condemn and degrade others. For those in the helping professions, racism undercuts their work with consumers and creates schisms among colleagues.

Pain, confusion, and strong emotions will accompany any serious examination of racism—particularly in a context that engages us personally and professionally and is not merely an analytic or academic endeavor. Fear of emotional pain can lead people to approach the subject of racism with wariness or detachment. In engaging in this work, we accept the risk of becoming vulnerable to being wounded along the way.

Because the spectrum of racism is vast, deep, and far-reaching, some readers may feel overwhelmed or resigned to it. These reactions are understandable, but we should keep in mind that racism has been challenged successfully, in the United States and elsewhere, and maintain the belief that all aspects of racism can be overcome someday. We cannot allow the complexity of racism to overpower us.

Racism is pervasive in the United States today, and helping professionals are obligated to work to dismantle racism and overcome its insidious effects. Ultimately, all human beings are entitled to equal rights, and we must visualize a nation in which all are validated and respected. To that aim, readers should strive to accept the strong reactions and feelings that this exploration is likely to engender. Profound feelings can be a source of motivation and inspiration for changing ourselves and our social world. As we confront racism and struggle to undermine it, we empower ourselves.

Ultimately, dismantling racism will benefit us all individually and will support a better society and nation collectively. In reading this book and working against racism, we also must acknowledge that each of us has had different experiences of racism and privilege. For some, this is a new area for consideration, and for others it has been a daily struggle throughout life. This book is for all helping professionals, regardless of race.

Some of the content is geared more toward one group or another. This is part of the challenge of writing and talking about race and racism. We come to the topic with a range of experiences. Some of us have been targets of racism and others have race privilege. Whether we identify as a person of color, white, biracial, or multiracial, or have a strong or weak ethnic identity, as individuals we resist being categorized or being subjected to assumptions that do not respect us as unique and intricate beings. At times, though, generalizations are needed when discussing race and racism. We also offer examples to illustrate specific points and concepts, and these should not be construed as conveying the dynamic, multidimensional complexity of people's lives and experiences.

When studying or discussing racism—including while reading this book—you may feel frustrated that your personal experience is overlooked. You should channel this frustration into continued learning and communicating and use the frustration as motivation for anti-racism activism, including offering feedback and contributing to teaching and leadership roles.

Ultimately, no one reading this book is responsible for the systemic racism that has hobbled our nation from its inception. As professionals and citizens, however, we are responsible for how we respond to racism today—in our own lives and in the lives of our clients. Thus, when learning about the nature of racism and counteracting the impact that racism has had on us, we should strike a balance between pushing ourselves to do more while also being gentle with ourselves and others. In any case, we must press ourselves past our comfort zone to our learning edge and be open to absorbing new content, skills, and insights about ourselves and society.

Racism has a long history and deep tentacles, and overcoming it will take time and persistence. We may learn and explore things about ourselves that we do not like, some of which will be unpleasant or even abhorrent. And we will encounter bias and prejudice in others. Although self-awareness and self-monitoring are important and critical to this process, excessive self-criticism can be detrimental. It can lead us to shut down or, if we are unduly impatient with others, cause them to shut down. This does not further the cause of anti-racism.

Beyond confronting ourselves and others and taking responsibility for what we say and do, we should work to develop patience and compassion for the struggle that anti-racism work involves. We are imperfect beings trying to be decent people doing good work. We will make mistakes. We may hurt people inadvertently or be hurt ourselves. At times, we may think we have regressed or feel more angry or confused than enlightened. All of these reactions are normal and predictable when undertaking a project as complex, challenging, and important as this one. Thus, a balance between pushing ourselves to do more and accepting our limitations is helpful in this work.

SOCIAL IDENTITY

Most of us want to be viewed as individuals and not placed in social categories or be typecast by others. We do not appreciate people making assumptions about who we are, particularly based on our appearance. This is part of what is so pernicious about racism: It stems from a social construction of race, a system of categorizing and generalizing about people based on physical characteristics and the alleged deeper meanings. We will consider this concept in greater detail in Chapter 2, but for now it is important to note the tension between the understandable wish to author our own identities and the social reality of how our identities can be assumed or even imposed by others.

When talking about race and racism, we do not want to be viewed solely as racial beings. We are far more complex than that. Our social identity has many facets—gender, social class, race, ethnicity, sexual orientation, religion—which together constitute who we are as social beings. Social identity is a useful construct as we approach the topic of race and racism. It helps us situate ourselves and be mindful of who we are in relation to students, colleagues, consumers, and others.

What is meant by social identity? This is a central topic in Chapters 6 and 7, but it is helpful to introduce the concept now so we can "situate" ourselves. Tajfel (1981) described social identity as that part of our self-concept that comes from our membership in social groups, the value we place on this membership, and what it means to us emotionally. For example, one of the authors identifies as white and Jewish and the other as Puerto Rican, Black, and a person of color. These are statements about our race and ethnicity. The first author is racially constructed as white, while he identifies himself ethnically as Jewish. The co-author identifies herself racially as a person of color and ethnically as Puerto Rican and African American.

Each of us has a range of feelings associated with these social categories. The statements about who we are also contain an assumption about another social category—gender—as one author is male and the other female. Although observers might be able to tell that one of us is white and male and the other is a person of color and female, they might not be able to discern that one of us is Jewish or one of us is part Puerto Rican. They also would not be able to say how we feel about our gender, ethnicity and race, unless we tell them. But, like it or not, people will be making assumptions about us when they see us, as this is a normal human response.

Tajfel's definition of social identity has been criticized for being too individualistic (Eriksen, 2001; Kelman, 2001). People do not always choose their social identities. Social identities emerge at certain times under specific conditions; they are shaped by social and cultural contexts, public discourses, national myths, and intergroup relations. For example, the meaning of being Jewish in Europe shifted before, during, and after World War II. A Jewish person who was no longer observant and whose ethnic or religious affiliation as a Jew had little or no personal meaning would have been defined as Jewish during the Nazi era, like it or not. In Rwanda, with its recent genocidal conflict, the meaning of being a Tutsi or a Hutu is woven inextricably into the relationships, perceptions, and history between the two ethnic groups. As we consider in Chapter 3, throughout U.S. history people have been granted privileges or have encountered barriers or overt oppression based on social constructions of their race.

Social identity is how we see ourselves in relation to others. It reflects two powerful social motives: our desire to be included and be part of a group, and at the same time our need for individuation and separateness (Brewer, 2001). This is how we internalize being part of our social world and influences how we position, align, and categorize ourselves, how we join with and individuate ourselves from others. It is the sense of self that we bring with us to work, to school, in public, at home—every environment and system that we are part of—although what we bring and share about ourselves varies considerably among cultures and depends upon social contexts. Some aspects of our social identity are self-selected, customized, and individualized. Others are collectively constructed, shared with others, and at times imposed.

SITUATING OURSELVES

Rather than talk abstractly about social identity, let us explore our social identities together. Figure 1.1 presents a diagram encompassing social identity: age, sexual identity, chosen interests, nationality, social class, economic status, gender, health status, religion, ethnicity, race, and political affiliation. Also, pieces of our identity reflect our personal history (such as growing up on a farm in South Carolina) and personal interests (such as amateur jazz musician). Already we can see how some of our social identity is chosen, some is inherited, other parts are imposed, and all aspects have meanings that are socially constructed. On the outer edge of the pie we have listed environmental factors that shape social identity: family, culture, institutions, political climate, economy, history, community, religion, and geography.

This might be a good time to draw your own social identity pie (see Exercise 1.1). If you do this exercise in class or in a group, it can be productive to discuss the questions listed in Exercise 1.1 in pairs. After thinking or talking about the questions, some of the following points might emerge:

- *Identity changes over time.* If we had drawn our pies 5 or 10 years ago, would they have looked the same as they do today? Probably not. Some aspects are enduring, and others have changed or shifted in importance. As we encounter new experiences and the world around us changes, our social identity evolves. It is dynamic, not a static part of ourselves. (We will consider phases of social identity development in Chapter 6.)
- *Some of our identity is chosen, some is imposed, and at times identity is a combination of the two.* We have choices over some parts of our social identity, but we receive other pieces from others and society. Also, there is a dynamic interaction between the parts that are imposed and the parts

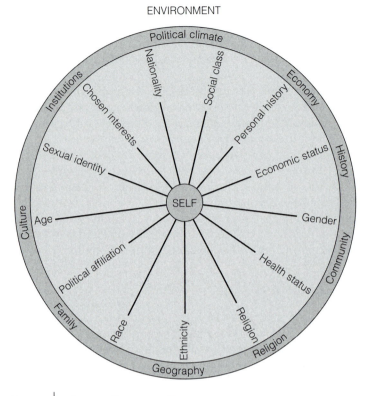

FIGURE 1.1 | SOCIAL IDENTITY PIE

that are chosen. Although our race may be socially constructed by society, the meaning we make of it is our choice.

- *Some of our identity is conscious, and other parts are unconscious.* We are always aware of some parts of our identity, and others we take for granted or think about only when we are doing an exercise such as this. It is useful to reflect on *why* we are so aware of some parts of our identity and unaware of others.

- *What is salient in our social identities differs among people.* For example, although my friend and I both may be female and African American and Puerto Rican, the meaning that either of these facets of our identity has for each of us may differ considerably. One of us may identify strongly with both of her ethnic heritages, and the other of us may identify only with one heritage and be identified most with being a lesbian.

- *What is salient in our social identities is influenced by context.* If a white man is in a classroom with a lot of other white men, he may not be conscious of his race or gender. If he is the only man in a class full of women, he is likely to be highly aware that he is male, or in a class where he is the only white person, very aware of his race. Eriksen (2001) offered the construct that social identity is relational, situational, and flexible.

- *Conflict and oppression can heighten our awareness of our social identity.* Social identities forged in conflict usually are salient, while those that are part of the mainstream or carry a lot of privilege are often less visible. (We will consider this dynamic in greater detail in Chapters 5, 6, and [7.)]

- *Social identity is co-created in micro relations.* Moffat and Miehls (1999) made the point that how we construct our social identity varies from relationship to relationship and from one interaction to another. The parts of self that emerge with an old friend may be very different from the parts that are prominent when meeting with a supervisor.

These points about social identity can be helpful to keep in mind when taking a course on racism, talking about racism in groups, or even reading a book like this. It is helpful to position ourselves, to think about our social identity, and to consider the social identities of people with whom we are interacting or reading about. We all have social identities, which vary considerably from person to person and have different significance and meaning for each individual. We must respect our diversity and appreciate our different experiences.

POWER, PRIVILEGE, AND SOCIAL IDENTITY

If diversity of social identity were only about difference, we would understand and appreciate one another more readily. But some aspects of our social identity carry social privileges and power while others are targeted or disparaged. One way to conceptualize this difference is the notion of agent and target (Hardiman & Jackson, 1997). *Agent status* denotes power, privilege, and the capacity to define and determine what is "normal." *Target status* means that social identity places a person with a group that is discriminated against, marginalized, and oppressed. Figure 1.2 illustrates which aspects of identity are privileged or oppressed, using an agent/target line. Agents (privileged) are shown above the line, and the targets are shown below the line.

Although the diagram presents agent and target status as dichotomous, they rarely are that clearcut. Some people of color have a great deal of target status because of their race (or skin color, hair texture, accent, or language) and are harassed and oppressed constantly. Others experience racism only occasionally. A multiracial person may experience both target and agent status at different times. Further, most people have social identities that are mixed, in which some aspects are targeted and others are privileged (Hardiman & Jackson, 1997). Some people with a similar mixture of target–agent status in their social identities feel privileged, and others in similar circumstances

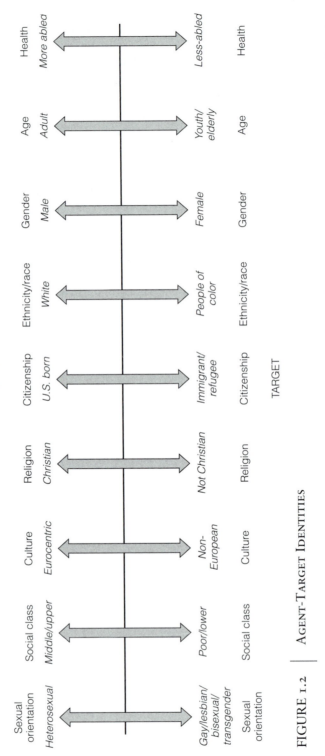

AGENT

Sexual orientation	Social class	Culture	Religion	Citizenship	Ethnicity/race	Gender	Age	Health
Heterosexual	*Middle/upper*	*Eurocentric*	*Christian*	*U.S. born*	*White*	*Male*	*Adult*	*More ablea*

Gay/lesbian/ bisexual/ transgender	*Poor/lower*	*Non-European*	*Not Christian*	*Immigrant/ refugee*	*People of color*	*Female*	*Youth/ elderly*	*Less-abled*
Sexual orientation	Social class	Culture	Religion	Citizenship	Ethnicity/race	Gender	Age	Health

TARGET

FIGURE 1.2 | AGENT-TARGET IDENTITIES

Source: "Conceptual Foundations for Social Justice Courses," by R. Hardiman and B.W. Jackson, in *Teaching for Diversity and Social Justice: A Sourcebook* (New York: Routledge, 1997), pp. 16–29.

consider themselves to be targeted. We cannot assume that we understand the meaning of another person's social identity.

Despite these caveats, it makes a huge difference whether a person's social identity is mostly privileged or is targeted. This explains why racism is much more profound than individual biases and prejudices (discussed in Chapter 2). Differences in social identity reflect differential social privilege, power, and access to resources. When talking about social identity and difference, these disparities always should be taken into account. It is not a level playing field of difference but, rather, a crater-pocked landscape of inequality. Those with the most privilege usually are the least aware of it, as culture and society mirror the centrality of these forms of status. People who have parts of their identity targeted find quite the opposite. This is one of the greatest challenges in talking about race and racism. For further work on social identity, see Exercise 1.3.

COMFORT ZONES, LEARNING EDGES, TRIGGERS, AND CREATING A CONTEXT FOR LEARNING

Certain concepts can assist us when we are trying to learn about racism and other forms of oppression, including the notions of comfort zones, learning edges, and triggers (Griffin, 1997). *Comfort zones* are the safe places from where we generally operate, where things are familiar and predictable, and where we feel most in control. If we stay inside our comfort zones, we have little impetus for change, we surround ourselves with the well known, and we do not challenge ourselves with new information or experiences. Moving too far away from our comfort zone can feel threatening and evoke a great deal of anxiety. This can lead us to withdraw or shut down.

Griffin (1997) suggests that the balance we should strive to achieve is our *learning edge*—that place where we are on the edge of our comfort zone—not so far out that we panic, but looking out at the world and taking small steps away from our safe place. At the learning edge we try to remain open to new perspectives, enhancing our awareness of self and others and ultimately learning new information that we can integrate into new understandings. We have achieved a balance between comfort and discomfort, stability and instability, having an anchor while allowing ourselves to sail into new waters.

As we move to our learning edge, we usually encounter some internal mine fields that can be activated by *triggers*: words, ideas, or statements that set off a strong emotional reaction (Griffin, 1997). Triggers often strike an emotional vein, either unconscious or conscious, that holds reservoirs of pain, frustration, confusion, guilt, or shame. We all have triggers and should not be alarmed by them. The key thing is to learn about what they are, recognize them when they arise, and learn to handle them rather than have them manage you. Exercise 1.2 offers some suggestions.

Identifying comfort zones, learning edges, and triggers requires self-reflection. It can be useful to identify what fears and hopes people have in group situations, such as when taking a course on racism or working in an agency exploring racism or a related topic. Identifying hopes and aspirations enables individuals to define and express their goals for the course, workshop, or discussion; indicates areas of convergence and divergence; and allows teachers and facilitators to clarify realistic goals for the group.

Expressing fears and concerns also is helpful, as this allows for venting anxiety, as well as providing an opportunity for members to collectively generate ideas for managing the group process effectively. It also can lead to suggestions and ideas about how to proceed if the group becomes stuck or if excessive conflict breaks out.

SETTING GUIDELINES

The group discussion can lead to a consensus about guidelines or norms for the group—which is why you may want to engage in the process early on. Guidelines help to create structure based on a group contract that supports the establishment of a learning culture and clarifies expectations. This, in turn, serves as a platform from which to explore racism. Helpful guidelines include

- maintaining confidentiality (only themes, not names, will be taken outside of the group),
- listening carefully,
- treating one another with respect,
- confronting without trying to shame,
- taking responsibility when making statements, and
- not having to represent one's racial/ethnic group.

Emerging norms will be unique to the group, and these are valuable to identify and practice. Having this discussion and allowing the norms to surface usually is a more successful approach than imposing a boilerplate set of norms. The group must take ownership of its guidelines and not view them as merely being the responsibility of the instructor or facilitator.

JOURNAL WRITING

Another way to further a group or classroom climate of authentic introspection is the use of journals. Dealing with racism evokes strong feelings, and classroom discussion can be supplemented by keeping journals. Sometimes feelings arise when reading a book or article, or a person may have a delayed reaction to something that came up in a workshop or class. The act of writing allows us to become more aware of our thoughts and feelings and to be able to reflect on what we find.

A journal also can represent a safer space to process difficult, confusing, embarrassing, and conflictual material. Trusted people, including instructors and others, might be invited to read the journals and offer comments and encouragement. Journal writers, of course, are not to be judged or evaluated for what they write. Journal writing must be done with an "anything goes" attitude.

CREATING A SAFE ENVIRONMENT

Often, people embarking on an exploration of race and racism will say they need to feel safe when processing difficult material. The suggestions presented here lend themselves to creating safer learning contexts that are conducive to learning and growth. As should be clear by now, learning about racism is not merely an academic enterprise. It combines substantive knowledge with self-awareness. This involves taking risks, moving out of our comfort zones, and being open to new experiences and to feedback.

Although the risk of hurt feelings or bruised self-esteem is always there, these reactions can spur growth and self-awareness. Ultimately we cannot learn about racism without taking some emotional risks, keeping in mind that the risks of exploring racism in a book or class are minor in comparison to the risks that racism poses to people of color day in and day out. Ultimately, exploring racism in a class can be beneficial to everyone, especially when this leads to action to dismantle racism.

CONCLUSION

This book and courses and workshops on racism and other issues of diversity are likely to engender strong emotional reactions, influenced and moderated by a sense of one's social identity. The following exercises can help in identifying and investigating aspects of social identity. Three relevant concepts are comfort zone, learning edge, and triggers. The learning environment should encourage openness to new information and experiences, appreciation of difference, recognition of differential social power and privilege, and self-awareness and examination.

The next three chapters will explore how racism is conceptualized, review the history of racism in the United States, and explore the manifestations of institutional racism today. Using the concepts and techniques presented in this chapter should provide a structure and foundation for engaging with this challenging material.

EXERCISE 1.1   SOCIAL IDENTITY

On a blank piece of paper, draw your own social identity pie. Look at the pie presented in this chapter and think about which parts are relevant to you. You might draw certain pieces of your pie as being very big and others very small. Some pieces of the pie in this chapter may not be relevant for you, or some aspects of your social identity may be missing. You may want to draw your pie to reflect these differences. Draw your pie in whatever shape, with whatever contents and in whatever proportions, best describes you.

Either on your own or in pairs, consider the following questions:

1. Which parts of your social identity are most important and meaningful for you and why?
2. Which parts are apparent to others and which are more hidden?
3. Which parts did you consciously choose and which parts do you feel were imposed upon you?
4. Which parts of your identity give you the greatest source of pride and satisfaction?
5. Which parts of your identity cause the most confusion or ambivalence?
6. When you are in classes or at work, which parts of your identity come to life and which parts are in the background?
7. Do you ever have to monitor whether you present or hide certain parts of your identity?

EXERCISE 1.2   EXPLORING TRIGGERS

This exercise can be done in pairs, in small groups, or individually.

1. *When discussing race and racism,* what triggers you?
2. What triggers you?
3. What responses are most typical for you when you are triggered?
4. What gets you stirred up for you when you are triggered?
5. What do you find helps you or works for you when you are triggered?
6. What guidelines for classroom discussion would you find helpful?

EXERCISE 1.3   RACIAL IDENTITY FORMATION

This exercise should be done in pairs, with each member of the pair interviewing the other.

1. When did you first become aware of your race and ethnicity?
2. Did any "critical incidents" shape your awareness of your identity?
3. How has your racial or ethnic identity affected your life?
4. How does your racial or ethnic identity intersect with other aspects of your identity?
5. In what ways are you targeted? In what ways are you privileged? How do these different aspects of your identity interact?

After conducting the interview, write it up or discuss it in class. Consider how your partner's experience with racial identity formation is similar to or different from yours. What did you learn about your partner and yourself? In what ways are you similar and different?

WHAT IS RACISM?

CHAPTER CONTENTS

In a class on racism in a graduate school for social workers, students are asked to define themselves racially and ethnically. A white male student from a predominantly white suburb in the Midwestern United States responds: "I think of myself as an American. I treat everyone the same, and don't like to see race. I don't care if you're black, brown, red, orange, or purple. People are people!"

An African American woman from Los Angeles responds: "I'm Black, African American, part Cherokee Indian. All of my life I've been defined by my race. I'm proud of who I am. When you say you don't see race, you don't see me. It's as if you're telling me to be White, which is racist."

The first student responds, somewhat defensively: "This is what I hate about all of this focus on race and racism. People misjudge me and distort what I say, and before I know it, I'm called a 'racist.'"

A white Jewish woman from Boston adds: "I'm not White, I'm Jewish. I have never felt 'White.'"

A Chicana woman from south Texas responds passionately: "You're a racist! All White people are racists, because you don't even know that you have a race and that your race gives you thousands of privileges I never get!"

The class attendees shift in their seats, and an uneasy silence descends on the class.

This vignette is similar to discussions that have taken place in virtually every class about racism that we have taught. It illustrates the difficulty in talking about race and racism, and also reveals the lack of clarity about race and racism and the different perspectives about the salience of these concepts for people today. The conversation also raises questions about the similarities and differences between race and ethnicity and the experiences of people of color and white people, including those who view themselves as neither white nor people of color.

Sources of the tension and confusion are complex and very real for the participants. We also could have added that some people in the class consider themselves to be biracial, or multiracial, or multiethnic. They might think that the discussion was encouraging them to define themselves narrowly, and that they were being pressured to make choices that privileged one aspect of their identity while denying, even sacrificing, another. Others might say that neither race nor ethnicity is important to them; they are more concerned with their gender or sexual orientation. Some might think the discussion about race is misguided, as inequality and oppression are really about social and economic class.

What is racism? Is it feeling and thinking with prejudice and bias, or is it something much bigger? If someone treats everyone the same, is he or she not a racist? Or are all people from a social category racist? Can only white people be racists, or can anyone be a racist? Is racism active, or can it also be passive? We will respond to these questions in this chapter.

In Chapter 6 we will consider the complexities of racial and ethnic identity and how this intersects with other aspects of social identity, such as nationality, gender, class, and sexual orientation. And in Chapter 8 we will consider the challenges of talking about race and racism and suggest strategies for making these conversations more meaningful and productive. We will compare the historical experiences of people from Europe and those of other parts of the world in Chapter 3. Here, in this chapter, we will explore concepts, theories, and definitions about what race and racism are.

HOW RACE AND RACISM HAVE BEEN CONCEPTUALIZED

In 1999, the American Anthropological Association (AAA, 1998) published a statement about race that its executive board had adopted previously. The board explained that the statement did not have a consensus but that it was representative of current scholarly thinking by anthropologists about race. The conclusion was that race is not a legitimate biological or genetic construct; rather, it is an ideology used to justify the domination of one identifiable group of people by another—a rationale that has supported many forms of oppression, including genocide, slavery, ethnic cleansing, colonialism, and other forms of domination, mistreatment, and resource and opportunity hoarding.

Even people who do not believe in the innate superiority or inferiority of "racial" groups often assumed that there were distinct races: Caucasian, Negroid, and Mongoloid. Even though these terms are used rarely, the assumptions about discrete racial groups lingers. Today, the census continues to classify people by race. Yet, the American Anthropological Association stated:

> Human populations are not unambiguous, clearly demarcated, biologically distinct groups. Evidence from the analysis of genetics (e.g., DNA) indicates that there is greater variation within racial groups than between them. . . . Throughout history whenever different groups have come into contact, they have interbred. The continued sharing of genetic material has maintained all of humankind as a single species. (AAA, 1999, p. 712)

Thinking of all of humankind as a single species certainly is not how race has been conceptualized, particularly in the Western world. And it certainly does not mesh with how "racial" groups have been treated historically in the United States and many other parts of the world today.

So how did the notion of distinct races occur, and why did this conceptualization lead to a legacy of racism? This huge question has occupied many historians, anthropologists, sociologists, and psychologists, as well as politicians and citizens. It is such a complex question that it may never be answered completely, and certainly will always be contested. Further, it is not as if anyone who is studying or writing about this subject has a completely "objective" vantage point, because in a racialized society and world, everyone is racially situated. Therefore, all those who write about race and racism must share their assumptions, values, and biases.

What we will do here is explain some of the more prevalent theories about race and racism and how these came to be, and then describe the concepts and terms used in this book. We already have situated ourselves racially and ethnically. Our position, which follows, is that *race* is a social construction, and *racism* is a very real, multifaceted, historical, and contemporary force. We also believe strongly that ending racism is a moral, ethical, political, and social imperative. We have been guided in our research, work, and teaching by a body of scholarship known as "critical race theory," which we will describe as well.

HISTORICAL UNDERPINNINGS

The historian George Fredrickson, who has spent his career writing about race and racism, traced how racism was linked initially with religious intolerance in Europe (Fredrickson, 2002). Unlike religious bigotry, however, which always held the potential for people to be accepted if they were to change their faith, racism relies on an essentialist, fixed, unchanging view of human beings.

Fredrickson writes that some of the first stirrings of modern racism were in the Iberian Peninsula in the 15th and 16th centuries. During that time, the Spanish, while battling the Moors, conceptualized Jews as having "impure" blood. Along with the Portuguese, the Spanish were beginning to explore Africa and the Americas (Diamond, 1997). This led to Europeans having much more contact with Native American Indians in North America and with Africans in Africa who subsequently were enslaved systematically and shipped to North America.

In turn, this served as an economic underpinning for European colonization of the Americas, and later Africa and other parts of the world. This condition created a racially oppressive social structure, requiring a legitimizing rationale.

THE WESTERN CONCEPT OF RACE

The modern Western concept of race had its roots in these seismic historical dislocations and collisions but received a conceptual frame, buttressing the exploitation of distinct groups of people, from the European enlightenment. The Enlightenment viewed human beings as having descended from animals rather than as being children of God (Fredrickson, 2002). It also was a time of classification, of "scientifically" ordering the world, as well as establishing cultural and aesthetic norms.

All of this led to categorizing people into races, as well as to privileging the white (or Caucasian) race as being the most intelligent and having the highest standards of beauty, culture, and conduct. As Fredrickson has pointed out, this coalescing of European thinking about race had the ironic effect of serving as a foundation for the biological determinism and scientific Darwinism of the 19th century while also articulating ideals of equality and justice, which would be used later to question and undermine the rationale for racism.

Certain groups of people do have clear physical differences—such as skin tone, hair color and texture, and facial features. Nevertheless, the genetic evidence cited by the American Anthropological Association and others is that there is far greater genetic variation *within* "racial" groups than *between* them.

Genetic researchers estimate that 88% to 90% of genetic variation occurs within local populations, whereas only 10% to 12% is between populations (Angier, 2000). Much of the perceived variation between races resulted from migration and adaptations to increase survival in a specific region, such as having darker skin in sunnier areas (Angier, 2000; Begley 1995; Diamond, 1997).

Although the conclusions of geneticists and other scientists are not unanimous, the consensus is that all human beings descend from the same original ancestors and that we are all, ultimately, of the same race (Angier, 2000; Begley, 1995; Cartmill, 1999). Lopez (1994) concluded that

> the idea that there exist three races, and that these races are "Caucasoid," "Negroid," and "Mongoloid" is rooted in the European imagination of the Middle Ages. . . . (p. 13)

Perhaps during some periods of human existence, there was little commingle of distinct human groups, but this has not been the case for many hundreds of years. In the United States, all "races" have coexisted and interbred for centuries. Or, as Cartmill (1999) stated:

> If races are defined as geographically delimited conspecific populations characterized by distinctive regional phenotypes, then human races do not exist now and have not existed for centuries. (p. 651)

Yet, the concept of race, both scientific and cultural, has been used ever since the inception of the United States to justify severe exploitation and terrible economic and social inequalities. Dehumanization and racial denigration served to rationalize the murder and slaughter of American Indians, enslavement of African Americans, dispossession and loss of rights of Mexican Americans, exclusion of Chinese and Japanese immigrants, and pogroms against many of the above-mentioned groups (Miller & Schamess, 2000; Takaki, 1993). The wedding of racial essentialism, racism, and social Darwinism led to further justifications for social and economic exclusion, as well as to pathologizing the cultures and mental health of groups considered to be "inferior" (Jansson, 2005; Rollock & Gordon, 2000, Steinberg, 2001).

Sadly, social Darwinist tracts, although widely discredited, still survive today. An example is Herrnstein and Murray's (1994) book, *The Bell Curve: Intelligence and Class Structure in American Life,* which explains social inequality by virtue of genetic differences in intelligence (Taylor, 1997). The concept of race does not exist or make sense without considering the dynamics of racism. We now will consider some principal theories about the nature of racism and its relationship to the construct of race.

THEORIES ABOUT RACISM

A multitude of theories conceptualize racism and race. For the sake of organizational simplicity, we will group them here into the following metacategories: ethnicity theories, race relations theories, psychological theories (including theories of prejudice and disease theories), and structural theories (including neo-colonial, Marxist, and opportunity theories). We then will discuss in greater detail critical race theory, which is the theoretical framework for this book.

One of the conceptual fault lines that runs through most of the literature about racism and race, and which seems to defy theoretical categories, is whether the problem is conceived of in binary or multiracial terms. Scholars advocating the binary concept tend to examine racism as a black/white problem, using concepts and data that separate race and racism into these two categories. Multiracialists view race and racism as being part of a larger prism, with many racial and ethnic groups and a meaning of race historically that is continually shifting, fluid, contested, and contextual (Omi, 2001; Omi & Winant, 1994; Winant, 1997, 1998).

Ethnicity Theories

What unites the ethnicity theorists is their belief that racism should be seen as a form of ethnocentrism, which can occur in any ethnic group and can lead to conflict or oppression with any other ethnic group. Race is viewed as only one facet of a group's ethnic identity (Omi & Winant, 1994). This theory also emphasizes a group's immigration experience, how rapidly or slowly members of this group assimilate into mainstream U.S. society and the cultural capital they carry and have generated, and how well this assists the group in moving forward socially and economically. In keeping with this theory, Chinese Americans, African Americans, and American Indians are viewed as ethnic groups, as are Jewish Americans, Italian Americans, and Irish Americans, all with their unique histories of oppression, adaptation, survival, and success.

Some of the key scholars within this prototype are Daniel Patrick Moynihan and Nathan Glazer. who co-authored *Beyond the Melting Pot* (Glazer & Moynihan,1963); Milton Gordon (1964); and Gunnar Myrdal (1962). One of the achievements of this movement was to shift the predominant racial discourse away from biological determinism to a consideration of cultural pluralism and assimilation (Omi & Winant, 1994). This theory does not place a great deal of emphasis on power and opportunity; rather, the focus is on cultural differences and the degree of fit with Anglo-American culture (Feagin & Feagin, 1994).

Ethnicity theories fit well with a liberal conception of democracy, in which everyone should be afforded equal rights and opportunities. Thus, ethnicity theorists supported the Civil Rights movements of the 1950s and 1960s, concerned that ethnic groups such as African Americans were being denied full participation in American society, including the capacity to assimilate. They advocated removing legal and institutional barriers and were for equal opportunity (Omi & Winant, 1994).

The ethnicity paradigm has contributed to the discourse on race and racism by elevating the focus from biological determinism to a consideration of culture, values, beliefs, and worldviews. The backing of civil rights and equal opportunity helped to articulate a post-War consensus in much of the United

States that overt discrimination, racism, enforced segregation, and other forms of racial exclusion and bigotry were wrong and socially destructive. The casting of racial groups in an ethnic framework illuminated the ethnic dimensions of those groups: the importance and structure of family ties, religious meanings, linguistic styles, worldviews, customs, and practices.

The ethnic group paradigm has received a great deal of criticism, which over the past 30 years has been seen as a limited and conservative way of understanding racism. A major critique is that viewing people of color as similar to white ethnic groups does not allow for the level of oppression, exploitation, and exclusion that people of color have experienced in the United States (Feagin & Feagin, 1994; Omi & Winant, 1994; Steinberg, 2001). Genocide, slavery, loss of legal rights, and legal exclusion are qualitatively different experiences from facing discrimination, stereotypes, de-facto quotas, and living in a poor neighborhood for one or two generations. Racism is not the same as ethnic discrimination; the former is more systematic, entrenched, and insidious. To equate it with the negative experiences of some white ethnic groups minimizes its potency.

Another criticism of this model is that it considers Eurocentric, Anglo-American culture as the norm, and that assimilation into this culture is a goal. If a group resists assimilation, the implication is that its members are not embracing this country and is erecting barriers to their own success and achievement. In general, this paradigm tends to center on the group's own agency and responsibility for its success or failure, neglecting an analysis of power and structural barriers that oppress and limit the opportunities of people of color. The emphasis is more on culture, and which cultural traits lead to social and economic success and which inhibit a group's advancement.

This stance tends to neglect an examination of the advantages that some ethnic groups have in capital, skills, connections, and power and raises the question: Does culture breed success, or does success shape culture? An associated risk is that the alleged cultural superiority of one group becomes reified in a similar way to biological justifications of racial oppression.

Also, a racial grouping (e.g., black) may subsume many ethnic groups (e.g., African Americans, Haitian Americans, Jamaican Americans), which is quite different from a white ethnic group (such as Irish Americans) (Omi & Winant, 1994). Ethnic theories on their own are unable to explain the advantages or disadvantages associated with skin color, or the phenomenon of white privilege (considered in greater detail in Chapter 5). Now we turn to some theories that, along with ethnic theories, examine more fully the ideas that form the underpinnings of race superiority and race relations.

RACE RELATIONS THEORIES

The 1950s through the 1970s saw a burgeoning sociological literature about ethnic and race relations (Berry, 1958; Blalock, 1967; Epps, 1973; Kinloch, 1974, 1979; McDonagh & Richards, 1953; Segal, 1966; Simpson & Yinger, 1953; Vander Zanden, 1963). Race relations theories form a broad category that encompasses many different perspectives. Some are aligned with ethnicity theorists, others focus on prejudice, and still others consider structural factors that shape race relations. What they have in common is that they recast racism as race relations. The conceptualization and concentration of study is how different ethnic and racial groups interact with one another.

Questions that are considered include the initial contact situation between groups; how groups interact and the role of prejudice and discrimination; and the dynamics of conflict, cooperation, and competition between groups. One of the conceptual advantages of this approach is that it goes beyond viewing racism as an individual problem of prejudice or discrimination and recognizes that people have group memberships and statuses that transcend their personal situations.

These theories usually conceptualize racism in terms of majority–minority group relations; however, the definitions of majority and minority are contested. Are Jews of European descent a minority group because of their religious and cultural status, or are they a majority group by virtue of white privilege? If a group is numerically superior, yet its members are neither white nor of European descent, do they still constitute a minority group? Does the term "minority" imply less-than, and, if so, does this mean that this group always will be viewed as existing peripherally to some assumed center or normative mainstream? Are members of minority groups "minorities"? This may burden individuals with a negative identity and can foster a sense of marginalization and alienation.

In addition to these questions are concerns that the term "race relations" does not adequately describe the institutional, political, and legal basis of racism. The race relations paradigm can focus on relationships between two or more ethnic and racial groups, without acknowledging the power arrangements that shape the interactions. Prejudice and discrimination can be seen as qualities of majority and minority groups. This lends itself to viewing racism as a reflection of group attitudes and behaviors, minimizing social context. Within this framework, any group potentially can subjugate or discriminate against another group. Despite the way the concept of race and the dynamics of racism have shifted over time, there has been a pattern of enduring inequalities, which constructs privileged people as "white" and disadvantaged people as "people of color."

THEORIES OF PREJUDICE

After World War II, psychologists and social scientists became more interested in understanding the nature of prejudice. Prejudice was defined as

> . . . the holding of derogatory social attitudes or cognitive beliefs, the expression of negative affect, or the display of hostile or discriminatory behaviour towards members of a group because of their membership in that group. (Brown, 1995, p. 8)

If prejudice could be understood, perhaps the roots of virulent racism and anti-racism would be exposed. How could the Jewish Holocaust have happened?

How do ordinary people become complicit in such irrational, hostile, and destructive social movements? What underlying psychological dynamics were at play to explain American racism and anti-Semitism? These were some of the questions that sparked the theory, and research was directed to the psychological aspects of racism and the social psychology of intergroup relations. Freudian and neo-Freudian concepts were employed to further this understanding.

EARLY RESEARCH Some of the most notable scholars in this tradition were Gordon Allport, Theodor Adorno and his research associates, and Ashley Montagu. They concentrated particularly on prejudice; psychological mechanisms that fueled prejudice, identity, and personality; and how all of this influenced group membership and intergroup dynamics. Allport's (1954) book, *The Nature of Prejudice,* still is regarded as a classic and has spawned much research on psychological facets of racism. Allport's (1948, 1954) work considers drives, attitudes, feelings, and defense mechanisms and how these contribute to stereotypes, prejudice, and discrimination.

This led to articulating the concepts of in-group (where a person sees commonality and sameness) and out-group (where a person perceives difference and possible threat). In addition to psychodynamic theory, learning theory was applied to explore the mechanisms by which prejudice was learned and transmitted.

Adorno and his associates (1950) also were interested in the concept of "in" and "out" groups. From their research, they concluded that a certain character type, an "authoritarian personality," predisposes people to prejudicial beliefs and behaviors. Utilizing Freudian concepts, they described how family socialization, particularly harsh discipline, leads to displaced aggression toward members of out-groups. Part of this dynamic is a predilection for ethnocentrism (inordinately favoring and elevating one's in-group) and the tendency to generalize about negative attributes of out-groups.

Building on these insights, Montagu (1965) described character traits, such as weak identity and sensitivity to social injury, that predispose people to display prejudice and participate in discrimination. These character traits, coupled with repressed anxiety and displaced aggression, lead to submerging one's identity in groups that are hostile to other groups and engage in racist or anti-Semitic beliefs and actions. Kovel (1970, 2001) also used psychoanalytic theory to describe the psychological need of whites to pinpoint a group—people of color—to view as inferior and feel aversion to, including projecting socially unacceptable drives and bodily functions on them.

RECENT SCHOLARSHIP A more recent manifestation of the search to understand the psychological mechanisms of racism is to think of it as a disease or addiction (Skillings & Dobbins, 1991; Dobbins & Skillings, 2000). This approach explains how white people are infected with racism and become addicted to white privilege. Surrounded by white privilege and Eurocentric biases that seem to be normative and ubiquitous, whites develop cognitive distortions about the nature of the world and their place in it.

Some have criticized the metaphors of disease and addiction as explanations for racism. Medicalizing racism has its risks: It depoliticizes racism, depicts it as aberrant rather than normative, and implies the need for psychological and/or medical responses rather than social action (Wellman, 2000).

Defense mechanisms, such as denial and rationalization, help whites to sustain illusions, such as the belief that society is fair for all, or that racism is a thing of the past (Miller & Schamess, 2000). When confronted with realities that challenge assumptions such as these, some whites feel guilt and shame.

Psychological theories of prejudice and racism have offered important insights and opened illuminating windows. It is important to discern the psychological genesis of racism and to map how it is internalized, managed (or mismanaged), and projected on to the world as a template. Extrapolating these insights to examine how people identify with groups and how identity, drives, impulses, and feelings become part of the fabric of intragroup cooperation and intergroup tensions has offered fertile seams of research and wisdom for social psychologists, anthropologists, political scientists, and other scholars.

MODIFYING STEREOTYPES Stemming from the study of prejudice, excellent research has been undertaken about the nature of stereotypes and how to modify them. This framework sheds light on how prejudice and stereotypes become mechanisms that help white Americans rationalize their position of privilege and disparage people of color, blaming people of color, rather than racism, for their own racial oppression (Feagin & Feagin, 1999; Miller & Schamess, 2000). Any understanding of racism is incomplete without an appreciation for its psychological dimensions, and we shall consider this in depth in subsequent chapters.

Still, this approach is incomplete, and by itself is insufficient to grasp the scope of racism in the world today. Racism is much more than the sum of individual prejudices and attitudes; it is systemic, institutional, and sustained by a collective discourse of privilege and denigration (Miller & Schamess, 2000). Is the mistrust that blacks feel toward whites, after repeated negative encounters, the same as the prejudice that many whites feel toward blacks, some of it conscious, some of it below the surface of cognition? We think not, but reducing racism to simply being a form of prejudice can open up such disparate comparisons.

In their consideration of prejudice, many believe that, although the imbalance of power and the differential lack of opportunity and access for people of color—essential components of racism—are included, prejudice is not adequately emphasized or fleshed out because the locus of examination is the individual and the group. Also, questions have been raised about the role of social conformity (Brown, 1995): Is prejudice solely a function of personality, frustrated drives, and family upbringing, or does it have a strong element of trying to fit with prevailing social norms? Otherwise, how can we account for the rise and fall of public expressions of prejudice and intolerance and the differences both across and within societies?

STRUCTURAL THEORIES OF RACISM

The structural theory metacategory encompasses a diverse range of conceptual traditions in the study of racism:

- internal colonization,
- Marxist theories of class and racism,
- split labor-market theories,
- economic and social opportunity theories, and
- power and group conflict theories.

Although they have different points of emphasis and, in some instances, challenge one another, they also overlap and share some common assumptions. We will describe these subsets only briefly but first want to highlight what most of them share and how this distinguishes them from the theories mentioned thus far:

- Racism is more than the sum of individual or group prejudices. Historical, sociological, political, and economic analyses identify racism as being pervasive, thorough, systemic, and institutional.
- Like all "durable inequalities" (Tilly, 1998), racism involves "exploitation" and "resource hoarding" by privileged groups—in this instance, whites at the expense of people of color.
- This leads to widely divergent opportunities for white people and for people of color, with people of color having less access to jobs (particularly well-paying jobs), a range of residential neighborhoods, quality schools, political office, and other positions of power and influence in society.
- The experience of people of color is qualitatively different from that of white ethnic groups in the United States. Racism and racial oppression are more than merely ethnocentrism and discrimination.

The internal colonialism model compares the experience of racial minorities in the United States with those of colonized, non-European peoples. In both instances, people of European heritage are in positions of power and privilege relative to indigenous peoples in colonies or people of color at home. Whites maintain an economic advantage by exploiting the labor of people who have limited economic options and, therefore, are coerced into working for low wages (Blauner, 1969; Feagin & Feagin, 1994), often accompanied by social isolation and cultural stigmatization. Those who are oppressed are forced into having contact with their oppressors, indigenous culture is decimated as part of the process of suppression and subjugation, and racism ultimately is employed as an ideology to justify it (Blauner, 1969).

ECONOMIC AND CLASS ISSUES   Other structural theorists emphasize economic and class issues (Omi & Winant, 1994). Racism is viewed not as a central, independent social process but, rather, as an outgrowth of capitalism and a complicating factor in the exploitation of all workers. Instead of workers making common cause with one another across races, together advocating for their rights and benefits, racism offers the lure of white privilege, which splits the working classes.

Relative to people of color, white workers have higher status and advantages in securing occupational niches, from which they expend energy on protecting, rather than fully recognizing and challenging, their own areas of social disadvantage. For example, the history of trade unions in the United States has been one of discrimination by white workers against people of color and women (Schiller, 1998), despite recent efforts by trade unions to become more inclusive and less discriminatory. Allen (1994) has described how the genesis of this dynamic during colonial times led to the "invention of the white race," in response to the threat of economic and social disorder posed by alliances between poor whites and present and former slaves.

Some structural theorists emphasize social stratification, status, economic opportunity, mobility, and access to resources (Omi & Winant, 1994). The role of the state in maintaining social divisions is part of this analysis. The mismatch between skills and available jobs—as well as lack of access to where jobs are located because of segregation, social isolation, the movement of jobs from cities to suburbs, and poor public transportation—create large swaths of severely disadvantaged people of color, particularly African Americans, Puerto Ricans, and other Hispanic groups living in older urban areas (Wilson, 1973, 1987, 1996).

When members of these communities do have jobs, many are in the service sector or in the "secondary" labor market (Schiller, 1998), which is unregulated, is poorly paid, lacks benefits and standards for occupational health and safety, and does not lead to occupational mobility in the primary labor market, where most workers hold jobs. The emphasis on the interaction between class and race is extremely important for a complex understanding of racism. This includes recognition of the economic and social burdens of racism for large segments of people of color, as well as the costs of racism for poor and working-class white people.

CRITICISMS OF STRUCTURAL THEORIES   Scholars of racism in the structuralist tradition have contributed greatly to our understanding of the pervasiveness of racism and how embedded it is in institutions, the economy, the political system, and society at large. More than any group, this one has mapped out the contours of institutional racism.

A criticism of those who downplay race and emphasize class is that everything cannot be reduced to class conflict (Omi & Winant, 1994). Racism is a force in its own right and, though perhaps intertwined with class exploitation, operates at all levels of society. Many middle- and upper–middle-class African Americans experience racism regularly in the workplace and in their communities (Cose, 1993); moving up in class does not dissolve racial oppression. And although neo-colonialism and domestic racial oppression are analogous, they are not exactly the same. Most people of color are U.S. citizens and, at least in formal law, have the same rights as other citizens, although this does not translate into equal treatment under the law.

As we shall see in later chapters, seemingly race-neutral laws, such as drug-sentencing laws, disproportionately discriminate against and encumber people of color. Another criticism is that structuralist explanations can be too deterministic and do not acknowledge the agency of oppressed people and their capacity to form cultures of resistance (Omi & Winant, 1994).

Describing the social and economic lines of racism is essential, yet incomplete. Racism also is an ideology that is part of public discourse. There are meanings, signs, and symbols that convey, represent, reproduce, and transmit racism through decades, even centuries, and across regions and communities. Racism in the media, for instance, is not solely about ownership and whose interests are represented (as important as these are) but also concerns what assumptions are embedded in projects, stereotypes that are presented, as well as what is ignored and left out. And racism is—as scholars of prejudice have articulated—a process of attitudes, emotions, and intergroup dynamics.

Much of racism today is less blatant than it was 50 years ago and is more subtle, although equally damaging. There is aversive racism (Dovidio et al., 2002; Dovidio, Gaertner, Nieman, & Snider, 2001), racial micro-aggressions (Solorzano et al., 2000), and "discrimination in contact" rather than discrimination in "contract" (Loury, 2001). Racism is a "project" that is constantly shifting, migrating, and "racial formation [is the] sociohistorical process by which racial categories are created, inhabited, transformed and destroyed" (Omi & Winant, 1994, p. 55). Racism has subjective as well as objective dimensions, and this is captured in critical race theory, the framework that we use primarily in this book and to which we now shall turn.

CRITICAL RACE THEORY

What is race? How does the way that race is constructed change over time? What are the social, economic, legal, and political implications of how race is constructed? What are the prevailing discourses surrounding race and racism? What is centralized and marginalized in the interrogation of race and racism, visible and invisible? What is outside, concrete, and observable about racism; what is internal and subjective; and how do the public and the personal interact? What can be done to dismantle racism?

These are some of the questions explored by critical race theorists, a loose amalgamation of scholars and social activists. Although the origins of critical race theory are traced to the late 1970s (Delgado & Stefanic, 1997), an outpouring of books and articles have been published under this umbrella since the 1990s. The impetus for development of this paradigm was an attempt to reconceptualize and reformulate the understanding of race and racism that had become common wisdom as a consequence of the civil rights movement and had seemed to stall and even backslide. Many people committed to ending racism wanted to grasp this phenomenon in a complex, holistic fashion that would contribute to more effective amelioration.

The primary inspirations for this new approach were critical sociology and postmodernism (Delgado & Stefanic, 1977). Scholars (McDowell & Jeris, 2004; Solorzano et al., 2000) have identified the following five common strands of critical race theory:

1. the significance of race and racism and how this intersects with other forms of social oppression;
2. the importance of deconstructing and challenging the dominant racial ideology, which normalizes racism;
3. a commitment to social justice;
4. the importance and validity of learning from experiential knowledge and recognizing the unique perspectives of people of color;
5. the use of an interdisciplinary perspective to understand race and racism.

Esposito and Murphy (2000) add that knowledge, understanding, and meaning evolve from inter-subjective processes: the interaction of personal meaning systems with historical and social realities and the identities, discourses, and connotations drawn from the interactions of racial groups, where race and identity are always relational.

Omi and Winant's seminal work in 1992, *Racial Formation in the United States: From the 1960s to the 1990s* (2nd edition, 1994) helped to reconceptualize the meaning of race and its implications for racial formation in what the authors referred to as the American "racial project." They described race not as a fixed, essentialist entity but, rather, a historically determined, fluid, unstable, contested social construction, continually being deconstructed and reconstructed.

The meanings of race change over time and in different social contexts. For example, the Jewish, Irish, and Italian people were considered racial "others" when they first immigrated to the United States, but over time were socially constructed as white (Guglielmo & Salerno, 2003; Ignatiev, 1995; Sacks, 1996).

As Winant (1997) has stated, race is real and illusory; it can both establish and deny one's sense of identity; racial categories can neither be frozen and reified nor completely dissolved. The process of racial construction is not only social and psychological, but legal as well. Some "requisite cases" in U.S. jurisprudence have struggled to define "white" and "Caucasian" by law, allegedly drawing on biological sciences and common sense (Lopez, 1994, 1996; Taylor, 1997). Laws such as these literally have shaped how the population looks, by defining who could enter the country and become a citizen and by prescribing who could and could not intermarry (Lopez, 1996).

Race is a social construction necessary to racism, which has a concrete existence and impact, as well as profound social and psychological consequences. Racism is neither an accidental nor an inevitable process. It arises from human ideas, actions, and interactions and is part of a complex human web of interactions imbued with social meanings (Lopez, 1994). Memmi

(2000) has described the construction of race and racism as a four-part process:

1. A group of people is perceived as being different (physically, culturally).
2. Value is placed on such differences; the "other" group is thought of as being less advanced, less worthy, less civilized, less trustworthy, and in some instances, not fully human.
3. The negative differences are generalized to all members of the group.
4. All of this is used to dominate, oppress, and marginalize the targeted group.

Although this is a helpful way to conceptualize the dynamics of racism, we also must recognize the strengths and agency of targeted groups despite these forces and their capacity to resist and undermine dominant racial discourses and racist practices.

This description of racial oppression acknowledges the interaction of psychological and social dimensions, integrating concepts from structural theorists and purveyors of the dynamics of prejudice. In a racialized society, we all have racial identities whether we wish to or not. Our sense of ourselves as racial beings and our consciousness about this informs our perceptions of others and social actions. White people, who have little awareness of white privilege, inhabit a world by gliding through life without encountering the closed doors or hurdles that people of color navigate daily. This shapes worldviews, values, judgments, behaviors, and beliefs about what is true and fair. One implication, drawn from critical race theory, is that an interrogation of white privilege, and what it means to be white, should be opened. Often, books about race and diversity address people of color while omitting a large swath of the maelstrom of racism.

RACIAL CONTRACT   Critical race theorists also investigate how racism is encoded in institutions, organizations, cultural practices, and the everyday interactions of people. Racism is so ubiquitous and endemic to the fabric of social life that it appears to be ordinary and, for some white people, invisible. The familiarity and imperceptibility of racism for many people is sustained by a public, cultural discourse that subjugates and marginalizes narratives of racism. Racism is reduced to egregious acts of personal prejudice and bias. Whiteness and European culture are elevated to "normal" stature, placing other cultures and people of color in a status of "minority," located on the borders, as deviations from the center.

One way to understand this concept historically is that a "racial contract" has existed from the inception of colonization of the new land, and encoded in the nation's social contract (Mills, 1997). The racial contract from the beginning determined who was fully human and who was considered to be "savage," "inferior," and not fully human. It determined who had the rights of full citizenship and who was denied those rights. According to Mills (1997), the racial contract is the reality that underlies the lofty ideals and aspirations of the social contract, in which "all men are created equal" were words written by slaveholders. The contract structured all of society—what is permissible, what is fair, what is normal, what can be debated, and what is rendered invisible or unthinkable.

Mills calls this an agreement to "misinterpret the world," the legacy of which obfuscates and obscures the nature of reality for those who benefit directly from the contract. This leads to white people acting and behaving in ways they believe are ethical and moral without being able to see how they themselves are, consciously or unconsciously, complicit in maintaining a society that benefits them while disadvantaging others—an idea that they would abhor in the abstract.

DECONSTRUCTION AND RECONSTITUTION   This sketches out the wide range of territory examined by critical race theorists. It involves reexamining and rethinking dominant historical and social narratives. It calls for deconstruction and reconstruction of racial categories and the many meanings they carry. It seeks to map out subjective states of mind and identity and to link them with the social realities experienced by the targets of racism, which are invisible to the vast majority of white people.

Critical race theory leads us to explore and understand the experience of being socially targeted, as well as being socially privileged, and how this meshes and buckles, interlocks and creates discord, within the dynamic complexity of social identity. It urges us to examine the hidden "dissensus," veiled by a dominant discourse of accord and consensus. And critical race theory is a call to action, a recognition that we are not neutral observers but, rather, embedded actors, woven into the social fabric and therefore able to make choices about what we accept or do not tolerate, what we ignore or decide to confront, and whether we are bystanders or social activists. This is the framework that we are drawing upon for this book, although we also will utilize elements of all the theoretical approaches summarized in this chapter.

THE CONTOURS OF RACISM

We conceptualize racism as existing along a spectrum, with many different types and forms. Part of the confusion about racism—as the introductory vignette to this chapter illustrates—is that the term is used to describe many different phenomena and is laced with multiple meanings. There are different levels of racism, direct and indirect racism, intentional and unintentional racism, varying sites of racism, and a range of frequencies of racism. We will describe these contours briefly before presenting the spectrum of racism.

LEVELS OF RACISM

Racism traditionally has been viewed as having at least three levels: (1) individual, (2) group, and (3) institutional. *Individual racism* refers to biases, prejudices, beliefs, or actions that participate in or collude with racism. An example of individual racism is demonstrated by a person who harbors stereotypes of inferiority or difference toward a person who is a member of a group that is different from his, which leads to exclusionary behaviors or actions, or even telling racist jokes.

Group racism alludes to actions on the part of one group—often referred to as a dominant, privileged, or agent group—that discriminates against, marginalizes, or in any way oppresses another group that is constructed as being racially different. An example is a white ethnic group that controls an occupational niche or a residential area and will not allow an ethnic group of color to integrate these domains.

Institutional racism indicates systemic, societal, durable racism that is embedded in institutions, organizations, laws, customs, and social practices. Institutional racism forms a web (see Chapter 4) that blocks opportunities for some while offering privilege to others. It leads to a cumulative effect in which groups that are racially targeted are excluded from living in certain neighborhoods and working in numerous jobs and professions, have less access to social assets such as quality schools, and have greater health risks and other negative consequences and outcomes because of a variety of interacting legal, illegal, direct, and indirect practices.

A final level of racism, *ideological racism,* is pervasive and interwoven into social discourses and narratives. Virulent ideological racism is demonstrated by the hateful and degrading messages about Muslims in Kosovo, the Tutsis in Rwanda, and Jews in Nazi Germany, and is used to justify horrendous actions against a racial or ethnic group. By contrast, subtle ideological racism is so familiar that it often passes unnoticed, yet it sustains stereotypes or discriminatory practices. Ideological racism can be used to reinforce or justify any of the levels of racism mentioned here.

Direct and Indirect Racism

Some racism is overt and direct. Examples of this were the Jim Crow laws and practices in the southeastern United States, which prohibited African Americans from riding in the front of buses, from voting, and even from using the same water fountains as white people. Direct, overt racism can occur at any level. An individual can actively and directly express racial bias or discrimination toward another person and cause bodily, emotional or psychological, or psychic harm to the target of racism.

Indirect, or covert, racism seems on the surface to be more passive, but in practice it serves to sustain and maintain racism. An example is seen in the attitudes and biases that inhibit homeowners in a predominantly white suburb from selling their homes to people of color. The cumulative effect can be a segregated neighborhood. Another example is the difference between sentences for possession of cocaine versus crack cocaine, which have no overt indication of racial bias, yet carry the consequence of African Americans being incarcerated disproportionately, more frequently, and for longer periods than their white counterparts.

INTENTIONAL AND UNINTENTIONAL RACISM

Intentional and unintentional forms of racism are related to active and passive types of racism. The important variable here is motivation. The men who murdered James Byrd in Texas consciously tortured him because of his race. But many well-intentioned and well-meaning white people engage in racist behaviors of which they are unaware unless confronted. This often comes from unexamined stereotypes or attitudes that we all carry inside of us.

For instance, a white professor, when talking about poverty or single parenthood may direct her gaze consistently to African American students in the class—a behavior of which she and many white students are unaware but is painfully evident to most African Americans in the class, as well as some white students. We will consider the dynamics of unintentional racism in Chapter 5.

SITES OF RACISM

Racism occurs in many different places—on highways when dark-skinned people are stopped "randomly" by the police while light-skinned people drive by, in classrooms, courtrooms, neighborhoods, streets, television shows, the nightly news, in mental health agencies, in conversations between people, in segregated or racially homogenous neighborhoods, in the privacy of people's homes. When we consider in Chapters 8 through 13 the various ways to dismantle racism, we will be mindful of the many sites where racism is manifested.

FREQUENCY AND MAGNITUDE OF RACISM

Frequency and magnitude refer to the incidence and scale of racism. Is it an everyday occurrence, a legacy that has persisted for decades, or is it an isolated incident? Does a television show consistently portray Asian Americans in a stereotypical fashion, or did a typecast emerge in a single episode? Is the racist narrative conveyed in a news discussion a part of the network's pervasive culture or more a reflection of individual editors and presenters? When analyzing racism and how to respond to it, an analysis of the frequency and magnitude of racism is useful.

THE SPECTRUM OF RACISM

Racism does not fit into neat, exclusive categories. Individual and institutional racism coexist side by side and also are interactive; they potentiate one another. The racist attitudes of individuals become reified in institutions, and racist institutions normalize prejudice and oppression, shaping the way in which individuals view the world. Societally, racism is a fluctuating, shifting process, with many examples of societies that have been at the extreme end of the spectrum of oppression during certain eras but not during others.

The United States has experienced all of the types of racism described by the spectrum. The spectrum of racism has a core set of practices and a range of levels, as shown in Figure 2.1. The bottom line indicates the level of racism,

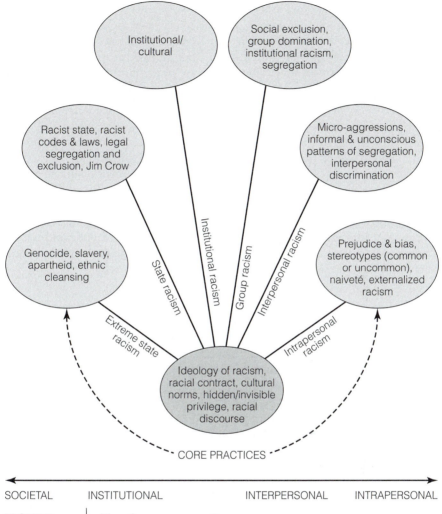

FIGURE 2.1 | THE SPECTRUM OF RACISM

ranging from the intrapsychic/intrapersonal, to the interpersonal, through the institutional, to the societal/nation state.

In the center of the spectrum is the core, consisting of a racial contract, an ideology of racism, cultural norms, and the oft-times hidden, invisible privileges of those who benefit from the advantages of the racial contract. The core of racism is part of any facet of the spectrum. The heart of racism is what powers any type or form of racism. Like a human heart, it pumps blood to the various regions of racism, and from them the blood returns.

INTRAPERSONAL

At the intrapersonal end of the spectrum are prejudice and bias, attitudes, beliefs, emotions, ideas, and cognitions. This is what we think of when we see a news story about an armed robbery or what we feel when we pass someone on the street. It is our internal process. It is the reservoir of the stream of messages that we have received from birth, from parents, books, teachers, songs, films, and pictures—messages as ubiquitous as the air we breathe. This leads to internalized stereotypes, some of which we are aware but many others that are unconscious. This can be a reservoir of internalized superiority or inferiority—what sometimes is referred to as "internalized racism."

INTERPERSONAL

At this point along the spectrum, we see racism expressed in interactions between people. Racial "micro-aggressions" occur, unintentional acts of racism often unrecognized by the perpetrator but often agonizing and hurtful to the target of the interaction. Or intentional hostile acts take place, resulting in many potential levels of injury. The challenges of having respectful and meaningful interracial conversations and dialogues lead to poor and missed communications. Interpersonal levels of racism create tensions in the workplace and fear and isolation in the community.

INTERGROUP

Intergroup racism refers to the place on the spectrum where people are identified with groups that carry racial categories. The act of identification shapes the formation of racial identity, and the collective interactions of group members result in domination, exclusion, discrimination, and other forms of group-based oppression.

This level of racism can be manifested in voting patterns, competition for jobs and neighborhoods, and marriage and friendship patterns. This is not a playing field of equals; one group (whites) has more power, resources, and privilege and is prepared to exercise this advantage at many levels of interaction and many sites of competition.

INSTITUTIONAL

Institutional racism is well documented and will be discussed at length in Chapter 4. Institutional racism leads to exclusion from neighborhoods, jobs, schools, politics, health and mental health care; greater exposure to environmental hazards; higher risk of arrest and incarceration; and lower life expectancies. We also include dominant cultural patterns of prejudice and oppression as a form of institutional racism. Institutional racism can occur in any form of society, including democracies.

OFFICIAL AND STATE

Official and state racism describes situations in which the state is overtly racist. Examples of this, unfortunately, abound. This level of racism includes state-sponsored racism at any level of government. Legal segregation, racist codes and laws, and Jim Crow are all forms of state-sponsored racism that are part of U.S. history. Nowadays, we witness state efforts to give privilege to one group over another or to strip members of a targeted racial or ethnic group of their civil rights.

EXTREME, STATE SANCTIONED

The gloomiest, most appalling end of the spectrum of racism is at the state-sanctioned extreme. Examples include genocide, ethnic cleansing, slavery, and racial apartheid. Sadly, these forms of racism persist in the world to this day.

CONCLUSION

In this chapter we have traced the historical underpinnings of race and explored the many meanings and interpretations of racism. Several theories of race and racism have evolved, of which this chapter highlights structural theories. Subsequent chapters will consider in depth many of the concepts and ideas presented here. The spectrum of racism will be explored in all of its facets but always with an eye toward anti-racism.

Our understanding of racism, both complex and comprehensive, should not leave us feeling hopeless or overwhelmed. Racism, in its most virulent manifestations, has been undermined, dismantled, and defeated. The work ahead is hard and challenging, and we must often take the long view, but the stakes are high and the risks to us all of remaining bystanders and not taking action is even higher.

EXERCISE 2.1   APPLYING THE SPECTRUM OF RACISM

1. Take each type of racism from the spectrum of racism and apply it to either a current or a historical situation. Consider what types of racism exist in your home town, college or university, worksite, the United States at large, and other parts of the world. What levels of racism are present in each example (individual, group, institutional)? Can you identify direct and indirect types of racism in your examples? What specific sites of racism are evident in the examples? Note the frequency and magnitude of racism described in your examples.
2. After completing the exercise, reflect on what thoughts and feelings emerged for you as you applied the spectrum of racism. Were any of these reactions surprising or unexpected? Were any parts of this exercise particularly difficult? What questions about racism has this exercise raised for you?

CHAPTER 3

A Brief History of Racism in the United States and Implications for the Helping Professions

CHAPTER CONTENTS

The United States is now well over two centuries old. Considered a nation with an Anglo-Christian tradition, it has been aligned politically and culturally with Europe for much of its history. Waves of immigrants from Europe have melted into the mainstream of "white" American society. Yet the land mass of the United States has been inhabited for thousands of years by Native Americans (American Indians), who settled North America and created tribes, confederations, and nations. For the United States to be established, the native peoples had to be subjugated, dispossessed, and in many instances murdered and annihilated.

From early on, the United States was settled with slave labor, which quickly evolved into the institution of chattel slavery, reserved exclusively for people seized from the African continent. Thus, the white race was "invented" in opposition to the dark-skinned people who were shackled (Allen, 1994). This, along with the near genocide of Native Americans, stands as the most extreme form of racism associated with the United States.

This was by no means the only state-sanctioned racism in the United States, though. Mexicans, who inhabited what is now Texas, New Mexico, Arizona, Colorado, Nevada, and California, lost their land and rights of citizenship after the Mexican-American War, with the Treaty of Guadalupe Hidalgo in 1848. Chinese workers in the United States, who were instrumental in constructing the transcontinental railway line, were subject to pogroms in cities such as Seattle, where the entire Chinese population was forced to flee at the hands of mobs. Eventually, Chinese people were excluded from immigrating to the United States by the Chinese Exclusion Act of 1882. Japanese immigrants were prevented from entering the United States by Executive Order 9066, commonly known as the "Gentleman's Agreement" of 1907.

Meanwhile, immigration from Ireland, Germany, Sweden, Poland, Italy, and other European countries was being encouraged, as many cities in the United States industrialized and required cheap labor. So, from the beginning of this nation state to the present, some groups have been encouraged and recruited—gaining important economic advantages by cornering occupational niches—while other groups have been barred from entering the country, or attacked and shackled within the realm.

Although this is not a history book, helping professionals will benefit from a brief examination of the past, as its legacy reverberates through our society today. We will begin by reviewing the relationship between Native Americans and European settlers, as well as the institution of slavery in the United States. Then we will then consider racial dynamics in the 19th century as the U.S. industrialized and developed major urban centers, followed by a comparison with European immigrants during this same time span. We also will consider how the development of the helping professions, particularly social work, both reflected and challenged the evolving racial project in the United States. The Progressive Era and the New Deal will receive particular attention, along with the modern Civil Rights Movement and the Great Society of the 1960s.

THE RACIAL CONTRACT

The United States was founded on a bedrock of racial exploitation and subjugation. Although most Americans are familiar with the history of "heroic settlers from Europe," braving fierce winters and surviving long journeys to the West across deserts and mountains, Americans are less familiar with the savagery, relentless slaughter, and displacement that accompanied the colonization of North America and the founding of the United States. And while most Americans are able to recall, even recite, the ideals and values of the Declaration of Independence and the U.S. Constitution, the reality of racism during that era remains obfuscated and clouded. We cannot understand racism in the United States today without examining its historical roots and foundations.

The United States was founded on certain principles and values that were ascendant in the European Enlightenment—the rights to freedom, dignity, security, and equality. These aspirations mask the reality of genocide and slavery upon which the republic was founded. By virtue of their race, neither Native Americans nor African Americans were treated with dignity, were afforded security, or were eligible for freedom and equality. They were not considered fully human—an underpinning of severe racism. This dehumanization and social and economic exclusion formed the underbelly of the social contract, the "racial contract" (Mills, 1997), which was used to justify the most extreme forms of state-sanctioned racism while masking its existence for generations to come.

In reviewing some of the most painful chapters in U.S. history, we must not lose sight of the many ways by which subjugated peoples resisted and survived. Whether they were engaged in large-scale conflicts, open rebellions, and massive civil rights movements, or in the day-to-day interpersonal interactions with white people, Native Americans and African Americans have endured the most dreadful conditions imaginable, yet always refused to give in, utilizing whatever means were available to them to care for one another and struggle for dignity and survival.

NATIVE AMERICANS

Native American Indians were living in both North America and South America at least 13,000 years ago, and by some estimates, tens of thousands of years earlier (Stannard, 1992). Between 75 million and 100 million people were thought to live in both continents, 8 to 10 million of whom were north of what is now Mexico. The number of people living in the Western Hemisphere was comparable to the population of Europe during the same period (Wilson, 1998). The more than 600 autonomous societies in North America had worldviews and a cosmology emphasizing the sacred, interconnectedness, interdependence, and equilibrium. Where farming was practiced, it was extensive, and land was not viewed as private property but, rather, as a public resource to be shared.

When the Spanish explorers first encountered the "New World," they were arriving from a country (and continent) that had seen many large-scale wars, the religious and ethnic battles against the Moors, the Crusades, and the expulsion of Jews because of their religious beliefs (Diamond, 1997; Stannard, 1992; Wilson, 1998). They brought sophisticated weapons and a willingness to fight in a brutal, effective fashion—a style of warfare that, unlike that of Native Americans, resulted in huge numbers of casualties.

The Spanish and other European invaders also brought with them devastating germs and illnesses. Diamond (1997) hypothesized that the reason the European diseases were so much more destructive to Native Americans was that the Europeans' exposure to many different peoples from Africa and Asia, as well as Europe, along with the density of the population and the domestication of large farm animals, had "hardened them." In any case, the mortality among Native Americans was overwhelming.

In addition, settlers from all of the major European nations who established colonies and settlements engaged in warfare and, in many instances, genocide. Stannard (1992) estimates a 95% death rate of Native Americans "within no more than a handful of generations following their first encounter with Europeans" (p. x) and declares that this might have been the single worst holocaust in world history. The destruction of Native American villages and communities occurred from the 17th century, when Pequots and Narragansetts were being slaughtered by Puritans, to massacres by the U.S. cavalry in the late 19th century.

Native Americans often could do nothing to prevent being massacred. Although the Moravian Delaware Indians converted to Christianity in an effort to comply with their white subjugators, their food was destroyed and they were rounded up by American troops and told that they would be taken to safety and offered food. Instead, they were tied up, massacred, and scalped—29 men, 27 women and 34 children (Stannard, 1992).

In Eastern Colorado in 1863, the *Rocky Mountain News* newspaper urged the extermination of Native Americans a year before what became known as the Sand Creek Massacre of Cheyenne and Arapahoe Indians (Stannard, 1992). When a family of settlers was killed by unknown Indians, some small skirmishes led to deaths on both sides, although the American Indian losses were much greater. Colonel John Chivington, who likened killing American Indians to delousing, led 700 heavily armed soldiers to Sand Creek, where there were about 600 American Indians, mostly women and children, as the men were away on a buffalo hunt. The residents of Sand Creek had disarmed themselves voluntarily to show that they were not a threat. Despite repeated efforts by the residents of the village to hoist white flags and other symbols of peace and nonviolence, the soldiers attacked and killed everyone. Stannard (1992) describes how mothers were frantically digging holes to hide their children, but all, from infants to the elderly, were killed and their bodies scalped and further mutilated.

These are but two small examples of widespread and wholesale massacres of Native Americans, ranging from New England to the Southeast, across the Plains to the Pacific Coast. In this way, the land of this nation, which now is occupied mostly by non-Native Americans, was cleared by mass killings and involuntary relocations. Annihilations were led by high-ranking officers in the colonies, and later the nation. Andrew Jackson, who went on to become President, led a particularly brutal massacre of nearly 800 Creek Indians, including women and children, at the battle of Horseshoe Bend in 1814 (Takaki, 1987).

When Indians were spared death or made peace, they were still subjected to broken treaties and forced relocations when settlers coveted the land they occupied. In the first 90 years of the American republic, white people broke *all* 370 treaties with Native Americans (Wilson, 1998). The Indian Removal Act of 1830 led to five tribes (Cherokee, Choctaw, Chickasaw, Seminole, and Creek) being moved from the Southeastern United States to the Oklahoma Territories, resulting in thousands of deaths during the brutal march (Lum, 2000).

Once the Indians were resettled, the white settlers made further land grabs, especially if the land was found to have natural resources such as oil. The Dawes Act of 1887 allocated land to relocated Indians, attempting to instill a sense of private ownership despite tribal traditions of shared and communal land use, but unscrupulous profiteers cajoled and defrauded the Native Americans. Between 1887 and 1932 most of the land grants had passed from Indians to whites (Lum, 200; Wilson, 1998).

Once they were "pacified," Native Americans were subjected to additional actions that sought to divest them of their cultural heritage and force them to assimilate into Anglo-American society. From the late 19th century to the present, contested government visions of what would be best for Native Americans have continued. The Bureau of Indian Affairs, led primarily by non-Indians, lurched from one policy to another. Well-intentioned reformers, such as Captain Richard Pratt, sought to "kill the Indian and save the man" through forced assimilation to white ways of living (Wilson, 1998, p. 312). Pratt founded the Carlisle Indian School in Pennsylvania, in 1879, which became the prototype of more than 300 schools, serving nearly 22,000 Indian students, which at the time was about 10% of the Native American population.

The schools attempted to change the students' identity by cutting their traditional hairstyles in favor of the short styles of the whites; dressing the students in Anglo-American rather than traditional Native American clothing; substituting foods for the traditional Indian foods; using unfamiliar forms of physical punishment; and even changing the pupils' names. The psychological and emotional consequences of this forced assimilation were profound, leading to depression, alienation from family and community, severe identity conflict, and high rates of mortality for the children. Finally, in 1924, after losing more than 90% of their people, most of their lands, their capacity to hunt and farm, and much of their traditional cultures, Native Americans were granted full citizenship.

AFRICAN AMERICANS

The history of African Americans in the United States is one of survival, resiliency, and collective solidarity despite encountering extreme forms of racism. Slavery is a profound aspect of the American racial contract. Many of the crafters of the Declaration of Independence and U.S. Constitution, some of whom went on to serve as U.S. President, were slaveholders and have become iconic, heroic figures.

Sadly, slavery has existed in one form or another throughout human history (Davis, 1997; Fredrickson, 2002). Slaves often were captured in wars and used by their conquerors as cheap labor. In earlier times, slavery, for the most part, was not racialized. It was deemed bad luck to have been defeated and captured, but the captives were not considered subhuman, inferior beings. The magnitude, duration, and scale of slavery in the Americas was unique in the history of the world. Spanning 423 years, it was the largest involuntary movement of people ever (Davis, 2001). Although we cannot know exactly how many people were transported from villages in Africa to ships that transported them across the Atlantic Ocean to plantations in New World colonies, an estimated 2,130,000 slaves were imported to the colonies in the New World between 1680 and 1786 (Foner, 1975).

Many European countries participated in the slave trade, including Portugal, Spain, Holland, France, Sweden, Denmark, and England (Foner, 1975). The trade formed a triangle (Foner, 1975; Klinkenborg, 2002), in which manufactured goods first were shipped to Africa from Europe. There, they were traded for people, who in the second leg were transported to the colonies. In the final leg, raw goods such as sugar, rum, and tobacco were transported back to Europe from the colonies. Because of its ascendancy at sea, England eventually came to dominate the slave trade (Foner, 1975), and more slave ships departed from Liverpool than from any other port (Klinkenborg, 2002). Although slavery came to flourish in the Southeast plantation economy of the United States, it was legalized first in Massachusetts in 1641 (Johnson & Smith, 1998).

INDENTURED SERVITUDE AND CHATTEL SLAVERY   In early Virginia, plantation owners sought cheap and stable labor (Allen, 1994; Foner, 1975). Indentured servants from England and Ireland were sold to work on plantations alongside Africans. In the 17th century, 75% of Virginia's settlers came to the state as indentured servants (Takaki, 1993). Indentured servitude was a far cry from chattel slavery, as the former could possibly work off their debts in their lifetime and go on to live freely in society. The evolution to chattel slavery, in which people were treated as property or livestock and they and their descendents could be slaves in perpetuity, heralded the institution of slavery in America. This had a profound influence on our racial history.

Indentured servants in Virginia during the 17th century were a force to be reckoned with, balking at the yoke of overly harsh working conditions and becoming restive when the prospects of attaining freedom and becoming landholders failed to materialize. Plantation owners and officials feared insurrection, mob violence, and social chaos. This condition culminated in Bacon's Rebellion of 1676, when a multiracial force of indentured servants mutinied over their working conditions and fought with Crown and colonial forces before being subdued (Allen, 1994; Takaki, 1993).

As a result, a full use of the law secured chattel slavery—prohibiting meetings, instituting strict oversight and supervision of slaves, disarming slaves, institutionalizing slavery as a system of intergenerational and perpetual bondage, and barring social and sexual unions between races. This marked the racialization of slavery for only African Americans. Allen (1994) describes this as the "invention of the white race": In return for the possibility of social mobility—as illusory as this may have been—and backed by the fear of returning to slave status, poor, working whites exchanged their economic grievances for the privilege of being members of the white race. Plantation owners succeeded in dousing the flames of social unrest while ensuring a steady source of captive labor.

The institution of chattel slavery, reserved solely for African Americans, was fully formed by the time the American Republic was established. George Washington, Thomas Jefferson, James Madison, and James Monroe were all slaveholders, although they expressed ambivalence or misgivings about the institution. Andrew Jackson was a slaveholder as well. These men all went on to become Presidents and are among the "founding fathers" of this nation. The "three-fifths rule," in which each slave gave the owner an additional three-fifths of a vote in elections, further cemented the disproportionate dominance of the South in American political life, extending the life of formal slavery until the Civil War (Wills, 2003).

Post–Civil War   Although slavery was officially ended at the end of the Civil War, oppression of African Americans in the South was far from over. Immediately following the war, all southern states passed "Black Codes" in 1865–66. These codes were a blatant attempt to continue the indentured, servile status of African Americans (Montgomery, 1993): All black adults were required to contract for their work in advance each year, and if they quit, they could be arrested and returned to their employers. If they wanted to work commercially or as artisans, they were required to obtain licenses from district courts. Orphans and children under 18 years of age who were deemed to be living with parents unable to support them could be contracted out to white families as laborers and servants.

When these codes were challenged by the federal government under the 14th Amendment to the Constitution, strict vagrancy laws were passed, resulting in high incarceration rates for African Americans (Steinberg, 2001). "Convicts," including children, then could then be leased out for labor. One convict in four was a child, and children as young as age 6 were leased out (Oshinsky, 1996). Poll taxes and literacy tests also were also established to prevent black people from voting while exempting white voters through "grandfather clauses" (Parillo, 1996). And anti-miscegenation laws prohibited interracial marriages and sexual liaisons (Fredrickson, 1981). After Reconstruction fizzled, "Jim Crow" laws instituting strict segregation saturated the states of the Confederacy and lynching became a gruesome version of southern racial justice. Between 1892 and 1921, about 2,400 African Americans were lynched in the South (Parillo, 1996).

After the end of the Civil War, African Americans could not migrate to the North because racism in employment prevented them from obtaining jobs. While millions of immigrants were arriving from Europe to work in northern factories, African Americans were stranded in the South (Steinberg, 2001). During and after World War I, however, African Americans could move north more successfully, because the flow of European immigrants dried up. Between 1900 and 1930, 2 million African Americans migrated north (Jones, 1985).

The migratory spigot truly opened between the late 1930s, when World War II fueled a strong demand for factory jobs, and the 1960s, with about 5 million people making the journey (Edsall & Edsall, 1991; Leman, 1991). Those who did make it to the North faced de-facto segregation, hostility from unions, the worst working conditions and the lowest paying jobs on occupational ladders, and were most prone to layoffs when white workers returned from the wars (Jones, 1985).

All of these structural impediments in the South and North constrained the capacity of African Americans to accumulate capital and inhibited their social mobility. They also propelled African American women into the workforce in far greater numbers than white women, as African American men had difficulty finding well-paying jobs because of Jim Crow in the South and racial discrimination in the North (Jones, 1985). The ability of African American women to find work as domestic employees led them to an unregulated niche in the low-paying labor market, where echoes of the unequal relationships between blacks and whites predated the Civil War.

In addition to lynching, overt violence continued, in which white mobs attacked black communities. There were pogroms in East St. Louis; Tulsa, Oklahoma; and Rosewood, Florida. More than 100 African Americans in East St. Louis were massacred by white workers in 1917 (Arnove & Zinn, 2004). In Tulsa, in 1921, whites rioted, destroying 35 square blocks in an African American neighborhood, murdering about 300 people (Staples, 1999). Days of violence by white mobs in Rosewood, Florida, in 1923, completely destroyed the town. Although the exact number of casualties is unknown, it is thought that dozens perished (Carnes, 1995). African Americans continued to struggle for their rights, despite physical violence, economic exclusion, segregation (official and unofficial), legal disenfranchisement, and overt and covert racism at all levels of the spectrum. After World War II, the modern-day Civil Rights Movement coalesced, gathering momentum in the 1950s and leading to dramatic political responses in the form of the Great Society in the 1960s.

LATINOS/HISPANICS

The terms *Latinos* and *Hispanics* refer to people from Latin America or Spain. This population is large and extremely diverse, ranging from Mexico to Argentina, and Peru to Venezuela, as well as many islands conquered by the Spanish, including Puerto Rico and Cuba. Although settled by the Portuguese, Brazil often is considered as part of Hispanic America as well. Hispanics include people from all "racial" groups, encompassing indigenous peoples

(Native Americans) from Latin America, and many religions and nationalities. Although Hispanic groups have some cultural similarities, and certainly linguistic unity in the predominant use of Spanish, they also show a wide spectrum of diversity between cultures and nationalities and ethnic diversity within nations, as well as class variations. In any case, when exploring racism in the United States, we have to understand some critical historical events and how they led to the creation of Hispanic minority groups within the United States, who were constructed as nonwhite, people of color and thus experience continued racism in the United States.

We will direct the discussion here to two major themes: (1) the conquest and control of land occupied by Hispanics and how the people occupying these territories were treated, and (2) the colonization of Hispanic lands, notably Puerto Rico and Cuba. The legacy of these conquests is of prime interest. Although there have been many instances of U.S. intervention and neo-colonialism in other parts of Latin America, we will not be able to cover these events, although immigrants from these countries have been inducted into a racial calculus already in play between Hispanics and white Americans of European descent.

MEXICAN AMERICANS   Spanish colonists, and subsequently Mexicans, were living in much of what is the Southwest part of the United States for many decades before English, Irish, and other pioneers from Europe settled in their territories. Although the antecedents of the Mexican-American War are complex, with provocations and human rights abuses on both sides, a racialized discourse was in play even before the outbreak of overt hostilities.

One of the issues was the reluctance of Mexico to allow slavery in the disputed lands; however, American cotton growers had migrated into Mexican territory (what is now East Texas) and were agitating to use slaves to work in cotton fields. Famous Texans used racial imagery to justify the struggle against Mexico: Stephen Austin talked of the "mongrel Spanish-Indian and negro races" versus the civilized "Anglo-American race," and Sam Houston believed that Texas in American hands reflected "glory on the Anglo Saxon race" (Takaki, 1993, pp. 173–174). In California, an 1856 vagrancy statute aimed at Mexican Americans referred to them in the text of the law as "greasers" (Shorris, 1992).

After defeating Mexico, the Treaty of Guadalupe Hidalgo in 1846 gave the United States what is now California, Texas, New Mexico, and Nevada, as well as parts of Colorado, Utah, Wyoming, Oklahoma, Kansas, and Arizona (Shorris, 1992; Takaki, 1993). The many Mexicans living in these territories were systematically dispossessed from their lands and livelihoods through laws, taxes, and concerted efforts to challenge their property deeds. Eventually they were forced to work as cheap laborers, hired cowboys, ditch diggers, and miners, at wages significantly below their Anglo counterparts (Feagin & Feagin, 1999; Lum, 2000; Takaki, 1993). Income went down and infant mortality rose (Shorris, 1992). Their language was also suppressed, contributing to social and cultural marginalization (Healey, 1995). Texas Rangers harassed Mexicans both north and south of the border, meting out their own standards of vigilante justice (Carnes, 1995).

PUERTO RICANS   Like the story of Mexican Americans in the United States, the chronicle of Puerto Ricans is one of creating a desperate and dispossessed workforce. In 1898, barely a year after the island had been granted autonomy from Spain, U.S. troops occupied Puerto Rico (Feagin & Feagin, 1999). Puerto Rico became a U.S. territory with patronage-appointed governors, who often knew little of the island's history, culture, and people. At the onset of American occupation, Puerto Rico was an agricultural country, with many Puerto Ricans producing sugar, coffee, and other crops from their own plots of land. But an inexorable process of corporate takeover through agribusiness and industrialization destroyed this economy, forcing farmers off the land and into the low-wage, dependent workforce (Feagin & Feagin, 1999).

The collapse of industries such as sugar and needlework in the early to mid-20th century led to high unemployment and migration to the U.S. mainland in search of work (Glazer & Moynihan, 1963). This migration did not abate. Now, about 3.5 million Puerto Ricans are living in Puerto Rico and about 2.5 million are working and residing on the U.S. mainland (Shorris, 1992). In addition to enduring economic hardship, Puerto Ricans have been subjected to racial and ethnic stereotypes that depict them as docile, overly emotional, and lazy (Feagin & Feagin, 1999).

CUBAN AMERICANS   Although Cuban Americans have not been burdened with the same stereotypes as Puerto Ricans, they, too, have been subjected to type-casting and discrimination in the United States. Many people have considered them a favored minority, and they have achieved a stronger economic position than either Mexican Americans or Puerto Ricans. Still, Cubans have encountered housing and employment discrimination. Many refugees have been unable to retain their occupations and professions in the United States, resulting in a lowered economic status (Feagin & Feagin, 1999).

Cubans had settled in the U.S. already during the 19th century, often as a result of political upheavals in Cuba and attracted by jobs in Florida (Feagin & Feagin, 1999). Shortly after the Spanish American War, Cuba became a U.S. protectorate in 1902. The United States was strongly involved in influencing Cuban politics and, as in Puerto Rico, controlled the Cuban economy. This resulted in many low-paid, vulnerable workers (Feagin & Feagin, 1999).

After the Cuban Revolution in 1959, many of the country's elite fled to Florida. Successive waves of immigration from Cuba swelled the Cuban American community in Florida, and eventually in other states such as New York, New Jersey, Texas, and California (Parillo, 1996). There was a marked difference in how the 1980 cohort of Cuban refugees was viewed, compared to their predecessors, with much attention paid to the numbers of convicts and ex-mental patients in this group (Steinberg, 2001). Most were not criminals or mentally ill but, unlike previous waves of Cuban immigrants, significant numbers of these refugees were of African heritage and darker skinned (Feagin & Feagin, 1999; Shorris, 1992).

Sadly, racism has divided the Cuban community in some instances. *The New York Times* ran a story about two friends who immigrated in the early 1990s—Joel, who is dark-skinned, and Achmed, who is light-skinned (Ojito, 2000). Although they attempted to remain friends in Miami, they both were inducted into the racialized world of the United States. They settled in different neighborhoods that reflected their skin privilege and moved in different cultural directions. Ultimately, Achmed felt uncomfortable visiting Joel in a predominantly black neighborhood and the friends drifted apart. Of course, one story cannot explain everything, but it does illustrate the complexity and pain accompanying racism in the United States and how it can intersect with other aspects of social identity, such as nationality, ethnicity, and social class.

Asian Americans

The history of Asians and Pacific Islanders in America is rich, complex, and diverse. It is a story of many nationalities and their experiences of immigration and settling in the United States from the world's largest and most populated continent. For the purposes of this brief historical review, we will concentrate on two national and ethnic groups, the Chinese and the Japanese, and their experiences of race and racism in America.

The Chinese   The Chinese came in large numbers to the United States in the mid-19th century, because of push factors such as wars and political upheaval, and high taxes and poor harvests in China (Takaki, 1993). They were attracted by the lure of jobs with higher wages, as well as the prospect of finding gold. Labor brokers even recruited them. They built railroads; mined; constructed agricultural canals, dams, and irrigation systems; and were active in farming (Parillo, 1996). At one point, 90% of workers building Western railway lines were Chinese, and in 1870, 29% of the population of Idaho was of Chinese descent. Because of federal law in 1790 restricting citizenship to whites, the Chinese were not able to become citizens.

Although they were welcomed initially, the Chinese encountered nativism, resentment, and eventually outright hostility, discrimination, and violence. In the 1890s there were anti-Chinese riots in California (Takaki, 1993) and during the same period, pogroms in Seattle forced all people of Chinese descent to flee from the city (Morgan, 1962). Racism was further institutionalized by the Chinese Exclusion Act of 1882 (renewed in 1892 and 1902), which prohibited further Chinese immigration and denied citizenship to Chinese already in the country. U.S leaders set an ominous and stentorian tone, just as they had with Native Americans and African Americans. President Rutherford Hayes referred to the "Chinese invasion" as being "pernicious," compared the Chinese with other, "weaker" races (African Americans and Native Americans), and committed himself to discouraging further immigration (Takaki, 1993, p. 206). The Chinese Exclusion Act was not repealed until 1943, and large-scale Chinese immigration to the United States did not resume until the 1960s (Feagin & Feagin, 1999).

The Chinese who were already in the United States did band together and form and maintain mutual support networks. Denied access to jobs and farming, they formed their own businesses and settled in what became Chinatowns (Takaki, 1993). Today, Chinese Americans are living in all sectors of society and are a socially and politically diverse group.

THE JAPANESE   Feagin and Feagin (1999) have observed that Asians immigrated to the United States serially. When immigration for one group was halted or reduced, employers sought Asian immigration from other sources. The Japanese came to the United States later than the Chinese. Many of them initially went to Hawaii to work on the sugar plantations. Then they emigrated to the mainland United States in large numbers from the 1880s until the "Gentleman's Agreement" of 1908.

Unlike the early Chinese immigrants, who were largely males planning to return home, the Japanese émigrés included significant numbers of women. Japanese settlers were employed mostly in agriculture, railroad construction, mining, and canneries (Feagin & Feagin, 1999; Takaki, 1993). Some worked as farm workers, and others became truck farmers, selling their own produce from truck stands. By 1910, these Japanese people were producing 70% of California's strawberries.

Like the Chinese before them, the Japanese were recruited by employers who valued their work ethic, skills, and willingness to work in difficult conditions for low wages. But the Japanese encountered hostility from white workers and stereotypes and nativism in society at large. A common accusation against the Japanese was that they were "inassimilable" (Feagin & Feagin, 1999; Takaki, 1993). Yet California had statutes prohibiting the Japanese from owning land, intermarrying with whites, and obtaining citizenship. Similar examples of "blaming the victim" have afflicted many targeted social groups: Legal and structural barriers deny them access to the rights and privileges enjoyed by other groups and cause them to rely on themselves, which confirms the stereotype that they are alien and unable to assimilate.

Laws and Supreme Court rulings have codified this process. From the inception of this country, a series of Supreme Court decisions, known as the "requisite cases," determined who was eligible for citizenship, predicated on who was considered to be "white" (Lopez, 1996; Taylor, 1997). One such decision was the Ozawa case in 1922, which denied naturalized citizenship to the Japanese plaintiff because he was not Caucasian. This was followed by an immigration law in 1924 prohibiting the entry of those ineligible for citizenship.

Before this, however, the rising anti-Japanese fervor, fueled by stereotypes in the press, led to what was known as the "Gentleman's Agreement," which essentially was a compact initiated by President Theodore Roosevelt between the United States and Japan that ended new Japanese immigration. It was buttressed by the Immigration Act of 1924, which was not altered significantly until a new immigration act in 1965 prohibited the quotas and restrictions that favored whites over other ethnic and racial groups (Feagin & Feagin, 1999).

During World War II, one of the most egregious modern acts of racism in this country occurred in 1942. Under Executive Order 9066, Japanese American citizens were barred from "sensitive" places and eventually were interned in concentration camps (Feagin & Feagin, 1999; Takaki, 1993). Although this was a response to the bombing of Pearl Harbor by the Japanese, it is the only time in the 20th century that an ethnic group was singled out for such treatment. German Americans were not interned despite the United States being at war with Germany. This shameful incident led to the confinement of 110,000 Japanese Americans, often in degrading camps, where they were leased out to perform menial work at low wages (Feagin & Feagin, 1999; Takaki, 1993).

The involuntary detention caused great economic, social, and psychological harm. Many Japanese Americans lost their businesses, relinquished their farms, and, after release, found their homes vandalized and damaged. Despite this, 33,000 Japanese Americans served in World War II (Takaki, 1993)! Not until 1987 was a bill passed apologizing to Japanese Americans for this indignation, including the offer of monetary reparations.

FACTORS COMMON TO ANTI-IMMIGRANT RACISM

Many other national and ethnic groups from Asia and the Pacific Islands experienced success as well as concerted efforts of prejudice, intolerance, and discrimination after immigrating to the United States. Filipinos, Koreans, and South Asian Indians immigrated in large numbers in the 19th century, followed by modern waves of Vietnamese, Laotians, Hmong, Cambodians, Thai, Malaysians, and Indonesians.

The Japanese experience illustrates a cycle of anti-immigrant racism with four factors common to most non-white American groups. This is not a linear process, but all of the elements are usually in place.

1. The media stoke a public discourse of targeting, scapegoating, and hatred.
2. Nativist groups join the conversation with dire warnings about alien cultures and stereotypes about inscrutability or lack of trustworthiness. Some of these nativist groups are considered quite mainstream, such as the American Legion and major trade unions.
3. Social groups that perceive themselves as victims direct their pent-up anger at the visible racial or ethnic minority. Examples are the white construction and railway workers in the Old West, whose working conditions were abysmal and who blamed Chinese or Japanese workers as being responsible because of their willingness to endure such conditions without complaint. The white workers' anger was directed at other workers rather than at the employers and owners who created the deplorable conditions.

4. National and local leaders support the targeting and legitimize or even stoke the flames of bigotry. American Presidents who have engaged in racist demagogy, denigration, and scapegoating include, among others, Thomas Jefferson, Andrew Jackson, Rutherford Hayes, and Theodore Roosevelt.

WHITE ETHNIC GROUPS

After summarizing the experiences of prejudice and racism of a number of ethnic and racial groups of color in the United States, we turn to a comparison of these experiences with those of white immigrant groups, such as Jews, Italians, Irish, French Canadians, Armenians, Poles, Greeks, and other groups that have encountered hostility and bias upon arrival in America.

All whites are immigrants to the United States. Early immigrants included Puritans, Quakers, and other settlers who left England because of religious persecution. Among the early residents of U.S. colonies were also many Dutch, French, Spanish, and German settlers. Immigrants from Scotland and Ireland, as well as the Scot-Irish from the area now known as Northern Ireland, were well represented among the early colonists. Class was a critical issue, particularly in the South, as many poor English and Irish émigrés entered as indentured servants.

PUSH AND PULL FACTORS

With all immigrant groups, regardless of race or ethnicity, varying push and pull factors influenced immigration (Steinberg, 2001). Push factors occur in the country of origin and include famine, political persecution, poverty, religious or ethnic intolerance, wars, and other conflicts. Pull factors are the jobs, land, political freedom, recruitment by employers (which can be voluntary or involuntary), and the draw of family or friends who have already immigrated.

In the early United States, major pull factors were land, religious freedom, and economic opportunity. During the 19th century, as the country industrialized, many jobs in mills and factories lured immigrants to the United States. While Native Americans, African Americans, and many Hispanics and Asian Americans were being denied access to these jobs, waves of immigrants from Europe and Canada were filling them.

As an example, in Holyoke, Massachusetts, a city that developed as a mill town, first the Irish and Germans were recruited to work in the factories. They were followed by French Canadians and, later, Poles (Miller, 1999). Puerto Ricans did not enter the city in large numbers until after the 1960s, when most of the blue-collar jobs had fled to the South or offshore as part of the process of industrialization. This municipality has never had a significant African American population.

DISCRIMINATION AGAINST WHITE ETHNIC GROUPS

Many white ethnic groups migrating to the United States encountered prejudice and hostility, as well as intergroup conflict. Some, such as the Irish, Jews, and Italians, initially were labeled as "non-white" by whites already in the United States. The Irish were arriving from a region where the English had socially constructed them as racial inferiors. The English had brutally suppressed them for centuries and had allowed appalling numbers to starve during a failure of the Irish food staple potatoes, while the British exported the rest of the Irish food supply for themselves (Takaki, 1987). Upon arriving in large numbers to Boston and New York, the Irish were met with signs stating that they should not apply for jobs or rooms in boarding houses.

Jews arrived in this country after enduring centuries of religious and ethnic hostility, prejudice, and violence throughout the European continent. Many of the groups who harbored strong anti-Semitic attitudes were well represented in the United States already or were immigrating here at the same time. Jews, too, found certain neighborhoods "unavailable," jobs not open, quotas limiting their attendance at colleges and universities, and inflammatory anti-Jewish rhetoric in newspapers and on the radio (Dinnerstein, 1994).

Further, Jews were subjected to hatred and violence from groups such as the Ku Klux Klan. Anti-Semitism has been a theme in intergroup relations ever since Jews arrived in the United States, and many negative ethnic and religious stereotypes have been promulgated and confronted. Jews still are targeted by extreme right-wing organizations such as the Aryan Nations, and incidents of graffiti involving swastikas and anti-Semitic statements still occur.

Italians and Greeks and other immigrants from Mediterranean countries also have encountered discrimination and nativism. Because many are dark-skinned, they initially were not accepted as white (Guglielmo, 2003). This led to difficulty finding well paying work, residential discrimination, overt hostility from other ethnic groups, and enduring stereotypes and ethnic caricatures.

All ethnic groups need to survive, and they seek upward mobility and prosperity to thrive. When legal and socially acceptable means of success are closed off, groups will move into opportunity structures available to them, including illegal businesses (Cloward & Ohlin, 1960). This surely occurred with Jews and Italians, in particular, upon their arrival in the United States, in which both groups took advantage of criminal opportunities when legitimate economic prospects were sealed off. This is another example of how structural factors in society lead to choices and adaptive strategies that then can be used as evidence of a group's predilection for antisocial behavior.

One of the forms of prejudice that white immigrant groups experienced in the 19th and early 20th centuries was to be viewed as childlike, dependent, and unable on their own to live up to the standards of American civilization. Often forced to live in squalid, overcrowded neighborhoods, with dismal sanitary conditions, they were held responsible for creating those conditions. New immigrants were seen as not being as intelligent as native-born Americans, unable to care for themselves, prone to excessive drinking and violence, having gross food habits, and even smelling different—the metaphor of "vile bodies" being one of the most enduring icons of the canon of racism. Social workers and their predecessors were summoned to maintain a semblance of social control through casework and child protective services (Gordon, 1988).

Italians, Jews, and other recent immigrants often lived in neighborhoods in close proximity to African Americans and felt compelled to distance and distinguish themselves by claiming "whiteness." In Chapter 5 we discuss in greater detail what it means to "become white." Put simply here, for an ethnic group that has experienced hostility and oppression, to assume whiteness means to begin to work toward racial assimilation.

Although the group may retain its ethnic identity and practices, racial assimilation means that the group now expects to be treated as white—able to move into affordable neighborhoods, be admitted to colleges and universities, assume that jobs will not discriminate against them because of their race or ethnicity, enjoy the privilege of not being stopped by the police because of skin color, and not be subjected to laws or informal barriers that limit intermarriage. Many of the ethnic groups that initially encountered prejudice, stereotyping, and social exclusion now have assumed the status of mainstream whites, despite retaining aspects of their ethnic identities.

ETHNICITY AND RACE

Several historical factors distinguish white ethnic groups from ethnic groups of color. Although many white ethnic groups encountered and endured serious disapproval and prejudice upon arriving in the United States, there are still some qualitative distinctions between their experiences and those of ethnic groups of color. Exercise 3.1 offers a series of questions to ask members of any ethnic or racial group for comparative purposes. The answers may help to distinguish between the experiences of racism in the United States as encountered by people of color and by whites. We will highlight some of the most important differences next.

Voluntary versus involuntary immigration or contact. The conditions of the initial contact situation are influential to the dynamics of intergroup relations, the trajectory of a group's success, and a group's identity. All white ethnic groups chose to immigrate to the United States, with the exception of early indentured servants, who were able to discharge their obligations of servitude. This signals group agency and autonomy, some control over one's group narrative, and it offers a much better opportunity to carry resources during immigration, maintain and develop those assets, and acquire new social and economic capital.

Native Americans and Mexican Americans were stripped and divested of the resources they had before their hostile encounters with whites. African Americans were transported here involuntarily without any belongings, just the resources they carried inside of themselves and the bonds that endured between people. Chinese, Japanese, and other Asian Americans were subject to laws and practices that inhibited their capacity to develop and accumulate resources and secure occupational niches.

Human versus not fully human. Although some white ethnic immigrant groups were not considered civilized and were viewed as being uncouth, pagan, greedy, lazy, stupid, and immoral, they were never denied the recognition of their humanity. The same cannot be said for Native Americans and African Americans. Latino Americans and Asian Americans also have been viewed as coming from inferior and less civilized cultures, and their integrity with reference to genetics has been questioned during certain historical epochs. They historically have been viewed as being less able to assimilate than white ethnic groups, although there are certainly trends today, such as rates of out-group intermarriage, which indicate that this myth is eroding.

The depth and breadth of discrimination. The quality of discrimination is hard to measure, but some differences are important to note. Slavery lasted for centuries, and after it was abolished in this country, Jim Crow and severe discrimination persisted. Native Americans were nearly exterminated by Europeans. This is qualitatively different from the experiences of white ethnic groups, who experienced initial discrimination but within two or three generations were able to move out of poor neighborhoods and gain access to the full opportunities of American society. These groups (e.g., Irish, Jews, Italians) who initially were constructed as not being white eventually were able to claim membership in the "white race" (Guglielmo & Salerno, 2003; Ignatiev, 1995; Sacks, 1996).

Even while living in poor ethnic enclaves, white immigrants were never as segregated as African Americans and never encountered the same depth of social and economic isolation and exclusion (Iglehart & Becerra, 1995; Jansson, 2005; Katz, 1986). All white ethnic groups had opportunities to achieve social mobility much more rapidly than ethnic groups of color, despite initial hurdles and barriers.

Control or influence over the group narrative. As white ethnic groups have gained power and resources and have achieved social mobility, they also have gained more control over their group narrative, the story of their ethnic group. The ability to have some efficacy is important for a group's internal sense of self-esteem and worth, as well as in shaping how others view one's group (Thomas, 1994). This does not happen overnight, and success occurs on many fronts. One factor is who owns or produces public narratives, such as television shows, news broadcasts, books, and songs. Another variable is in having watchdog groups, such as the Anti-Defamation League or the Order of the Sons of Italy, to publicly challenge offensive stereotypes or ethnic misrepresentations.

Group leaders and role models can influence public discourse in the way they describe or characterize various social groups. They can extol virtues or exaggerate deficits, include members as part of an in-group of Americans or distinguish them as outsiders and aliens. Control or influence over group narratives is never absolute: White ethnic groups still find that their members are caricatured, just as ethnic and racial groups have experienced extreme racism and yet have struggled boldly to assume some authorship over their own stories.

LIMINALITY

The construction of race and ethnicity is fluid, contested, and contextual. As we have discussed, even the notion of who is white or of color has shifted over time. One of our examples was of two Cubans who immigrated to Miami. Even though Latinos fall within the metacategory of being of color, one Cuban was considered "white" and the other Cuban was considered "black". Contradictions, inconsistencies, and irregularities arise whenever we try to group people for the sake of categorization or discussion. People do not appreciate being lumped into a group in a way that is inconsistent with how they define themselves. Yet that is exactly what has happened to many groups in the United States. They were offered or denied access, rights, and opportunities based on how they were socially constructed and categorized.

We must acknowledge that some groups more than others occupy a liminal space in the world of socially constructed race, at the boundaries and frontiers of racial typologies. Although there are many examples, we will briefly consider three: Arab Americans, Asian Americans, and Jewish Americans.

ARAB AMERICANS   For many years, and according to the U.S. census, Arab Americans have been considered white, based on racial categories that include Caucasian. Although many Arab Americans consider themselves to be Caucasian or white, significant numbers believe that Arab Americans are treated like people of color and subjected to racism and discrimination. The wake of 9/11 has seen many instances of anti-Arab sentiment, stereotyping, and hostility. This has been exacerbated by the unending "war on terrorism" and military conflicts with Afghanistan and Iraq, as well as in the severe, unresolved tensions between Arabs and Jews in the Middle East. It illustrates how international events increasingly shape the contours of race and racism in the United States.

ASIAN AMERICANS   Although we have described the strength of racism experienced by Chinese and Japanese Americans, as well as other Asian nationalities in the United States, there are differences within the diverse Asian American community over their connections and common experiences with people of color or whites. Many Asian Americans feel the sting of racism, whether it is through racial stereotypes portrayed in the media or outright hostility from whites in society.

Further, because Asian Americans have a high rate of out-group intermarriage with whites (nearly 50%), many of them do not consider themselves to have a lot in common with other ethnic groups of color and may not consider themselves to be people of color. There is no right or wrong here; rather, this is a statement about the complexities and vicissitudes of how we define ourselves and others racially in a racialized society.

JEWISH AMERICANS   Many Jews have experienced forms of racism and oppression. Most, although not all, Jews in the United States are descendants of Ashkenazi Jews in Europe. Many Jews acknowledge that, at this stage in U.S. history, they have access to most if not all of the benefits of other white citizens. Nevertheless, Jews have a lengthy history of oppression and suffered one of the most destructive and egregious acts of racism in modern history, the Jewish Holocaust of World War II.

Jews also have also encountered severe anti-Semitism in the United States, and this form of oppression endures, although it is marginalized. Jews are a religious minority in a highly Christian country. And Jews, like Arabs, are impacted by a world context of tremendous tensions and acts of violence stemming from the conflict in the Middle East, which have spread to other parts of the world such as Europe. So some Jews can have a hard time considering themselves as white Americans, despite the predominant experience of white skin privilege.

In short, the historical experiences of groups and the ways by which these experiences shape social identity are laced with tensions, contradictions, and anomalies. In addition, many individuals claim multiple group heritages with their complex racial and ethnic identities. Thus, we will ever be cautious about generalizations and respectful of the tremendous diversity within groups.

RACISM AND THE HELPING PROFESSIONS IN HISTORICAL PERSPECTIVE

In the United States, the helping professions were born and grew within a racial contract (Mills, 1997) in an evolving, fluctuating, and mutating racial project (Omi & Winant, 1994). All durable inequalities involve adaptation and institutional emulation of structured disparities (Tilly, 1998). Thus, it is not surprising to find the nascent helping professions reflecting the racism of society and participating in its maintenance. We will consider three major eras of social policy enactment: the Progressive Era, the New Deal, and the Great Society, focusing on the influence of race and racism on legislation and social programs, as well as the impact on racism of the policies and reforms.

PROGRESSIVE ERA

In late 19th-century America, major and profound social trends interacted, and the helping professions emerged within this milieu. Industrialization was a major economic and social force, attracting large numbers of immigrants, particularly from Europe, and cities became swollen with working and poor people. The fact that most of the immigrants were from Europe in itself reflected the depth of racism in U.S. institutions and the American consciousness.

The period from the end of the Civil War to the turn of the century has been called the "Gilded Age" (Jansson, 2005). It was characterized by the development of major cartels and monopolies, the ascendancy of an industrialist elite, corruption and greed, extreme economic inequality, and profound labor and social unrest (Axinn & Levin, 1992; Jansson, 2005; Katz, 1986; Trattner, 1999; Zinn, 1980). The extreme economic disparities and the precarious plight of workers and immigrants were justified by "social Darwinism," which saw society as an arena for survival of the fittest. This, in turn, justified the lack of government intervention, because it would buoy and protect the weakest. This social philosophy was fueled by nativist reactions to the masses of immigrants, as well as being overtly racist toward people of color while offering a framework to shape perceptions of the poor, as well as to guide reform efforts.

Cities during this period were squalid, with overcrowding, extreme poverty, poor sanitation, health hazards, and exploitation of children. Urban residents were buffeted by economic depressions and their vulnerability to financial fluctuations. Even reform and social movements had racist and nativist overtones: Trade unions were hostile to people of color; suffragists fought mostly for the right of white women to vote; and the birth control movement was associated with the move for eugenics, which espoused overtly racist ideologies (Jansson, 2005; Trattner, 1999).

The main thrust of the Progressive Movement—which extended from the turn of the century until the end of World War I—was legislation focusing on anti-trust activities, instituting economic reforms, introducing a federal income tax, producing health and sanitation standards, enacting women's suffrage and child labor laws, and establishing juvenile courts. Although these universalistic reforms and protections were in theory of benefit to all, they did not challenge institutional or societal racism, which in turn was fueled by prejudice and intergroup hostility. The two major presidential figures of this period, Theodore Roosevelt and Woodrow Wilson, courted white southern racists as their part of their political base and overtly expressed racist attitudes in speeches and public statements, as well as in their actions (Iglehart & Becerra, 1995; Jansson, 2005).

The Progressive Era did not respond to Jim Crow in the South or discrimination against the Chinese and Japanese in the West and Mexican Americans in the South, and it was a period of continued land grabs from Native Americans, as well as attempts to destroy their culture. *Plessy v. Ferguson*—the Supreme Court decision in 1896 enshrining the doctrine of separate but equal—stood as the law of the land. African Americans continued to have drastically higher infant mortality rates and shorter life expectancy than whites, despite the poverty of many white immigrants (Iglehart & Becerra). Within this context, many helping professions were growing—in particular, social work, public health, juvenile justice, and those associated with public education. We will briefly explore two forerunners of social work—the Charity Organization Societies and the Settlement House movement.

CHARITY ORGANIZATION SOCIETIES   The Charity Organization Societies represented a well-intentioned response by upper-middle-class, Christian, white reformers, primarily women, to save and elevate the poor, particularly white immigrants. Rather than offering material assistance, the philosophy advocated using social assessment to identify social pathologies and the relationship (a forerunner of the casework relationship in social work) to effect change. The approach, which was riddled with class biases and would be considered patronizing by today's standards, was predicated on and fueled by many ethnic and racial stereotypes. White immigrant groups, and not racial and ethnic groups of color, were the primary targets of the COS.

SETTLEMENT HOUSES   Settlement houses were founded to elevate the poor through contact with their social betters. This movement was spearheaded by upper-middle-class women, but there was minimal social distance between the reformers and their clients, as many settlement house workers actually lived in the settlement houses. The emphasis was on efficacy and empowerment, with a less punitive, morally judgmental attitude. Their use of groups and education and their willingness to fight for needed social reforms reflected an appreciation for the environmental causes of poverty, sickness, and social problems.

Although settlement houses pressed for political and economic protections, they did not work to further social integration or challenge the structure and dynamics of racism (Berman-Rossi & Miller, 1994). And, though some of the settlement house leaders—notably Jane Addams (Jansson, 2005) and Sophonisba Breckinridge (Iglehart & Bercera, 1995)—acknowledged racism, settlement houses for the most part were established by white reformers, served white clients, and did not respond adequately to the needs of African Americans and other people of color (Berman-Rossi & Miller, 1994). Carson (1990, p. 195) summarized this by saying that

> . . . institutionally the settlements failed to make any significant contributions to white Americans' consciousness of racism or the furthering of black people's rights and opportunities.

Consequently, African Americans worked to establish their own social networks, social service programs, and settlement houses. Unlike white settlement houses, black settlement houses attempted to foster race pride, promote mutual aid, and tried to integrate micro (personal) issues while responding to macro-level social problems (Carlton-LaNey, 1999). There was less social distance between workers and clients, more support for the need of women to work than in white-run settlement houses, and stronger efforts to create the social institutions and programs in the black community that were more manifest in white communities (Gordon, 1991).

Taking care of one's own people in the face of white indifference and hostility also spurred Japanese and Chinese Americans to form community networks and pool their economic resources. Newly arrived Mexican immigrants in the Southwest often looked back to Mexico for supports and services unavailable in the United States (Jansson, 2005).

Neither the Charity Organization Societies nor the white-run settlement houses responded adequately to the needs of people of color. As institutions, they re-created and perpetuated the dynamics of racism found in other sectors of society.

THE NEW DEAL

The New Deal, with its unprecedented number of employment projects and social insurance programs, heralded a new era of government response to need. For the first time in the nation's history, the federal government provided massive grants for people in need, created huge public works projects to provide jobs, and established a system of social insurance and welfare. Yet this, too, was a period in which the racial project was not questioned seriously or undermined and serious acts of racism continued to be perpetrated, including one of the greatest blots in the history of racism in the United States.

The New Deal, more than anything else, was a response to the Great Depression that began with the stock market crash of 1929 and persisted for 12 years. Business and bank failures were staggering, the magnitude of unemployment was unprecedented, the economic challenges to the country were catastrophic, and the social unrest challenged the nation's economic and political systems. When Franklin Roosevelt won the presidential election in 1932, the rate of unemployment in many cities and communities across the country was 20% to a staggering 60% (Jansson, 2005)!

Roosevelt's response in the form of the New Deal was based on three premises (Axinn & Levin, 1992):

1. a belief in the efficacy of the free market system,
2. an attempt to maintain a balanced budget, and
3. an attempt to create an effective demand for employment and consumption through massive government spending.

The New Deal also offered three types of relief (Jansson, 2005):

1. grants to states for direct emergency relief through the Federal Emergency Relief Agency (FERA),
2. public works programs to stimulate investment, employment, and consumption, and
3. eventually, social insurance for the elderly and welfare for children and the blind.

Legislation also was passed to reform the economic system, such as the National Labor Relations Act (the "Wagner Act") and the Fair Labor Standards Act, which encouraged unionization, raised the minimum wage, and limited workweeks (Jansson, 2005). The model for all of the programs of the New Deal was for the federal government to funnel resources through states and cities.

Herein lies a fundamental problem for a racially stratified society: Roosevelt sought to retain the political support of many regions of the country, certainly of the South. He also promoted universal programs, because these garnered greater political support. He instituted a few efforts to support fairness for people of color, such as a nondiscrimination statement in the Works Progress Administration (WPA), and African American men eventually did constitute about 10% of the Civilian Conservation Corps (CCC) and 15% of the WPA (Jansson, 2005). But the CCC camps and housing at other work relief programs remained segregated (Jones, 1985)—which is illustrative of the tensions and contradictions caused by not challenging racism directly.

This pattern rippled throughout the programs of the New Deal. Local agencies administering programs often discriminated against blacks and Hispanics, including delaying the processing of their applications, maintaining racial quotas, and demoting workers to positions that were lower than their education and training warranted (Abramovitz, 1988). Structurally, the programs excluded many people of color, as the benefits did not extend to those who worked in agriculture, as domestics, or in unregulated, secondary economic sectors (Jansson, 2005; Jones, 1985). By some estimates, three-quarters of African Americans were not covered by the social insurance benefits of the New Deal (Brown et al., 2003).

Roosevelt and the New Deal did not challenge poll taxes or lynching in the South (Jansson, 2005). Mexican Americans, who had been recruited from Mexico to do agricultural and ranching work, were forcibly repatriated, while those living in Los Angeles were subject to attacks by whites and to police brutality (Jansson, 2005).

Native Americans were grappling with the Native American Reorganization Act of 1934, which, although perhaps well-intentioned, caused problems. The Act sought to establish semi-tribal governments and encourage economic development but still fostered a client-like, dependent relationship between tribes and the federal government, ceding a great deal of authority to the Secretary of the Interior for Indian affairs. Many Native Americans viewed this Act as another step toward losing their culture and heritage, as local chiefs were replaced with tribal councils. As for Asian Americans, most still were unable to immigrate to the United States. As described previously, Japanese American citizens were placed in concentration camps.

So where were the helping professions during this turbulent period? This was a time of growth and expansion for social work and other helping professions. Groupwork expanded, and the specialty of community organizing was becoming popular. For the most part, social work and other allied professions supported the Roosevelt administration and the New Deal programs (Jansson, 2005). A number of social workers, such as Eveline Burns and Mary Switzer, were active in the Roosevelt administration. A radical group of social workers known as the "Rank and File" criticized the New Deal for propping up capitalism and failing to deal with profound social inequities and injustices, including racism (Abramovitz, 1988). But this small group did not represent the profession as a whole.

In sum, racism was not challenged seriously during the period of the New Deal, and because of a lack of willingness to confront it at the highest levels and the tendency to dispense programs through states and cities, societal racism structured and shaped the contours of the New Deal. Many racial and ethnic minorities continued to suffer from levels of prejudice and discrimination and relief, public works, social insurance, and welfare programs did not reach people of color in the same way that they assisted whites. Executive Order 9066, establishing Japanese-American internment camps, was one of the worst acts of American racism in the 20th century and was not atoned for until a half a century later.

THE CIVIL RIGHTS MOVEMENT AND THE GREAT SOCIETY

After World War II, seismic societal changes took place in the United States. People of color served with distinction in segregated military units and were not prepared to resume a subordinate social status; their expectations of fairness and social justice were higher. This was accentuated by the Cold War between the United States and the Soviet Union, in which the United States was presenting itself as a democracy—and racism is decidedly undemocratic. Japanese Americans were freed from their internment and quickly asserted themselves by challenging California's Alien Land Act through legislation in 1948 (Takaki, 1993).

Major demographic changes were at work as well. The dramatic expansion of highways during the Eisenhower years, coupled with the boom in housing fueled by the GI Bill, led to a striking expansion of the suburbs, accompanied by white flight from cities and de facto segregated neighborhoods. People of color all over the nation and from Puerto Rico migrated to cities seeking jobs, but they encountered poverty, discrimination, and ethnic and racial ghettoes (Jansson, 2005). The great migration of African Americans from the South to cities in the Northeast, upper Midwest, and West continued, and between 1940 and 1970, 4.5 million African Americans made this journey (Jansson, 2005).

Major executive orders and Supreme Court decisions furthered the cause of civil rights. President Harry Truman desegregated the armed forces by executive order in 1948 and the *Brown v. Board of Education* ruling in 1954 upended the "separate but equal" decision of *Plessy v. Fergusson* and led to a movement to desegregate schools. One of the consequences of the migration of people of color to urban areas was that they had greater access to one another, fostering a sense of solidarity and furthering their ability to communicate and organize to protect themselves and advocate for their own needs (Jansson, 2005).

The Civil Rights Movement that originated in the South often is referred to as the "Second Reconstruction," following the first reconstruction immediately after the Civil War. In 1955, Rosa Parks refused to give up her seat on a bus to a white person, leading to a bus boycott in Montgomery, Alabama, and eventually to court-ordered desegregation of public transportation (Takaki, 1993). Demonstrations at segregated lunch counters and "freedom rides" challenged segregation on buses and at bus terminals. In 1963, Dr. Martin Luther King, Jr. led a massive civil rights march in Washington. Social workers were active in the Civil Rights Movement, and in 1964 a Columbia University social work student, Michael Schwerner, was murdered in Mississippi, along with James Chaney and Andrew Goodman.

Although the Civil Rights Movement initially focused on civil rights rather than economic rights, the two were soon linked. The emergence of Malcolm X as a black spokesperson and subsequent riots by African Americans feeling

trapped and frustrated in many cities furthered the impetus for civil and economic rights (Takaki, 1993). In 1967 the National Advisory Committee on
Urban Disorders reported eight major uprisings, 33 other serious rebellions,
and 123 minor outbreaks, in which racism was cited as the major cause of this
massive social unrest and disorder (Zinn, 1980). Black militant groups, such as
the Black Panthers, emerged, advocating armed struggle.

The conditions of racism and economic exclusion in cities led to high rates
of African American unemployment as migration from the South continued
(Miller, 2003). Social workers responded by actively organizing programs to
serve people and also precipitated a crisis in the inadequate social welfare
system. Richard Cloward, George Brager, Harry Specht, and Sherman Barr, all
social workers, were instrumental in converting anti-gang programs, such as
Mobilization for Youth, into anti-poverty operations. They devised a strategy
of enrolling all those who were eligible for welfare in New York City, most of
whom were not receiving benefits, by learning about the city's welfare regulations and educating clients about their rights. The goal was to bankrupt the
system and force the federal government to step in with adequate resources, or
even establish a guaranteed annual income (Edsall & Edsall, 1991; Katz, 1989;
Leman, 1991; Miller, 2003).

All of the strong social currents described thus far, along with the assassi-
nation of President Kennedy in 1963 and the ascendancy of Lyndon Johnson—
who won a landslide victory in 1964 and whose party controlled both houses of
Congress—created an unprecedented tide of social change and legislation
addressing racism, under the awning of the Great Society. The Economic
Opportunity Act of 1964 established Community Action Programs, designed to
combat poverty and engage citizens with "maximum feasible participation"
(Katz, 1989; Miller, 2003; Trattner, 1999).

Programs that emerged from this legislation included VISTA, Job Corps,
Neighborhood Youth Corps, Operation Head Start, and Upward Bound. Food
stamps were introduced, and Model Cities legislation in 1966 targeted poor
urban neighborhoods with federal resources for public schools, nutrition, and
health care for women and children. This Act, as well as the HUD acts of 1965
and 1968, boosted low-income housing (Axinn & Levin, 1992). Medicaid and
Medicare were established in 1965.

All of these programs were aimed at reducing poverty, which indirectly
addressed the consequences of institutional racism. Additional legislation
directly confronted racial discrimination and supported civil rights. The Civil
Rights Act of 1964 prohibited racial, ethnic, or sexual discrimination in
employment and established the Equal Opportunity Commission (Axinn &
Levin, 1992; Jansson, 2005; Trattner, 1999). Under this Act the Attorney
General could file suits against racially segregated court systems and the U.S.
government could withhold federal funds for schools and hospitals that practiced racial discrimination (Edsall & Edsall, 1991). The Voting Rights Act of
1965 guaranteed all citizens the right to vote, and Executive Order 11246
established Affirmative Action to redress current and historical patterns of
racial discrimination.

The Great Society did not redistribute wealth dramatically; programs were underfunded and there was mismanagement and corruption (Leman, 1991; Trattner, 1999). A guaranteed annual income did not materialize. Although the Great Society did not extinguish the virus of racism, its legacy is profound in the struggle against racism in the United States. The programs aimed at helping the poor and strengthening urban areas benefited people of color as well as poor whites and those who were city dwellers. Poverty rates were reduced for people of all ages, discrimination was curtailed dramatically, and affirmative action opened doors sufficiently to allow more people of color to enter the middle class (Katz, 1989).

Perhaps one of the Great Society's most notable accomplishments was not in the specific programs that were enacted but, rather, in the attempt by the federal government to challenge and dismantle racism directly. Not since the Civil War and the immediate aftermath of Reconstruction had such a focused and concerted effort to dismantle racism emanated from Washington. As a result of the passion for social justice generated during the 1960s, social workers, lawyers, and other helping professionals often entered their professions. Not since Abraham Lincoln was presidential leadership exercised on behalf of people of color as by Kennedy and Johnson.

In today's times, it is difficult to believe that a President, let alone a President from the South, could make speeches endorsing affirmative action with vigor and passion. And herein lies the tragedy of the Great Society—the political and social backlash that has followed it. The Deep South moved inexorably from Democrat waters to become a Republican sea of red, led by white voters associating Democrats with the rights of people of color (Edsall & Edsall, 1991). Across the country, working-class and middle-class white Democrats, angered by what they viewed as preferential treatment for people of color through efforts such as affirmative action, revolted and backed the conservative Republican presidential candidate, Ronald Reagan. The country became increasingly conservative, cutting taxes and social welfare programs, and dismantling or underfunding many of the Great Society programs. Today, many white people in this country view racism as a past legacy rather than a present reality, which we will examine more closely in the next two chapters.

CONCLUSION

Racism has been part and parcel of the history of the United States, from the earliest European settlers to the present. Many ethnic groups, including some considered to be white today, encountered prejudice and social exclusion, but the ethnic/racial groups socially constructed as people of color experienced racism that was significantly more extreme and persistent. Painful as it may be, to understand the extent and dynamics of racism today, we must explore and revisit this history. This also is necessary if we are to accomplish true racial healing and reconciliation in this country. Although we have made tremendous progress in confronting racism since the founding of the American Republic, the capacity of racism to adapt and endure, and to render itself increasingly invisible to those who are most privileged by it, is a challenge that will be considered throughout the rest of this book.

EXERCISE 3.1   DIFFERENTIAL GROUP EXPERIENCE

The following questions can be applied to any U.S. ethnic or racial group, to understand and compare their historical experiences. This exercise can highlight significant differences between ethnic and racial groups of color and those constructed as white, as well as differences between groups within those categories. Select a white ethnic group and an ethnic group of color and consider the following questions:

1. Was contact or immigration voluntary or involuntary for each of the two groups?
2. Were members of each group ever legally defined as not being fully human?
3. What resources did each group have—linguistic, cultural, economic? Was there a fit of skills with job opportunities?
4. How destructive was the oppression (e.g., genocide, slavery, exclusion, internment, dispossession, lack of civil rights)? Have members of each group ever been forcibly repatriated or barred from emigrating to the United States? Were there laws justifying each group's subordinate status?
5. How far-reaching and severe was the damage caused by racial and ethnic oppression of each group—economic, social, family, psychological, cultural, legal?
6. How long did each group experience severe oppression in the United States? Was the oppression transitory, in that the group later was enabled to become "white"? Did significant numbers of group members live for generations in socially and economically isolated and deprived neighborhoods? Have poverty rates and other indicators of social well-being been consistently lower for each of these groups than for other groups?
7. Does the oppression of either group endure today?
8. Does either group continue to lack access to resources, as well as to cultural, social, economic, and political capital?
9. Are there enduring denigrating stereotypes and cultural scapegoating for each of these groups?
10. Do members of each group consistently encounter harassment by law-enforcement officials? Are members of each group overrepresented in the criminal justice system and underrepresented at universities and in many occupations and professions?

THE WEB OF INSTITUTIONAL RACISM

In the video "True Colors," Diane Sawyer leads a team of journalists/researchers for the ABC television show *Primetime Live* to "test" whether racism is still alive in a "typical" U.S. city (True Colors, 1991). Two testers, one black and the other white, are filmed secretly while sampling the economic staples and rewards of American society. It becomes clear that the two are consistently treated differently. An advertised job is open to the white man, with great encouragement from the employer, and the same employer denies that the job is available when the black man with the same credentials applies for the job. The same happens with an apartment that is allegedly for rent.

And in a music store, the white man browses without notice while the black man is followed by an employee wherever he goes. A used car dealer jacks up the price of the same car for the black man. As the two men leave the television studio after debriefing, a taxi ignores the black man and screeches to a halt to take the white man. Many white people who watch this video have expressed shock, while many people of color nod their head because these experiences are all too familiar.

For a significant number of white people, racism *is* a relic of the past and not a salient social issue today. Many whites believe that we have moved to a color-blind society. True racism is associated with the overt, Southern white variety of hostility, aggression, and discrimination that was challenged by the Civil Rights Movement after World War II. Certainly there has been a great deal of movement toward diminishing overt forms of racism and most U.S. citizens, whatever their race, now believe that racism is wrong (Bobo, 2001).

As visible signs of progress, more people of color have gained access to universities, many police departments now are desegregated, and significantly more people of color are serving in public life as business leaders, actors, athletes, Supreme Court justices, cabinet officers (including two secretaries of state and an attorney general appointed by a conservative Republican President).

At the same time, some whites have resented civil rights accomplishments. School busing in the wake of the *Brown v. Board of Education* decision in the 1950s spurred white anger and flight from cities to suburbs, and from public schools to private and parochial schools—in many instances reinstituting de-facto segregation. And some whites now feel victimized, believing that their chances of being admitted to elite colleges or of securing jobs are diminished by too much emphasis on race, which they think favor people of color.

To be sure, many white people are well aware of the persistence of racism in the United States. Still, whites and people of color show marked differences in their beliefs about the extent of racism today, and these disparities indicate a significant perceptual racial divide in this country (Shipler, 1997). African Americans and Hispanics overwhelmingly believe that there is occupational discrimination in favor of whites, while less than a fourth of whites agree; and people of color view racism as a deeply entrenched, institutional phenomenon, while many whites see it as a question of attitudes and behaviors (Bobo, 2001).

These different observations perhaps belie fundamentally dissimilar experiences with racism, but the perceptual chasm itself becomes a factor in sustaining racism. A danger in having such divergent views about the nature of social phenomena in a highly segregated society is that many people exist in homogenous environments in which it is easy to mistake mirrors for windows.

Revisionist historians and critical social scientists, such as Takaki (1993), Ignatiev (1995), Allen (1994), and Steinberg (2001), have illustrated how members of certain ethnic groups gained access to resources, were granted full citizenship and assumed the privileges of whiteness in short order while members of other ethnic groups who were socially and legally constructed as "other" experienced barriers, exclusion, and even extreme and brutal repression at times. As is still the case today, those who encountered severe social oppression were, in turn, held responsible for their own misfortunes.

A political backlash has erupted in response to the Great Society. One form of this backlash has been the growth of predominantly white exurbs and gated communities, as well as concerted assaults on affirmative action, questioning its use to ensure diverse student representation on college campuses and in social work programs. This backlash also has resulted in a stalling or even backsliding of the gains and momentum created by the civil rights movements of the 1950s and 1960s.

In this chapter we will map out the contours of the web of institutional racism in the United States today in the wake of this backlash, illuminating its stubborn and tenacious tendrils. We will focus on nine types of institutional racism: residential, educational, employment, accumulation of wealth and upward mobility, environmental and health, mental health, criminal justice, political, and media The emphasis here is on how racism remains institutionally embedded in U.S. society and what remains be done, as opposed to what has been accomplished. We are well aware of other severe forms of social oppression in the United States—for example, class inequities, sexism, heterosexism—and that these (and other types of social oppression) are intricately entwined with racism. To completely separate out, for example, the effects of class inequities or those due to racism, is difficult. We will consider these intersections of oppression in Chapter 7.

THE NATURE OF THE WEB OF RACISM

We have diagrammed the web of institutional racism in Figure 4.1. This figure does not cover every type of institutional racism; instead, each circle encapsulates a critical area in which institutional racism is manifested through laws, policies, and formal and informal practices. Each nodule is connected to all of the others, although some are attached by large, thick cables and others by thin but strong threads. Some strands of the web restrain certain ethnic or racial groups of color more than others, and some individuals and subgroups succeed and prosper despite the web. The web is metaphorical but, as we will illustrate, also very real.

Durable inequalities, such as racism, are replicated in all institutions and practices of a society, although their form adapts and changes (Omi & Winant,

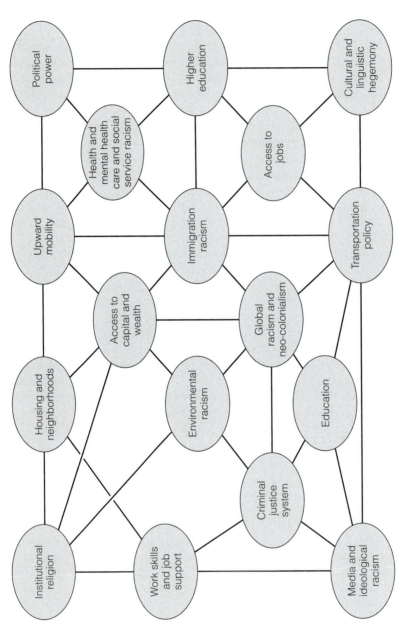

Note: Connecting lines are arbitrary and for illustration; in reality, each form of institutional racism connects with each other form in multiple ways.

FIGURE 4.1 | WEB OF INSTITUTIONAL RACISM

1994; Tilly, 1998). The United States was founded on a "racial contract," which was the shadow side of the social contract (Mills, 1997), topics that were explored in Chapter 3. The social contract stressed the Enlightenment values of equality, citizenship, and human rights, and the racial contract defined who was human and who was not, who was free and who was enslaved, who could be dispossessed of their lands and often slaughtered, and who would take their place. Thus, we should not be surprised that in a nation founded on a racial contract, racism is reflected in institutions and policies. It is as if the "public DNA" contains this mutation, which is regenerated and reproduced. Because the racial contract is ubiquitous, it becomes central, the norm, a given, which makes it all the more difficult to see by those unimpeded by it (Mills).

In the film *The Matrix*, the hero (who is white) lives in an illusory world that appears pleasing and benign until he has a transformative experience (guided by an African American man) that enables him to view the deceptions and corruption that have always surrounded him. In presenting the web, we hope to make visible the semi-hidden matrix of racism and also to examine its scope, depth, and its many connections. Any one chamber of this maze is problematic and of concern, but taken together the sites and locations of the web of racism potentiate one another, increasing their ability to exclude and deny. Although some parts of the web, such as racial profiling (in which motorists are stopped because of their race) are overtly racist, what is particularly insidious is that much of the web includes institutions and policies that are viewed as race-neutral, such as transportation and environmental policy.

We emphasize five aspects of the web here:

1. It is systematic and comprehensive, not a case of isolated pockets of "leftover racism."
2. It exists on many levels. For example, educational racism at the macro level shows a racialized pattern of unequal funding for schools and also (at the mezzo level) insufficient teachers and administrators of color working in many school districts, to racial microaggressions (at the micro level) being perpetrated against students by other students and teachers.
3. It combines formal and informal practices, some overt and others covert. For example, residential segregation is maintained by formal lending policies; many people of color, particularly African Americans, have more difficulty than whites qualifying for mortgages. More informally, some real estate agents guide prospective homeowners to some properties and neighborhoods and not to others, or landlords and property sellers are willing or unwilling to do business with people by virtue of their race. Predominantly white communities, in which many white people grew up or live, were not formed by accident or coincidence; they resulted from many strands of the web of racism.
4. It is cumulative, not just contemporaneous. Today's web is built on webs going back hundreds of years, resulting in disinvestment and disempowerment; it is the legacy of generations of outright oppression, systematic exclusion, and loss of opportunity. It has resulted in an inability to

generate and maximize social and economic assets (Brown et al., 2003). Thus, the web is historical, as well as reflecting current social phenomena.

5. It contains the molecules of power—the power to make laws and policies, to enforce them, to fund them, to define and present them, and to create a public narrative and discourse that normalizes them.

The web of institutional racism encompasses neighborhoods and housing, education, employment, upward mobility, environment and health, mental health, racism within the criminal justice system, political racism, and media racism. We will explore each of these webs in turn.

RESIDENTIAL RACISM: NEIGHBORHOODS AND HOUSING

We discuss residential racism first because it is a bedrock of racism, "normal" yet insidious, influencing other strands of the web and casting a long shadow over those excluded from some neighborhoods and trapped in others. Although there have been instances of desegregation—ever since the Great Society, significant numbers of African Americans and other people of color have moved to suburbs and middle-class neighborhoods—residential segregation still is a fixture of American life. Many poor African Americans continue to live in hypersegregated, deprived, and isolated neighborhoods, at times called ghettoes, and continue to be the most residentially segregated racial group in the country (Brown et al., 2003; Feagin, 1999; Massey & Denton, 1993).

The phenomenon of white flight has been a social trend since the end of World War II, and the majority of white people now live in neighborhoods that are predominantly white (Squires, 1999). They rarely have contact with poor, urban neighborhoods of color and imagine life in those neighborhoods through the filters of media-amplified, white, middle-class stereotypes. How does this happen?

Although the home-ownership rate for African Americans has grown to 49%, it still lags well behind the rate for whites, which is 76% (Pelletiere, 2005). Since the late 1950s, federal lending policy has favored loans to predominantly white suburbs (Brown et al., 2003) and transportation policy has privileged the building of highways that serve suburbs over public transportation in metropolitan areas. Shapiro (2004) argues that segregation is supported by racial discrimination enacted by real estate brokers and mortgage lenders, along with white racial attitudes that restrict people of color from trying to move into neighborhoods. This is reinforced by zoning regulations that exclude rental and public housing from some neighborhoods and result in high concentrations of such housing in others.

Real estate agents engage in informal "redlining" that determines which homes and neighborhoods are shown to prospective homebuyers. Mortgage lenders are less likely to grant mortgages to people of color, particularly African Americans (Brown et al., 2003; Feagin, 1999; Massey & Denton, 1993; Shapiro, 2004). According to the Urban League (2004), African

Americans are denied mortgages at twice the rate of whites. Credit is harder to establish and the terms of loans are more severe for African Americans (Manning, 1999). Middle class African Americans also face higher hurdles with home financing than their white counterparts. These African Americans often have less equity than whites to begin with and are more likely to borrow "subprime" loans, which allow them to make a lesser down payment but saddle them with significantly higher interest rates (Brown et al., 2003; Pelletiere, 2005; Shapiro, 2004).

Social and psychological factors have fueled segregated housing as well. In the 1950s, overt manifestations—including mob violence, intimidation, and acts such as burning crosses on the lawns of African Americans—frightened people of color from moving into predominantly white areas (Brown et al., 2003). As the numbers of people of color increase in a community, so does white hostility and the urge of whites to move to another neighborhood (Taylor, 1998). Entire communities, such as Sherman Park, Wisconsin, and Yeadon, Pennsylvania, which once were predominantly white, became predominantly black as African Americans moved in (Steinhorn & Diggs-Brown, 1999). Whites today seem to feel more comfortable with Asian and Asian American neighbors than with African American neighbors, with Latinos falling somewhere in the middle (Charles, 2001). This pattern is similar to the rates of intermarriage between whites and people of color.

The consequences of segregation are profound, affecting education, access to jobs, health and economic well-being, and upward mobility. For people of color trapped in hyper-segregated "ghettoes," a vicious cycle ensues that further ensnares them and diminishes their life opportunities. Because neighborhood stores are sparse, shopping is difficult and prices at those few stores often are higher. Also, there is a also a dearth of banks, so residents have to resort to check-cashing establishments and loan sharks for financial transactions, incurring high fees and rates of interest (Calhoun & Bailey, 2005).

Because fewer jobs are available in these areas, residents turn to secondary and illegal job markets for employment (outside of the mainstream and the law), and crime rises. As property values fall, residents lose even more of their equity—if they had any to begin with (Shapiro, 2004). Loans from banks and mortgage companies for repair and renovation become less available, and disinvestment stalks the community, which deteriorates further (Massey & Denton, 1993; Feagin, 1999).

As communities become less safe, people avoid being out in public and keep their children off the streets, which makes the neighborhood even more dangerous (Massey & Denton, 1993; Miller, 2001). Further, the police patrolling the neighborhood often feel threatened, alienated, and prone to overreaction, which contributes to an escalating cycle of tensions between residents and authorities. As residents become more socially isolated, fueled by the absence of adequate transportation and well-paying mainstream jobs, there are fewer role models for prosocial behaviors. This is a climate in which self-destructive subcultures can evolve, including the rise of gang activity (Wilson, 1987; 1996). In sum, the integrity of the community is fractured and the implicit social contract between families and their neighborhood becomes frayed and tattered (Miller).

This is one side of the tragedy of residential segregation. Another side is the cocoon of whiteness surrounding many children who grow up in predominantly white lower-, middle- and upper-class neighborhoods, suburbs, and exurbs. Socialized into a world of whiteness where people of color are often defined as a denigrated "other," whites are apt to fear and avoid them (Miller & Schamess, 2000). Even in families that espouse the values of equality, nonprejudice, and good will toward all, the actual social arrangements of their lives belie these values. Their behaviors and lifestyles conflict with their social ideals.

Residential isolation ensures that significant numbers of white people will have little or no awareness of their race privilege. They will internalize a sense of entitlement to live in a predominantly white world. They will hold stereotypes unchallenged by reality, undisturbed by those who are different from them, and unperturbed by those who suffer the consequences of racism.

EDUCATIONAL RACISM: PUBLIC, PRIVATE, AND HIGHER EDUCATION

Segregated neighborhoods are accompanied by segregation in public education. It would be bad enough if public schools literally reflected residential segregation, but parents have choices about where they send their children to school, and this leads to a pattern of educational segregation that is worse than residential segregation. This is the result despite determined efforts following the Supreme Court's 1954 *Brown v. Board of Education* decision to desegregate schools. Efforts to achieve integrated schools, such as school busing, which was designed to offset residential segregation, often provoked a large white backlash. Many white parents withdrew their children from public schools in favor of private schools or moved to whiter school districts.

These trends emerged in the wake of the court-ordered desegregation of Boston schools in 1974, in which by 2000 only 25.4% of children under the age of 18 living in Boston were white, and half of those children attended private schools (Logan, Oakley, & Stowell, 2003). The Harvard University Civil Rights Project found that schools are becoming *more* segregated and, on average, whites are attending schools in which more than 80% of students are white. White racial homogeneity is even more pronounced in private schools (Frankenberg, Lee, & Orfield, 2003). The same project described a significant number of apartheid schools, characterized by few white students, substantial rates of poverty, and limited educational resources—a return to "separate and unequal."

Schools are funded primarily by property taxes, with additional aid from state and federal governments. Thus, the wealthiest communities, which usually are predominantly white, are able to pay more for their school systems and typically spend more per capita per pupil. Kozol (1991) observed what he described as "savage inequalities" in public school systems: Poor students were taught in unsafe, overcrowded, decrepit buildings, did not have enough school supplies, and did not have access to technology. These schools were less able to attract and retain qualified teachers. Longitudinal studies of teachers in New York State indicate that those that have the best educational backgrounds and test scores and the most teaching experience usually are teaching white, middle-class students (Brown et al., 2003).

All of these factors contribute to lower quality education for many children of color, particularly those who are poor. Dropout rates and school suspension rates for Hispanics and African Americans are higher than for whites. College attendance rates are considerably lower. In 1998 nearly 95% of whites aged 25–29 had a high school diploma, and for Hispanics it was just over 60% (Council of Economic Advisors, 1998). Guidance counselors in predominantly white, middle-class school districts, more so than their counterparts in poor school districts of color, expect and encourage their students to attend college. Further, the former have more experience in navigating the application process and far more contacts in college admissions offices to boost the chances of admission for the students that they recommend. Predominantly white schools also are more likely than predominantly non-white schools to have advanced, college preparatory classes (Renner & Moore, 2004).

As if white students did not already have enough advantages over students of color in the college admissions process, state anti-affirmative action efforts have cut minority admissions in colleges. In California's two flagship state schools (UC Berkeley and UCLA), non-Asian minority freshman dropped from 21.93% to 10.54% in one year after the universities were banned from taking race into account in their admissions decisions (Bronner, 1998). Cut-backs in federal support of financial aid for college also have hurt students of color disproportionately (Brown et al., 2003). In 1995, although African Americans and Latinos comprised 28% of all 18-year olds, they constituted only 12% of the freshman class in "selective" institutions (Carnevale & Rose, 2003).

Once on campus, students of color frequently face stereotyping, cultural exclusion, and "racial microaggressions" from white students and white faculty (Solorzano et al., 2000). As one consequence, students of color strive to avoid confirming the stereotypes, which creates tension and performance anxiety among them (Leary, 1999). This dynamic is exacerbated when students of color find themselves few in number in the classroom, at times the only non-white student in a class (Thompson & Sekaquaptewa, 2002). Stereotypes, lower social status, and isolation contribute to their feeling alienated and disengaged and not trusting the fairness and validity of the educational enterprise (Schmader, Major, & Gramzow, 2001).

Poor students of color are less likely to have had access to computers and the Internet before entering college and are less likely to have computers once they attend college (Harmon, 1998; Komar, 2003). In the end, far more whites than blacks or Hispanics graduate from college. In 1998, 33% of whites aged 25–29 had a college degree, compared to only 15% of blacks and 11% of Hispanics (Council of Economic Advisors, 1998).

These factors have major implications for employment prospects and for the accumulation of wealth. We will consider these two areas of institutional racism next.

EMPLOYMENT RACISM

Historically, racism has limited the job opportunities for people of color. Legislation has prevented African Americans, American Indians, Mexican Americans, Chinese Americans, and Japanese Americans, among other non-white ethnic groups, from competing with white people in an allegedly free-market economy. These barriers continued with exclusionary immigration and labor laws, hostility from trade unions, and a range of roadblocks limiting access to jobs. All of these factors conspire to limit economic opportunity. As we mentioned earlier, many well-paying jobs have moved to the suburbs and exurbs. In the absence of adequate public transportation linking them to urban centers, many residents are stranded without the means to earn a living (Wilson, 1987, 1996).

This circumstance has been exacerbated by deindustrialization. For example, Holyoke, Massachusetts, a small industrial city, has seen an influx of Hispanic, primarily Puerto Rican, residents, drawn by the low cost of housing (rental apartments built for mill workers) and family networks (Miller, 1999, 2001). The Irish, French Canadian, and Polish immigrants who preceded them, and also arrived poor and without resources, were able to gain a foothold on an economic ladder through factory work. Now, however, the mills are moribund, with no entry-level jobs. Also, public transportation is insufficient to take people to jobs in surrounding cities and communities. Further, the Puerto Ricans are young and poorly educated. They often do not have the qualifications to be hired for some of the high-tech and white-collar jobs in the area. Finally, the quality of the public school system is far below that of more affluent nearby communities, and the rate of college attendance is low. This pattern stalks many older, metropolitan areas.

Among other daunting barriers to getting jobs, people of color do not have the necessary connections. As important as qualifications, merit, and access are, many jobs are landed through the connections of family and friends. This is how, over time, various ethnic groups have cornered occupational niches and have accessed specific businesses, trades, and professions (Steinberg, 2001; Sullivan, 1989).

Another barrier is not having the requisite cultural capital to thrive in the workplace. Many people of color living in poor, isolated urban neighborhoods have few role models in how to talk, dress, and act in ways that fit with many mainstream business establishments (Wilson, 1996). Discouraged, some may feel more comfortable operating in the informal, secondary labor market, which is less humiliating but carries more risks and little security (Bourgois, 1995). Cultural norms, too, erect a barrier to middle-class people of color, who may feel pressured to conform to white, middle-class norms at work (Cose, 1993).

But employment racism goes beyond culture. Promotional opportunities are fewer and salaries lower for people of color engaged in the same professions as whites. College faculty members of color earn about 75% of what their white colleagues make with similar qualifications. Kivel (1996) explains this by referring to a number of factors: the legacy of past discrimination that keeps people of color out of the academy; inadequate public schools and needing more time to complete postsecondary studies; having fewer colleagues of their race, ethnicity, and culture to form support networks within universities; and prejudice and discrimination by white faculty and administrators. All of these factors form a web of discrimination.

People of color are underrepresented in many professions and occupations. Retail and construction jobs, which do not require high educational levels still present major barriers to African Americans (Brown et al., 2003). The U.S. Census Bureau (2000) provides many examples of this pattern, keeping in mind that African Americans make up about 12% of the U.S. population and Hispanics about 13%:

- Only 8.4% of architects are black and 4.5% are Hispanic.
- In health care, 5.7% of doctors and 1.9% of dentists are black, and the figures are 1.9% and 3.1% for Hispanics.
- In teaching—slightly better—9.9% are black and 5.4% Hispanic.
- Social work is an exception for African Americans, who compose 24.2%, but only 7.4% of social workers are Hispanic.
- In the legal profession, 5.1% of lawyers are black and 4% are Hispanic.

The Urban League (2002) has found that African Americans are twice as likely as whites to hold low-paying, low-prestige service jobs, and though 30% of whites are professionals and managers, only 20% of blacks hold such jobs. These indicators are stark and powerful reminders of the barriers that still exist for people of all ethnicities and races to participate fully in the entire range of occupational opportunities.

Once people of color have made it into law firms and corporations, they often do not progress as quickly as their white peers (Cose, 1993). For example, General Electric, representative of many other major U.S. corporations, has little racial or ethnic or gender diversity in the top echelons of management. In 2000, only 6.4% of its corporate officers were women and of the 20 businesses that contributed 90% of the company's earnings, only one was headed by a person of color (Walsh, 2000).

All of the nodes of institutional racism mentioned thus far—residential, educational, and occupational—contribute to the next nexus of institutional racism. We turn to disparities in accumulation of wealth and upward mobility.

RACISM AND WEALTH ACCUMULATION AND UPWARD MOBILITY

We must acknowledge significant progress in lowering the income differential between people of color and whites (Roberts, 1995). From 1960 to the mid-1970s, the gap between the median income for African Americans and whites narrowed because of the Civil Rights Movement, legislation from the Great Society including affirmative action, and a tight labor market (Stoll, 2004). In the 1990s, African Americans also made some less dramatic gains toward reducing the wage gap; however, there are still significant disparities in earnings by virtue of race. According to Stoll, in 2003 the average black family earned $.64 for every dollar earned by a white family, better than the equivalent $.55 earned in 1989 but still less than two-thirds of income parity. Yet these divergences pale when compared to racial discrepancies by virtue of net worth, or cumulative assets held by families.

Assets are accumulated over time, and are passed down from one generation to another in the form of college tuition payments and loans, gifts, and, of course, inheritances. The capacity to accumulate wealth is so racially disparate that it is one of the most profound examples of the opportunity-hoarding that characterizes durable inequalities (Brown et al., 2003).

Two of the most important assets in accumulating wealth are home ownership and higher levels of education. As we have learned, home ownership is more difficult to achieve for African Americans and Hispanics, and the web of racism prevents many African Americans, Hispanics, and American Indians from educational achievement comparable to that of whites. Even when they own their homes, interest rates for mortgages are higher and property values lower, contributing to a hemorrhaging rather than an increase in assets (Brown et al., 2004). "The way homes are bought and sold, where they are located, how the market values them, provides a contemporary foundation for racial inequality" (Shapiro, 2004, p. 53).

The same holds true for small businesses. African Americans are less able to secure loans and capital, denying them another way by which families and communities grow their assets (Urban League, 2004). All told, residential and occupational segregation continue to further the existing racial wealth divide (O'Connor, 2001) because of historical barriers and disadvantages.

No matter what measures are used, African Americans earn less than whites and have significantly fewer financial assets (Oliver & Shapiro, 2000). In 2001, the typical black household had a net worth of $19,000, compared to $121,000 for a white household. Although African Americans constituted 13% of the U.S. population in that year, they owned only 3% of the assets (Muhammad, Davis, Lui, & Leondar-Wright, 2004).

Financial assets can be "transformative" over the life cycle, helping family members purchase houses and attend college without incurring massive debt, which can boost a family beyond where their jobs and earnings alone would land them socially (Shapiro, 2004). The flip side is that poverty rates are higher for all groups of color, particularly American Indians, blacks, and Hispanics, than they are for white families (Blank, 2001). The gap in wealth between whites and African Americans, Hispanics, American Indians, and some Asian American groups is a profound consequence of racism. Shapiro (2004) concludes that "it is virtually impossible for people of color to earn their way to equal wealth through wages" (p. 2).

ENVIRONMENTAL AND HEALTH RACISM

Although all forms of institutional racism are abhorrent, two particularly insidious forms of institutional racism are environmental racism and health racism. Together, they expose people of color to greater health risks; injuring, hurting, and maiming their bodies and spirits; depleting and devastating communities; and abrogating life chances—a graphic reminder that racism literally kills people. Another facet of environmental racism intersects with residential racism as white families continually move farther from communities of color, leading to ribbon development, longer commutes, and further environmental degradation and pollution (Powell, 1999).

Environmental racism correlates with race and class. Poor people of color are more likely to live in neighborhoods sandwiched by highways, where they are subjected to increasing levels of noise and air pollution. And they are more likely to live near toxic chemical dump sites, in neighborhoods with elevated rates of cancer and other major diseases. Some of this is a consequence of class. In Massachusetts, communities with a median household income of less than $30,000 have triple the cumulative exposure to hazardous locations and facilities than communities with higher income levels (Faber & Krieg, 2001). Race exacerbates the problem: If people of color make up more than 25% of a community's population, the hazardous exposure rate is nine times the rate of communities with less than 5% people of color (Faber & Krieg).

Poor people of color are more likely to live in areas prone to natural disasters, such as low-lying floodplains, as was sadly illustrated by the "social ecology" of Hurricane Katrina (Park & Miller, 2006). Poor people of color are more apt to live in apartments with lead paint, more likely to live in roach-infested apartments, and they have much higher rates of asthma than do white, middle-class children (Acevedo-Garcia & Osypuk, 2004; Yinger, 2000).

A report by the Natural Resources Defense Council (Quintero-Somaini & Quirindongo, 2004) documented environmental health risks for Hispanics. Many Latinos live in cities with high levels of air pollution, which increases the risks for cancer and asthma, and older housing stock results in Hispanic children having twice the rate of dangerous lead levels as white children. A significant number of Latinos live in "colonias," unincorporated communities near the U.S.–Mexico border, where inadequate drinking water and sewage disposal increase the risks of water-borne diseases such as giardiasis, hepatitis, and cholera. In Western states, many Latinos drink water contaminated by arsenic, chemicals, and fertilizers. Those working as farm workers face high exposure to pesticides, which increases the risks for cancer.

Taken together, these environmental hazards create major health risks for Hispanics, who as a group are least likely to have health insurance, although this also is a problem for African Americans and some Asian American groups such as Koreans (Brown, Ojeda, Wyn, & Levan, 2000). These are a few examples of the many environmental perils faced by people of color.

People of color, particularly African Americans, Latinos, and American Indians, receive lower quality health care than whites (National Academy of

Sciences [NAS], 2002). In addition to having less insurance, people of color have less access to health services. Health facilities that are used are often more crowded, with longer waiting periods and in older and less well-kept facilities. People of color are less likely than whites to find doctors who mirror them ethnically and have a good understanding of their culture. People of color also are more likely to be misdiagnosed and less likely to have necessary tests, while being more vulnerable to undergoing intrusive surgery such as amputations and castration.

Doctors and other health care providers, as with the population at large, may be unaware of their own stereotypes, biases, and prejudices. Tervalon and Murray-Garcia (1998) report that emergency-room doctors give Latinos analgesia for long-bone fractures half as often as white patients; yet a follow-up study with the same physicians indicated that they did not think that Latinos were in any less pain.

Despite progress in public health initiatives over the years, people of color endure more illness and injury from birth until death. African Americans babies are more than twice as likely as white babies to have a low birthweight (Acevedo-Garcia & Osypuk, 2004; McLoyd & Losoff, 2001). This, in turn, contributes to higher rates of infant mortality and lifelong developmental challenges and learning difficulties. This trend is exacerbated as poor children of color face higher risks of injury in hazardous living situations, along with more exposure to lead paint (Acevedo-Garcia & Osypuk, 2004). Poor, isolated neighborhoods also are more dangerous, placing residents at higher risk for being victims of violence. All of these factors have negative consequences for developmental, behavioral, educational, and social outcomes.

Adults of color have higher rates of disease and injury because of their greater exposure, yet they have less adequate health care when they are stricken (NAS, 2002). Blacks are more likely to die from heart disease (Williams, 2001), have a significantly lower survival rate from cancer (Joiner, 2004), and, along with American Indians and Hispanics, have higher death rates than whites from diabetes (Williams, 2001). African Americans also have much higher rates of hypertension, which may be related in part to the ongoing stress of racism (Kingston & Nickens, 2001).

In research by Woody and Green (2001), African Americans of all social classes reported that they confront constant stereotypes and discrimination and are concerned about losing jobs. Thus, they work longer hours and take less time for vacations, which affects health as well as family life. African American men in particular report strong feelings of vulnerability as well as an acute awareness of their lower life-expectancies and higher risk factors in all aspects of life, leading to a diminished sense of well-being compared to whites.

African American men also are more likely than whites not to have a doctor, a consequence of the conditions mentioned above and also borne of mistrust about the aims of the medical profession, generated in part by revelations about medical abuse. A prime example is the infamous Tuskegee experiment, in which black men were left with untreated syphilis for research purposes (Joiner, 2004). Given this accumulation of risk factors, it is not surprising that 40% of black men die prematurely, compared to 21% of white men, and that blacks have significantly shorter life expectancy than whites (Joiner, 2004; Muhammad et al., 2004).

MENTAL HEALTH RACISM

The same structural barriers to health care that affect people of color disproportionately also apply to mental health services. Mental health services, however, sometimes are offered on a sliding-fee basis, a policy that expands the pool of people who are covered. At the same time, managed care has reduced the number of counseling sessions available to consumers, except those with the means to pay out of pocket. Provider biases and prejudices are the same for mental health workers as they are for medical personnel. Internalized, unconscious stereotypes loom large when white practitioners engage in cross-racial or cultural counseling because of its intimate, interpersonal nature.

Wade (1993) has argued that institutional racism is present in mental health policy and has a significant impact on diagnostic and treatment issues. Institutional racism is at hand in the following areas: (1) access, (2) services offered, (3) who provides services, (4) the structure of services, (5) theoretical biases, (6) racism in the clinical encounter, (7) culturally insensitive counseling facilities, (8) lack of representation on policy-making boards, and (9) lack of access to private practitioners.

ACCESS

The same issues of access apply to mental health services as to other health services (Davis, 1997). The uninsured have fewer mental health options, and the rates of insurance coverage are lower for many groups of color, as discussed previously. Other considerations include the location of clinics and whether they are easily accessible by public transportation.

Middle-class consumers have choice when selecting providers, whereas poor communities of color often have access to only one mental health agency. A recent emphasis on faith-based initiatives may lead to more religious agencies offering counseling services. Some people will welcome these services, but they will exclude some people of different denominations. Another inequity is that waiting lists for clinics serving poor clients of color are often longer.

SERVICES OFFERED

Managed care has remedicalized counseling. To receive reimbursement, a client requires a diagnosis acceptable to Medicaid or to a managed care company. Less counseling is available for the stresses of daily living, to help people cope with the consequences of illness and disability, to improve interpersonal communication, and to address developmental delays and learning disabilities—all of which are needs exacerbated by institutional racism.

WHO PROVIDES TREATMENT

The issues facing community mental health centers are similar to those in public education who are concerned about the quality of services offered and who provides them. Counseling in clinics located in poor communities of color is stressful, with low pay, long hours, and stringent productivity requirements. Although some dedicated clinicians remain in these agencies, more often we see an exodus of qualified counselors seeking better working conditions and salaries by going into private practice or working in agencies in more affluent communities. This leads to high staff turnover. Overall, clinicians with less experience and training work in poor communities of color.

Also, when clients speak languages other than English, there is a need for translation, which is difficult to arrange and frequently unavailable. In some agencies, when indigenous workers are hired, cultural competency increases but clinical services may be offered by people with less professional training. Also, agencies have racial hierarchies. Although a significant number of line workers may be people of color, the staffing pattern whitens in the supervisory, managerial, and leadership ranks. The exceptions are agencies run by people of color, for people of color, with representative boards of directors.

THE STRUCTURE OF SERVICES

Individual counseling and 50-minute sessions make certain assumptions about cultural styles, worldviews, and values. Many Asian American, Hispanic, and African American communities have more of a collective orientation, which deemphasizes the individual. Yet most U.S. counseling centers offer individual counseling in a 50-minute hour. This is reinforced by a financing and billing structure in which most clients are seen individually rather than in families (nuclear and extended), friendship clusters, or groups.

The emphasis on regular appointments, though important to staff, assumes a certain level of organization, adequate transportation, and does not allow for irregular working patterns or sudden and debilitating stressful events. The length of sessions, with an emphasis on starting and ending on time, also reflects middle-class Eurocentric norms of communication and social behavior.

THEORETICAL BIASES

The counseling enterprise in the United States is founded on values, expectations, and beliefs derived from European psychologists and white practitioners in this country. As mentioned above, the focus on the individual and the value placed on separation–individuation is a clear example of this cultural and social bias.

These assumptions are exacerbated by expectations about disclosure and communication, as well as by Western notions of egalitarianism, which sometimes run counter to expectations about deference and hierarchy in other cultures. Even the notion of confidentiality, as important as it is, reflects cultural norms about privacy and the rights of the individual transcending those of the family.

RACISM IN CLINICAL ENCOUNTERS

A danger in working with people of color is that non-Western cultural patterns and behaviors might be pathologized or viewed as dysfunctional. This contributes to the potential for nonempathic, unhelpful services, ranging from culturally insensitive services to actual racist encounters during sessions (Carter, 1995; Pinderhughes, 1989; Ridley, 1995).

Therapists already hold a great deal of power in their relationships with clients, and this is magnified when clinicians are not mindful of the power and privileges that their race or ethnicity convey. Clinicians, like most people, have internalized stereotypes and biases that often unconsciously manifest themselves in clinical interactions. Racial transference and counter-transference is operating in all cross-racial and cultural work, whatever the race or ethnicity of the client or therapist.

CULTURALLY INSENSITIVE FACILITIES   Waiting rooms and offices, like the clinicians themselves, typically reflect cultural biases and assumptions, as well as power relationships. Where a receptionist sits, how he or she treats clients, and how he or she is treated in return by professional staff send many messages. The reception area also communicates respect or disrespect for clients. What pictures, if any, are on the wall, and what do they convey? Is there a television in the waiting room and, if so, what channel is it tuned to? What toys and magazines are in the waiting room? Is the telephone message in English only?

LACK OF REPRESENTATION ON POLICY-MAKING BOARDS   Most mainstream clinical agencies that are not established specifically to serve a specific ethnic or racial group do not have adequate representation of people of color on their boards, even when their clients are predominantly people of color. Boards of directors often do not offer enough board positions for consumers. Managed-care panels and Medicaid decision-making committees also are prone to exclude people of color or to have only token representation.

LACK OF ACCESS TO PRIVATE PRACTITIONERS   Very few private practitioners work with poor people of color, and if they do, they often limit the hours of availability. This leads to a tremendous gap in potential clinical services for clients. It also limits the options of poor clients of color. If a consumer has had a bad experience with the only mental health agency serving his or her neighborhood and does not want to return to that organization, or if in turn the agency has dismissed her or him as a client, the option of seeing a clinician in private practice is often not available.

In short, institutional racism, particularly when combined with class inequities, is pervasive at all levels of the mental health system, from policy making to what happens in the consulting room. The result is that people of color, who suffer the additional life stresses of racism, often have the fewest options for mental health services. And when they do receive counseling, it often reflects cultural biases and leads to further racist encounters and experiences.

RACISM IN THE CRIMINAL JUSTICE SYSTEM

All forms of institutional racism are wrong and dangerous. Criminal justice racism is a stain on American society akin to apartheid. African Americans constitute only 13% of the general population, yet comprise nearly 50% of the prison population. When people of color number about one-third of the population but make up three-quarters of the prison population, something is terribly amiss. When African Americans comprise the majority of death-row inmates, an appalling caricature of justice is enacted in the name of all U.S. citizens.

These discrepancies cannot be explained by nationality or culture. What is taken as a normative pattern today was not yesterday's prototype. In 1950, at the height of Jim Crow and virulent Southern racism, African Americans constituted 30% of the prison population while by the early 1990s they constituted more than half (Hawkins, 2001). Ultimately, this is a crushing indictment of the web of institutional racism, in which all of the strands contribute to more vulnerability for involvement in the criminal justice system and rampant racism within it.

A vicious cycle ensues: Segregated, isolated, economically depleted neighborhoods lack opportunities for quality education, well-paying jobs, and pathways to economic self-sufficiency (Massey, 2001). Lacking legitimate opportunity, some residents turn to illegal activities, such as drug dealing. As these activities become more prevalent, the neighborhood becomes more dangerous. This, in turn, leads to fewer citizens venturing out to public places, which makes streets even more dangerous (Geis & Ross, 1998; Miller, 2001).

Police officers, many of whom are white, patrol these neighborhoods and develop or reinforce negative stereotypes toward people of color, who report far more negative interactions with police than do white people (Weitzer & Tuch, 2004). The police guard these neighborhoods in much the way the military guards occupied territory. They may overreact and sometimes commit brutal and sadistic acts, such as the well publicized beating of Rodney King, the slaying of Amidou Diallo, and the rape and torture of Abner Louima. Residents then not only fear drug dealers and gangs but also the law enforcement officers who supposedly "protect" their community. This is all a prelude, occurring before institutional racism in the criminal justice system comes into play.

Prior involvement with the child welfare and juvenile justice systems are risk factors for adult association with the criminal justice system. African American children are more likely to be the subjects of protective investigations, more likely to be placed out of their homes, less likely to have permanent placement or reunification plans, and on average spend a longer time in foster care (Lu, Landsverk, Ellis-Macleod, Newton, Ganger, & Johnson, 2004; Roberts, 2002). In Chicago, 95% of foster children are black (Roberts, 2002).

There is also a shortage of black foster homes and, thus, greater likelihood that African American children will be placed in homes that are culturally and ethnically unfamiliar.

Black children, too, are more likely to be moved from one foster home to another. Children without family or stability in substitute care, living in more dangerous neighborhoods, and attending underresourced schools are more prone to educational difficulties. This leads to a greater likelihood of becoming involved with gangs and, thus, more risk of police harassment.

African American children are disproportionately represented in the juvenile justice system. Youth of color are treated more severely at every stage of the juvenile justice system (Building Blocks for Youth [BBFY], 2001; Poe-Yamagata & Jones, 2000). African American youth are more likely than white youth to be charged for the same offense, and more likely to be placed out of home. They are given longer sentences, are more likely to be referred to adult court, and are less likely to receive probation (Poe-Yamagata & Jones, 2000). In Cook County, Illinois, 99% of juvenile offenders referred to adult courts are African American or Latino (BBFY, 2001).

One of the single most important factors in determining whether a youth offender does not reoffend as an adult is to be able to change either the peer group or the community (Laub, 2000). But with disproportionate sentencing and incarceration of youth of color, combined with less social mobility, the peer group becomes entrenched and increasingly deviant. These factors increase the risks for engagement with the criminal justice system as adults (Laub, 2000).

Adult African Americans and dark-skinned Latinos are more likely than others to be stopped by the police (Kennedy, 2001). Once stopped, a person is always at greater risk of arrest, but racism does not end there. Once arrested, an African American is more likely to be charged and brought to trial; if tried, more likely to be convicted; and if convicted, more likely to receive a longer prison sentence. Accordingly, black men are five times more likely than white men to be under the supervision of the criminal justice system (Council of Economic Advisors, 1998; Human Rights Watch, 2000). A black person arrested for possession of drugs is three times more likely than a white person to end up in prison (Oliver, 2001). Once in prison, black people are less likely to have their sentence reduced or to be paroled.

Among other contributing factors—although African American men do have slightly higher rates of engagement in violent crimes than white men, this difference is not large enough to explain the discrepancies in the demographics of the prison population. The majority of prisoners are not incarcerated for brutal crimes, and while the prison population has grown dramatically over the past 20 years, the murder rate has been dropping (Massey, 2001). Many people are in prison for violating drug laws, which have built-in racial biases. Crack cocaine carries mandatory minimum sentences, whereas powdered cocaine does not (Kennedy, 2001). Because whites use powdered cocaine proportionately more than blacks do, the sentencing patterns are racially divergent.

Other contributing factors are states' "three strikes" laws, which dispro-portionately affect African Americans because they are more likely to have been arrested and charged in the past for reasons already stated. This is part of a trend that favors punishment over treatment. Once in prison, there has been a move to deny prisoners educational services (Boyd, 2001; Western, 2001).

Consequences of racism in the criminal justice system amplify racism in the political process, as more and more states are depriving felons of the right to vote—in some instances for the rest of their lives. By 2000, more than 4.2 million Americans had been disenfranchised from voting because of past or present incarceration; and in Alabama and Florida, 31% of African American men have lost their right to vote (Sengupta, 2000). The United States is the only democracy in the world that disenfranchises convicted felons, which has dis-turbing echoes of the Jim Crow era (Boyd, 2001; Simson, 2002).

The costs of all of this to communities are immense. Many men who are socially integrated in their communities and who are fathers are taken out of their communities (Sabol & Lynch, 1997). This means that potential bread-winners are no longer available, which contributes to the family's inability to accumulate social capital, as discussed. It also leads to a loss of eligible mar-riage partners. Children lose father figures. Re-integration programs are few and inadequate, so those who try to return to their communities after incar-ceration often lack skills, counseling, training, and other necessary supports, all of which contribute to high rates of recidivism. And because of hyper-segregation, most of the men in prison come from a small number of urban communities of color (Sabol & Lynch, 1997).

By the middle of 2003, the United States had nearly 2.1 million people in U.S. state and federal prisons, earning the dubious distinction of having the most people incarcerated in the world (Sentencing Project, 2004). The United States incarcerates 25% of the world's prisoners, and if all prisoners were brought together in one place, they would constitute the 35th most populous American state (Boyd, 2001). Black men in the United States are incarcerated at four times the rate that black men were imprisoned during the apartheid era in South Africa, and that number is now approaching that of black men enslaved during the height of the U.S. slave era. In the past quarter century, the United States has created a racial gulag through its criminal justice system (Boyd, 2001).

POLITICAL RACISM

Power in society resides in many sites—industry, the military, the media, among the wealthy, and—when there are social movements—among the people. One of the most visible and significant locations of power lies in government and politics. Over the course of its history, this nation has repeatedly denied political representation and power to people of color, such as denial of citizenship and the right to vote by legal and illegal means. Accordingly, racism not surprisingly extends throughout the political system. It is manifested in who is elected (and who is absent), who is appointed, who can and cannot vote in elections, and who wields power behind the scenes.

The United States has not had a non-white (or female) President. Neither political party has nominated a person of color as its candidate for President or Vice President. After the Civil War, the first African American senators and representatives were elected, but the backlash to Reconstruction and successful efforts by white Southerners to restrict voting meant that shortly afterward, no African Americans served in Congress until the election of an African American representative from Illinois in 1928 (Patrick, Pious, & Ritchie, 2001).

Since the beginning of the 20th century, only three African Americans have been elected to the Senate. In the history of the Supreme Court, there have been two black justices. In recent years there have been a number of firsts: Colin Powell became the first African American to serve as the head of the Joint Chiefs of Staff and the first black Secretary of State under the second President Bush. The numbers of people of color in cabinet-level positions increased under both Presidents Bill Clinton and the George W. Bush.

The few Hispanic congressmen and senators do not mirror the percentages of Hispanics in the general population, which is more than 13%. The first Latino cabinet members were appointed in the 1970s. There has never been a Hispanic Supreme Court justice, and Hispanics constitute only 5% of federal judges (Patrick, Pious, & Ritchie, 2001). There have been three Native American congressmen, two of whom went on to serve in the Senate, although at this writing there are no Native American senators. There have been no Native American Supreme Court justices. Asian Americans were not elected to Congress or the Senate until the 1950s, when their numbers were boosted by the admission of Hawaii as a state in 1959. There has never been an Asian American Supreme Court justice. Few staffers of color work for elected officials. For example, in Massachusetts, of 151 Congressional staffers, only 15 are "minorities" and no congressional office is headed by a person of color (Associated Press, 2000).

The lack of adequate representation of people of color does not stop with the federal government. Many cities and states lack a fair proportion of elected and appointed people of color. One mechanism that supports this inequity at the local level is the practice of electing at-large candidates to city councils and school committees. In a city where one-third of the residents are people of color, this practice can mean that people of color will be in the minority for every contested seat and, therefore, unable to elect people representing their interests.

In suburbs around Hartford, Connecticut, for example, people of color have moved to Bloomfield, East Hartford, West Hartford, Newington, Wethersfield, and Windsor in significant numbers; yet a number of these communities have only or mostly white city councilors and school board members (Altimari, Budoff, & Davis, 2001). This under-representation goes beyond elected officials, extending to the warrens of commissions and city departments, often staffed by people who are patrons of the elected people who appoint them. For example, in Holyoke, Massachusetts, of 79 appointed officials listed in the Chamber of Commerce's city guide book, only three had

Hispanic surnames—this in a city where at least one-third of the population is Hispanic (Miller, 2001).

This lack of access to political offices at the local level means that people of color do not gain the experience and develop resumes propelling them to state and national office. The high costs of campaigning also hamper the capability of people of color to forge political careers.

Voter disenfranchisement also creates difficulty for people of color to exercise political power. The stunning statistic that nearly a third of black males are denied the right to vote in certain states because they have been convicted of a felony is but one way to deny votes. The presidential election of 2000 raised many concerns about attempts to suppress the black vote in Florida, either by striking people of color from voter registration rolls before the election or by making it difficult for them to vote during the election (Fritz, 2001).

A congressional investigation found that voters in "low-income, high-minority" districts were sometimes 20 times more likely than voters in other districts to have their votes discarded in the 2000 election (Waxman et al., 2001). In South Dakota, American Indians complained that certain maneuvers, including complicated registration procedures and dubious identification requirements, were attempts to suppress their vote (Cohen, 2004). Tactics such as these are eerily reminiscent of voting restrictions that characterized the Jim Crow era.

The lack of adequate representation has consequences for people of color. The nation's leaders do not fully grasp the experiences and implications of racism. Consequently, at best, these issues are neglected, and actually exacerbated by support for anti-affirmative action initiatives and stiff, unequal drug penalties. There has not been a serious attempt to implement an urban policy since the Great Society.

Meanwhile, schools have become segregated again. Although government policy is not entirely responsible, it certainly is a major contributor. Part of the problem is that the political party dominating national politics over the past 25 years has used a consciously racist electoral strategy to woo white voters—a tactic that paid off handsomely (Edsall & Edsall, 1991; Polikoff, 2005). Republicans have employed a discourse of denigration, particularly directed at poor African Americans, defining them as "other" and different (Miller & Schamess, 2000). They are described as lacking a work ethic and in need of sanctions, not government "coddling."

President Ronald Reagan talked about "welfare queens," and the first President Bush appealed to similar sentiments in his now infamous Willie Horton advertisements while running for president against Michael Dukakis. This raised the specter of unbridled sexual and physical assault by black felons, a stereotype promulgated throughout the history of the racial project of the United States. Although his son, George W. Bush, has a better track record of appointing a more diverse cabinet, both of his election campaigns were marred by numerous efforts to suppress the black vote, and many of his policies have increased the tax burden on poor people of color while cutting health and human services.

Leaders set a tone and offer role models. When leaders legitimize coded racist imagery, they encourage and permit others to do so as well. Leaders can divide and exacerbate social schisms (Miller & Schamess, 2000). They are highly visible opinion shapers in what becomes a public discourse that no longer is concerned about racism and inequities but, instead, how people of color are "cheating the system," gaining unfair advantage through government programs and affirmative action policies, while the rights of "good, hard-working" white people allegedly are under siege.

"Tax relief" is proposed for the wealthiest, thereby reducing federal expenditures on development if assets by the poorest. This one-dimensional discourse closes off legitimate social and political options as economically unfeasible or politically untenable. Opposition leaders who try to speak for the marginalized are discredited, and when the oppressed speak for themselves, they are viewed as touting their own interests—as if they are the only group in society that advocates for their own interests (Miller & Schamess; Whillock, 1995).

The not-so-silent majority that benefits from white privilege assumes its entitled position in the center of the political discourse, claiming reason and fairness even as its own privileges increases. This "elite discourse" is essential to forming an "ethnic consensus," which engages white consent toward maintaining the domination and status of whites in society (van Dijk, 1995).

MEDIA RACISM

What inner models do people internalize to understand race and racism, and where do those images and concepts come from? People are exposed to a racial discourse from birth. The discourse is not hegemonic, but the dominant narrative is one that privileges white people and presents doing so as fair and normal. This narrative is transmitted by parents to children, and they are not alone: Children's books help to tell the story with racialized choices of characters, settings, and plots (van Dijk, 1995).

The narrative is furthered in preschool and school, where teachers, books, videos, and other media presentations continue the racial saga, often without reference to race and racism. Children are exposed to an idealized history, such as the story of Thanksgiving and the relationships between Pilgrims and Indians, that neglects to describe the Native American holocaust. This discourse forms attitudes and encodes stereotypes that people often carry with them for life. The narratives subtly diminish people of color and establish white people as society's dominant group (van Dijk, 1995). This racialized discourse is complemented by the actual encounters white people have with people of color, or more often do not have because of the patterns of residential and educational segregation described in this chapter.

Adults are exposed to the racial discourse through television shows, news broadcasts, films, books, magazines, advertisements, music, and the Internet. Most people have internalized stereotypes from childhood, and they continue to be bombarded with complementary stereotypes: whites presented as heroes, leaders, decision makers, central characters, experts and talking heads; while people of color frequently are constructed as "other," different, deviant, quaint, exotic, and stereotyped (van Dijk, 1995).

Television shows and films often deal with race and racism as if it is a question of individual attitudes and behaviors determined by whether white people and people of color can talk to one another and be friends (DeMott, 1995). The realities of the web of institutional racism and the legacy of the "racial contract" are rendered invisible. A fantasyland of individual relationships without reference to historical and sociological legacies and constraints dominates many storylines.

When it comes to the news, people of color consistently are portrayed in a negative, stereotypical fashion. Sometimes this is done through codes that do not refer to race and yet have racial meanings for readers and viewers. The terms "broken families," "teenage mothers," "welfare mothers," "inner-city crime," and "crack" all conjure up racial stereotypes (van Dijk, 1995), as did the Willie Horton advertisements used in the election campaign of the first President Bush.

One reason is that most of the editors and television producers who are responsible for promulgating such images are white and may not recognize that they are colluding with racial stereotypes (Gillens, 1999). Some media executives, however, do know what they are promoting, and they strive to maintain high ratings through news that titillates and stirs people up (Westin, 2001).

Whatever the motivation, the choice of images and words, how stories are presented, and who presents them create a racialized tapestry of meaning. When people of color are used as presenters or "talking heads," they often are enlisted to talk about issues seen as pertinent to "minorities," while mainstream, allegedly nonracialized issues more often are the domain of white experts. When people attempt to present programs that feature people of color in a positive light, they encounter barriers, including concerns from producers that the programs will not appeal to whites and, thus, will not fare well in the ratings derby (Westin, 2001). Advertisements, too, are prone to portraying white men in leadership roles and African American men as aggressors (Coltrane & Messineo, 2000).

The saturated ubiquity of whiteness in the media promulgates an ongoing narrative of racism while rarely drawing attention to racism as a central social problem. It is nearly impossible to withdraw or escape from this unending drumbeat of culture, style, morality and meaning. It is the cloak that shrouds and obscures the web of racism by normalizing it. Recognizing, decoding, and resisting take a great deal of time and effort.

IMPLICATIONS OF THE WEB OF RACISM FOR THE HELPING PROFESSIONS

The web of institutional racism is painfully obvious to the people of color caught in its strands, yet nearly invisible to many white people who pass through it unimpeded. White people hold the illusion that many societal institutions, policies, living and working arrangements, programs and organizations are race-neutral. As we have argued, this is not possible in a racialized society. Thus, identifying and mapping the web of institutional racism, pinning it on the wall of individual and collective consciousness, is a step toward confronting racism. It no longer can be denied or relegated to museums and history.

Recognizing and understanding institutional racism is particularly essential for the helping professions. Clinicians must appreciate that racism affects everyone. No one is immune. Some are targeted by it, others benefit from it, and still others have experiences of both privilege and oppression. Even though some can ignore racism, it is always present and certainly is a dynamic involving those in the helping professions. Essential questions include: Who is offering the services, and to whom? How are the services being provided? What assumptions are being made, and where do they come from?

A second implication is that every organization is affected by the web, and in some ways is part of it. The web influences which agencies or programs are funded and under what conditions. Racism is part of the mission statement of every organization, whether by commission or omission: Is there an explicit commitment to anti-racism, multiculturalism, and social justice, or are these factors absent in the organizational mission? The web shapes who works in organizations, what qualifications they have, how they enter the organization, what capital they bring with them, and how quickly or slowly they progress after they arrive.

A third implication is that the web shapes interactions between providers and consumers and also between colleagues. The web operates in everyone's lives, but differentially. It influences worldviews, values, and assumptions. One's experience with the web will shape one's beliefs about how fair and equitable the world is, which in turn will influence how open or guarded people are. One way that social service organizations can deal with this dynamic is to have ongoing dialogue groups among staff members, as well as workshops that help them identify their cultural and social assumptions and values.

The web also influences training and qualifications. Racism increases the challenge for some people of color to gain an education or acquire the resources necessary to become professionally qualified. The web enables many white people to receive a college education, increase their professional training, and find jobs where they gain important experience. In turn, these inequities influence what jobs people are qualified to take within organizations, what they are paid, even with similar credentials and work history, and, of course who is positioned to move into supervisory and management positions.

The web of racism also determines what is taught when people receive their training, how they are trained, and what is viewed as normative professional behavior. In the helping professions, racism is always present and may be tackled, partially confronted, or ignored. As Kivel (1996) has written, institutionalized racism in organizations determines what gets addressed, how it is addressed, who participates in addressing it, and what options are considered viable or untenable.

CONCLUSION

The web of institutional racism limits opportunity for many people of color and is a profound manifestation of racism in our society today. Many white people are unaware of it. It is a direct descendent of the implicit racial contract undergirding the foundation of the United States. Although public and political discourses place the locus of responsibility for racial differences in wealth, power, incarceration rates, and success with individual effort and cultural and ethnic work ethics, the web of racism demonstrates that society is structured unequally, and how racism continues to privilege white people and oppress people of color. That the web is so ubiquitous and yet so invisible to the majority of white people in the United States is perplexing. The reason that racism in the United States remains so entrenched is the subject of the next chapter.

EXERCISE 4.1   THE WEB OF RACISM AND PASSPORTS OF PRIVILEGE

Consider the web of racism. Have you had experiences where you have been caught in the web, or have you had a passport of privilege that has permitted you to pass through it? For those who have experienced the web, which parts have been most problematic? For those with passports of privilege, which parts were you least aware of?

Discuss your experiences with the web in small groups. Are parts of the web evident in your school or agency? What steps could be taken to unravel the web of racism on a local level?

Why Is It so Difficult for People with Privilege to See Racism?

CHAPTER 5

CHAPTER CONTENTS

Thus far, we have considered what racism is, its lengthy and central place in the history of this nation, and the pervasive web of institutional racism today. People of color often face racism daily. Although racism has been statistically documented and consistently confirmed by research, most white people and some people of color have sufficient privilege to buffer them from the onslaught of racism and believe that racism is essentially a thing of the past. Bobo (2001) cites the Los Angles Survey of Urban Inequality, conducted in 1994, which found that slightly more than 20% of whites believe that discrimination prevents blacks and Hispanics from getting good-paying jobs, compared with 65% to 70% of blacks and Hispanics believing that they face such discrimination. Many other surveys continue to reach similar findings. How is this possible?

In this chapter we will discuss how racism has become so "normal" and central in our society that, for those with race privilege or partial race privilege, it is accepted as the way things are—as familiar as the air one breathes. So it shapes the streets we walk down, the neighborhoods we live in, the offices where we work, the food sold in supermarkets and who sells it, the news we watch, and the characters and stories in television shows, books, and films. Racism is the "invisible knapsack" of race privilege that white people carry.

The blindspot is reinforced by a constant "discourse of denigration" and the creation of "other," which produces narratives that manage to both deny and justify racism. This denial and obfuscation of racism is encoded in the mental and cognitive maps that people use to navigate their social worlds—maps that shade and distort so that racism is barely a shadow or a whisper, maps that make it difficult for many well-meaning and well-intentioned white human service workers to accept the extent of racism that some of their clients experience or to recognize how they themselves have benefited from race privilege.

CONSCIOUSNESS

Understanding the nature of consciousness is an ongoing human quest that perhaps never will be completed successfully. But recent progress in neuro-biological imaging and advances in our knowledge about how the human brain works have generated new hypotheses and understandings about consciousness. Damasio (2000) persuasively speculated that consciousness has two essential components: (1) an awareness of self as an actor who is both the author and reader of any narratives that constitute consciousness and self-awareness; and (2) an awareness of "objects" outside of ourselves that impinge on us and modify and alter how we think and feel. Thus, we have a sense of ourselves as actors and of objects outside of us; and consciousness involves a secondary, meta-awareness of the interaction of self and object and the resulting transformations.

If we apply this model to consciousness about race and racism, it helps to explain why people of color are more aware of racism than white people. People of color have two advantages with race consciousness:

1. They are more likely to have an ongoing racial self-awareness.
2. They are highly aware of the social world outside of them and how it can encroach upon them.

Consequently, people of color are more likely to be aware of racism and themselves as racial actors.[1] White people can move through the world believing that they are deracinated, that they are just people, or Americans, but with little core awareness of being white and what that means in this society. It means that white people can view themselves as individuals rather than as members of groups whose identities are imposed on them by society (Groot & Marcus, 1998). White writers can think of themselves as American writers and not have to respond to assumptions that they are writing white books for white people because of their race, while writers of color often are seen as being black writers, or Latina writers, or Chinese American writers. Their perceived group membership is inseparable from who they are.

Let us explore this a bit further. If a white person grows up in a predominantly white suburb, attends a predominantly white school, encounters mostly white teachers and administrators, sees mostly white actors on television and in films who for the most part are not portrayed as stereotypes or deviant, there is little dissonance between their positive sense of self and the world they experience. Whether people of color grow up in a racially or ethnically homogenous neighborhood or in a predominantly white neighborhood, they are likely to come up against racism that is at odds with their positive sense of self. Children of color who grow up in a predominantly white neighborhood most likely encounter racial stereotypes and slurs from other children, interact with mostly white teachers and administrators, and observe that students of color have higher detention, suspension, and expulsion rates and are saddled with lower expectations.

If children of color grow up in a racially homogenous neighborhood, it is more likely to be poor, and the schools probably will have significantly fewer resources than those in white neighborhoods. These children are more likely to have had negative encounters with the police, many of whom are white. People of color, when watching television news, will find people of their color largely absent from some stories and featured stereotypically in others. This will be true of other media as well.

In Demasio's (2000) theory of consciousness, he also asserts that people strive toward a homeostatic state when they encounter outside influences that stir them up. It follows that people of color will be more aware of the salience of

---

[1] Some people of color have experienced sufficient partial race privilege, which can derive from a variety of factors (class privilege, having grown up in another country, being able to pass for white, etc.), so they do not have a highly developed racial consciousness. We will consider this in more detail in Chapter 6.

their race and how this can threaten their well-being in a racist society. Race is more likely to be on the radar screen of their consciousness. Meanwhile, white people will encounter less dissonance between their race and their social world and experience less disequilibrium, so they likely will not have to be conscious of their race constantly. If they do experience discomfort, it is more likely to consist of feelings of confusion, guilt, or shame, which can lead to attempts to re-set their equilibrium through strategies such as withdrawing from discourses about race, becoming angry at those who draw attention to issues of race, dismissing accounts of racism, or blaming and deprecating the victims of racism. In truth, in a racialized society, no one can escape a racial discourse, but people of color are more likely to recognize this.

INVISIBLE KNAPSACKS OF PRIVILEGE

One of the best metaphors for illuminating the cognitive challenges that white people face in regard to racism was coined by Peggy McIntosh (1989, 1992). She described how whites carry an "invisible knapsack" of white privilege. As a white woman, she drew an analogy from her frustrations with males who are taught not to recognize their gender privilege, and realized that she had learned to ignore her race privilege. White people carry race privilege as "an invisible weightless knapsack of special provisions, maps, passports, codebooks, visas, clothes, tools, and blank checks" (1989, p. 10).

This invisible knapsack has been available to white people since the inception of this country, the implicit racial contract upon which the nation was founded (Mills, 1997). The "special provisions" have been encoded into laws from the outset, when white people were granted citizenship and this right was denied to people of color (Lopez, 1996). The social construction of whiteness was reaffirmed consistently, although reinterpreted by U.S. courts, which have had a profound influence on who could enter this country and what rights they were afforded if they did get in (Lopez, 1994, 1996).

McIntosh (1992) listed up to 46 examples of the knapsack's provisions. Here is a sample:

- To be able to consistently arrange to be in the company of people of your own race; this would not be true of a person of color working in a mostly white office.
- To be able to move to live in whatever neighborhood you could afford.
- To not be followed when shopping.
- To see yourself widely (and for the most part positively) represented in the media.
- To be taught that people of your race had created a civilized democracy.
- To not consistently have to prove your credit-worthiness (such as when shopping) because of your race.
- To not have to protect your children from racism.
- To not be considered a "credit to your race" when you excel.
- To not be viewed as representing or speaking for your racial group.

- Not to have to worry if stopped by the police or audited by the IRS because of your race.
- To find greeting cards, dolls, and toys depicting people who look like you.
- To see that "flesh-colored" adhesive bandages more or less correspond to the color of your skin.
- To be able to be late for a meeting without it reflecting on your race.

McIntosh could have added: to have your way of speaking assumed to be the correct way and not to have your speech monitored (Hill, 1999). Ultimately, these privileges allow white people to feel "more at home in the world" and to "escape penalties or dangers that others suffer" (McIntosh, 1992, p. 76).

Why does this knapsack remain so invisible? There are many possible reasons, and understanding them might help us as human service professionals to work more effectively against racism. Many pressures and social and psychological forces combine to minimize the visibility of white privilege. Deconstructing white privilege threatens the ideals and myths about this nation that many take for granted; it challenges the notion of meritocracy and equal opportunity, which are cornerstones of democracy (McIntosh, 1992; Miller & Schamess, 2000). Examining white privilege can threaten a person's sense of self—the belief that he or she is a good person who does not condone nor collude with racism.

McIntosh (1992, p. 76) believes that the knapsack remains invisible because of the erroneous assumption that its contents are "neutral, normal and universally available to everybody." This view echoes the myth that racism results from individual acts, perpetrated by bad people, and not from a web of systemic privilege.

Another factor that we and others (Goodman, 2001; Kaufman, 2001) have noticed is that many, if not most, white people do not feel powerful. Actually, many feel disempowered because of their gender, social class, sexual orientation, religion, and personal misfortunes and tragedies, so there is resistance to assuming the mantle of race privilege. Our adaptation of Damasio's (2000) theory of consciousness illustrates that it is often easier to be aware of how advantages are structured when we feel disempowered because we do not have passports of privilege.

SOCIALIZATION INTO WHITE PRIVILEGE

To further our understanding of why the knapsack remains so invisible, we should examine ways by which are all socialized into a racialized society, founded on the racial contract and structured by the web and discourse of racism. To paraphrase anti-racism activist Andrea Ayvazian (personal communication), it is in the air we breathe, and we all need to breathe. And as with air, it seems normal and taken for granted that many Americans live in virtually segregated communities or attend segregated schools; it is the world they know.

Thus, by as early as age 4½, white children have begun to internalize a sense of white racial superiority (Group for the Advancement of Psychiatry [GAP], 1987). By adolescence, teenagers are forging their identities, which are closely related to their sense of who is inside and outside of their group.

In her book *Why Are All the Black Kids Sitting Together in the Cafeteria?* Beverly Tatum (1997) considered this process and what it is like for students of color who are minorities in predominantly white environments. Sitting together can reflect a need of students of color to bond, support a positive sense of identity, and buffer themselves from the stresses and wounds of racism, as well as be a response to being considered out-group members for many white students. In Chapter 6 we will explain this process in greater detail, but now we will consider the role of the family in socializing white people into taking their race privilege for granted.

THE ROLE OF THE FAMILY

Families are nested in the racialized society that we have been describing. The relationship between family and community is reciprocal, and to completely filter out societal racism from the family is difficult if not impossible. Society and community provide parameters for what families can and cannot access, such as safe streets and superior schools, and they influence how families think by offering discursive narratives about the meaning of living in this society. Families and communities have a profound influence over our development and daily lives, instilling in us with values, sorting out what is normal and abnormal, defining what is possible and impossible (Miller, 2001). Many of the inner maps that we carry to orient ourselves to the world are minted by our families.

Families have explanatory systems, internal to the family system although strongly influenced by systems external to the family (e.g., families of origin, workplaces, ethnic groups, churches, the media), which become a shared meaning-making process to interpret (or misinterpret) the world (Reiss, 1981). This is important to keep in mind when we consider the nature of stereotypes, below. According to Reiss, these explanatory systems form "naïve psychologies," in that they are subjective and often untested and uncontested, but they are *experienced* as being truthful and objective maps of the world. When naïve psychologies are carried outside of the family, they are liable to clash with different or contradictory explanatory systems or may be inadequate to explain phenomena outside of the family. This can lead to confusion, a state of disequilibrium, a form of cognitive dissonance.

Allport (1948, 1954) considered ways by which people deal with the tension caused by this discord. One of his strategies is to "refence," to explain the difference as an exception without changing the explanatory system. A classic example is the white person whose explanatory system orients him to believe that African Americans do not work as hard as white people, yet one of his work colleagues is a hard worker. He might "refence" by concluding that his colleague is an exception, that he is not like "those people," while the prejudiced belief system remains in place. Another way of dealing with the tension caused by racial cognitive dissonance is to blame victims for their own misfortune, which can lead to a discourse of denigration.

For people of color, the process also is one of dissonance between family explanatory systems and the outside world, although for different reasons. From their parents and extended families, children of color learn explanatory systems about their self-worth and value. Some families attempt to prepare their children for the racism they are likely to encounter and also provide strategies for responding to it. Even if forewarned, however, most people of color are unprepared for the magnitude, depth, and persistence of racism. This leads to an even greater consciousness about how society devalues people and does not treat them fairly or equally by virtue of race and ethnicity. It also can cause strong emotional reactions, such as anger, rage, despair, sorrow, estrangement, isolation, and confusion. To be the "other" in the discourse of denigration is a particularly uncomfortable and alienating feeling.

THE DISCOURSE OF DENIGRATION AND THE CREATION OF OTHER

The "normalcy" and invisibility of the racial contract, the web of racism, and white privilege coalesce in a discourse of denigration and creation of "other" (Miller & Schamess, 2000). Most societies project an image of fairness, particularly if the society views itself as a beacon of democracy for the world. And members of society want to feel good about their country because this also makes them feel better about themselves (Brewer, 2001). Thus, a discourse that emphasizes a nation's greatness, magnanimity, generosity of spirit, and commitment to equal justice serves to enhance both social stability and collective self-esteem. Citizens feel proud about being members of a compassionate, just, and great nation. Often, such a discourse emphasizes the unique nature or character of a nation, such as "manifest destiny."

So if there is dissonance between the narrative and reality, how is this resolved? How do citizens who are proud of their country reconcile slavery, annihilation, exclusion, subjugation, and a pervasive system of race privilege? If feelings of confusion, guilt, or even shame are present, how are these expressed or resolved?

RENOUNCED TARGETS

One psychological strategy, be it individual or collective, is to have "common renounced targets" (GAP, 1987; Kaufman, 2001; Volkan, 1988). These become receptacles for projections of what is too painful or conflictual for an individual, or society, to tolerate. These unacceptable aspects of self or society are passed on to individuals or groups who are denigrated and fulfill the role of "other." Thus, politicians will extol the virtues and greatness of a nation while directly or implicitly targeting subgroups within a society for approbation. They have managed to craft a discourse that elevates the country in the face of discrimination and unearned race privilege, connecting some people to its success and greatness and enhancing collective self-esteem while marginalizing and denigrating others.

As individuals, we also construct discourses about our lives, authoring stories of ourselves, which are revised and rescripted (Bruner, 1990). Because we want to feel good about ourselves, we will go to great lengths to avoid censure and blame (Douglas, 1995), including self-criticism. Then, when confronted with unearned privilege or complicity in the oppression of others, particularly when we view ourselves as good, nonprejudiced, well-meaning people, we tend to split off those parts of ourselves that are incompatible with our self-narrative and project them onto denigrated targets (GAP, 1987; Miller & Schamess, 2000; Volkan, 1988). The targets and victims of racism become the problem: They are "lazy," "demanding," "overly sensitive when it comes to race." (In the past, the terms were "inferior," "savage," and "sub-human.") This process occurs on all levels—intrapersonally, interpersonally, between groups, and on societal and national levels. It serves to strengthen social cohesion and makes those who are not targeted feel better about themselves.

TRIANGULATION

Bowen's (1976) concept of "triangulation" furthers our understanding of this process. In triangulation, two parties (individual or groups) join together against a third party, which brings the two groups together at the expense of the scapegoat. It is a way to reduce or oversimplify complex reality and can lead to an "emotional cutoff" from the pain and suffering of the scapegoated party, who is held responsible for their social oppression. When it comes to race, it is a process that allows people and groups with race privilege to come together to feel good about themselves, denying any gains or benefits from their race while lacking empathy for those facing racial discrimination.

Conversely, when people of color are confronted with an unfair society, such as a biased school or organization, they can, in turn, psychologically disengage, resulting in less investment in systems where they are experiencing the hypocrisy of racism, or from society at large (Schmader, Major, & Gramzow, 2001).

On the positive side, this can be part of a process of shedding and disowning an imposed, falsely negative identity and developing a positive identity—an act of rebellion and self-empowerment. But it also can lead to disengagement, alienation, and even self-destructive and oppositional behavior—what Dr. Richard Majors termed the "cool pose" of young African American men, creating the illusion of control in the face of severe environmental threats (Goleman, 1992). We will explore racial identity development in greater detail in Chapter 6, but now will consider how all of the above manifests itself in internalized stereotypes, and how to respond to them.

STEREOTYPES AND WHAT CAN BE DONE ABOUT THEM

We all harbor stereotypes. Stereotypes are a set of beliefs and cognitions about the characteristics of members of a social group (Bobo, 2001). Some are positive, and others are derogatory. They stem from our need to generalize and form categories as we navigate the world. Stereotypes do not evolve in a vacuum. They reflect and contribute to public discourses about groups, encoding attitudes, guiding behaviors, while staking out social boundaries. So, in our racialized society, stereotypes have been used to discredit the victims of racism and to justify mistreatment and social exclusion, masking privilege and unequal and unfair access to resources.

As with "naïve psychologies," those who hold stereotypes often assume them to be objective truths rather than subjective prejudices. They appear as fixed reference points and involve group generalizations. They go beyond merely being cognitive constructions, drawing on deep emotions while operating as programs filtering what we see and how we make meaning of what we perceive. They often are unconscious and can be at odds with our conscious values and beliefs. Although all people harbor stereotypes, these are particularly toxic when supported by power and group dominance, as they then go beyond personal attitudes and justify and reinforce societal oppression.

One form of stereotyping, known as "group attribution theory" (Brewer, 2001), involves giving people in your own group the benefit of the doubt when they encounter misfortune while blaming members outside of your group for their travails. So if a white person knows of another white person receiving public assistance (welfare), it may be assumed that the recipient encountered some bad luck or was treated unfairly; when a person of color collects the same benefit, that recipient is assumed to be lazy or manipulating the system. Racialized attitudes such as these are shaped by segregation and family explanatory systems, and inflamed by media depictions and discourses.

Gillens (1999) found that newspaper editors and television producers, who were mostly white, helped to manufacture deprecating stereotypes about African Americans and welfare, thereby influencing the white public to become unsupportive and antagonistic to the social value of offering such assistance to families in need. This undoubtedly contributed to survey results in the mid-1990s, which found that between 65% and 70% of whites believed that blacks and Hispanics preferred welfare to working (Bobo, 2001).

SOURCES OF RESISTANCE

We discussed earlier the cognitive dissonance or emotional conflict that can result from confronting evidence about one's unearned privilege or the pervasiveness of racism in society. Stereotypes can allay the tension caused by cognitive contradictions and emotional discomfort because they relieve the holder of responsibility, projecting culpability for misfortune onto those who are oppressed. It follows that white people need not feel guilty about social inequality or the benefits of race privilege if they rationalize that they worked hard for what they have achieved and that people of color have not tried hard enough (an example of group attribution theory). This is one reason that people resist challenges to their stereotypes.

If stereotypes are at odds with people's conscious view of themselves or with their values and principles, they may feel shame or discomfort about actually holding a stereotype and, therefore, attempt to deny or suppress it. If white people view themselves as enlightened, liberal, fair, and lacking prejudice, a recurring negative stereotype about people of color can be disturbing if it is recognized. It can cause an identity crisis, leading a person to try to stifle the stereotype as it challenges his or her positive self-identity.

This can be problematic, as the stereotype is still operating but now below the radar screen of self-awareness. For people of color, holding stereotypes—particularly if they are about their own group or other groups of color—can be unsettling when they also have been on the receiving end of such distortions.

Resistance to examining and challenging stereotypes is stiffened further by the source of many stereotypes—trusted, respected, even beloved relatives, friends, teachers, and colleagues. Confronting stereotypes can cause us to lose faith in people we have believed and relied on and can lead to our feeling alienated from important relationships. Even acknowledging stereotypes, then, can cause an identity crisis, casting a flawed light on essential people in our lives as well as on ourselves.

CONSEQUENCES OF UNEXAMINED STEREOTYPES

One of the greatest risks of unacknowledged stereotypes is that rather than being reflected upon, they will be acted out, often in ways that are unconscious but having the potential to wound and harm others. They are the source of aversive racism and racial microaggressions.

AVERSIVE RACISM   Aversive racism is not intentional, aggressive racism. It occurs when white people hold implicit attitudes about people of color—often at odds with a white person's conscious beliefs or intentions—that lead to negative interactions with people of color. Aversive racism is prejudice, and its consequences are subtle, unintentional, and grounded in unconscious biases. It reflects a lack of awareness by whites in general about the realities of racism for people of color (Dovidio, Gaertner, Kawakami, & Hodson, 2002). When it occurs, it often is enacted by white people who hold egalitarian views and who would be defensive, upset, even shocked to be confronted with racism. It can, however, influence hiring and admission decisions, support or lack of support for public policies. The tension between conscious beliefs and implicit attitudes may make people unaware of their biases or discomfort, as already described. In interactions with people of color, however, the anxiety, discomfort, or prejudice can be manifested sufficiently to be picked up by the person of color, much to the surprise and dismay of the white person, leading to interpersonal strains and difficult interactions. In turn, people of color can become increasingly watchful about their interactions with whites, and wary of the impact of subtle biases (Dovidio et al., 2002).

When one of the authors (Miller, 2001) was conducting research in a liberal Northeast city, he interviewed a Hispanic police officer who had run unsuccessfully for political office. The respondent described how, when he entered white, suburban neighborhoods to campaign, he would have to wear a t-shirt emblazoned with his campaign logo, so as not to cause undue alarm to residents or to the police patrolling the neighborhood. Yet the majority of white respondents living in that neighborhood viewed themselves as being mostly without prejudice.

Kaufman (2001) describes the subtlety of interactions with an underlying current of aversive racism:

> The actions that create the racist atmosphere in society can be so small that each action in itself is almost imperceptible. For many people of color, whenever they walk into a mostly white space, they are looked at. The looks are not necessarily hostile. But they are looks nevertheless. The person of color's presence has a charge and, if the tension is to be eased, it falls on the person of color to initiate this. Each individual white person doesn't do much. A meeting of the eyes that is broken off a split second too quickly; a slight pulling in of the arms; a smile that is just a millimeter too forced at the edges. Each action is almost imperceptible. Together they are enough to create a force field of discomfort. (p. 33)

RACIAL MICROAGGRESSIONS   Racial microaggressions are similar to aversive racism. They are "subtle, stunning, often automatic," verbal and nonverbal put-downs and social assaults that wound people of color unbeknownst to the perpetrator (Pierce, Carew, Pierce-Gonzalez, & Wills, 1978). As with aversive racism, microaggressions often are unconscious acts, but they have painful consequences. They occur repetitively, and their impact can be cumulative, like a thousand paper cuts as opposed to one deep wound. Examples of racial microaggressions are: ignoring people of color in a group or classroom, having lower expectations, being mistrustful, expecting people of color to speak on behalf of their own race, expecting a person of color to "act and talk white," denying the relevance of race and racism (Solorzano et al., 2000).

A hypothetical illustration is a Korean American student whom other students and the professor look at every time of Asian Americans are mentioned in a sociology class. Or a Native American student describes how racism contributes to the high poverty rates in her community and is told by other students that she makes too big a deal about racism and uses it as an excuse to justify the plight of her people.

Being on the receiving end of racial microaggressions can leave people of color feeling hurt, mistrustful, angry, beleaguered, and exhausted (Solorzano et al., 2000). One way of dealing with such regular and commonplace assaults is to seek refuge in groups that are composed predominantly of people of color to lessen the chances of encountering microaggressions and to offer buffering, mutual support, and positive validation and confirmation (Solorzano et al.; Tatum, 1997).

| BOX 5.1 | STRATEGIES FOR CONFRONTING STEREOTYPES |

1. *Monitor dissonance with conscious beliefs.*
   - Do not suppress the stereotype. Examine it.
   - Experience the discomfort and discord with values and beliefs to create motivation to confront the stereotype.
2. *Monitor thoughts and feelings that accompany the stereotype.*
   - How did you learn the stereotype?
   - How did you come to disagree with it?
   - What feelings accompany the stereotype?
   - What feelings accompany your desire to counter the stereotype?
3. *Take a perspective.*
   - Think of individuals who defy the stereotype.
   - Imagine how *you* would feel if you were them.
   - Practice empathy in groups as well as alone.
4. *Use replacement thoughts.*
   - Think of something that contradicts the stereotype.
   - Whenever the stereotype emerges, try to associate the thought.
5. *Practice.*
   - Recognize that unlearning stereotypes takes time.
   - Keep in mind that any of these techniques must be practiced.
6. *Develop egalitarian goals.*
   - Cultivate goals that contradict racial stereotypes.
   - Use professional codes of ethics and standards, as well as organizational mission statements and commitments to support egalitarian goals.
7. *Surround yourself with allies.*
   - Find allies to support you in unlearning racism.

This, is turn, can lead to white people thinking that people of color are preoccupied excessively with race, are excluding themselves and fostering racial divisions, are manufacturing problems that do not exist, or are exacerbating conflicts because they are seen as being unwilling to discuss issues with whites. We will consider these dynamics in greater detail in Chapter 8, when we explore intergroup dialogue.

CONFRONTING STEREOTYPES

Thankfully, research by social psychologists has confirmed a number of effective strategies for confronting stereotypes and minimizing their impact. We will discuss each of these tactics, as they are essential for workers in the helping professions to use with themselves and others.

1. *Dissonance with beliefs.* We must have conscious beliefs that counteract stereotypes. People who are comfortable with their stereotypes will either not recognize them as such or have no motivation to modify them. This is why it is so important to expose people to experiences that confront their prejudiced, but often unconscious explanatory systems. To create the dissonance necessary to motivate people to work to dispel their stereotypes and to enable self-monitoring, people have to acknowledge, examine, and explore a stereotype rather than try to suppress it and act as if it does not exist (Monteith, Sherman & Devine, 1998; Moskowitz, Gollwitzer, Wasel & Schaal, 1999). One of our students put it this way: A stereotype is like a pop-up screen on your computer desktop—you have an urge to click the X and close it. The more the stereotype conflicts with one's conscious beliefs and positive self-image, the greater is the impulse to stifle it. But we are suggesting that it is better to leave it open and examine it, comparing it with what you consciously value and believe.

   Suppressing stereotypes usually is not helpful, because it can interfere with self-awareness (Moskowitz et al., 1999), and there also is a danger of a "rebound effect" (Galinsky & Moskowitz, 2000). By trying so hard to smother a stereotype, the stereotype gains more potency and resonance than if it is aired and explored.

2. *Self-monitoring.* Related to allowing the stereotype to surface and to experience the discord with conscious ethics and viewpoints is the value of self-monitoring (Monteith, 1993). This self-awareness has two aspects: (1) the cognitive component; and (2) the feelings that accompany the stereotype. Self-awareness about the "thought" part of a stereotype can involve tracking back the source of the stereotype—where it was learned, who also holds this stereotype, what experiences you have had that reinforced the stereotype, how you came to disagree with it.

   The emotional self-awareness can take the form of exploring what feelings accompany both the stereotype and your awareness that you hold the stereotype. Do feelings of fear and anxiety spark the stereotype? Do feelings of guilt or shame immobilize you when you are trying to work on the stereotype? Are there other people who hold this stereotype with whom you have strong emotional attachments? Do you have feelings that cause you to resist letting go of this stereotype?

3. *Perspective taking.* Empathy is an excellent antidote to stereotypes (Stephan & Finlay, 1999). Empathy puts us in the shoes of others, infusing their humanity with our personhood, so constructing them as a denigrated "other" becomes much more difficult. When stereotypes are operating, empathy often is lacking and will not flow easily. Thus, a conscious effort is necessary to try and empathize to offset a racial stereotype.

   You can leaven the process of empathy by: (1) treating people as individuals and trying to empathize with the individual, rather than attempting to make a general connection with a group; and (2) imagining how *you* would feel and experience the world if you were the other person, rather than empathizing only with how that person experiences the world (Galinsky & Moskowitz, 2000).

Empathy can be achieved in different ways: (1) Participate in diverse groups and form relationships with people who are racially or ethnically different, and structuring conversations to evoke mutual and reciprocal empathy; and (2) use techniques such as focused, single-point meditation to concentrate on putting oneself in another's place and to experience, as nonjudgmentally as possible, what this feels like.

4. *Replacement thoughts.* One way to confront a stereotype is to substitute another thought in its place, which negates or contradicts the stereotype (Kawakami, Moll, Hermsen, Dovidio, & Russin, 2000). This is a way of "imagining a stereotype away" (Blair, Ma, & Lenton, 2001).

The first step is to consciously think of something that contradicts the stereotype, bringing into conscious awareness a positive association (e.g., a friend, colleague, public figure) who is inconsistent with a negative stereotype toward an ethnic group.

Next, practice tagging this thought to the stereotype every time the stereotype arises, so eventually when the stereotype bubbles up, so does its antidote. If you do this repeatedly and self-consciously, it eventually may become a process of automatic self-monitoring in which the replacement thought becomes ascendant (Kawakami, et al., 2000).

Ultimately, the replacement thought can cancel out the stereotype even before the stereotype reaches the level of consciousness (Moskowitz, et al., 1999).

5. *Practice.* With all of the above techniques and strategies, practice is of paramount importance (Blair et al., 2001; Monteith et al., 1998). Stereotypes have accrued over many years and are reinforced constantly by the webs and discourses of racism. Thus, it is not as if a person can just decide to expunge a stereotype and—poof—it's gone! It also is frustrating to work on challenging a stereotype only to have it pop up again.

Thus, it is important to engage in a variety or combination of the above strategies and continue to identify dissonance, develop self-monitoring, actively engage empathically, and substitute replacement thoughts over time. This may take years and may never be complete; however, the research cited thus far indicates that these strategies do work and are worth the investment.

6. *Developing egalitarian goals.* All of the stereotype-reduction approaches discussed here are dependent on developing egalitarian goals that clash with the stereotypes. This is not always as easy as it sounds, because the stereotypes themselves can inhibit a person from developing empathy or egalitarian goals (Monteith et al., 1998; Moskowitz et al., 1999). This is where professional codes of ethics, training, and standards of practice can be helpful. They provide a mandate for ethical practice, as well as templates for achieving that standard. All human service and helping professionals are expected to practice according to the principles of their professions, and this can be the incentive for learning about content that

challenges assumptions and stereotypes and can facilitate the development of nonprejudicial goals.

Another helpful tool is for organizations and institutions to make a formal commitment to social justice and/or anti-racism. This serves as a constant reminder to all staff about the vision and aspirations of the organization, with expectations of staff commitment.

7. *Surrounding oneself with allies.* Because motivation, time, and persistence are required to unlearn stereotypes, surrounding oneself with allies, people who have already done similar work, or are also engaged in an unlearning process, is beneficial. This creates a space where people can take risks and collectively explore internalized stereotypes about themselves and others. Allies can set an example for one another and together create an impetus and momentum for unlearning racism. Confronting stereotypes is an emotional endeavor and requires courage and persistence.

CONCLUSION

Because of the cognitive and emotional tensions between explanatory systems and the reality of the historical and social worlds that people inhabit, all people, regardless of race, are conscripted as actors in a racialized social discourse, which grants in-group status to some while casting others into socially targeted and maligned roles. All of these processes lead to stereotypes about oneself and others, internalizations of external social inequities and ideologies. Unexamined stereotypes can lead to aversive racism and racial microaggressions. A variety of strategies can be used to counteract stereotypes.

Two exercises further the experience of self-awareness and detoxification of stereotypes. Exercise 5.1 is a cultural audit that permits you to explore how you learned about yourself as a social actor and your encounters with people from different cultural and racial backgrounds. Exercise 5.2 can be done alone or in groups, with discussion enabling participants to examine their stereotypes and begin the process of empathy, perspective taking, and replacement thoughts.

EXERCISE 5.1   PERSONAL AUDIT

This is a tool to explore your socialization with people from different racial and ethnic groups—often a source of positive and negative stereotypes.

1. Describe your first contacts with members of other racial and ethnic groups. When did these occur?
2. What values and attitudes did you learn from your family about people from other racial and ethnic groups? Were there discrepancies between what was said and what was done?
3. How diverse was your neighborhood? School? College?

4. What other experiences have you had with people of different races and cultures?
5. What were some positive encounters with people from other ethnic or racial groups?
6. What were some negative encounters with people from other ethnic or racial groups? What did you think or feel? If you could replay the tape of what happened, what do you wish you would have done differently?
7. Which clients from different racial and ethnic groups have you found to be most challenging. Why?

EXERCISE 5.2   CONFRONTING STEREOTYPES

1. Think of a racial stereotype you hold that makes you feel uncomfortable. If you have difficulty identifying one, try to think of something about a person from a different racial or ethnic group that you would *not* want to discuss with him or her but would be willing to confide to somebody who shares your racial or ethnic identity.
2. What is the stereotype? If you were trying to teach this stereotype to someone else, how would you explain it?
3. What uncomfortable feelings surface when describing this stereotype? It can help to list them.
4. Where might you have learned this, and from whom? (Include multiple sources if you like.)
5. What might have been the historical and social contexts from which this stereotype evolved?
6. What in society or your daily life perpetuates and reinforces the stereotype?
7. What do you *know* or *believe* that contradicts this stereotype?

Social Identity Formation and Group Membership

CHAPTER CONTENTS

When did you first think of yourself as having a race and ethnicity? Were you aware of this as a child? When you went to school? College? How well do you think your race or ethnicity is respected and validated in society? Are you able to be your complex self, or does society try to label you or restrict you to one category? Do you have regular interactions with people of different racial backgrounds? If so, do you sense that they are mostly comfortable or uncomfortable? If not, what are some reasons that cross-racial interactions occur much less often than those of the same race?

These questions address our racial and ethnic identities. They invite us to reflect about who we are, who we identify and interact with, how we perceive our group's place in society, and all of the feelings that accompany these contemplations. For some, these questions will be fruitful, and the questions will make others feel awkward or uncomfortable. In any case, they help us explore and validate our sense of self while at the same time highlight our differences and social divisions. We believe that these are essential lines of inquiry for all who work in the helping professions.

Chapter 1 introduced the concept of social identity and asked readers to situate themselves and reflect on how various aspects of our identity carry differential power and privilege. In the previous chapter we described the paradox of white privilege, ubiquitous yet often invisible to those who benefit from it. In this chapter we will continue to explore the internalization of racism and examine how this influences group allegiances and intergroup dynamics. We present a comprehensive model of social identity that is holistic, flexible, adaptable, and useful in the work of the helping professions.

Because all of the helping professions involve interpersonal contact and the use of self, exploring our social identity and how we came to be who we are is essential as we try to work across race and culture. We also have to try to understand the identities of the people with whom we work and how they are similar to and different from us.

After considering classical notions of identity and some major principles of racial identity theory, this chapter will present a model of social identity development, building on the theories and concepts of racial and social identity theorists. Identity is related intricately to the groups we feel attached to and those we feel different or excluded from, so we also will look at the dynamics of group membership and how this affects intergroup relations. Last, we will consider the implications for work in the helping professions.

IDENTITY

We all have an identity, a sense of who we are in relation to other people. Identity is an integral part of self. It is a consistent way by which we organize the various aspects of ourselves as we negotiate relationships and the social world. Identity can be adaptive or maladaptive. It can be a vehicle for successfully negotiating relationships, social roles, and social tasks or a train on the wrong track that never seems to be cruising at the right speed or in the right direction. Some aspects of identity are stable and enduring, while others are fluid or situationally activated. Identity engages us as both actors and observers; we reflect on ourselves and are able to name and classify who we are and what we do in relation to other people and how we fit with social categories (Stets & Burke, 2000). Identity is the narrative we construct about who we are, which we present to ourselves as well as to others.

Identity shapes what we see, think (about the world, ourselves, and others), feel, believe, and value. It also directs our social roles, skills, occupations, and our group affiliations and allegiances (Erikson, 1963; Stets & Burke, 2000).

Erik Erikson (1963, 1968) is by far the most recognized identity theorist over the past half-century. He offered a developmental, epigenetic, psychosocial model of development from birth until death. He believed that identity is the resolution of adolescence, the bridge between childhood and adulthood. Adolescence is a time of physical, endocrinological, and social turbulence, which involves dismantling our child-self and laying down tracks for our adult-self, but we are neither beyond our childhood nor have we reached adulthood. It is a period of transition.

This transition involves a heightened sense of self-awareness. We are concerned with how we look and present ourselves, sensitive to how others perceive us. During this period we clarify what is good and bad, whom we feel attached to and to which groups we belong, and whom we distance ourselves from and scorn and disparage.

The process of individuation and differentiation, along with the desire to belong, are powerful sources for creating in-groups and out-groups and fueling social divisions. According to Erikson (1963, 1968), identity is formed by the interaction of a developmental process and the cultural and social context in which this occurs. In the United States, identity is fashioned in a relatively heterogeneous society. Even if many neighborhoods are segregated and socially homogenous, society at large is quite diverse ethnically and racially. This contrasts with identity formation in many other societies, which are ethnically and racially homogenous (Hoare, 2003).

Identity formation incorporates a sense of power, privilege, and marginalization. Erikson (1968) believed that those with privilege project their unconscious, negative identities onto those who are oppressed, which has the effect of buttressing their sense of superiority at the expense of those who are "other" and, further, socially constructed as "less than." Identity formation involves internalizing a subjective sense of social order, a hierarchy with a "we" and "they" (Smith, 1991). Thus, in a society riddled with racism, people have difficulty achieving a positive sense of self without denigrating others or being recipients of unowned and unacceptable projections from others (Myers et al., 1991; Volkan, 1988).

Erikson's sense of identity reflected a localized, Western notion of self that is not representative of many of the world's cultures. Although he was aware of this, his own thinking and the preponderance of his clinical experience was in a Western, Eurocentric context. Thus, his strong emphasis on an autonomous, individuated self, with its roots in Western history, philosophy, and culture, is at odds with most of the world's cultures, which emphasize a more collective and interdependent sense of self and identity (Roland, 2003; Yeh & Hwang, 2000). It also is a very male vision of identity (Gilligan, 1977, 1982).

Another criticism of this vision of identity is that it is often written from the perspective of society's privileged, rather than from the vantage point of those who are socially targeted. Partially in reaction to these concerns, racial identity theory emerged.

RACIAL AND ETHNIC IDENTITY THEORY

Racial and ethnic theories of development go beyond generic conceptualizations of identity and attempt to consider the impact of cultural differences and societal oppression. Ethnic and racial identity theories originally had different premises, focusing on cultural differences in worldview, values, and relationship of self to family. Power, privilege, and oppression were taken into account by considering how identity formation was influenced by reacting to a racist environment (Sellers et al., 1998). Racial identity theory took as its starting point the experience of African Americans (Cross, 1978, 1991; Helms, 1990; Helms & Cook, 1999) and, later, other people of color, seeking to understand how a positive and adaptive sense of identity could emerge for black people living in a racist society. The perspective was the internal experience of people of color (Sellers et al., 1998).

Racial identity theorists disagreed over whether a theory could be applied to only one specific racial or ethnic group or if universal theories could be developed for people with race privilege and those who are racially targeted. But theories of ethnic and racial identity development also had much in common. The distinctions between ethnicity and race are far from clearcut. For example, African Americans are an ethnic group, with traditions, customs, and other cultural distinctions, but also are the targets of racism and have been socially constructed racially as black (Taylor, 1997).

On a personal level, some people distinguish between their race and ethnicity and others do not. For example, a Mexican American born in the United States could view herself as Mexican American, American, Chicana, Latina, or a person of color. She also may identify with Native American, European, Asian, or African heritage. As both race and ethnicity are social constructions and a person's identity includes personal, subjective meanings, the distinction between race and ethnicity is not always clear. Thus, we find it more useful to consider ethnic and racial theories of identity formation together rather than as separate entities.

All theories of ethnic and racial identity map out phases or stages that a person moves through. Stage theories tend to be more linear and epigenetic, with a clear progression of stages in which each stage subsumes previous stages in a hierarchy of stages. In most stage theories, a person is in one stage at a time.

Phase theories are more fluid and can view a person as having certain statuses or constellations of attitudes and behaviors. These theories allow more leeway for a person to have qualities of more than one phase and for development to proceed in a nonlinear fashion.

Most theories of ethnic and racial identity development, whether stage or phase, have different trajectories for white people and people of color. In this context, we will consider both stage and phase theorists together.

Phinney and Kohatsu (1997) have summarized some of the most prominent theories of racial and ethnic identity development for adolescents of non-European descent (Atkinson, Morten, & Sue, 1993; Cross, 1991; Helms, 1990; Marcia, Waterman, Matteson, Archer, & Orlofsky, 1994; Phinney, 1989, 1993; Sue & Sue, 1990) and collapsed and synthesized them into four major phases: initial, transition, intermediate and final (see Table 6.1).

- *Initial phase.* Different theorists have described this as "pre-encounter" (Cross; Helms), "unexamined" (Phinney), and "conformity" (Atkinson, Morten, & Sue; Sue & Sue). All refer to an unexamined identity. In this phase adolescents have not yet reflected on the meaning of their ethnicity/ race in society and for themselves.
- *Transition phase.* This phase has been termed "encounter" (Cross; Helms), "exposure" (Phinney), "dissonance" (Atkinson et al.; Sue & Sue), and "identity crisis" (Marcia et al.). It implies a critical reevaluation, a period of transition, often precipitated by a crisis or intense encounters that challenge previously held assumptions. This often is accompanied by cognitive confusion and emotional distress.
- *Intermediate phase.* This phase often is characterized by "exploration" (Phinney) of a new identity and its implications, as well as "immersion/ emersion" (Cross; Helms), which means wanting to be with people, groups, and cultures that reflect one's new identity and avoiding painful encounters with those who are different or antagonistic. This involves self-protective, self-validating, and buffering maneuvers.
- *Final phase.* The final phase involves internalizing and establishing a positive and adaptive identity and a means of functioning within the dominant culture and being able to manage racism and other threats to self.

Hardiman (1994) performed a similar service for models of white racial identity development, comparing her own model (Hardiman, 1982) with those of Marcia (1980), Helms (1990), Ponterotto (1988), and Sabnani, Ponterotto, and Borodovsky (1991). All illustrate movement from being racially unaware, to encounters that create crisis and confusion, to eventually achieving a nonracist, positive racial identity—an awareness of what whiteness and white privilege mean in society, without subscribing to the tenets of racism.

Hardiman employs the metaphor of wearing new eyeglasses at each stage, enabling people to see themselves and the world with greater clarity. As with models of racial identity for people of color, the steps involve reevaluation, immersion, and emersion. Helms (1990) and Helms and Cook (1999) include a stage called "reintegration," which is a time of great resistance to acknowledging racism, understanding one's place in a racist society, and accepting a nonracist identity. This is consistent with what we described in the previous chapter about the difficulty many white people have in seeing and acknowledging the extent of racism and their white privilege.

TABLE 6.1 | COMPARISON OF ETHNIC AND RACIAL IDENTITY MODELS

Title	Initial Phase	Transition	Intermediate Phase	Final Phase
Ego Identity[1]	Diffusion/Foreclosure	Identity Crisis	Moratorium	Identity Achievement
Ethnic Identity[2]	Unexamined	Exposure/Experience	Exploration	Achievement
Racial Identity Theory[3]	Pre-encounter	Encounter	Immersion/Emersion	Internalization/Commitment
Minority Identity Model[4]	Conformity	Dissonance	Resistance and Immersion	Introspection/Integrative awareness

[1]Ego Identity: Handbook of Psychosocial Research, by J. Marcia, A. Waterman, D. Matteson, D. Archer, and J. Orlofsky (New York: Springer-Verlag, 1994).

[2] "Stages of Ethnic Identity Development in Minority Group Adolescents," by J. Phinney, Journal of Early Adolescence, 9 (1989), 34–49; "A Three-Stage Model of Ethnic Identity Development," by J. Phinney, in Ethnic Identity: Formation and Transmission Among Hispanics and Other Minorities, edited by M.E. Bernal and G.P. Knight (Albany: State University of New York Press, 1993).

[3]Shades of Black: Diversity in African-American Identity, by W. Cross (Philadelphia: Temple University Press, 1991); Black and White Racial Identity: Theory, Research and Practice, by J. Helms (New York: Greenwood Press, 1990).

[4]Counseling American Minorities (4th edition), by D. Atkinson, G. Morten, and D. Sue (Dubuque, IA: W.C. Brown, 1993); Counseling the Culturally Different: Theory and Practice, by D.W. Sue and D. Sue (2nd edition) (New York: Wiley and Sons, 1990).

Source: Adapted from "Ethnic and Racial Identity Development and Mental Health, by J. Phinney and E.L. Kohatsu, in Health Risks and Developmental Transitions During Adolescence, edited by J. Schulenberg, J.L. Maggs, and K. Hurelmann (New York: Cambridge University Press, 1997).

Theories of racial identity development share many characteristics: They are developmental, have discrete stages or phases, and ideally lead to a positive and adaptive sense of self. Phinney (1992) identified four common elements found in most theories of racial/ethnic identity:

1. how a person self-identifies;
2. the ethnic behaviors and practices that accompany identity;
3. how strong or weak a person's sense of belonging to a group is, and an affirmation of one's own ethnic or racial identity; and
4. the actual process that one goes through to achieve an ethnic or racial identity.

Adolescence clearly is a fertile time for developing a racial and ethnic identity, but the process actually begins in childhood and is lifelong (Smith, 1991). As we described in the previous chapter, the family plays a crucial role by shaping attitudes, conveying ethnic practices and values, and employing explanatory systems and narratives to explain how family members fit with their social world. As children attend school, socialize with friends, play sports, are exposed to the media, and eventually move on to college, the circle of influence widens and the opportunities for encounters and challenges to assumptions about self and others increases.

Although all theories of racial and ethnic identity development have some elements in common, they also have fundamental differences in the tasks assigned for white people and for people of color. People of color work to develop an identity that encompasses self-esteem and positive self-regard despite societal ambivalence or hostility toward their identity; white people do not face the same challenges related to race. People of color face the dual challenge of understanding how whiteness operates in society and how they can survive in this world, while also having to learn about their own racial and ethnic group, resolving their relationship to both.

With so many negative stereotypes in society at large, it is difficult for people of color not to internalize some of them. Therefore, part of the task of developing racial identity is to dislodge internalized stereotypes and to externalize them. Ultimately, the hope is that people of color will achieve an identity that will enable them to survive and prosper in a social world where they encounter oppression and to feel good about who they are.

White people face the challenging task of unlearning racism. This involves forging a nonracist white identity. As we described in the prior chapter, white people do not see racism or the scope of white privilege for many reasons. Racial identity formation relies on being able to perceive this eventually and to place oneself in this racialized matrix. One of the biggest challenges for white people is that unlearning racism and coming to terms with white privilege cuts across the grain. Racism, not anti-racism, is reinforced in society, with many pressures, both overt and subtle, to continue to assume white privilege and to discourage white people from challenging entrenched racial systems of advantage. This is one reason that support groups for unlearning racism can be so helpful, in the same way that groups and associations for people of color can offer mutual support and buffering from racism.

MULTIRACIAL/BIRACIAL IDENTITY DEVELOPMENT

One dilemma confronting theories of racial and ethnic identity development is that many people today identify as biracial, multiracial, and multiethnic. Some multiracial and multicultural people grow up in an environment that predominantly stresses one side of their heritage, because of family dynamics, or perhaps the nature of the community in which they grow up (Poston, 1990). For other people, all aspects of their racial and ethnic identity are acknowledged and validated. Even in this situation, though, they can face tremendous tensions in school, where they may be pressured to choose between different and competing groups. Shifting contexts, such as moving from one community to another or attending college, also can validate or invalidate one aspect of a multiracial/ethnic person's identity (Aldarondo, 2001).

Family is another critical context for everyone's racial and ethnic identity development, but particularly for multiracial people. For example, whether a bi/multiracial person grows up with one parent or both parents or is adopted (either by someone from his or her own or different racial/ethnic group) is likely to have a significant impact on his or her racial/ethnic identity development.

Another factor for multiracial people is physical appearance. Students who are light-skinned Latinos or African Americans have described to us how they have been able to "pass" as white while their siblings or parents with darker skin are treated as people of color. Shirley Taylor (1995), who came from a multiracial family, described how a light-skinned wing of her family denied its African American heritage, cut off contact with their darker-skinned relatives, moved to a new region, and essentially became white people. This is a good example of how racism can cause internal conflicts and ambivalence for multiracial people, even estranging them from their own family members. But many multiracial people do gain a great deal of strength and support from their family, community, and cultural traditions.

Racial and ethnic identity theory should not be binary, as if people are only white or of color. Otherwise multiracial people are pressured to choose one aspect of their identity over another (Aldarondo, 2001; Poston, 1990; Rockquemore & Brunsma, 2004), which is painful and fragments the identity rather than integrating it. A task for multiracial and multiethnic people is to integrate the various parts of racial and ethnic identities in a way that feels authentic to multiracial/multiethnic people and connects them, as much as possible, with family and friends. They may identify with one aspect of racial/ethnic identity, all aspects, no aspects, or, in some instances, shift from one identity to another, depending on context (Rockquemore & Brunsma, 2004).

Helping professionals should be careful not to privilege any specific resolution of racial identity development for multiracial people, as this creates additional pressure to conform to the others' expectations. As with any racial identity development, a transcendent goal is for people to feel positive and secure about themselves and to feel competent in negotiating their social world.

THEORETICAL ASSUMPTIONS

We have mentioned goals and tasks for the development of racial identity. These theories have a prescriptive element based on the assumptions of the theorists (Sellers et al., 1998). One is the belief that it is better for a person to move to the higher stages from the lower stages. Another is that people will be happier if they can integrate their racial identity so they neither feel negatively about themselves nor feel perpetually angry or guilty. The highest stages usually describe those who feel positively about who they are while also being able to appreciate and respect people from different cultures and races. Myers et al. (1991) describe the importance of identity integration and expansion, leading to what they consider an "optimal" identity resolution.

Most racial identity theories assume that it is better for white people to become racially aware than to continue to operate beneath a veil of ignorance about their race and privilege. Because much of this theory has emerged from clinical work and is written by counselors and therapists, it focuses on the therapist's racial identity, the client's racial identity, and how these mesh and clash during the process of therapy. We will consider this in greater detail in Chapter 11.

CONCEPTUAL EXPANSIONS OF ETHNIC AND RACIAL IDENTITY THEORY

Building on racial and ethnic identity theory while also questioning some of its assumptions, several theorists have offered alternative scenarios or have revised or made conceptual modifications to a racial and social identity framework. Following are some of the concepts consistent with the model of multidimensional identity development that follows.

- *Identity is internal and external* (Kwan & Sodowsky, 1997). Internal concepts of identity include people's views of themselves and their ethnic group, as well as their awareness of the history and values of their ethnic group. External identity refers to observable customs, behaviors, cultural practices, traditions, and rituals.
- *Parts of identity are fixed, and others are fluid and flexible* (Arredondo, 1999; Sellers et al., 1998). For most people (although not all), some aspects of identity, such as gender, are consistent (fixed) from birth onward. Even if the *meanings* associated with gender evolve, the actual gender remains constant. Other aspects of identity may change over time (fluid), such as one's spiritual or religious beliefs or racial and ethnic identity.
- *Identity connects us with our past and future* (Myers et al., 1991). Having a sense of racial and ethnic identity can tie people to ancestors, as well as descendents, with whom they can identify. If children or grandchildren modify or abandon their ethnic and racial identities, this can be viewed as

rupturing this connection—which often is why there are such emotional struggles over retaining historical and traditional identities.

- *Some aspects of identity take precedence over others* (Reynolds & Pope, 1991; Sellers et al., 1998). Most people have a hierarchy of aspects of their identity, in which some parts are more conscious and important for the individual. We often hear white students describe their social class, gender, or sexual orientation as being more significant for them than their racial identity. This is less common for students of color. When parts of identity are socially targeted, they tend to be salient and are more likely to enter conscious awareness.

- *Helping professionals should accept the validity of an individual's definition of his or her own identity* (Sellers et al., 1998). Identity is subjective and socially constructed, and when using relationships to help people, we must honor a consumer's self-constructions of identity. Unfortunately, society defines and generalizes about people, placing them in categories whether they choose to be in these groupings or not. The dignity and worth of each individual is affirmed when we begin by asking them how *they* socially define themselves. Validation in interpersonal relationships is vital to achieving a positive sense of identity (Rockquemore & Brunsma, 2004).

- *Identity development is not linear* (Henriksen & Trusty, 2004; Myers et al., 1991; Sellers et al., 1998). Identity does not progress neatly through a series of linear steps. It is most helpful to track each person's own journey through identity development, which may proceed elliptically, in a spiral or zigzag formation, as well as step by step. Some people skip phases or stages altogether, and at other times people revisit earlier identity phases.

- *A person's identity has many dimensions* (Arredondo, 1999; Myers et al., 1991). Examples of identity dimensions are self-regard, salience and meaning, affect, opinion, and values and beliefs about one's identity.

MULTIDIMENSIONAL SOCIAL IDENTITY DEVELOPMENT

We have created a model of social identity development that draws on many of the concepts just presented, the work of Reynolds and Pope (1991), Donner & Miller, 2007, as well as our own clinical and teaching experience. We have opted to present a model of social identity development rather than a narrower view of racial and ethnic identity development, as we have found that race and ethnicity are inseparable from other aspects of identity.

The model is holistic and values the complexity of social identity, the conflicts and contradictions among different aspects of a person's social identity, an individual's phenomenological experience and meaning, and the significance of the historical and material context in which identity emerges. We will share the assumptions that underpin our model and then present its

BOX 6.1 | ### SOCIAL IDENTITY VARIABLES

Dimensions

1. *Social:* Who you affiliate with
2. *Emotional:* How you feel about who you are
3. *Cognitive:* How your social identity influences how you see the world (and vice-versa)
4. *Ego-self:* How you view and describe yourself

Lifespan Context

Social identity is influenced by and shaped by lifespan development: phase of life, health status, social situation, living situation.

Environmental Context

1. *Macro:* Social identity is shaped by history, politics, nationality, cohort, economics.
2. *Mezzo:* Social identity is shaped by where we work, live, our professions, schools, social groups.
3. *Micro:* Social identity is contingent and interactional and is activated (or deactivated) by relationships, interactions, places, billboards, songs, books, films.

Resolutions/Stances

1. Integrated versus unintegrated
2. Complex versus simple
3. Flexible/adaptable versus fixed/rigid
4. Activist versus passive observer
5. Collaboration versus conflict
6. Stable versus fluid

Axes of Social Identity

Race, ethnicity, gender, sexual orientation, class (both social and economic), religion, nationality, regional identity, immigration status, language capacity, physical ability/health

Source: Adapted from "The Complexity of Multidimensional Social Identity Development," by J. Miller and S. Donner, *International Social Work: Social Problems, Cultural Issues and Social Work Education*, edited by S. Borrmann, M. Klassen, and C. Spatscheck (Opladen, Germany: Barbara Budrich Publishers, 2007).

various components: axes of social identity, dimensions, contexts (both lifespan and environmental), and potential resolutions and stances for each axis. We will then describe possible developmental phases for both targeted and privileged parts of identity. (See Exercise 6.1 for a framework to explore this model.)

ASSUMPTIONS

Most theories of identity development are predicated on assumptions about what is healthy and normal. Following are some of the assumptions underpinning the multidimensional social identity development model.

- *Identity goes through phases.* We believe that phases are more variable, less categorical, and more applicable to the vicissitudes of human experience than are stages. We consider phases to be a cluster of perceptions and behaviors that generate meaning. They are not fixed or objective realities but, rather, are subjective, contingent, and contested frameworks.
- *Identity development is not linear.* Our schema of phases, although having a possible direction or trajectory, should not be viewed as a linear process, nor should it be assumed that all people go through all phases. Some people progress through all phases, others only through some phases. One person may seem to have many characteristics of a given phase, and another seems to have attributes of multiple stages.
- *There are targeted and privileged identity statuses.* Each aspect of social identity development has the potential for either targeted or privileged status, using objective social measures. For example, heterosexual people can marry, but gay, lesbian, and bisexual people are unable to marry in most states.

    Many people have a mix of targeted and privileged statuses. For example, someone feels targeted by virtue of being a woman but is privileged by being middle class and white. Having a targeted or privileged status is a matter of degree and falls on a continuum rather than being limited to absolute categories.

    The extent of racial oppression that people of color experience varies considerably, as does the amount of privilege for white people. For example, a dark-complexioned African American man may experience many forms of racism that a Japanese American woman does not, although each of them identifies as a person of color and has encountered some degree of racial prejudice. Similarly, a dark-complexioned woman of Jewish and Italian descent may have a great deal of white race privilege, yet also encounter some racial prejudice, based on her appearance. This would not be the experience of a light-complexioned woman of Scandinavian descent.

    How people view themselves in relation to others is highly subjective, as is their personal sense of having privilege or being socially oppressed. Much depends on which parts of their identity are most salient over time, as well as on their exposure to specific social and historical contexts. Croteau, Talbot, Lance, and Evans (2002) found that having mixed social identity statuses, including privilege, mitigated the impact of oppression.

    They also found that having some aspects of identity that are socially targeted helps people connect with people from other oppressed groups, as well as having a more realistic understanding of the dynamics of oppression. Many variables, including how various axes of identity interact, personal experience, available resources, and the meaning one ascribes to one's identity, render a person's identity more complex than a binary classification of oppressed or privileged.

Those with privileged aspects of social identity may have the capacity to understand the experience of those with oppressed identity statuses by virtue of intimate and personal relationships. A white partner of a person of color can empathize deeply with the experience of racism. A white mother of biracial children can better understand her own racial identity and privileges through her children's experiences with oppression (O'Donoghue, 2004).

There are also aspects of identity in which a person experiences both privilege and being targeted within the same axis. Examples are biracial/bi-ethnic or multiracial/multi-ethnic people and those who identify as bisexual who might experience privileged and targeted aspects of their identity simultaneously. Also, some people change an aspect of their social identity—such as those who are transgendered or transsexual—and in the process modify their social status. A transgendered woman experienced herself as being male during one phase of her life before becoming female. Even within the category of "women," she may experience minority status. A working-class white male who becomes a college professor has shifted his social class and, although his inner sense of self still may be working-class, his economic and social status have risen in society.

We have given these examples to illustrate how targeted and privileged identity statuses are relative, fluid, and not always clearcut. Therefore, although societal privileges are attached to different social identity statuses, virtually any axis of social identity can change over time and can be personally reconstructed or redefined in different contexts.

- *Identity is holistic and personal.* People may be highly aware of race or gender, and this may be central to their self-concept and lived experiences. But most people do not appreciate being characterized by one aspect of their identity, because they view themselves as more complex and holistic beings. All aspects of identity intersect, including those parts that are unconscious. As well, people do not appreciate when other people make assumptions or judgments about who they are.
- *Identity development is vital for helping professionals.* Although we have tried to honor the phenomenology and subjectivity of social identity development, we are writing to an audience of helping professionals. To enhance their capacity to help others without conscious or unconscious prejudice, helping professionals must strive to reach a point of personal comfort and self-esteem, as well as respect and empathy for those who are different. Helping professionals should strive to understand their own social identity development, as well as that of clients and consumers.

AXES OF SOCIAL IDENTITY

Our model of social identity development posits that we all have social identities, which can be separated into distinct axes. Among the more common coordinates that form a person's social identity are race, ethnicity, gender, social class, economic class, sexual orientation, nationality, religion, age, and health or disability status. This is not an inclusive list. For example, we have worked with clients and students whose regional identity, such as coming from the southeastern United States, was salient for them. One of us also consulted with a social service agency staffed by Asian and Asian American clinicians, for whom immigration status and linguistic preferences and competency were significant social identity factors.

And even within our list of social identity coordinates, the valence and relevance of various aspects of social identity vary considerably among individuals and groups. Helping professionals should understand the meaning that each aspect of social identity has for themselves as well as their clients, and appreciate the social advantages and baggage carried by each axis.

DIMENSIONS

The following four dimensions—social, emotional, cognitive, and ego-self—are part of each axis of social identity:

- *Social.* The social dimension refers to groups and people with whom a person identifies or disidentifies and which groups of people they spend time with. This includes what people often refer to as their "community," which is more a socially constructed sense of community and less a geographic rendering of area or district.
- *Affective.* The affective dimension of identity development refers to the feelings people have about an aspect of their identity, such as pride, joy, ambivalence, shame, rage, sorrow, acceptance, indifference, attraction, and denial. Feelings about our identity are influenced as well by the affective reactions that *others* have in response to our identity.
- *Cognitive.* Feelings influence thoughts (and vice-versa), and people have cognitive reactions at different phases of social identity development. This literally means the way one thinks about and understands the world at large. Social identity influences perception and analysis—how one sees, what one hears, the sense and meaning one makes of experience.
- *Ego-self.* The final dimension refers to how we perceive, think about, and describe ourselves. We observe ourselves as actors engaged with the social world and this, in turn, leads to meta-narratives, the story of our identity in action that we tell ourselves and others. The ego-self dimension responds to the question, "Who am I in relation to others?"

Social identity dimensions interact and cluster together in any identity phase. Sometimes they are synchronized and in accord and contribute to a sense of clarity and consistency but may also clash and lead to internal conflict. There is no right or wrong assemblage for these dimensions, but how they coalesce has implications for the course of identity development as well as the salience of a given axis of social identity.

LIFESPAN CONTEXT

Social identity development occurs throughout the lifespan. The meaning and sense of one's gender probably will be quite different at ages 2, 5, 16, 25, 40, and 65. Yet everyone does not have the same experience at a certain age. Some women become aware of their targeted gender status as children or adolescents, others in middle age, and still others may not have moved beyond the phase of awareness of gender difference. At whatever age people grapple with some aspect of their social identity, their lifespan development influences how they process and come to terms with their social identity. Age is itself an axis of social identity.

Lifespan development can also influence a person's social status. For example, older couples who are still in the workforce tend to be wealthier than younger, single people who have been employed just recently. Health and psychological tasks vary considerably throughout the life course and have a bearing on social identity development. Thus, the meanings of race and ethnicity are likely to be very different for an adolescent, who is struggling to establish an identity and joining peer groups, than for a retired person, who is grappling with retirement and impending issues of mortality.

ENVIRONMENTAL CONTEXT

Who we are and how we see ourselves is influenced profoundly by environmental contexts, past and present. Even future contexts shape the contours of social identity, as we imagine where we want to go or who we hope to be. Environments affect who we encounter and what we see or do not see, and create a gestalt in which some aspects of identity become figure and others, ground. For example, a white teenager from a predominantly white suburb may not have thought much about her racial identity until she finds herself taking a subway through a predominantly African American section of a city, with few other white riders. Or a working-class male may not have thought about his agent social status until he attends a social work program that is predominantly female. Middle-class participants in the same program may not have paid much attention to their class status until they are engaged in discussions with the aforementioned working-class male.

Environmental contexts fall into the following three categories:

- *Macro contexts.* Macro contexts encompass large historical and societal contexts. For example, if a country is at war, its people may be much more aware of their citizenship, gender, and age than during peacetime. Political environments affect social identity, as witnessed by the influence of the Civil Rights Movement and the Great Society on raising awareness about racial oppression and racial identity. Another macro-context is geographical—one's community, region, or country.
- *Mezzo contexts.* Examples of mezzo contexts are professions, schools, agencies, and other organizations in which we find ourselves throughout much of our lives. Children attending highly diverse and integrated

schools are likely to have a very different consciousness about their racial identity than are students who attend homogeneous schools. A social service agency in San Francisco is likely to have an entirely different discourse about sexual orientation than one in a rural town in Mississippi—which will influence how workers think about themselves and interact with one another.

- *Micro contexts.* Micro contexts include families, as well as the small, quotidian, and ubiquitous fabric of everyone's lives. They are the streets we walk down, the stores we pass or shop in, the songs we hear on the radio, the food available (or unavailable) in the supermarket. Micro contexts contain social and cultural markers that privilege certain social identities while marginalizing others.

    Although identity has autonomous and enduring aspects, it also is co-constructed and reconstructed in the micro-context of relationships with others (Moffat & Miehls, 1999). Each interaction has symbolic meanings in which we are aware not only of how we want to present ourselves but also how the other person expects us to present ourselves (Cooley, 1922; Goffman, 1959; Pfuetze, 1954). All of us have found that some aspects of ourselves come to life in one friendship but not in other friendships or in a work environment. Thus, the aspects of our social identity that are present, conscious, understood, and validated vary between relationships and even in different encounters with the same person or groups.

RESOLUTIONS/STANCES

We have identified six resolutions/stances in social identity development that transcend any one axis of social identity. Exploring these factors can be useful when considering interpersonal and intergroup relationships. We do not place a value on these stances, and they are not binary, either/or dichotomies. Rather, they cover a range of possibilities located within the polarities that we describe.

- *Integrated versus unintegrated.* Some people integrate most aspects of their social identity, and others have less integrated parts, which may include blindspots or areas of great ambivalence. For example, one person may feel passionately about his class background and work to challenge class oppression while having done little thinking about his racial identity, gender, and sexual orientation. Another person may have made many connections between the various parts of her social identity and been able to integrate her targeted and agent axes, gaining a sense of how her identity reflects her privileges and areas in which she also is oppressed.
- *Complex versus simple.* The complexity or simplicity of a person's social identity relates to the previous discussion. A person with a clear sense of one aspect of her identity but not others may have a straightforward sense of who she is in the world, while someone else might see himself as having

many identity strands that cohere in intricate, multifaceted ways. Environmental contexts influence this stance. Heterogeneous societies are more likely to foster complex identities than are more homogeneous or fundamentalist societies.

- *Stable versus fluid.* In addition to some social identities being integrated or unintegrated, simple or complex, they may be stable or fluid. This resolution is influenced by lifespan development and environmental contexts. Some people have identities that endure over time, while others experience a great deal of flux and transition, which raises more questions about who they are than provide answers.

- *Flexible/adaptable versus fixed/rigid.* Although this stance relates to stability, it is not exactly the same. Some social identities, even when stable, are able to take in new information about oneself and others continually and have the capacity for plasticity and adaptation. For example, someone's ethnic identity may remain stable in its central importance to the person but has been modified in terms of what it means and how it is integrated into a person's lifestyle. By contrast, another person's social identity may have cohered at a certain lifespan phase (e.g., adolescence) and be constructed in such a way that new information or critical experiences will do little to change or alter it.

- *Active versus passive.* The stability, adaptability, and complexity of a social identity can have implications for how empowered people feel and whether they believe they have the capacity to work to change personal and social conditions or are resigned to the status quo. This also is influenced by a cognitive appraisal of the social conditions in which their identity is grounded and whether they believe that change is feasible and worth attempting.

- *Collaborative versus confrontational.* The final stance that has implications for interpersonal and intergroup dynamics is whether social identity inclines people to approach change through collaboration with others, including people with diverse social identities, or wariness about working with those who have divergent social identities, which is more likely to lead to confrontation. This can be manifested in interpersonal relationships, small groups, and large groups, all the way up to how nations conduct their affairs with other nations.

SOCIAL IDENTITY DEVELOPMENT PHASES

Thus far, we have described the various dimensions, contexts (life-span and environmental), and resolutions/stances of each axis of social identity development. We will now consider how social identity moves through different phases.

Each aspect of social identity has corresponding degrees of social status, and these statuses carry different levels of privilege and degrees of oppression.

| BOX 6.2 | SOCIAL IDENTITY DEVELOPMENT PHASES |

Target: Aspect of identity that corresponds with social oppression*

Agent: Aspect of identity groups that corresponds with unearned privilege*

Social identity moves through different axes (e.g., race, gender, sexual orientation, religion, social class) at different rates, although different aspects of social identity interact and become integrated into a sense of self.

Targeted Identity

1. *Awareness of difference*: recognition that not all people are the same and that there are differences in race, religion, sexual orientation, etc.
2. *Recognition of targeted status:* realization that not only are people different, but an aspect of one's social identity is socially targeted
3. *Affective reactions:* a range of explanations and emotions that can result in different stances (e.g., withdrawal, passing, assertion of difference)
4. *Denial or seeking group support*
   a. *Denial:* not acknowledging one's targeted status, which may involve denying identity or attempting "passing"
   b. *Seeking group support:* searching for assurance from those who share some of one's social identity; can involve withdrawal from and aversion to people who are agents
5. *Shedding internalized oppression:* feeling better about oneself, and having pride; embracing one's identity without internalized feelings of oppression
6. *Comfort with self, comfort with others:* feeling comfortable and at peace with one's own identity while respecting and valuing the identities of other people
7. *Social activist:* commitment to working with others for social justice

Agent Identity

1. *Awareness of difference:* recognition that not all people are the same, there are differences in race, religion, and sexual orientation
2. *Assumption of agent status:* internalization of assumptions about privilege and power as being normative
3. *Encounters with people with targeted identities:* interactions or encounters that challenge one's assumptions and worldviews; can lead to emotional and cognitive dissonance
4. *Retreat, regression, and/or painful realizations*
   a. *Retreat and regression:* going back to the familiar, retrenching former assumptions, blaming victims for one's problems
   b. *Painful realizations:* experiencing guilt and shame, and responding with humility to realizations; may seek support from other agents experiencing similar reactions
5. *Aggressive distancing from the privileges of agent status:* putting space between oneself and agent status and attempting to forge a nonprivileged, nonoppressive identity; may idealize people in target status and have little tolerance for agents who are perceived as being less aware of their privilege.

6. *Achieving a non-oppressive identity:* no longer feeling overwhelmed by guilt, and able to accept one's social identity but not the unearned privilege that accompanies it; able to respect and appreciate people with different identities.
7. *Working as a social activist:* being committed to working with others for social justice.

*"Conceptual Foundations or Social Justice Courses," by R. Hardiman and B.W. Jackson, in *Teaching for Diversity and Social Justice: A Sourcebook,* edited by M. Adams, L.A. Bell, & P. Griffen (New York: Routledge, 1997), pp. 16–29.

Although we do not subscribe to a binary, either/or way of conceptualizing the differences in these social statuses, for the purposes of illustrating this model, we have presented potential phases of social identity development using the concepts of *target* and *agent* identities (Hardiman & Jackson, 1997). Target identities are those aspects of identity that correspond to social statuses that are marginalized and scapegoated, in which groups of people suffer exclusion and oppression. Agent identities correspond to social statuses that are privileged by society and reflect dominant norms and assumptions and are afforded unearned and unequal rights by virtue of this status.

The phases we are presenting are prospective and not definite or automatic; people do not always pass through involuntary or obligatory phases. Nor do we believe that a person always goes through one phase before the next—people can skip phases—or that this transpires in an invariable, linear sequence. People can return to phases or move through them out of progression. We also have applied the concept of phases to illustrate that a person may be in more than one phase at the same time and that different contexts will stimulate or highlight a given phase. If social identity is like climbing a mountain, it entails different routes of ascent and descent, and the ease and risk of the climb is influenced strongly by environmental factors, as well as the person's personal capital and equipment.

Even though we will be presenting only one aspect of a person's social identity development to illustrate our model, we should keep in mind that each axis of social identity is interacting with other axes; most people are grappling with a process that involves a solitary aspect of their social identity but with a concert of identity axes.

Targeted Identity

The most important task for those wrestling with a targeted aspect of their identity is to ultimately embrace their identity while externalizing and rejecting the webs of social oppression they may have internalized in the form of stereotypes, low self-esteem, self-doubts, and self-alienation. Internalized social oppression is destructive to individual and collective well-being, and a primary task of social identity development for those who are targeted is to have pride in, respect for, and comfort with their social self.

- *Phase one: Awareness of difference.* At some point, a person becomes aware that he or she is similar to and different from other people. This consciousness can occur during any chronological period of a person's life. For some axes of social identity, this awareness comes in childhood, and for others in adulthood. For example, a child might recognize that her skin color is darker than that of some of her friends in daycare, while a man might not be aware that he is bisexual until he is married.

- *Phase two: Recognition of targeted status.* This phase can occur immediately after the first phase, or it can take some time. During this phase, a person becomes aware that some aspect of his or her social identity has possible negative consequences such as social isolation, stigmatization, and social oppression.

   The feelings evoked during this phase can be dispiriting and painful. Awareness can occur through memorable encounters or critical incidents, or through more solitary experiences, such as reading or watching television. For example, a Jewish first-grader in a predominantly Christian school learns that Christmas, not Chanukah, is what the class will celebrate in December.

- *Phase three: Reactions to targeted status.* A person begins to generate feelings and thoughts about his or her targeted status. This often is quite painful and can lead to attempts to withdraw, hide, or minimize this aspect of social identity, or conversely through a strong statement affirming these differences. This phase also can generate feelings of pride if a person receives sufficient validation and social support.

- *Phase four: Denial or seeking group support.* We have identified two possible aspects of this phase. For some, only one may occur, or a person can move through them both sequentially, but it is unusual to have them occur simultaneously. They are similar to what Helms (1990) has called immersion and emersion.

   The first aspect involves denial. If people are flooded with overwhelming or negative affect in association with their targeted identity, they may deny their targeted status. This process can be conscious, such as trying to appear like a person with agent status, or unconscious, such as repressing one's actual social identity. Attempts to conform to agent group members, or "passing," are common at this phase. An example might be straightening or dying one's hair so it does not stand out.

   The second part of this phase can be to seek social support from other people who share one's targeted social identity and status. Cross (1991) has called this buffering. Buffering can be accompanied by withdrawal, as much as is possible, from contact or interactions with people with agent status. Solorzano et al. (2000) has described this reaction occurring on college campuses when students of color experience "micro-aggressions." The title of Tatum's (1997) book, *Why Are All the Black Kids Sitting Together in the Cafeteria?*, captures this response.

- *Phase five: Shedding internalized oppression.* This phase is critical to people's sense of self, how they view themselves in relation to others, who people affiliate with and how they feel about their identity. During this phase, those with targeted identity take on less responsibility for the targeted status, externalizing the reasons for it while becoming more aware of societal inequities and social injustice. They recognize that they, as well as others like them, have been unfairly victimized. Feelings of pride in one's identity can accompany this phase, although there may still be strong negative feelings about people with agent status.

- *Phase six: Comfort with self, comfort with others.* In this phase, people have internalized a sense of pride about their identity and feel as if they know who they are. The security in this can make it easier for a person to now appreciate people who are different. Sometimes it is easier to value people with other (but different) targeted statuses before feeling comfortable with people who have a great deal of agent status. It may always prove challenging to trust or feel at ease with people who have agent status, particularly people who have not examined that status.

- *Phase seven: Social activist.* This phase reflects the ethics and values of human service professionals. This phase is different from phase six in that people go beyond feeling good about themselves and others and make commitments to work for social justice and the amelioration of social conditions that maintain their targeted status. This commitment can be generalized to other forms of oppression—even in domains in which the person has agent status—working in concert with people who have varied social identities.

AGENT IDENTITY

While the task for people with a targeted identity is to shed internalized stereotypes and negative self-images, for people with agent identity, the charge is to recognize their agent status, which often is invisible to them initially, and to discard internalized feelings of superiority. Although people with targeted identity status usually have to confront that status in the face of oppression, those with agent status can ignore their privileged identity and social group membership more easily. Thus, it also is easier *not* to move through many of the later phases, as society is structured to mirror the agent identity status, and to disown agent status poses risks and challenges.

- *Phase one: Awareness of difference.* Although this understanding can occur at any age, a person with agent status is more likely to recognize this difference at a later age than a person with a targeted identity. Many of our white, straight, middle-class students have told us that they did not meet a person of color until they went to high school, or someone who was poor or not heterosexual until college.

- *Phase two: Assumption of agent status.* Interestingly, the assumption of agent status and the sense of entitlement and privilege that accompanies this can occur even before people become aware that many others do not share their identity or enjoy the same privileges. This internalized sense of superiority may be unconscious because it is so socially reinforced.

- *Phase three: Encounters with people with targeted identities.* Interactions or exchanges with people with targeted social identities are likely to challenge or confront a person's agent-saturated worldview and assumptions. Perhaps a student says, "We Americans believe in fairness," only to find that some in the class are from South America and not U.S. citizens, and have not experienced the United States as a "fair" country. Or a person may ask a friend when he plans to get married, only to find that the friend is unable to marry because same-sex marriages are not legal in his state. These encounters can be "critical experiences" that are memorable and induce a sense of discomfort.

- *Phase four: Retreat, regression, and painful realizations.* During this phase a person may find initially that the identification of his or her agent status is too cognitively dissonant and emotionally charged to want to pursue this further. These awakenings can lead to denial, rationalization, retreating to what is more familiar, even anger toward and blaming people with targeted status. Again, as this is reinforced by social structures, leaders, and social discourses, many people with targeted status become mired in this phase.

  Some, however, stay with their pain, guilt, shame, and confusion and allow their agent status to become part of their ongoing, conscious awareness. Because this phase can be challenging and humbling, it can be helpful to seek social support from other people with agent status to explore these reactions. It also can also be a time when people with agent status seek to have more contact with people who have target status, to "learn" from them (which may or may not be welcomed by the recipients of the overture).

- *Phase five: Aggressive distancing from the privileges of agent status.* During this phase, people with agent status can become angry and resentful over unearned privileges. This is a time when there can be attacks against people with agent status who appear less enlightened or willing to interrogate their privileges. Sometimes these attacks are against family members or close friends. While the person is trying to forge a nonoppressive identity, forceful, at times antagonistic, confrontations with other people with agent status can mask his or her fears, guilt, or shame. During this phase, people with targeted status may become idealized.

- *Phase six: Achieving a nonoppressive identity.* During this phase, people accept who they are while not accepting the unearned privileges that accompany this status. They have less personal guilt and more of an appreciation of the historical and social forces that bestowed the unearned privileges that now are being challenged and discarded. They also appreciate people with a social identity different from theirs without idealizing or romanticizing them.

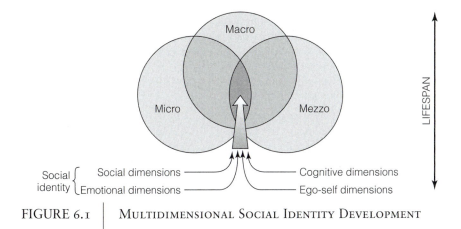

FIGURE 6.1 | MULTIDIMENSIONAL SOCIAL IDENTITY DEVELOPMENT

- *Phase seven: Working with others for social justice.* During this phase, people go beyond their emotional and psychological realizations and resolutions and work with others, as allies, to change the social conditions that granted them the privileges in the first place. The person may take a leadership role in forming an "unlearning racism/deconstructing whiteness" support group, for example. Working as an ally implies that a person with agent social identity does not usurp leadership positions and is able to work collaboratively and respectfully with people with differing social identities.

We realize that this model of social identity development is complex and offer the schematic diagram in Figure 6.1 to represent the process of identity development for each axis of identity. Exercise 6.1 will help readers map out their own social identity using this model.

IDENTITY AND INTERGROUP RELATIONS

So far, we have been considering the process of social identity development from the perspective of the individual. And social affiliations—how people feel part of or separate from groups—make important contributions to identity development as well. We also have described the process of racism as one of group inequality. Thus, it is useful to consider how social identity leads to group affiliation and how this contributes to durable inequalities such as racism.

"Optimal distinctiveness theory" postulates that humans have a need to both individuate and affiliate (Brewer, 2001). Groups potentially offer members many benefits: a sense of identity and belonging, validation, support, resources, security, buffering, and a source of meaning. Inclusion in a group can meet the need for belonging but, in turn, the group can meet the need for differentiation by stressing the differences between in-group and out-group members. Feeling a sense of in-group pride and solidarity can be healthy and validating, but when it is predicated on demeaning members of the out-group, it can lead to intergroup strife and conflict.

This can be accompanied by disowning negative and undesirable traits from the in-group and displacing them and projecting them onto the out-group, members of which are described as being diabolical, morally deficient, less than human (Erikson, 1968; Fisher, 1996; GAP, 1987; Miller & Schamess, 2000; Volkan, 1988). Viewing members of another group in such negative terms can enhance the positive identities of members of the in-group (Crocker & Luhtanen, 1990; Triandafyllidou, 1998). This in turn can accentuate differences between in-group and out-group members, further fueling intergroup mistrust and tensions (Brewer).

Accentuating positive attributes to in-group members and negative connotations to out-group members can lead to "misattribution" of motives of out-group members (Brewer, 2001). An example is imputing malevolent intent to another group—surmising that its members mean to do harm to "us"—which can justify engaging in destructive, preemptive actions toward "them," legitimized by fear of those categorized as "other."

A similar dynamic can lead to ascribing positive motivations to in-group members and bad behavior to out-group members. As an example. someone might construct meaning about a person who is unemployed and requires public assistance. If the unemployed person is a member of the same racial or ethnic in-group as the observer, the narrative may stress circumstances outside of one's control—the person was unfairly fired, or the economy was tight—making that person a worthy victim of external forces. For out-group members, however, the storyline might stress the lack of a work ethic and tendency to seek government handouts. Misattributions such as this further fuel a sense of group differences and distinctions and increase the difficulty for members of one group to respond empathically to members of another group.

Leaders can exploit group conflict by further demonizing and demeaning out-group members. This dynamic has many historical examples, one of the most egregious of which was the Nazis' targeting of Jews as being subhuman. Nazi propaganda focused on the threat posed by Jews to non-Jewish Germans, which then was used to justify unspeakably brutal treatment toward Jews.

In the United States, leaders fanned similar flames in the United States to justify slaughtering Native Americans, enslaving African Americans, and placing Japanese Americans in concentration camps during World War II. To this day, invidious group distinctions have been used to justify wars and civil rights violations

Group conflict reinforces in-group and out-group distinctions and fosters in-group solidarity, making dissent and disagreement more difficult, with less tolerance for difference. The rights of the individual are sacrificed in the name of group security. Many factors can either promote or reduce group conflict. For example, competition for scarce resources or territory (such as jobs or apartments) can heighten group conflict. This has been referred to as "realistic" group conflict, as contrasted with "unrealistic" group conflict, which occurs by virtue of the symbolic demonizing of another group (Bayor, 1988).

Unequal power and privilege between groups can deepen group conflict, as can exploitation and monopolization of resources. Intergroup conflict does not occur only between majority and minority groups, or between those with power and those facing oppression. The 1930s in New York City saw fierce ethnic conflict between the Jews and the Irish, both recent immigrants, as they competed for jobs, apartments, occupational niches, and political power (Bayor, 1988). A similar process is occurring today in major U.S. cities between African Americans, Latinos, and Asian/Asian Americans because of "demographic restructuring, social dislocations, and spatial isolation" (Johnson & Oliver, 1994, p. 197).

The perception of having efficacy can buffer the stress of perceived hostility from members of other groups (Dion, 2002), so another factor in intergroup relations is the control, or lack of control, over a group's narrative (Thomas, 1994). It is often remarked that history is written by the victors, and this dynamic certainly is true of racial and ethnic relations. Although there are revisionist history books, such as Takaki's (1993) *A Different Mirror*, most U.S. citizens have been schooled on historical narratives emphasizing the positive virtues of early white European settlers.

The demonizing of people of color has abated in contemporary historical narratives, but the stories of their exploitation and suffering are accorded insufficient space in mainstream history courses and public discourse. The ability to tell the story of one's group and to present it to others, and for it to be received empathically, is an important step toward resolving intergroup conflict, as we shall consider in Chapter 9.

What Can Prevent or Alleviate Intergroup Conflict?

Conflict between groups and exploitation of one group by another is not inevitable, nor is it a hopeless historical inheritance. Just as processes of identity and group behavior foster mistrust and tension, steps can be taken to reduce this conflict. Ultimately, stressing our commonalities and similarities can bridge differences and offer a framework to heal wounds. We will mention briefly some steps that work in this direction.

- *Overarching, common goals.* We must establish superordinate objectives and purposes that unite, rather than divide (Brewer, 2001). For example, a course that uses this book should establish that the purpose of conducting an in-depth examination of racism, which is such a divisive social force, is to prepare all readers entering the helping professions to be better professionals. We are united in our desire and commitment to become better social workers, counselors, therapists, nurses, and social service workers. We all share this goal, and even if we have had experiences that divide us or face challenges when trying to talk about this topic, we are unified in our professional identity and codes of ethics.

| BOX 6.3 | WHAT CAN PREVENT OF ALLEVIATE INTERGROUP CONFLICT? |

1. Having overarching, common goals that emphasize what members from different groups have in common.
2. Separating positive group identities from negation of members of other groups.
3. Fostering healing and reconciliation rather than demonizing and accentuating differences.
4. Fostering empathy for the pain of members of other groups and recognizing the historical narrative of their suffering.
5. Resolving both the practical and symbolic issues that foster conflict.
6. Establishing a process for intergroup dialogue, taking group responsibility, reconciliation, and reparations.

- *Positive identity not predicated on negation of the "other."* It is normal for people to want to feel good about the groups of which they are members, as this increases their own sense of self-esteem (Brewer, 2001; Crocker & Luhanten, 1990; Kelman, 2001). But this need not lead them to denigrate other groups. Thus, we must distinguish between having pride in oneself and one's group and needing to disparage other groups. Actually, vilification of others is frequently a warning sign that collective self-esteem is low and requires an external target to boost it.

  An example on a national level is Staub's (2001) distinction between "constructive" patriotism, which is thoughtful pride in one's nation, and "blind" patriotism, which views the outside word as inherently dangerous or evil and does not question the policies or actions of one's own nation.

- *Relationships.* People from different ethnic and racial groups have more commonalities than differences, so actual relationships, whether they are between individuals or within groups, create more opportunities for exploring what people have in common. Working on overarching goals places people in the position of working together, and intergroup dialogue creates structured opportunities to listen and share.

  Friendships have the effect of making it more difficult to misattribute motives and intentions (Shelton & Richeson, 2005). Being in relationship with people is not without its challenges, particularly when there is a history of mistrust and outgroup denigration, but actual connection is preferable to the dehumanization that is more possible when there is no affiliation.

- *Leadership that fosters healing and reconciliation.* Leadership can sow seeds of divisiveness and hatred or can be a voice for compassion, empathy, and healing (Staub, 2001; Whillock, 1995). We have witnessed this phenomenon repeatedly in the United States and throughout the world. Leaders shape public narratives and give voice to fears and hopes.

Leadership can humanize those who are different or can demonize them, justifying oppression and aggression.

- *Empathy for the suffering of the other group and recognition of its historical narrative.* The absence of empathy is most apparent during times of group exploitation and intergroup conflict. When people are described as "insects," "vermin," "diabolical," "inscrutable," "subhuman," "savages," or "wet-backs," it is difficult to engender understanding and compassion. "Brother," "sister," and "fellow human being." conversely, prompt compassion. Groups must develop processes to listen to one another empathically and to hear and validate the suffering and wounds that are related (Staub, 2001). The group also should control the narrative it presents and have autonomy and authorship of the story being told (Thomas, 1994).

- *Resolving practical and symbolic issues alike that foster conflict.* Intergroup conflict often involves "realistic" areas of competition and disagreement, as well as powerful symbols, historical and contemporary, that hold great meaning for group members. Failure to respond to both of these areas of divergence can lead to partial or unresolved clashes (Kelman, 2001).

- *Establishing a process to take group responsibility.* Most intergroup conflict has arisen between groups with unequal power and resources, resulting in the subjugation and domination of one group by another. Reconciliation requires acknowledging past wrongs and taking responsibility for prior exploitation and current reparations.

Yamamoto (1999) conceptualized a four step process involving:

1. recognizing the humanity of the other group,
2. taking responsibility for past wrongs,
3. reconstructing fractured relationships, and
4. establishing a process for reparations and healing.

Each of these steps is challenging and requires enlightened leadership and collective commitment, but the rewards can be to heal wounds that have festered for centuries.

IMPLICATIONS FOR THE HELPING PROFESSIONS

The process of racial identity formation and of intergroup relations is a central, ongoing dynamic for workers in the helping professions. All human service work and health care occupations rely on interpersonal contact and the centrality of worker–consumer relationship. In a multiracial, multiethnic society, professionals must be committed to fairness, equity, and for some professions, social justice, to take race and culture into account when providing services.

Racial identity and social identity theory is helpful in understanding ourselves, as well as our clients and colleagues. Ultimately, using relationship to help people prospers when we have a good understanding of who we are, who our consumers are, and how this influences our relationships with one another. If we can situate and position ourselves by reflecting on our social identity, we are more likely to have a sense of self-awareness and less likely to act out our prejudices unconsciously or to think and behave in a way that meets our own identity needs rather than responding to those of our clients.

If we can develop a greater sense of comfort with ourselves, as well as an awareness of and respect for cultural differences, we can own our assumptions and worldviews without imposing them on others. If we are mindful of our own experiences of power, privilege, oppression, and marginalization, we can respond more empathically to our clients, who have had their own mix of these experiences and are engaged in their own quests for identity and self esteem.

Some theorists have attempted to map out the potential dynamics between clients and workers, depending on the racial identities of both parties (Carter, 1995; Helms, 1990; Helms & Cook, 1999). We are reluctant to present such equations, as they can lead to prejudgments and overgeneralizations. Nevertheless, we do share our belief that practitioners—on their own, as well as through supervision and consultation—should explore and assess their social identities and, when working with clients, be mindful of how social identities interact in the helping relationship.

We all can benefit from the perspectives of trusted others, whether they are similar or different from us in their social identities, as we reflect on ourselves and in our work with clients. People with similar social identities can be empathic and understanding of challenges and struggles, blindspots, and areas of resistance, as they may have traveled over similar terrain. Consulting with colleagues of different social identities offers diverse perspectives, encouraging us to view things in different ways and to leave familiar comfort zones. Also helpful is to consult with colleagues who are familiar with the social identities of consumers.

Working with social identity is not just about working with clients. It involves our relationships with colleagues, too. At work, we interact as individuals, and midsize and larger organizations have subgroups and cliques of workers. Interpersonal tensions and misunderstandings at work often are related to differences in social identity and the consequent intergroup dynamics.

Workplaces often fail to recognize these dynamics, or they do not have the capacity to explore and respond to intergroup discord when it arises. Often these tensions escalate beyond individual miscues and become part of an organizational culture characterized by mistrust and group splintering, which ultimately harm professional cohesiveness and productivity. It also can lead to low morale, suspicion, wariness, and alienation from the agency. Understanding the dynamics of intergroup conflict can shed light on tensions between subgroups of colleagues working together within an organization, as well as interactions between staff and consumers.

CONCLUSION

It is important for helping professionals to have a good sense of their own identity as well as those of their clients. As social identity is closely aligned with groups, it also is useful for helping professionals to appreciate the dynamics of conflict and cooperation between groups with differing social identities. Social identity is a foundational concept for helping professionals trying to work effectively cross-racially and concerned with undoing racism. Therefore, we develop this concept in subsequent chapters.

In Chapter 7 we continue our consideration of social identity by exploring intersectionality—the relationship between racism with social class, gender, sexual orientation, and immigration status. We will build on this foundation in Chapter 8, further examining the impact of social identity on relationships with colleagues and how to talk about racism and other issues surrounding social identity.

The discussion of social identity and intergroup conflict will be helpful in understanding Chapters 9 and 10, as we consider anti-racism work by human service professionals in the community and in agencies. Social identity also is a central concept in Chapter 11, where we discuss cross-racial/cultural clinical work, and Chapter 12, which describes teaching about race and racism. All anti-racism work is enhanced by an appreciation of the complexity of social identity.

EXERCISE 6.1   MULTIDIMENSIONAL SOCIAL IDENTITY EXERCISE

This exercise will help you map out your own social identity.

General Questions/Lifespan Context

1. Which axes of your social identity have the most meaning for you today?
2. Which axes had the most meaning for you during the following periods of your life: preschool, elementary school, high school, college?
3. What experiences or social and historical factors have been most influential in the evolution of your social identity?
4. What family influences have had a strong effect on your social identity?
5. When you are with your best friend, which parts of your social identity most come to life?
6. When you are in a public situation (e.g., work, school), which parts of your social identity are you most aware of? Least aware of? Which parts are other people aware of?

Dimensions

Taking one axis of your social identity that is relatively *privileged* and one that is relatively *targeted*, respond to the following questions:

1. When you have a choice, which people do you seek to be with?
2. What groups do you feel a part of that connect with this aspect of your social identity?
3. What feelings do you have about this aspect of your social identity? Do some situations evoke certain feelings about this aspect of your social identity?

4. How does this aspect of your social identity influence how you see the world?
5. What does this aspect of your social identity say about who you are in relation to others?

Contexts

1. Think of a macro context (historical events, social movements, wars, community, etc.) that had a big influence on some aspect of your social identity. How did it influence your social identity development? Can you imagine living in a different place or at a different time and how your social identity development might have been different as a result?
2. Think of a mezzo context (school, workplace, organizational setting) that influenced your social identity development. What occurred in this context that had an impact on your identity?
3. Think of a relationship (a form of micro-context) in which you find certain aspects of your social identity coming to life, then think of another relationship in which these aspects of your identity are not expressed. Which factors in the two relationships have an influence on your identity expression?

Resolutions/Stances

Think about how the following statements apply to you. What are some reasons they do or do not apply?

1. All parts of my identity are integrated and fit well together.
2. My social identity is straightforward and easily explained to other people.
3. My social identity has not changed much in the past 20 years.
4. I am happy with the way my social identity fits me and am not seeking to adapt or change any aspects of it.
5. I believe that I have the capacity to change and improve the social conditions that shape my social identity.
6. I feel completely comfortable and like working with people on issues of social identity and social oppression, however similar or dissimilar they are to me.

Targeted Identity Development

Take one aspect of your social identity that is less privileged than other aspects of your social identity. Trace your identity development using the phases mentioned in the targeted identity model in this chapter.

Agent Identity Development

Take one aspect of your social identity that is more privileged than other aspects of your social identity. Trace your identity development using the phases mentioned in the agent identity model in this chapter.

Questions

1. For both the targeted and agent aspects of your identity, were the models consistent with your experience? If not, how did your experience differ?
2. Did your identity development progress in a linear fashion? If not, what pattern did it follow?
3. From your application of the model to your own development, do you find it to be valid? If not, what model of identity development would be truer to your experience?

In addition to reflecting on these questions on your own, it is valuable to discuss the answers in pairs or small groups, or to write them in a journal and share them with someone.

7 CHAPTER | INTERSECTIONALITY: RACISM AND OTHER FORMS OF SOCIAL OPPRESSION

CHAPTER CONTENTS

Racism is very real, and although based on a fiction—the social construction of race—it has profoundly damaging consequences for individuals, groups, and society. Because racism has such a deep impact on people's lives, race is a significant dimension of social identity, but racism, although an independent social and psychological force, does not stand alone. Nobody is defined solely by race. This dimension of social identity interacts with gender, social class, sexual orientation, and other axes of identity. The same holds true for racism in society. It is strongly interconnected with other forms of social oppression.

In this chapter we will discuss four social forces that interact significantly with racism: socioeconomic class, gender, sexual orientation, and citizenship–immigration status. Although we will consider each one separately in its relation to racism, in truth all interact simultaneously, although to different degrees. Therefore, considering even two forms of social oppression and how they interact leaves out their interaction with other sorts of social oppression.

So, even though we will consider each of these factors and their conjunction with racism separately, we will describe briefly how all forms of social oppression have certain similar qualities. We use the term "intersectionality" to describe the relationship between these factors because it captures the connections and junctures that occur both inside a person (manifested in their identities), and in society (as evidenced by inequities and disparities in power and privilege).

COMMON ASPECTS OF SOCIAL OPPRESSION

First we will examine Tilly's model of categorical inequalities. This leads into a discussion of Bell's major features of social oppression.

TILLY'S MODEL OF CATEGORICAL INEQUALITIES

Tilly (1998) sought to extract the essential dynamics and structures of "durable inequalities" and came up with four enduring traits:

1. exploitation,
2. opportunity hoarding,
3. emulation, and
4. adaptation.

He argued that these "categorical inequalities" are manifest in many organizational and institutional settings, and evidenced by categorical disparities (e.g., by race, gender, class) in wages, health care, political power, and all of the institutions described in the "web of racism" in Chapter 4.

Although each class of categories has its own historical legacy, the categories have a common pattern:

> Over and over again, exploitation by powerful people and resource hoarding by less powerful people combine to favor the establishment of unequally rewarded categories, while emulation and adaptation secure such categories in place. The creation

of interior categories and the matching of interior with exterior categories build durable inequality into organizations and attach them to networks—internal and external—in ways that favor their reproduction, even their transmission to new members of the categories. (p. 169)

Readers are familiar with the notion of *exploitation,* which involves centralization and use of power, controlling and deploying resources, granting rights and privileges, and creating categories that include and exclude groups of people (Tilly, 1998). Implicit in *opportunity hoarding* is ideological control, as well as domination of social institutions and resources (Hardiman & Jackson, 1997). Tilly describes how "networks" of less powerful people who have been granted privileged status by decision makers and power holders

> ... reinforce their control over hoarded resources by means of their power to include or exclude other members with respect to language, kinship, courtship, marriage, housing, sociability, religion, ceremonial life, credit, and political patronage.... Race, gender, schooling, professional training, political affiliation and sexual preference all, at times, constitute the networks and categorical distinctions on which opportunity hoarding builds. (pp. 154–155)

Emulation, in Tilly's model, refers to the structures of categorical inequalities operating in society at large that are replicated in various social sectors, institutions, and organizations. The pattern of inequality is found in most social units. As people are socialized into these familiar disparities, they become normative and commonplace. *Adaptation* refers to the interactive rituals, social scripts and narratives, and interpersonal practices that facilitate social interaction while maintaining categorical boundaries and their accompanying inequities. An example that Tilly (1998) offers is the use of humor in offices as males sexually harass females.

Adaptive strategies lead to compliance and complicity with the social structure of durable inequalities. Tilly's framework offers us the possibility that durable inequality is not only a macro-structural phenomenon but also is one residing in smaller-scale institutional forms, which then are extended to other settings. We have durable inequalities not because of the sum of economic and social transactions but, rather, because of the stability of structures.

BELL'S FEATURES OF SOCIAL OPPRESSION

Bell and Griffin (1997) have identified the major features of all forms of social oppression:

- *Pervasive.* Oppression is ubiquitous and "fuses institutional and systemic discrimination, personal bias, bigotry, and social prejudice in a complex web of relationships and structures that saturate most aspects of life in our society" (p. 4).
- *Restricting.* All forms of social oppression restrict opportunity, access to resources and privileges, and upward mobility.

- *Hierarchical.* Groups that have privilege because of the status of their social identities have a hierarchical relationship with other, less privileged groups.
- *Complex, multiple, cross-cutting relationships.* This characteristic corresponds with the points made in the previous chapter about the complexities of social identity; people have an intricate mix of privilege and of being targeted, which may confer privilege or barriers depending on the situational context.
- *Internalized oppression.* As discussed, people are prone to internalize the oppressive worldviews, beliefs, values, and attitudes that stem from the durable inequalities encountered throughout society.

Bell and Griffin go on to say that the features in this list are common to all forms of social oppression but that we also should consider the unique and specific ways by which each form, such as sexism or racism, is manifested.

Durable inequalities help to create in-group and out-group allegiances and identities (Tilly, 1998). The psychological and social psychological process of creating a denigrated "other" further justifies and rationalizes social inequality, reinforcing categorical group distinctions (Miller & Schamess, 2000). Social categories and social identity converge and intersect as internal identities reflect and reinforce external social divisions. This confers social roles and statuses on people, such as being targeted or having privilege (Hardiman & Jackson, 1997), as well those who try to sit on the sidelines as bystanders (Staub, 2001).

Harro (2000) has drawn a "cycle of socialization" to illustrate how individuals are taught their various social roles, the ways by which these are reinforced, and how this shapes identity, attitudes, and behaviors. Figure 7.1 depicts this cycle.

Another way to conceptualize these ideas is as a "social oppression matrix" (Hardiman & Jackson, 1997), reproduced in Figure 7.2. It diagrams the levels of oppression (individual, institutional, and societal/cultural), the psychosocial processes (conscious and unconscious), and how these are manifested in attitudes and behaviors. Keeping these concepts and processes in mind, we now consider the interaction of racism with other forms of durable inequality.

RACISM AND CLASS OPPRESSION

Perhaps the most difficult relationship to disaggregate is that of class oppression and racism. These forms have been intertwined from the inception of this country and are tightly woven together today. Theorists of class conflict and oppression, particularly Marxists, tend to emphasize the primacy of class, whereas scholars of racism often call attention to the significance of race. In our view, they are independent social forces that interact synergistically, potentiating their effects.

People of color in the middle class experience racism, whether at work or in how they are treated when they are shopping or driving (Cose, 1993), and many poor people are white. But class-based factors, when combined with race,

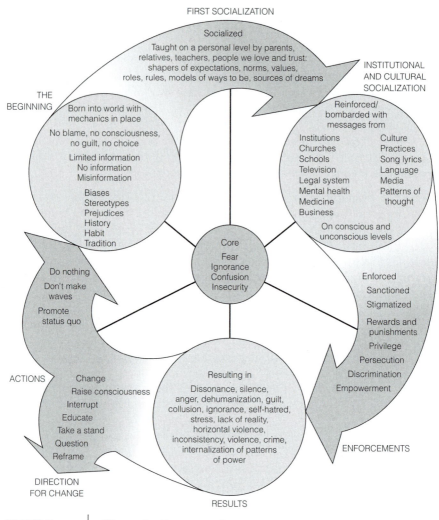

FIGURE 7.1 | HARRO'S CYCLE OF SOCIALIZATION

"The Cycle of Socialization," by B. Harro, in *Readings for Diversity and Social Justice: An Anthology on Racism, Anti-semitism, Sexism, Heterosexism, Ableism, and Classism,* edited by M. Adams, W.J. Blumenfeld, R. Casteneda, H.W. Hackman, M.L. Peters, & X. Zuniga (New York: Routledge, 2000).

make it even harder for people of color to achieve upward social mobility. And from the country's inception, being considered white has granted certain social privileges, even to those who were economically considered poor or working class (Allen, 1994; Fredrickson, 1988; Takaki, 1993). Economic success for people of color in the United States has not always afforded the same access to social privileges as it has for whites.

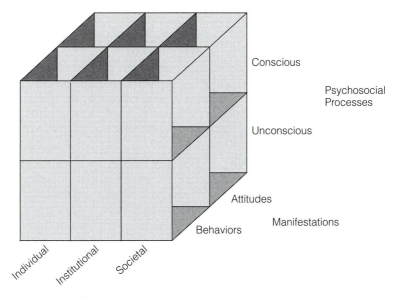

FIGURE 7.2 | SOCIAL OPPRESSION MATRIX

"Conceptual Foundations for Social Justice Courses," by R. Hardiman & B.W. Jackson, in *Teaching for Diversity and Social Justice: A Sourcebook* (pp. 16–29), edited by M. Adams, L.A. Bell, and P. Griffen (New York: Routledge, 1997).

We use the term "class" to mean socioeconomic status and positioning. This has an economic dimension as determined by employment, income, and assets, but also a social and spatial dimension, such as where people live, how they dress, what vehicle they drive, the level and quality of their education, how they speak, with whom they socialize, and the types of recreations they favor. As discussed in the preceding chapter, class also involves an axis of identity. Like race, class is a social construction, influenced by history and context, and its meanings are disputed, as are the ways by which people see and define themselves. Even the way that classes are conceptualized and discussed varies and is contested.

For example, how is class divided and measured? Is it by income or by lifestyle or some other factor? Why do so many people describe themselves as "middle class"—ranging from blue collar workers to highly paid professionals and managers? Socioeconomic class is a relative concept, and its meaning often is in the eye of the beholder.

RACE AND CLASS VISIBILITY

Within limits, class can be less visible than race. We can dress similarly and even learn to talk in the same way. As a result, people can carry "hidden injuries of class" and feel as if they are "passing" (Sennett & Cobb, 1972). For example, in the elite college where we teach, students from lower-middle-class or working-class backgrounds have expressed to us ambivalence over whether they "truly" belong here as much as students from higher-class backgrounds.

Class also influences developmental processes (see Chapter 6), and as such, we carry within us the memories and sense of self based on our constructions of class from earlier phases of our life into the present. Class, too, has a future orientation, as people set their sights on upward mobility. The belief in class mobility is what may diminish class resentment for some Americans, as they hold to the idea that they can alter their class standing. But we should not minimize the limits of opportunity that many people face by virtue of their social and economic class, regardless of race.

From the beginning of this country, race and ethnicity shaped which class positions were available and which were foreclosed. Native Americans, Chinese Americans, Japanese Americans, and Mexican Americans had less access to the full range of economic opportunities afforded to ethnic groups constructed as white, and faced restrictive laws as well as informal discriminatory practices. African Americans lost their economic mobility through the institution of slavery and, after the Civil War, through Black Codes, Jim Crow, and segregation, both formal and informal.

Ransford (2000) has proposed a racial/ethnic hierarchy that has characterized U.S. society, with Anglo Saxons at the top; next, white ethnic groups; then Asian Americans; and finally, African Americans, Native Americans, and Mexican Americans. The factors influencing those at the bottom of the socioeconomic scale include people with a history of having been enslaved or conquered, and people having less power and efficacy in their communities, who have a history of having to confront pervasive discourses that legitimize denigration.

Discrimination by labor unions was a mechanism that white ethnic groups used to maintain their rungs on the socioeconomic ladder, much to the disadvantage of people of color (Fenton, 1999; Omatsu, 2000). This was in the context of not being able to climb society's highest steps. Coupled with discriminatory hiring and employment practices, this practice severely limited the class mobility of people of color, particularly African Americans, Native Americans, and many Hispanic Americans.

Class mobility was blocked further by residential segregation, lack of access to good schools, being unable to attract as much credit for to obtain homes and businesses, paying higher interest rates for loans, and having homes and businesses situated in areas where their value was lower and appreciated more slowly (Oliver & Shapiro, 2000). Last, social policies—as in the example we gave of the New Deal in Chapter 3—had built-in inequities, disadvantaging low-income people of color by not covering many of the occupations in which they were employed (Jansson, 2005; Jones, 1985; Lieberman, 1998; Quadango, 1994).

Cox (1948) believed that racism is the inevitable byproduct of capitalism, but it also can be argued that race determines class relations and status (Omi & Winant, 1994). We cannot say whether racism or classism is the more preeminent social force; they are both powerful social dynamics in their own right. Ultimately, ethnicity and race have strongly influenced a group's socio-economic position in society (Eriksen, 1996). Conversely, an ethnic group's socioeconomic standing has profoundly influenced a group's ethnic character and interactions with other groups (Fenton, 1999). For example, African Americans as an ethnic group have been influenced by the race and class struggles they have endured, as well as by cultural practices brought from Africa and transplanted to and nurtured in the United States.

Because race and ethnicity are more visible than socioeconomic class, class exploitation often has been obfuscated by racial and ethnic scapegoating. During colonial times, as well as in the early days of the Republic, poor white workers felt a greater allegiance to the white elite of owners than to black slaves, who also were being economically exploited (Allen; 1994; Fredrickson, 1988; Takaki, 1987). Thus, the focus on race and the alleged inferiority of black slaves served to divide potential class allies and perhaps forestall and preempt a genuine class-based struggle that might have resulted in better conditions for all workers.

Racial and ethnic scapegoating as a subtext of public discourse continues to this day, while class-based inequities receive little attention from the mainstream media. Social ills are blamed on immigrants and violent people of color, and the struggle for gay and lesbian rights is seen as the demise of the traditional family (Yeskel & Leonard-Wright, 1997). These subtexts all occur as the government promulgates policies that redistribute wealth upward. All of this has been done by linking race and class in ways that distract from class issues.

RACE, CLASS, AND POLITICS

Politicians have been able to link race and class in ways that detract from class issues and that ultimately diminish the discourse on social class in the United States. There are political rewards for "playing the race card" and punishments for those who support civil rights. President Lyndon Johnson, more than any other modern President, actively sought legislation to respond to racism and ensure greater equality for African Americans and other people of color. He worried that his policies would turn the South into a Republican stronghold.

Thus far, President Johnson's concerns have been validated. Since 1968, when he declined to run for reelection, Republicans have won the Presidency in seven of 10 elections and will have will have held the Presidency for 28 of 40 years by 2008, with a substantial swing of southern states to support their success. President Nixon openly played the race card, fomenting white working-class resentment toward people of color who benefited from the policies of the Great Society (Edsall & Edsall, 1991; Quadagno, 1994).

Speaking of the Great Society, Quadagno stated,

> The positive liberties it extended to African Americans were viewed by the working
> class as infringements on their negative liberties, the liberty for trade unions to

discriminate in the selection of apprentices and to control job training programs; the liberty to exclude minorities from representation in local politics; the liberty to maintain segregated neighborhoods. (p. 195)

President Reagan used racially coded discourse when he described "welfare queens" and received working-class white support from so-called "Reagan Democrats" (Edsall & Edsall, 1991; Quadagno, 1994). During his successful Presidential campaign, George Bush I exploited the "Willie Horton" issue, blaming the release of a "dangerous" black felon on the liberal policies of his opponent. Even President Clinton, who had tremendous black support, had to prove himself to white people by publicly denouncing Sister Souljah when running for President and by taking the lead in dismantling the country's welfare system. Now, if critics complain that the tax policies of the current President George W. Bush have grossly redistributed wealth upward, they are immediately denounced as fomenting "class warfare."

INTERACTION OF RACE AND CLASS TODAY

On the level of political discourse, then, race is used to cloak and veil class exploitation. How does the interaction of race and class affect people who live in the United States today? We have identified seven major areas to explore in more detail.

1. *Residential apartheid.* Neighborhoods always are segmented by class, as determined by income, wealth, and the cost of homes. As we discussed in Chapter 4, however, neighborhoods are still segregated racially, leaving certain groups of people of color, particularly poor African Americans and Latinos, living in hypersegregated, poor neighborhoods (Feagin, 1999; Massey & Denton, 1993; Wilson, 1996).

2. *Access to jobs.* Working class people of color, particularly those living in highly segregated neighborhoods, have less entrée to decent jobs than other people, even poor or working-class whites. Deindustrialization, expanding suburbanization, and poor public transportation give them less access to jobs, and racism and discrimination add another layer of impermeability for poor people of color seeking employment.

    Blacks reside in neighborhoods and are engaged in social networks and households that are less conducive to employment than those of other ethnic and racial groups in the inner city. (Wilson, 1996, p. 111)

3. *Segmented labor markets.* Both of the previous factors contribute to segmented labor markets, with poor neighborhoods of color offering more illegal and marginal work and carrying fewer benefits, if any, greater risks, and little opportunity for advancement and employment security (Bourgois, 1995; Schiller, 1998; Wilson, 1996).

4. *Racialized financial services.* Credit and loans are essential for class mobility, yet both are less available and more expensive for people of color (Manning, 1999). Poor neighborhoods of color have fewer banks and more check-cashing companies and informal loan sharks, which

charge much higher rates of interest. People of color have more difficulty securing the credit to buy a home—which is one of the most basic assets that people acquire as they move up in class—and, as we have mentioned, when people of color acquire homes in these areas, the value of these homes is less likely to go up and more likely to fall (Shapiro, 2004). The PBS series *Race: The Power of an Illusion* (2003) documents the lasting effects of racist government and business practices in the post–World War II financial and residential limitations imposed on people of color who were eligible for funds through the GI Bill.

5. *Lack of assets.* All of the above conspire to hamper poor people of color in accumulating assets (Oliver & Shapiro, 2000; Shapiro, 2004; Wolff, 2001). More than income, assets create the great wealth divide in the United States between whites and African Americans, Hispanics, and Native Americans (Oliver & Shapiro, 2000; Shapiro, 2004). The status of middle-class African Americans reflects their income rather than their comparative net worth (Oliver & Shapiro, 2000).

6. *Racism and classism in state policy.* Federal policies can take class or race into account in a remedial fashion, such as having a progressive income tax or laws supporting affirmative action. But state policies can do the opposite, widening class and race divisions.

    The policies under President Reagan of reducing progressive income taxes while increasing flat payroll taxes did exactly this, as wealth was redistributed upward (Phillips, 1990), and predominantly to white people. Under President George W. Bush, policies that have reduced the income tax burden on the wealthiest dramatically, as well as the moves to reduce or eliminate wealth and estate taxes while cutting services for the poor, have further widened the class and race divide with respect to assets.

7. *A vicious cycle.* All of these factors leave concentrated neighborhoods of poor people of color with higher poverty rates and more social disorganization. This becomes "evidence" of the cultural dissoluteness of people living in these neighborhoods, reinforcing stereotypes and making them suitable targets for scapegoating (Wilson, 1996). A "discourse of denigration" then is used to mask the policies that contribute heavily to this situation (Miller & Schamess, 2000). It also fuels suburban sprawl, as white people of all socioeconomic strata and middle-class people of color seek to move away from the perceived sources of social disorder. This has the effect of despoiling the environment and also reinforcing residential segregation with all of its economic, social, and psychological consequences.

RACISM AND SEXISM

Racism and sexism are closely connected to the social construction of race and gender and have significant consequences as independent social forces. They are two of the most basic forms of durable inequalities and, in combination, have profound consequences for how a person experiences the world. Together, they straddle all aspects of social life—public and private, at the workplace, and in the home. Although everyone has a socially constructed race, as we have discussed, many white people are unaware of this.

But everyone is conscious of gender and, unlike racial and ethnic groups, some of whom have little direct contact with other groups, most people have interactions with men and women daily. (Although binary male and female categories have been contested, with emerging gender categories such as transgendered and transsexual, for the sake of simplicity we are focusing primarily on classic male and female conceptualizations of gender.) Many people have interracial and ethnic interactions at school or work, yet most do not have these interactions at home, as males and females live together in most households.

Class has profound consequences on physical appearance, influencing health, diet, weight, how we dress, and how we look. When we are born, however, our physical appearance does not reveal our class. Both gender and race (or at least the physical characteristics that fuel social constructions of race) are physical realities from birth. Thus, sexism and racism are forms of social oppression that reference the deepest core of our identity, our bodies.

For most people, gender is the earliest axis of social identity of which the person becomes conscious, and gender has immediate social consequences involving dress and playmates, as well as social roles and expectations. Every culture and society throughout history has had gender norms and expectations throughout the life course.

Racism requires a social construction of race, just as sexism relies on the social construction of gender. Although ethnic distinctions do not always lead to ethnic oppression and conflict, racial categories almost always incur racism. Theoretically, gender distinctions can exist without sexism, but this is rare in actual experience. Racism tends to divide and segregate, cutting down on intimate social interactions and relationships.

Despite sexism, women and men consistently have intimate interactions, and most people seek out these relationships. Despite the differences, sexism and racism have an intimate connection—involving blood ties, genetics, and their constructed meanings. Race, like gender, is socially constructed as a blood legacy, a genetic heritage, with attached meanings and value. The domestic domain, between women and men, is where race is inherited and passed on (Collins, 1990). This domain, in turn, is shaped by the social arrangements of racism—where people live, those with whom they socialize, and those with whom they procreate. Therefore, male and female relations in the domestic realm engender "racial" beings, but racism is a larger context influencing who mates with whom.

In considering the interaction of sexism and racism, we will concentrate on two important domains: (1) social, economic, and political consequences—the external, material costs; and (2) social roles and social identity. The previous chapter considered the contradictions and paradoxes: White women subjected to much sexism can be racists, whereas men of color who are subjected to racism every day can have sexist attitudes and behave in sexist ways toward women. These paradoxes can cause tensions and divisions between individuals and groups, splinter social movements, and fracture potential political alliances.

The ongoing discussion about why some have perceived the women's movement as primarily a white, middle-class movement exemplifies this fissure. Many women of color also have worked hard for women's rights, yet found that white women were not always invested in affiliating with them in the struggle for women's rights. Further, discussions of race were glaringly absent in the early days of the modern feminist movement.

SOCIAL CONSEQUENCES OF RACISM AND SEXISM

We have described in detail the social consequences of racism. The socioeconomic consequences of sexism include lower pay scales for women than men, under-representation in many professions and over-representation in lower-paying occupations, sexual harassment and sexual objectification, and domestic violence. Although females comprise more than half of the country's population, the U.S. Senate includes only 14 female senators. No woman has been a President or Vice-President. It is a newsworthy exception when a woman heads a Fortune 500 company.

Thus, women earn less than men and a greater percentage of the poor are women. Women also are more likely to have major child-rearing and other domestic responsibilities than men, often in addition to their work in paid employment.

The socioeconomic consequences of sexism are similar to those of racism in some ways: limited economic opportunities, stereotypes connected to alleged biological differences, restricted access to positions of power and influence. Women of all races and men and women of color have had to struggle for rights, opportunities, and the status of full citizenship. Repressive institutions, such as slavery, relied on an interaction of racism and sexism to create socially stratified roles and positions. As a result of discrimination and oppression, people of color and women have endured diminished economic, political, and social status (Reid & Comaz-Diaz, 1990).

Research seems to indicate that both sexism and racism operate as independent forces and are additive. A woman of color is disadvantaged twice—by race and by gender (Cotter, Hermsen, & Vanneman, 1999; Hardy & Hazelrigg, 1995). But there are differences between sexism and racism. Historically, in the United States, women have endured oppression and unequal treatment but were not targeted for extermination or slavery as a result of their gender. Today, women outnumber men as students in higher education while African Americans, Native Americans, and Hispanics are underrepresented. Women form the majority of the population while people of color still constitute a minority. And white women, despite experiencing sexism, as a group have greater economic success than men and women of color (Elmelech & Yu, 2004).

Wilkinson (1995) has stated that "whenever race is part of the mosaic, it outweighs all potential influences" (p. 175). In her view, racism is the prime reason for discrepancies in the lives of individuals and groups, particularly as it fosters segregation, which is foundational to social discrimination and inequality.

The effect of racism and sexism has documented economic effects. Taking data from the Current Population Survey, Elmelech and Lu (2004) found that black and Puerto Rican women suffered extreme economic hardship because of their race and ethnicity as well as their gender. These researchers proposed two hypotheses as to why this is the case:

1. Women of color have lower educational levels and less social and economic capital to acquire higher paying jobs.
2. Family structure—such as single parenthood and having many children—creates greater economic hardship.

What these authors did not explore are the interactive effects of racism and sexism. Why do women of color have less social capital than white women? As we have discussed previously, this is not an accident or a sign of lack of motivation but, rather, a reflection of systemic institutional barriers and resource hoarding.

And what of the role of sexism? Do women have the same entrée into jobs and occupations, similar rates of promotion, and equitable pay scales? The evidence is that they do not. Ultimately, all people of color are socially disadvantaged by racism, and all women by sexism, with women of color having the added burdens of race and gender discrimination (Cotter et al., 1999: Hardy & Hazelrigg, 1995).

SOCIAL ROLES AND SOCIAL IDENTITY

Gender roles are shaped by culture and historical and social contexts. The meanings of being male and female are far from fixed and have transmuted over time and across societies. Racial roles and gender roles both are contested by groups and social movements, as well as by individuals in their daily interactions. They also are intricately interconnected.

If we consider race and gender for African Americans, slavery initially placed severe constraints on the range of available social roles, and gender influenced what forms of labor slaves were expected to perform (Jones, 1985). This also meant that African American women worked outside of their families in jobs that white women did not—a pattern that continued for many decades following the Civil War, a clear example of how racism contributed to the construction of divergent gender roles by race.

Racism also contributed to public visions of stereotypical social roles for black men and women, although African Americans challenged and contested these distortions. This necessitated a great deal of struggle, requiring African Americans to create and value their own self-definitions over those that were foisted upon them and to generate collective self-respect and self-reliance (Collins, 1990).

Racism has affected black families in many ways, two of which are that (1) more African American women work outside of the home, and (2) the educational and job opportunities for African American men are constricted. Furstenburg (2001) notes that in the middle of the 20th century, the rates of marriage for blacks and whites were similar but that this similarity has diverged, and now 25% of black women in their 20s will never marry, compared to 10% for whites. And for those who marry, the rates of separation are high. Furstenburg's research in Baltimore, running focus groups and conducting interviews with low-income, young adult African Americans, led him to posit three explanations:

1. the high unemployment rate among African American males;
2. the shortage of "marriageable" African American males; and
3. a "culture of gender mistrust."

It is interesting to see how these three explanations interact. African American men are in a more economically precarious position, for the reasons described in Chapter 4; all of the barriers in the web of racism conspire to limit their economic opportunities. Economic stability is a major foundation for a stable marriage, so this is linked to the shortage of marriageable males, as well as other vulnerabilities caused by the web of racism—high rates of arrest and incarceration and higher death rates.

Furstenburg (2001) posits that these social conditions consequently lend themselves to a culture of gender mistrust. The women he interviewed described men as immature, not self-reliant, and unreliable, while the men complained that women expect too much of them and don't respect them. He concludes that "economic uncertainties make marriage a less desirable, predictable, and permanent social form" (p. 243).

Lack of respect is an important notion, as racism can be thought of as a collective lack of respect for the dignity and worth of human beings based on their race and ethnicity (Miller & Ferroggiaro, 1996). Lack of respect makes it all the more difficult to achieve a positive sense of identity, including gender identity. Bourgois (1995) has described young Puerto Rican drug dealers seeking the respect that was absent from office jobs by becoming involved in their illegal but self-validating entrepreneurship. Cose (1995) has speculated that because men of color, particularly African American men, receive so little respect in society at large, they may, at times, feel as though they need to seek respect in ways that can be construed as very intense or damaging to themselves, or that others seek in an intense way with their domestic partners, as they are closest people at hand. This dynamic further weakens cross-gender relationships and provides an example of how racism and gender interact.

For people of color, particularly African Americans, Latinos, and Native Americans, gender becomes a second source of stereotypes to confront in addition to those based on race and ethnicity. Although all women are subject to sexist stereotypes, women of color find that these negative images are distorted further through the lens of racism, leading to exoticism, denigration, and visions of hypersexuality or hyposexuality. Idealized female images of body, weight, and dress are laden with Eurocentric distortions, compounding the challenges of developing a positive, integrated body image and gender identity.

Men of color also face racialized gender distortions with reference to their sexuality, fidelity, and potential for violence. People may internalize images such as these, with the result that many white women acknowledge fear if they pass an African American man on the street at night.

Thus, gender stereotypes have psychological consequences for women and men of color, affecting their sense of psychological well-being. To internalize a positive sense of both race/ethnicity and gender becomes more of a challenge, as the world is lined with distorted mirrors and narrated by demeaning discourses.

In their research, Woody and Green (2001) have found that the most salient factor in psychological well-being is race, followed by its interaction with gender, with African American men being the most adversely affected. They face a greater likelihood of police harassment while simply walking down a street, and they experience projections at work and elsewhere. Many of their leaders have been assassinated and their friends and relatives incarcerated. This lack of control over their life is further exacerbated if domestic relations are tense, conflictual, and unstable.

RACISM AND HETEROSEXISM

Shortly before the Presidential election of 2004 had begun in earnest, the Massachusetts Supreme Judicial Court reached a decision that ignited a firestorm around the nation. The court delivered an opinion that to deny gay and lesbian couples the right to marry was a violation of state law. Soon thereafter, lines of couples registered for marriage at town halls from Cambridge to Northampton, accompanied by public celebrations of marriage.

In other parts of the country, the scene was less cheerful. The court's decision sent a shockwave through many communities and homes, believing that marriage was a right reserved exclusively for heterosexual couples. Although a few religious denominations supported the decision, some believed that it violated fundamental teachings of their faith. Many politicians exploited the issue, seeking a ban on same-sex marriages through a constitutional amendment and placing anti–gay marriage propositions on state ballots. It was a factor in how some people voted in the Presidential election, although it is not yet clear whether it influenced the outcome.

Even though there have been tremendous strides in the movement for the rights of gay, lesbian, and bisexual people, including the right not to be seen as deviant from a heterosexual norm, this example illustrates the strong rivers of heterosexism and homophobia still flowing in our society. Heterosexism is a formidable form of social oppression, a durable inequality that intersects with sexism and racism, as well as other types of social oppression. Sexual orientation cannot be considered without also taking gender into account, along with gender roles and expectations. Also important to consider are the contexts of culture, ethnicity, and race.

The gay, lesbian, bisexual, and transgender communities comprise a highly diverse grouping of people—not a homogenous or monolithic cluster of the populace (Griffin & Harro, 1997). This heterogeneous nature is akin to trying to describe ethnic and racial communities: There is not an African American or black community—rather, many communities (hooks, 2000). What is shared by these groups is that they are not heterosexual, or "straight." Even within any one of these categories are many differences, as sexual orientation can refer to identity, sexual attractions, and behaviors that, although they overlap, are not exactly the same (Morales, 1990).

Diamond (2003, p. 491) describes *sexual orientation* as a stable and enduring pattern of sexual attraction and distinguishes this from *sexual identity*, a "culturally organized conception of the self." Sexual orientation describes attraction but does not necessarily tell us about a person's behaviors and lifestyle (Morales, 1996). For example, a man who is attracted to other men may marry and live his life as a straight, heterosexual person because of societal pressures, or live with a male partner, or work out a lifestyle that accommodates his sexual orientation while protecting him from homophobic harassment. Diamond also distinguishes sexual orientation and sexual identity from *same-sex sexuality*, in which a person may have a same-sex sexual liaison in certain situational conditions, such as living in a college dormitory or serving time in prison, but not have a gay sexual identity or sexual orientation.

For purposes of this discussion, we will consider anyone and any groups that do not see themselves fitting within the dominant paradigm of heterosexuality, and we will refer to them as GLBT (gay/lesbian/bisexual/transgendered) recognizing that this term involves lumping together a highly diverse, disparate group of people. We also will use the terms "straight" (to describe heterosexuals) and "queer" (in reference to those who are gay), as these are common terms within GLBT communities. The term that researchers use for all those who are not straight heterosexual is "sexual minorities" (Diamond, 2003), so we will employ that term as well.

HETEROSEXISM

Heterosexism is the presupposition that heterosexual relationships are normative and that all other sexual attractions and gender identities are divergent. Heterosexism is an ideology, a dominant discourse that is manifest on many levels. It is a set of attitudes and belief systems that organizes interpersonal relationships, particularly dating and family formation, while also evident in institutions and the social ordering of society. Many subcultures within society also have their own meaning-making systems about gender and sexual relationships, which are transmitted intergenerationally through families, influencing how people feel about their own sexual identity and how they react to those of others (Morales, 1996). For instance, in Latino and Hispanic culture even language is gendered, ordering an entire cosmology between masculine and feminine.

As with every form of durable inequality, a web of oppression covers those who are considered sexual minorities (see Figure 7.3). Heterosexism has many social consequences for those who are queer: being unable to marry in most

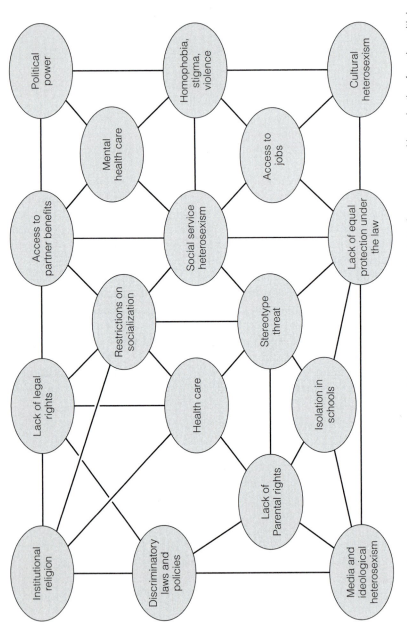

Connecting lines are arbitrary and for illustration; in reality, each form of institutional heterosexism connects with each other form in multiple ways.

FIGURE 7.3 | WEB OF HETEROSEXISM

states, being the target of stigma and violence, encountering discriminatory laws, lacking access to partner benefits, facing employment discrimination, having to fight for parental rights, and being denied the capacity to serve as foster or adoptive parents in many states—to mention a few. GLBT people encounter hostility, discrimination, and exclusion from a significant number of religious denominations. Many openly GLBT people also have difficulty succeeding in politics in most parts of the country.

Homophobia is an aspect of heterosexism that is expressed through fear or aversion to GLBT people. It can take the form of prejudice, discrimination, or harassment and can operate intrapersonally, interpersonally, institutionally, and culturally (Blumenfeld, 2000). Heterosexism does not rely on homophobia, although these two are often present together. Homophobia fuels and advances heterosexism.

Heterosexism and homophobia place pressures on GLBT people that people who are straight do not face. This causes those who are GLBT to have to make decisions about disclosure and lifestyle, weighing the risks and balancing them with their desire to live openly. Herek (2000) talks of "internalized homophobia," which accrues from a constant discourse of normative heterosexism, creating conflict and internal tensions. People can feel guilt or shame about their identity if they are "out," or experience the same emotions if they remain in the closet. Unlike social class, race, and gender, which are considered primarily inherited attributes, sexual orientation sometimes is constructed as a choice that people make about their lifestyle (Lim-Hing, 2000).

Although people do make decisions about the details of their lifestyle, most GLBT people strongly believe that their sexual orientation is part of their core self and being, that they are being themselves. Again, straight people do not have to justify their sexual and partnership lifestyles as "choices." It is *assumed* that they are being true to their genes and character.

The struggle against heterosexual norms and sanctions and to achieve one's authentic social and sexual self has its psychological costs. Many studies have documented higher rates of depression, drug use, and suicide in the GLBT population, particularly youth struggling to achieve their identities in hostile environments, such as high schools, and often without the support of their families (Consolacion, Russell, & Sue, 2004; Gipson, 2002; Harper, Jernewall, & Zea, 2004).

THE INTERACTION OF RACISM AND HETEROSEXISM

Racism and heterosexism are independent forms of social oppression that certainly are additive, creating a double filter of social exclusion and, for women, a "triple sieve." There is also a dynamic interaction between race and sexual orientation. Racism exists within GLBT communities, and homophobia is present in communities of color. Although experiencing social oppression can help to sensitize a person to the impact of being targeted, this does not necessarily negate internalized prejudice or discriminatory behaviors along another axis of social identity (Morales, 1990). And though all forms of durable inequalities have similar structures (Tilly, 1998), they also are distinct.

For example, for many people, the social construction of race is a visible characteristic that is obvious to all while their sexual orientation is often hidden and unseen. People of color can feel resentment toward white women or lesbians who believe they grasp the experience of racism because of their own social disenfranchisement (hooks, 2000). Although an "oppression Olympics" to determine the worst form of social exclusion may be unhelpful, it is important to understand the unique dynamics for each form of social targeting.

People of color who are GLBT usually have to operate in at least three communities—their ethnic and racial communities, GLBT communities, and society at large—which privileges whiteness and heterosexuality (Morales, 1990). GLBT people are both a visible and an invisible minority and often find that none of these worlds has the space for them to be their complete and complex self. GLBT people of color often encounter tensions that white people and straight people of color do not. These may be loyalty conflicts or pressure to choose one community over the other, as their GLBT and ethnic communities often do not overlap and may even be wary of one another (Harper et al., 2004).

Because of invisible white privilege and the internalization of racist stereotypes and prejudices, people of color may feel alienated from GLBT friends and even partners. At the same time, a GLBT person of color may feel estranged from his or her own family and community. People of color often find support from their families for their race and ethnicity, but this frequently is not the case for their sexual orientation (Consolacion et al., 2004). There are many reasons for this, in addition to general societal heterosexism.

Some ethnic and racial groups, such as Native Americans and African Americans, have survived systematic attempts to destroy their families and cultures, including enslavement and genocide. Homosexuality can be perceived as a threat to the survival of the race (Greene & Boyd Franklin, 1996). Some racial and ethnic groups have traditional values about gender roles and may see gayness as a threat to their culture (Morales, 1990), which can place a great deal of pressure on a person not to let down his or her family.

Merghi and Grimes (2000) describe a Vietnamese American man who was his family's only male heir, and he felt as if he were disappointing and undermining his family because he was gay. In another example, a Mexican American man was concerned about what the reaction would be in the town in Mexico where his family originated if the townspeople were to find out that he was gay. GLBT people of color may feel that their sexual orientation makes them "cultural traitors" (Parks, Hughes, & Mathews, 2004).

Such internal conflicts, accompanied by negative or even hostile reactions from loved ones, can make the coming-out process painful and tendentious and can alienate a person from family, culture, and ethnic community. This can result in GLBT people of color seeking support from people who are not ethnically or culturally similar but who also may not grasp the unique dynamics and strains being encountered. For example, a young Latino man may not act in a way that is visibly gay because in his family and community, this is linked with being alien, feminine, and inferior (Morales, 1996). His behavior, in turn, can precipitate a negative reaction from white gay friends who are disappointed that he is acting straight (Merghi & Grimes, 2000).

The emotional and psychological costs of various loyalties can cause GLBT people of color to act as if they are being segmented and parceled out into fragmented identities (Gipson, 2002; Harper et al., 2004). Yet there are anomalies and cross-currents. Balsam and her colleagues (2004) found that American Indians who were "two spirits" (having male and female spirits in one body) had more psychological symptoms and more mental health needs, but they also were highly identified with their traditional ethnic culture.

We should be mindful, too, that many GLBT people, of color and white, receive support and validation from their families. There are white allies to people of color and GLBT allies from communities of color. And though groups can be sites of tension, they also serve as a buffer from micro-aggressions and a locus of mutual aid and support. People gain many survival skills and sources of strength and resiliency from their experience of oppression, which can be of use when they encounter other types of discrimination. Even though they certainly experience high stress levels, people who encounter multiple oppressions do not necessarily have more emotional and psychological problems than people who have more social privilege (Consolacion et al., 2004).

Although it is important to explore the complex interactions of different axes of social identity and diverse forms of oppression, it also is prudent not to overly generalize. When working with individuals, groups, and families, it is most fruitful to seek to understand the unique constellations of identities and oppressions and how they are manifested with specific people in a given situation.

IMMIGRATION AND RACISM

Immigration has been central to racism in the United States. Without immigration, Europeans and Native Americans would not have come into contact. The forced immigration of African Americans led to slavery and its aftermath. Through immigration, Irish, Italian, Jewish and many other European ethnic groups came to the United States. This country has been called "a nation of immigrants." And immigration today, with huge numbers entering the country from Central and South America and Asia, is reconstructing the calculus of race, ethnicity, and racism.

As immigration brings more and diverse groups of people together, complex intergroup relationships are formed. Immigration raises questions of citizenship and rights (particularly since September 11, 2001), questions of culture and assimilation, and results in a reconfiguring of who is inside and outside and who has power and prestige. And in terms of race and racism in the United States, immigration and assimilation are vital to the social construction of who is white and who is of color.

Immigration tends to happen in waves, the largest of which in the United States occurred in the late 19th and early 20th centuries. Between 1901 and 1925, 17.2 million people immigrated to this country (Zhou, 2001). Between 1971 and 1995, nearly the same number of people, 17.1 million, arrived here, although this represented a smaller proportion of the total U.S. population. Immigration today is in the range of 1.1 million people annually (Goldsborough, 2000), with more than 28 million foreign-born residents— about one-tenth of the population (Ruiz, 2000). The new immigrants are socioeconomically diverse, ranging from highly educated and trained people from India to poor and illiterate migrants from Mexico and El Salvador (Zhou, 2001).

We currently are in a period of high immigration, which is contributing to a major shift in the ethnic and racial population of the United States. In the following discussion we will consider some of the dynamics of immigration, mention some significant recent legislation and its impact on immigration, and then examine how immigration and racism interact today.

DYNAMICS OF IMMIGRATION

Immigration is a process of push and pull factors. Push factors are the circumstances that lead people to want to move, and pull factors are the conditions that attract and lure them to specific locations. An example of macro factors is the demand for labor in one country corresponding to high unemployment in another. An example of a micro-level cause of immigration is wanting to live in the same locale as one's children who have migrated. Clearly, an interplay of macro and micro factors always is operating globally (Zhou, 2001).

Some immigration is done voluntarily and is part of a family's or individual's desire for economic advancement or finding a more compatible culture. Yet much immigration today is spurred by wars, famines, economic upheavals, and political dislocations (Zhou, 2001). Urbanization is occurring all over the world, resulting in large migrations from the country to the city (Gardner & Blackburn, 1996), where many social tensions and disarticulations prompt further migrations. Terrorism and the perceived threat of terrorism influences immigration patterns, policies, and the treatment of immigrants in their new homes.

Laws and policies that encourage or discourage people from entering the United States influence immigration and historically have shaped the national, ethnic, and racial make-up of newly arrived residents. Espenshade, Fix, Zimmermann, and Corbett (1997) identified four objectives of U.S. immigration policy.

1. economic, ensuring an adequate supply of workers with the skills necessary for certain jobs, as well as workers who will accept jobs that are difficult to fill;
2. humanitarian, such as reuniting families;

3. political, allowing certain refugees into the country, such as Cubans or South Vietnamese after the end of the Vietnam War; and

4. promoting greater cultural and ethnic diversity—although this contentious goal is not shared by major sectors of the population. Resistance to this goal has increased since 9/11.

The national myth is of America being a nation of heroic immigrants, but this is a paradox, as immigrants have been, and still are, treated as objects of scorn, distaste, mistrust, and disapproval (Kibria, 1998). Social work and other helping professions evolved out of a concern about the perceived immoral and dissolute lifestyles of recent European immigrants. Immigrants often are targeted and scapegoated, treated as alien and other (Ong Hing, 1998).

They also can be used as political fodder. A content analysis of national newspapers, citing statements by major politicians about Mexican immigrants between 1993 and 1998, revealed that 63% had referred to them as "illegals," 32% as "a welfare burden," and 30% as "a border invasion" (Ruiz, 2000). This evokes President Rutherford Hayes' warning of the "Chinese invasion" more than 130 years ago!

The language and symbolism of leaders exerts a powerful influence over how immigrants are perceived and treated. Even though the United States has a clear *immigration* policy, there is greater ambivalence about how immigrants are cared for once they are here, a lack of *immigrant* policy (Espenshade et al., 1996–97). This stance is unfortunate, as immigrants face many challenges in trying to settle in their adopted homes. They may have experienced disruptions in their original countries, and certainly the process of immigration is unsettling and disorienting (Gardner & Blackburn, 1996).

Once they arrive in the United States, they encounter many differences—in culture, customs, language, climate, lifestyle, and often economic well-being (Gardner & Blackburn, 1996; Padilla, 1997). Although some immigrants are well educated and find themselves economically secure in this country, many others come with little education and few employment skills and end up working in low-paying, often hazardous jobs (Padilla, 1997; Zhou, 2001).

Another consequence of immigration is the difficulty of access (Gardner & Blackburn, 1996). Many immigrants, particularly those living in the United States illegally, are denied work benefits and access to health care; thus, their health and mental health needs are seriously underserved (Padilla, 1997). They often lack familiarity with the system and confidence to lobby effectively for themselves. This carries over to the public education system, in which immigrant parents, because of many of the reason cited, as well linguistic and cultural barriers, are less likely to attend meetings about their children's educational progress or to advocate for them when they have problems or special needs. Interestingly, immigrants are required to pay taxes in most cases and are able to enlist in the armed forces and fight in foreign wars (Espenshade et al., 1997).

SIGNIFICANT LEGISLATION

The significance of the 1965 Immigration Reform Act and its impact on race and racism in the United States cannot be overstated. In Chapter 3 we discussed the laws that were intended to prevent immigrants from entering the country in the late 19th and early 20th centuries. By giving preference to immigrants from countries from which people already living in the United States originated, the distinctly white, European character of much of the United States was kept intact. During the peak period of immigration during the early 20th century, 90% percent of immigrants hailed from European countries (Zhou, 2001). In the wake of the 1965 law, 88% of immigrants originated from the Americas and Asia, and significant numbers from Africa (Zhou, 2001). This has had, and will continue to have, a huge impact on the ethnic and racial makeup of the United States.

Impetus to reform immigration stemmed from a presidential commission established by President Truman. Shortly before the 1965 Immigration Reform Act was passed, the commission reported that the three major problems with existing law were that: (1) it was predicated on a fundamental mistrust of all aliens, (2) it discriminated on the basis of race, and (3) it did not support U.S. foreign policy interests (Goldsborough, 2000). Still, it is difficult to conceive of such a revolutionary immigration act being passed without the momentum generated by the Civil Rights Movement and the consequent concern for racial justice (Kibria, 1998). This Immigration Reform Act was passed during the same wave of legislation that led to the Voting Rights Act, the Civil Rights Act, and the advent of affirmative action.

After this act was passed, legislation in 1980 and 1986 gave legal status to refugees and asylum seekers and, for a brief window of time, granted legal status to 2 million undocumented workers (Padilla, 1997). These measures have been accompanied by attempts to discourage immigration by denying benefits to immigrants. The most notorious effort was Proposition 187 in California, denying health and social services to illegal immigrants. This proposition passed with the support of 62% of the electorate, after a campaign led by then Governor Pete Wilson, who repeatedly characterized immigrants as "freeloaders," appealing to nativism and racism rather than acknowledging the economic contributions of those being targeted (Ruiz, 2000). This Act eventually was declared unconstitutional in a court challenge.

The 1996 Welfare Reform Act passed by Congress and signed into law by President Clinton initially banned immigrants, including legal immigrants, from receiving social welfare benefits, but health and disability benefits eventually were restored to immigrants who had lived in the United States before the legislation passed (Ong Hing, 1998). Since that time, federal support for immigrants has steady eroded, leading to a greater burden for the states (Padilla, 1997).

IMMIGRATION AND RACISM TODAY

The current wave of immigration is much more racially and ethnically varied than in the past as the complexion and customs of the country are changing.

Conceptualizations of race and racism are being rethought and reworked; old paradigms are being interrogated; and new patterns of intergroup relations are emerging—reshaping and reconfiguring the American racial project. The spectrum of racism has become more complex, and while African Americans and Native Americans continue to face enduring inequalities, race and racism are conceived of in more intricate and less dichotomous white and black terms.

Even though many of today's immigrants are socially constructed as people of color, the personal and social meanings of this designation are contentious and unstable. The shifting meanings of race and ethnicity are an important aspect of the disruptions and dislocations that immigrants experience. Jamaicans, for example, come from a country that is predominantly black and where African-Jamaicans have economic and political power and black people have social mobility. When arriving in the United States, are they to be viewed as a group distinct from African Americans? Certainly, they have ethnic and cultural differences, but the logic of racism constructs both African Americans and Jamaicans as black people. How does the child of Jamaican immigrants growing up in Brooklyn and attending school with other Jamaicans and African Americans identify himself? How is he viewed by his African American classmates? How is he treated by white police officers and by shopkeepers, who may be white, Indian, or Korean?

Or how does a Japanese social work student view herself racially in the United States? In Japan, a relatively homogenous society, she was part of a mainstream majority in which she had ethnic privilege. Now some of her fellow students and professors are telling her that she is a "person of color." What does this mean? What does she have in common with her Korean American, African American, and Mexican American fellow students—if anything?

And how about a light-skinned student from Colombia who is used to having race privilege and suddenly finds himself being grouped with Puerto Ricans and Dominicans as a "Latino"? What does this mean?

These are just three examples of the Charybdis and Scylla of identity navigated by immigrants, sometimes every day. These issues may lead to a more complex understanding of identity and the absurdities and contradictions of racism in society at large, and challenge a more dichotomous way of thinking.

Another area in which immigration intersects with racism is in the restructuring of intergroup relations with other immigrants, indigenous people of color, and whites. Nearly three-quarters of recent immigrants have settled in six states: California, New York, Florida, Illinois, New Jersey, and Texas (Zhou, 2001). One-third of Los Angeles and Miami residents are immigrants, significant numbers of whom live in economically and socially isolated neighborhoods, contiguous or coterminous with indigenous people of color, particularly African Americans.

Morawska (2001) has conducted comparative research of various cities with high numbers of immigrants, focusing on intergroup relationships between immigrants and African Americans. He cautions against generalizing, as each city has its own unique intergroup dynamics. Building on Bobo and Hutchins, and Blumer, he conceptualizes intergroup relationships as being a function of concrete economic and political circumstances in interactions with internalized opinions, sentiments, and judgments that have evolved historically and collectively and are specifically situated. What this implies is that concrete conditions of contact and competition intermingle with subjective conclusions and stereotypes, which have been shaped by contemporary and historical discourses. And though intergroup relations have some common themes and patterns, the unique social, economic, political, and historical conditions of each community produce variations in race relations.

Some arenas of competition and conflict are predictable: identity, status, jobs, power, cultural values, and competition for upward mobility (Morawska, 2001). The contours of these contested areas are influenced by cultural values, group perceptions, and the nature and tenor of the white power elite's relationship with African Americans and immigrant groups in the community. In New York City, Morawska found tensions between African Americans and Korean shopkeepers over identity, control of the community, and economic interactions; and struggles with Puerto Ricans involved competition over jobs and political power and influence. Between African Americans and non-Hispanic West Indians, Morawska noted the tensions and contradictions between race and ethnicity described above.

These findings differ significantly from relationships between African Americans and Cubans in Miami, where Cubans have a great deal more economic and political power than do Puerto Ricans in New York, and significantly outnumber African Americans. The white political establishment in Miami is considerably more conservative than in New York, so they tend to align with the predominantly conservative Cuban immigrants.

There is controversy about whether low-wage-earning immigrants compete with African Americans and take away jobs. Common wisdom says they do (Zhou, 2001). There are concerns that immigrants will work for less pay and under less desirable conditions, which has the effect of lowering wages and employment standards for everyone, to the advantage of employers. Immigrants also have been able to corner economic and occupational niches, blocking out African Americans while letting their ethnic compatriots in (Zhou, 2001). This experience is one that African Americans encountered with white immigrant groups in earlier times. Employers have been found to favor immigrant job seekers over African Americans (Wilson, 1996; Zhou, 2001).

Some dispute this analysis. Ong Hing (1998) argues that immigrants fuel the economy through their work and as consumers, stimulating demand and creating jobs. After reviewing the research about this controversial topic, Esphenshade et al. (1996–97) concluded that immigrants do not displace indigenous workers; rather, they occupy different occupational niches and complement local workers rather than displace them. They also found that the impact of perceptions far outweighs actual experiences and encounters.

Particularly painful and demoralizing for many African Americans is knowing the level of struggle and sacrifice they have engaged in to break down barriers and open doors for people of color. They are dispirited to see immigrants take advantage of these achievements, corner economic and occupational niches, and then collude with employers to keep African Americans out. Rather than having a united front of people of color, indigenous and immigrant, confronting racism and white privilege, there is competition, tension, and intergroup conflict.

Some have conceptualized Korean grocers, for example, as playing a classic "middleman" role (Kibria, 1998), much as Indians did as merchants and civil servants when the British Empire controlled large swaths of Africa and Asia. Cubans and Cuban Americans have formed political and economic alliances with conservative whites in Miami, often at the expense of blacks (Morawska, 2001), the same white elite class that colluded with Jim Crow and other racist practices. Yet immigrants, whatever their color, want to succeed, and cornering job markets and forming alliances with civic elites is an American tradition.

Despite the localized nature of intergroup conflicts, Morawska (2001) has identified a set of factors that influence relationships between African Americans and immigrants of color. They include structural factors, such as the scale of immigration, the power and influence of ethnic niches, and the nature of the local political system.

Economic factors, such as the extent of post-industrialization and the role and size of the public sector, are also important because African Americans have had success in working in the public sector of employment in cities, including New York and Washington, often in contrast to their exclusion from the private sector. When the public sector shrinks or other ethnic groups gain access to it, this change often comes at a disproportionate cost to African Americans. Other factors relate to the history of intergroup relations, incendiary issues that ignite conflicts, mechanisms that foster intergroup dialogue and cooperation, extent of cohesion of ethnic and racial groups, how the media constructs narratives about groups and their relationships, and how connected or alienated ethnic and racial groups feel to society at large.

Since September 11, 2001, there has been a significant rethinking of immigration in the United States. Federal agencies tightened up monitoring of immigrant status, and many immigrants were deported (Davis, 2004; Steakley, Rubin, & Reina, 2004)The government imprisoned an unknown number of immigrants without releasing their names or granting them access to lawyers, all in the name of national security. Some may have been shipped secretly to foreign countries or U.S. gulags, where they have been subject to torture (Mayer, 2005).

Following the events of 9/11, immigrants who looked "Arab" have been attacked, even causing their death. Restrictions on immigration and regulations on visitors from predominantly Muslim countries have been implemented (Paden & Singer, 2003). Arab immigrants and Arab Americans have reported feeling much less secure and have experienced anti-Arab and anti-Islamic fear and hostility. This has been exacerbated by the tension between Israel, the Palestinians, and other Arab nations in the Middle East.

The anti-immigrant climate has led to a dramatic decrease in the number of international students studying in the United States on student visas (Paden, & Singer, 2003; Steakeley, Rubin, & Reina, 2004). The Department of Homeland

FACTORS CONTRIBUTING TO IMMIGRANT–BLACK
CONFLICTS IN U.S. CITIES DURING THE 1980S
AND 1990S

National-Level Factors
- Effects of post-industrialization on the American economy
- Dwindling of the American public sector and the welfare state
- Shared sense of alienation from the larger society
- National media-propagated negative images reinforcing stereotypes of immigrants and racial groups
- Contagious incidents of intergroup conflicts occurring in and reported from other cities
- U.S. immigration policies and the impact of American foreign policy interests and priorities

Local-Level Factors
- Size and proportions of immigrant or racial groups over time
- Dynamics of a city's economy (job loss, labor market segmentation, enduring unemployment and underclass, size and areas of the informal economy, existence of ethnic occupational niches)
- Occupational location of immigrants and native blacks over time, including occupational niches
- Overt and covert competition for jobs and wages among immigrants and native blacks
- Residential concentration, segregation, and interaction of immigrants and native blacks over time; and intergroup competition for space, housing, and local social services
- Liberal versus conservative local civic-political climate, incorporating an exclusion of outsiders and newcomers
- Immigrants' and native blacks' participation in local politics and share of public offices
- Competition for public offices among immigrant and native black groups
- Institutionalized racism or constraints on achievement of nonwhite, particularly dark-skinned, groups
- Group sense of dislocation resulting from the factors already mentioned
- Beliefs and ideologies by either group about in-group superiority, rewards, and statuses that are due to the group, and about the openness or closeness of the American social structure
- In-group negative perceptions of other groups
- Local ethnic or racial group medial representations of other groups and their attitudes toward, and relations with, the in-group
- History of local intergroup hostility
- Absence of outstanding, reconciliation-oriented leaders
- Absence of tradition of instances of intergroup collaboration

Source: "Immigrant-Black Dissensions in American Cities: An Argument for Multiple Explanations," by E. Morawska, in *Problem of the Century: Racial Stratification in the United States*, edited by E. Anderson & D.S. Massey (New York: Russell Sage Foundation, 2001), pp. 47–96.

Security is experimenting with a controversial plan of having immigrants wear ankle bracelets so they can be tracked (Zwerdling, 2005). All of this illustrates how immigration and the treatment of immigrants are tied to complex and unstable global events and local political ideologies. The long-term impact of this on race relations in the United States continues to evolve.

Certainly, the ethnic and racial makeup of the United States has changed dramatically and continues to do so. Coupled with concerns about terrorism and the role of immigrants, it is uncertain how this will interact with the existing, racialized system of privileges and exclusions into which immigrants are inducted. Will the distinction between native citizens and immigrants be drawn more sharply, and will this discourage immigration? Will white privilege erode as people of color become the majority of the country (which already is the case with a number of major cities)? Or will some groups be admitted to the club of white privilege—much as Jewish, Italian, and Irish immigrants were after they initially were constructed as non-white—leaving others, such as African Americans, behind? Will lighter-skinned Hispanics and Asians become "white" while their darker siblings and cousins be considered "of color"? Or will there be a gradual shift toward a browner populace as intermarriage leads to further dissolution of rigid racial and ethnic categories?

CONCLUSION

Racial identity does not exist in isolation from other aspects of identity. It is connected intricately with other forms of durable inequalities and social oppression. Because the focus of this book is on racism, we have limited our consideration of these intersections by not considering many other forms of social oppression, such as religious intolerance, nor have we considered class, gender, sexual orientation, and immigration in great depth. All of these are worthy of many volumes of analysis and discussion on their own. What we have done in this chapter is to explore some of the most significant ways by which race and racism intersect with these social phenomena and how racism in the United States, whether inside or outside of us, touches and transforms everything else.

EXERCISE 7.1 INTERSECTIONALITY

Intersectionality involves the interactions between different axes of identity and of different types of social privilege or oppression.

Returning to the Social Identity Pie that you drew for Chapter 1, consider how your racial identity interacts with different aspects of your identity (e.g., gender, social class, sexual orientation). You can do this on your own, in pairs, or in small groups.

1. How significant is your racial identity for you in relation to other aspects of your identity?
2. With which parts of your identity does your racial identity feel most integrated? With which parts do you feel tension? How would you explain the places of fit and disjuncture?

3. What social forces have supported or undermined the different aspects of your social identity? What social policies would you like to see changed to support yourself, family, and friends?
4. As a helping professional, what about your social identity will you want to be particularly mindful of when working with consumers?

RACIAL DIALOGUE: TALKING ABOUT RACE AND RACISM

CHAPTER CONTENTS

"I say hi to everybody, touch everybody, but that's normal. I don't even see what color you are when I do that. But when a white student comes up to me in the cafeteria where I'm sitting, minding my own business, and wants to talk about her burning issues of race, that's another level for me, and I can't do that if I'm not in a good space.... It's hard when I get angry and voice it. I'm getting angry with the people I love and kiss. That's a horrible feeling for me."

—Latina participant in a racial dialogue

"I need to check my own internalized oppression and voice it. I need the opportunity to talk about how I feel and how offended I am by constant references to [white] people's privilege and safety that I don't ever have the safety to experience. I need to allow myself to be angry."

—African American woman participant in a racial dialogue.

"It's the longest process you are going to go through probably in your life, if you are really committed to it. It means unlearning something so codified in the culture. It's both interrupting a racist joke and making a racist joke and being interrupted and hearing that; somebody having the courage to say to me 'you're screwing up.'"

—White woman participant in a racial dialogue.

The above quotes are from a facilitated racial dialogue held at a graduate school of social work in 1998 (Miller & Donner, 2000). They convey many things: strong emotions such as anger and fear, the desire to be left alone, ambivalence about caring for someone who is intruding in an oppressive fashion, and the importance of confronting other people. The statements also suggest inner resiliency, the courage to face oneself and others, the importance of being authentic, and the value of listening and self-reflection. The quotes illustrate both the benefits and the challenges of having dialogues about race and racism.

Talking directly about race and racism in racially mixed groups does not occur often in society (Miller & Donner, 2000; Shipler, 1997). Residential segregation limits interracial contact in public. The web of racism opens doors for white people while creating filters for people of color, further limiting opportunities for interracial dialogue. Even when people are working or studying together, however, these dialogues usually do not take place, and if they emerge spontaneously, they can be so painful or difficult that people disengage and withdraw. Why is talking about race and racism so difficult?

This chapter explores the possible answers to that question, but begins by considering why racial dialogues are even worth the time, effort, and investment. We will look at the ways that people avoid talking about race and racism and the consequences of such evasion. We then will suggest ways to have fertile interracial conversations. Last, we will consider how these conversations can be part of a larger process of repair and reconciliation.

When we talk of racial dialogue, we refer to structured, group conversations and discussions that focus on race, racism, ethnicity, and culture. Some dialogues take place in large groups, others with small clusters of people. A racial dialogue can be a one-time event or a series of meetings, structured or unstructured. We will examine some of these variables and their potential impact. What all racial dialogues have in common is a commitment by all participants to listen respectfully, accompanied by a desire to learn about oneself and others in the milieu of a racialized society.

WHY UNDERTAKE RACIAL DIALOGUES?

What is to be gained by talking about race and racism? In many ways, racism itself is the antithesis of this question: Racism is predicated on *not* having respectful interracial dialogue. Racism is a condition of dehumanization and alienation and, by contrast, genuine dialogue relies on recognizing the fundamental humanity and equality of the person or groups of people engaged in dialogue.

Racism isolates and silences people, even alienating them from themselves. Dialogues connect people. Racism relies on obfuscation and masking privilege. Dialogue can lead to exploration and revelation. Racism justifies inequities by alleged genetic or cultural flaws. Dialogue unmasks these fictions while exposing people to personal stories and experiences. Racism is a system of power, privilege, and exploitation that benefits one or a number of groups at the expense of others. Dialogue, even if only temporarily, can establish a level playing field. Racism marginalizes the voices of people of color while promoting a hegemonic, white discourse. Dialogue allows all to tell their stories and to hear the narratives of other people. Racism depends on uninvolved bystanders. Dialogue encourages everyone to participate. Racism relies on ignorance. Dialogue contributes to knowledge. Without dialogue, racism seems to be the normal state of affairs. With dialogue, the madness of racism is laid bare. Racism leads to feeling overwhelmed and resigned to failure. Dialogue sparks optimism. Racism divides people and pits them against one another. Dialogue offers opportunities for cooperation and trust building that may lead to collaborative social action.

Dialogue will not dismantle racism on its own. The most significant civil rights victories have resulted from organized social movements and heroic struggle, in which lives were risked and lost. It took a Civil War to officially end slavery in the United States. Dialogue can challenge racism that has been internalized and that poisons interpersonal relationships, and can help groups of people, whether in the workplace, school or community, learn to understand, respect, and collaborate with people who are different.

Interracial and intercultural dialogue encourages individuals and groups to reflect on who they are in relation to other people (Miller & Donner, 2000). These encounters immerse our social identities in a social situation with people who have similar and dissimilar social identities. Dialogues take people out of their own ethnocentrism.

Dialogue has been used to enhance understanding and resolve conflict between groups experiencing severe tensions, misunderstandings, and conflict. Examples include discussions between Koreans/Korean Americans and African Americans in Los Angeles (Norman, 1994), Jews and Arabs in the Middle East (Bargal & Bar, 1994), Protestants and Catholics in Northern Ireland

(Templegrove Action Research Ltd., 1996), whites and people of color in many U.S. communities (McCoy & Sherman, 1994; Study Circles Resource Center, 1997, 1998), and in many other parts of the world marked by enduring patterns of ethnic, religious, or racial conflict (Fisher, 1990).

Dialogue groups also offer a forum to discuss charged and controversial issues, such as abortion and the death penalty (Becker, Chasin, Chasin, Herzig, & Roth, 1995; Chasin, Herzig, Roth, Chasin, Becker, & Stains, 1996). They have been held on a national level, such as President Clinton's national dialogue about race, as well as on the local level (Lawson, Koman, & Rose, 1998).

Zuniga, Nagda, and Sevig (2002) identified three beneficial consequences of dialogues:

1. sustained communication,
2. consciousness raising, and
3. bridging differences.

Sustained communication brings together people from diverse backgrounds and with varying social privilege, status, and power, and encourages them to keep talking with one another about their differences. This involves listening, taking risks, raising questions, and moving beyond static positions. It also requires developing a language and skills for participating in these conversations. Consciousness raising implies learning about history, sociology, and cultural differences, and further suggests the importance of self-awareness and learning about the experiences of members of different groups.

Consciousness raising also has a value orientation, as it is meant to lead to social-justice commitments and changes in how people think, act, and interact. A central goal of racial dialogues is to bridge differences. The dialogue offers a space where conflicting perspectives and strong emotions can be expressed, shared, and interrogated. The conflicts that arise in these exchanges can lead to greater understanding, self-awareness, and compassion for others.

Ultimately, dialogue is an alternative to the use of force as a means of conflict resolution. These conversations can offer hope, no matter how deep the conflict or how long the odds. Most participants in the dialogue referred to at the beginning of this chapter found "that the dialogue provided hope that constructive and substantive conversations could take place across racial lines," which encouraged them to take risks (Miller & Donner, 2000, p. 46). Optimism that people can work together and challenge oppression is an essential ingredient in the struggle against racism.

WHY IS RACIAL DIALOGUE SO CHALLENGING?

Because racial dialogues are not common and are not always successful, we should endeavor to understand why. Without awareness, we are likely to have sterile or fruitless conversations or to avoid the discussions entirely. One impediment to racial dialogue is pessimism on the part of people of color who believe that they will not benefit or gain anything by raising painful feelings, and that white people will remain uninterested and unmotivated. Another barrier is that some white people lack the incentive to participate in a process that could involve conflict or painful realizations.

Part of what makes racism so pernicious is how "normal" it seems and how everyone living in a racist society is socialized into roles and internalizes beliefs, attitudes, and values shaped by racism. Yet many people are willing to risk talking about racism because they are committed to challenging it. In our view, for anyone entering one of the helping professions, engaging in these discussions is imperative, because effective cross-racial and cross-cultural work requires the ability to talk about race and racism.

Chapter 4, "The Web of Institutional Racism," described how U.S. society continues to be segregated. This is one of the fundamental reasons that people do not have cross-racial conversations about race. This is not the only reason, because even when occasions present themselves, many people are wary or skeptical. Dominant public discourse often denies and masks racism, which in a sense amounts to not talking about it at all. Racism becomes a taboo subject, a discursive "third rail."

Some people may have tried to talk about race and racism with people of other races and had bad experiences that left them feeling vulnerable and misunderstood (Stone, Patton, & Heen, 1999). When our few experiences are negative, we begin to lack trust and confidence in the process, increasing the potential for misunderstanding. If people enter into such conversations with suspicion and their guard up, they face miscommunication and missed opportunities.

In addition to their fear of being misunderstood, people are dissuaded from engaging in racial dialogues because they think their identity is on the line (Miller, Donner, & Fraser, 2004; Stone et al., 1999). Race and racism pivot on the construction of racial identity. Most people seek situations in which their identity is affirmed and valued and avoid situations in which their identity is dismissed, disrespected, and denigrated. People of color often maintain a positive identity despite social stereotyping and cultural devaluation. As we described in Chapters 1 and 6, one strategy for withstanding assaults on selfhood is to form support groups with other people of color, which can serve as a buffer (Dion, 2002; it is Solorzano et al., 2000; Tatum, 1997). Engaging in racial dialogue carries the risk of painful social interactions with white people.

Most white people see themselves as tolerant. They resist entering social situations in which their view of themselves might be challenged, in which they may be called a "racist." This can threaten a person's identity and self-concept, as well as generate cognitive dissonance from being exposed to information that challenges both their identity and their perception of the world (Miller et al., 2004).

People of color and white people alike risk being emotionally hurt or wounded in conversations about race and racism. As the opening quotes illustrate, they also are concerned about inadvertently hurting other people or having to confront friends or colleagues. Shelton and Richeson (2005) found that whites held back from participating in intergroup dialogue for fear of appearing prejudiced, undesirable, and selfish; and blacks were reticent to risk confirming negative stereotypes held by whites. So it is not surprising that people try to avoid these situations.

Nevertheless, people have a concomitant desire to understand more about themselves and others, and those in the helping professions are concerned about serving their clients, as well as having a commitment to social justice. So people do enter into such conversations or take classes and workshops in which racial dialogues are a part. But as the conversation heats up, if someone feels under attack or misunderstood or becomes angry over another person's insensitivity, what happens?

At this juncture, the risk is that people will withdraw, shut down, or become pessimistic or even despondent. As people become guarded and mistrustful, defense mechanisms such as denial or projection can kick in (Miller et al., 2004). A climate of blame and shame can overshadow attempts to listen and be self-reflective. Sometimes this leads to frustration and anger directed toward the facilitator or teacher. A conspiracy of silence can settle over the group, as its members no longer feel safe to talk or take risks (Davis, 1992; Miller et al., 2004).

Another typical roadblock to productive racial dialogues is that the learning curve for white people is much steeper (Miller & Donner, 2000). While people of color are highly aware of racism, many white people are cocooned by their white privilege. This creates a paradox: White people need space to learn and explore about racism in the world and inside of them, where they will not be attacked or humiliated. Yet, when people of color observe this unfolding, it can be painful or frustrating, particularly during the early phases of discussion, which might expose significant white naïveté about racism and blacks' ambivalence about not wanting to have to teach white people about racism. One of the biggest challenges for racial dialogues is how they can be productive for all participants, not just a learning situation for white people while people of color bare their souls to help white people "get it" (Miller & Donner, 2000). We will reflect on this dilemma as we consider how to structure successful dialogues.

CONDUCTING SUCCESSFUL RACIAL DIALOGUES

What constitutes a successful racial dialogue? A number of criteria can be employed in responding to this question. One is that participants leave the dialogue thinking they have learned something about racism. What is learned will vary considerably among participants, but this may include enhanced self-awareness; greater understanding of others' experiences; more knowledge about the dynamics of racism; and a sense that one has been heard, respected, and understood. This will not always feel good. A successful racial dialogue can cause discomfort and unease, and these feelings can be overwhelming.

As we described in Chapter 1, to be able to experience deep learning, one must leave one's "comfort zone," but it is not productive to be so uncomfortable that defense mechanisms take over and shut a person down. Researchers have found that whites and people of color have different expectations for racial dialogues (Miller & Donner, 2000; Study Circles, 1998). White people often think a dialogue has been successful if race and racism were discussed openly and respectfully and they learned something. People of color may value this experience, too, but they also have reported that they think it is important to see how the discussion has led to action, more than just talk. Other criteria for successful dialogue include less suspicion toward and greater respect for others, a reduction in negative stereotypes, and lower levels of ethnocentrism (Miller & Donner, 2000).

The dialogue mentioned at the beginning of this chapter had 53 participants—11 people of color and 42 white people (Miller & Donner, 2000). It was co-facilitated by two women—Beverly Tatum, who is African American, and Andrea Ayvazian, who is white. Both had facilitated many racial dialogues, often together. They structured the dialogue by first mapping out the contours of the conversation and then having an exchange between themselves about race and racism, describing their own feelings, struggles, fears, and missteps, using anecdotes to illustrate their points. They modeled respectful listening and the courage to take risks and make mistakes and acknowledged their different experiences and expectations by virtue of their race.

Then they then set up a "fishbowl," a circle within the larger group circle. Six chairs were placed in the fishbowl with the expectation that one chair always would remain empty so people outside of the fishbowl could enter it to participate in the conversation. This meant that if someone were to enter the group, someone else would have to leave, to maintain the empty chair. Then the facilitators asked for volunteers to fill the initial fishbowl and asked the first question: "What do you need to be able respond to cross-racial dialogue at [this school for social work]?" After 15 minutes, they asked a second question: "How do I use what I have learned here beyond the gates of [this school for social work]?"

After this, the facilitators asked those in the larger group, who had not participated in the fishbowl, to relate their reflections about what they had heard. Next the facilitators had another conversation between themselves, reflecting on the discussions that had taken place, highlighting issues and themes. This was followed by moving to a "brainstorming" activity in which the participants were asked to generate examples of active and passive racism and ways to resist racism. They concluded with a video showing faces of different ethnic and racial groups melting into one another.

The participants filled out questionnaires immediately after the event, utilizing Likert-scale responses. The results are summarized in Table 8.1. As can be seen, all participants found the event to be helpful and gave it high positive ratings. But white participants were more enthusiastic about how helpful the event was and significantly more positive about learning to better talk about race and racism, being exposed to new perspectives, and feeling more motivated to engage in anti-racism activities. White participants also indicated that they felt more challenged about their feelings and opinions about

TABLE 8.1 | RESULTS OF QUESTIONNAIRE

Percent of Respondents Who Strongly Agree (1) or Agree (2).

	Total	People of Color[1] (n = 11)	White People (n = 42)
I found this event to be helpful	98.1	90.9	100
My experience in this dialogue increased my desire to participate in further racial dialogues	98.2	90.9	100
A person's race is a central element in one's experience in this society	98.1	90.9	100
Racial dialogues are one important way to deal with racism in this country	100	100	100
This dialogue increased my understanding of how people from a racial background different from my own think and feel about racial issues at SSW	77.4	45.5	85.7
Perspectives were put forward that I had not considered before	56.6	18.2	66.7
The dialogue increased my hope that people from different racial backgrounds can listen to each other	92.4	72.8	97.6
The dialogue gave me hope that people from different racial backgrounds can learn from each other	90.5	54.6	100
My experience with this event will better enable me to talk about racial issues on campus and in the classroom	80.8	36.4	92.7
The dialogue was just an exchange of monologues	0	0	0
The dialogue complements other anti-racism activities on campus	86.3	72.8	90
The dialogue helped me clarify some of my own thoughts and feelings about race and racism	84.6	45.5	95.1
The dialogue challenged some of my feelings and opinions about race	55.8	27.3	63.4
Participating in this event motivated me to want to become more involved in anti-racism efforts	82.7	45.5	92.7
The facilitators were skilled at assisting the expression of diverse points of view	100	100	100

[1] African American, Asian, and Latina

From "More Than Just Talk: The Use of Racial Dialogue to Combat Racism," by J. Miller and S. Donner, *Social Work with Groups*, (2000), 23(1), 31–53.

race and racism and more hopeful that people from different racial backgrounds can listen to one another. At the same time, more than 90% of the participants of color found the experience to be helpful and wanted to participate in more dialogues, and more than 70% indicated that the dialogue had given them hope that people from different racial backgrounds can learn from one another.

The results of this dialogue offer an example of one way that a discussion can be structured. The responses on the questionnaire indicate that the experience was different for whites and people of color, but the majority of the participants seemed to get something from it and, at the very least, this would motivate them to participate in further racial conversations. So what can we extract from this and the experience of others to suggest ways to manage effective dialogues?

IMPORTANT DIMENSIONS OF DIALOGUE

Before turning to how to conduct successful dialogues, some dimensions and parameters to consider in planning such conversations will be helpful.

- *The participants.* Dialogues can occur in small groups or large groups. People may know each other already or be brought together specifically to participate in the dialogue. This will affect the dynamics of the discussion as well as follow-up to the conversation. Some dialogues feature prominent people, such as President Clinton's national dialogue on race, and others consist of ordinary people sitting down and talking with one another.
- *The sponsor and the location.* The credibility of a dialogue often rests on the sponsoring organization and the perceived motives and intentions for holding a dialogue. If people tend to trust and respect the sponsor, this is more likely to carry over to the actual discussion. The location also is important, so all participants feel comfortable. For example, holding a dialogue in a public school may feel more familiar and comfortable for some participants than others; conversely, holding a dialogue at a public housing project might seem more secure for some and less genial for others.
- *The duration and frequency.* Some racial dialogues, such as the one we have described in this chapter, are single, contained events. Others are structured encounters that meet over time, often following a curriculum (Study Circles, 1998). A dialogue can take place as part of an ongoing class or as a part of a 2-day workshop. This dimension influences what is discussed, how it is talked about, and how deep the conversation will become, and also can affect who can participate or wants to participate.
- *The context.* What is the context for having the dialogue? Is it in response to tensions or conflict? Is it being offered to improve understanding in an effort to avoid clashes? Is it part of an organization's desire to be more culturally competent or to engage in anti-racism activities? Is the discussion the vision of a few people, or is it part of an organizational or community movement to increase interracial understanding? Is the

dialogue a required part of professional training, in which all students are expected to participate?

Whatever the reasons for having the dialogue, the context in which it occurs shapes the expectations and the actual discourse. Dialogue has more value and resonance when it takes place in the context of a strong institutional or community commitment to challenge racism.

- *The goals.* Clarifying the goals of a racial dialogue is helpful. Is the dialogue being used for educational purposes or to resolve conflict between two clashing groups? Is the goal to encourage people to think in a more complex and nuanced way about complicated issues or to motivate them to become more socially active? Will the dialogue have a follow-up, or is it a single event?

  For example, the dialogue described was a single event, whereas Study Circles (1997) offer a racial dialogue curriculum for interracial small groups that meet simultaneously for five sessions and conclude with a large-group session for all participants to plan action strategies.

  These are examples of goals that can shape how a dialogue is set and determine what questions are asked. Some dialogues combine many of these objectives. If one dialogue is attempting to accomplish too much, however, it can become confusing, so prioritizing goals can provide coherence and focus.

MODELS AND STAGES OF INTERGROUP DIALOGUE

Zuniga and Nagda (2001) have created a typology of four different types of intergroup dialogue.

1. *Collective inquiry model.* This model encourages participants to suspend their usual assumptions and judgments and examine challenging issues, such as race and racism, from new perspectives. In many ways, this model is one attempted in many educational classrooms teaching about diversity across the country. The Public Conversations Project (Becker et al., 1995; Chasin et al., 1996) falls within this category. With this model, participants all are given a chance to listen and respond to questions about challenging social issues. Engaging in this process will help participants loosen rigid thinking and be able to see and understand different perspectives. Ultimately, collectively interrogating and examining an issue will facilitate meaningful relationships.

2. *Critical-dialogical education models.* These models assume a social-justice perspective with multiple goals: increasing knowledge and understanding; raising awareness about social inequities; consciousness raising about privilege and oppression, which includes self-introspection and gaining perspectives about intergroup dynamics; and creating alliances among participants that lead to social action. Although these models are used primarily in classrooms, they also are found in campuswide orientation programs. They are allied with critical race theory, which is a major theoretical perspective informing this book.

3. *Community building and social action models.* These models seek to engage community members, citizens, and workplace employees in conversation about big issues, such as racism, but primarily to ground the discussion in local concerns and to mobilize people to take constructive collective action to redress social problems. A good example of this model is Study Circles (1997, 1998), summarized in Appendix 8-1.

4. *Conflict resolution and peace-building models.* These models apply when distinct groups are in conflict with one another, usually racial/ethnic, religious, or national groups. The goals are to identify sources of conflict, to understand competing group narratives, to engage in conflict mediation and resolution, and to eventually generate action plans that reduce conflict and promote intergroup understanding, healing, and resolution. Examples of this model are attempts to improve Korean American and African American relations in Los Angeles (Norman, 1994), to work with Arabs and Jews in the Middle East (Bargal & Bar, 1994), and to improve relations between Catholics and Protestants in Derry/Londonderry (Templegrove Action Research Limited, 1996). The model of racial reconciliation summarized at the end of this chapter (Yamamoto, 1999) falls within this category.

Zuniga et al. (2002) have developed a model for intergroup dialogue along the lines of the critical-dialogic educational model (see Appendix 8-2). It is designed as a class or ongoing workshop for small groups of 12 to 16 students who correspond to both targeted and agent identities within the topic being discussed, and if possible, both should be equally represented. The classes are co-facilitated and again, the facilitators represent each of the social-identity groups within the context of the dialogue topic. So for race and racism, the co-facilitators ideally would include a facilitator of color and a white facilitator.

All four of the models presented above have stages in common, although what actually transpires with each stage differs. Zuniga and Nagda (2001) represent this comparatively and schematically in Table 8.2.

The first stage creates an environment for dialogue and sets the stage for the type of dialogue that will ensue. The second stage involves developing a common base, which can include defining terms, identifying the issues on which to focus, clarifying the nature of problems, and identifying beliefs and assumptions that participants bring to the table. The critical-dialogic model places more emphasis on exploring the complexity of social identity at this stage.

In the third stage participants explore questions, issues, or conflicts, which may include consideration of conflict and social justice, the meaning and significance of social identity, and the nuances of intergroup dynamics. The final stage in all of the models is for the group to move from discussion to some form of alliance-building and action, whether that means changing the way people lead their everyday lives, planning local community events, or committing to major action plans to resolve conflicts and further social justice.

TABLE 8.2 | STAGES OF INTERGROUP DIALOGUE ACROSS MODELS AND APPLICATIONS

Stage	Collective Inquiry Model	Critical-Dialogic Education Model	Community Building and Social Action Model	Conflict Resolution and Peace Building Model
1. Setting an environment for dialog	Build a "container" for dialogue for safety and trust issues to emerge Develop group consensus on purpose, mission, and structure	Develop guidelines for dialogue Begin relationship building	Discuss, clarify, and set ground rules Share personal beliefs and experiences about race and race relations	Orient group members Decide to engage in dialogue
2. Developing a common base	Explore beliefs and assumptions leading to public suspension of judgments Talk about personal, work-related, or general topics	Develop a common language Explore multiple social identities—commonalities and differences	Ask what the state of race relations in our community is Ask what the nature of the problem with race is	Map and name problems and relationships Explore and clarify issues and group development
3. Exploring questions, issues, or conflicts	Increase suspension of judgment and trust in the dialogue process Inquiry and creativity flow in the container Talk about personal, work-related, or general topics	Explore and talk about issues of conflict and social justice Explore in and out group dynamics and issues	Ask what main changes participants would like to see in the community Ask what kind of public policies can help	Continue clarification of issues Probe relationships to choose direction for change Build scenarios—experience a change in the relationship
4. Moving from dialogue to action	Assess experiences Talk about transferring learning and skills into daily life	Plan action Envision and seek opportunities for action Build alliances	Ask what participants will do, as individuals and with others, to make a difference	Plan action Act together to make change happen Monitor and evaluate

"Design Considerations in Intergroup Dialogue," by X. Zúñiga & B.A. Nagda, *Intergroup Dialogue: Deliberative Democracy in School, College, Community and Workplace* (Ann Arbor: University of Michigan Press, 2001).

| BOX 8.1 | KEY INGREDIENTS FOR SUCCESSFUL RACIAL DIALOGUES |

- *Skilled facilitation*—preferably biracial or multiracial teams
- *Egalitarian space*—ensuring a group composition of parity of people of color and white participants, or at least having a "critical mass" of either group (30%)
- *Establishing a dialogic framework*—generating group norms that facilitate respectful listening and self reflection
- *Understanding the historical, social, and political context in which the conversation occurs*—presenting group narratives; distributing advanced readings for group discussion
- *Creating conceptual categories*—such as Racial Identity Development, Worldviews, Cultural Values, predicting strong emotions; seeing the dialogue as part of an ongoing process
- *Having mechanisms to deal with stuck conversations*
- *Engendering hope; considering solutions as well as problems*—considering strategies, action plans, and individual commitments

Source: Adapted from "Talking When Talking Is Tough: Taking on Conversations About Race, Sexual Orientation, Gender, Class, and Other Aspects of Social Identity," by J. Miller, S. Donner, and E. Fraser, *Smith College Studies in Social Work* (2004), *74*(2), pp. 377–392.

MANAGING EFFECTIVE RACIAL DIALOGUES

The important ingredients for establishing fruitful conversations are summarized as follows.

- *Skilled facilitation.* This is one of the most important factors in fostering a successful racial dialogue, often determining if a dialogue is a positive learning experience that engages participants or a negative encounter that wounds people, leading to alienation and withdrawal. Preferably, facilitators should be from the outside rather than members of the group. Group members should be free to participate rather than have to take on the dual role of facilitator and participant. The facilitator should not be someone who is in a position to evaluate participants, as this will inhibit honest conversation.

    Whenever possible, the dialogues should have co-facilitators and biracial or multiracial teams. Co-facilitators can plan together, support one another, and act as live consultants. They also can model respectful cross-racial conversation. Two facilitators can demonstrate sharing and collaboration and offer a variety of role models for various people in the group to connect with (Miller et al., 2004). Ideally, facilitators should know something about racism and about the nature of the participants in the conversation and have skills in presenting, facilitation, mediation, and creative problem solving. Good interpersonal skills are always an asset.

- *Egalitarian space.* A racial dialogue cuts against the grain, in that inequality and talking past one another is more the norm in many social venues. Racial conversations can take place in groups that are racially mixed, all white, or all people of color. The conversations should be adapted to the nature of the group and emphasize the experiences of the participants, not those of people who are not present for the discussion. Thus, for an all-white group, suitable topics for discussion include white privilege, or stereotypes, or the feelings associated with being white. For a group that is composed of people of color, topics might be internalized racism, racism between people of color, strategies for resisting white racism, and how to survive in predominantly white environments.

  Notwithstanding the benefits of homogenous caucus groups, we ultimately must move to interracial dialogues—and this is where egalitarian space becomes important. A racial dialogue composed of mostly white people and only a few people of color is not advisable, as this re-creates the demography of many social situations in which people of color find themselves. In such circumstances, the danger is that people of color will become marginalized as the needs of white students dominate, or find themselves in the roles of teachers or as exemplars for the experience of the racial "other."

  Proportion matters. Davis and Proctor (1989) found that African Americans prefer dialogue groups with equal numbers of whites and blacks, whereas white people feel more comfortable in groups that reflect the demographics of larger society. Miller et al. (2004) recommend striving for parity between people of color and white participants, but otherwise at least one-third of the group composed of people of color. Parity presents a greater likelihood of a balanced and complex conversation, as participants will be more likely to speak up, take risks, and present a greater variety of viewpoints.

- *Establishing a dialogic framework.* Many people are not used to talking about race and racism and can feel anxious when engaging in such conversations. And the expression of strong emotions can make people uncomfortable listening to other people and different perspectives. Sometimes participants deliver prepackaged speeches and are reluctant to embrace new ideas, grandstanding on soapboxes. To create a climate that fosters dialogue and deep listening, norms and guidelines should be established for discussion, and participants asked to abide by them (Miller et al., 2004; Muldoon, 1997).

  Miller et al. (2004) have suggested guidelines for establishing a dialogic framework. Facilitators may want to work with the group to generate the norms for discussion, as this leads to greater ownership. The facilitator also might suggest important guidelines if the group fails to identify them on their own, and to remind them that the purpose of the conversation is to listen and explore, promoting what Stone et al. (1999) have referred to as a "learning conversation" in which people do not already know all the answers. This promotes a stance of genuine curiosity, encourages empathy for people and positions that are different, and a commitment to self-reflection and respect for others (Miller et al., 2004).

| BOX 8.2 | NORMS FOR ESTABLISHING A DIALOGIC FRAMEWORK |

- *Maintaining confidentiality.* Outside of the group it is acceptable, even useful, to share the themes that emerged within the group, but it is important to strive to maintain the confidentiality of who said what about whom, particularly when participants have expressed strong emotions.

- *Sharing time and not taking up too much air space.* A few individuals dominating the discussion will choke and stifle a dialogue. Although facilitators should monitor the group process, group members should agree on this norm and observe it to ensure contributions by all members.

- *Speaking for oneself and not representing one's group.* In a dialogue, people should speak from their own experiences and not try to represent the views of others or think they must speak for all people of their racial or ethnic group. "I" statements are helpful here.

- *Listening carefully to others.* Dialogue depends on listening. Frequently, in other types of conversation, people are thinking about their responses while another person is talking. Allowing a moment of reflective silence after each speaker is a good idea. If listening is problematic, the facilitator might ask each speaker to paraphrase the remarks of the previous speaker to foster careful listening.

- *Striving for open-mindedness.* Group members should be asked to reflect on their usual positions and stances and to acknowledge areas of ambivalence and ambiguity. The facilitator might remind participants that if everyone already knows the answers, there is no need for dialogue.

- *Challenging behavior and ideas without attacking people.* Meaningful dialogue requires an exchange of ideas, including disagreements. If group members start attacking one another, however, participants will be less likely to take the risk of participating and the conversation may shut down. The distinction between challenging behavior and ideas without putting down the speaker is subtle but important. The facilitator should remind participants that everyone is imperfect and that they are permitted to take risks and make mistakes because this is how we learn and grow.

Source: Adapted from "Talking When Talking Is Tough: Taking on Conversations About Race, Sexual Orientation, Gender, Class, and Other Aspects of Social Identity," by J. Miller, S. Donner, and E. Fraser, *Smith College Studies in Social Work* (2004), 74(2), pp. 377–392.

- *Understanding the historical, social, and political context in which the conversation occurs.* Conversations about race and racism inevitably draw upon the racial axis of social identity (Miller et al., 2004). As these identities are grounded in subjective interpretations and group narratives about history and the nature of sociopolitical reality, some time must be allotted to discuss these topics. One way to do this is to allow different groups represented in the dialogue group to present their social and historical narratives while members of other groups listen (Bargal & Bar, 1994; Miller et al., 2004; Norman, 1994).

Another way to prepare the ground is to distribute articles before-hand, for participants to read and comment on. Chapters from revisionist history books, such as Takaki's (1993) *A Different Mirror,* can offer counter-narratives to prevailing historical discourses and elicit critical thinking and historically grounded dialogue.

- *Creating conceptual categories.* Concepts can help participants to cogni-tively grasp common challenges and dynamics that appear in racial dialogues. They can be used to predict misunderstandings before they occur, which renders them less disturbing and toxic. The nature of racism is that people have had different experiences and varied understandings about the role of race in American society. Strong feelings are attached to these differences, as well as perceived threats to one's social identity (Stone et al., 1999).

  Many concepts presented in this book can be valuable for promoting racial dialogues. The formation of racial identity is one such notion that can help participants understand varying phases of racial identity development and how these influence self-concept, emotions, meaning making, and interpersonal needs and relationships.

  Other examples of useful concepts include differences in worldviews and cultural values (Sue & Sue, 1990) and naming certain defense mechanisms, such as denial and projection (Miller & Schamess, 2000). Predicting strong emotions and perceived threats to identity also may reduce their potency. The conversation should be seen as part of an ongoing process in which participants engaged before the actual dialogue and will continue to do afterward, so they will face less pressure to solve and resolve everything in this encounter.

- *Having mechanisms to deal with "stuck" conversations.* Facilitators should enter racial dialogues with the expectation that misunderstandings, conflicts, or withdrawal and disengagement may arise. Fortunately, a number of strategies are available to prevent or respond to jammed conversations.

  1. *Divide into caucus groups.* *Temporarily* dividing the participants into separate caucus groups of people of color and white people allows them to discuss painful and challenging material without fear of hurting others or being attacked when expressing vulnerabilities. Whites can discuss racist stereotypes and ways to respond to them, while people of color can talk about their mistrust of white people or the psychic wounds of racism.

     One problem with dividing into caucus groups is that biracial or multiracial people may feel torn about which group to join, or invalidated as no one group represents the complexity of their identities. Another problem is that interracial relationships and friendships are interrupted temporarily by dividing the group in this fashion. Being flexible and allowing participants to choose which caucus group they wish to work in can be helpful, while also acknowledging that tensions can arise by dividing the group in this manner.

     A mechanism for summarizing the caucus group discussions and sharing them with the larger group is important. This should include the chance to debrief about what the experience of dividing up was like for different people. The large-group discussions about both the process and the content of caucus groups can uncover important issues and emotions that occur in daily social intercourse.

2. *Take a "fishbowl" approach.* We have already shared the use of this method in the racial dialogue described by Miller and Donner (2000). Having a smaller circle with five to eight people talking in front of a larger audience can allow for more focused and intimate conversation. An empty chair allows people outside of the fishbowl to enter the conversation. Allowing the larger group to comment on the conversation observed in the fishbowl is important.

3. *Use structured "go-rounds."* Sometimes dialogues become heated or unproductive when a few individuals become locked in conflict. This can freeze a conversation and lead to disengagement and alienation. One way of preventing this is to ensure that all participants are given a chance to speak by sequentially asking each person to respond to a question that has been posed. When using this method, facilitators should institute a "pass rule," so anyone who does not want to speak at a given moment can pass and wait for another round of questions. Going around in a circle also cuts down on reactive, defensive, and attacking responses and usually leads to a more complex and nuanced conversation (Becker et al., 1995; Chasin et al., 1996).

4. *Use structured exercises.* Having participants engage in a structured activity, such as brainstorming, can unify them in working toward a common target or goal. Or, when difficult material, such as white privilege, is being covered, a helpful exercise involves having participants stand up and walk a step forward as questions are posed about access to education, housing, jobs, and other resources, as this visually conveys the differential impact of racism and stimulates thoughtful and reflective conversation.

- *Engendering hope, considering solutions as well as problems.* Racism is pernicious but not hopeless, a common state of affairs but not an inevitable one. If people are led to believe that nothing can be done about it, they will feel demoralized and discouraged from taking action:

> Thorny and sensitive discussions about social identity can leave participants feeling dispirited and overwhelmed if the discussion ends in a thicket of unresolved problems; thereby fostering tendencies to blame rather than take responsibility. (Miller et al., 2004, p. 390)

This can be the consequence of a racial dialogue that discusses only problems and does not offer solutions. At least part of the racial dialogue should be devoted to considering resiliency, empowerment, and ways to dismantle racism. It must consider strategies, action plans, and individual commitments to engage in future anti-racism work. Racial dialogues are valuable, but they are not an end in themselves. They are just one part of a larger process of decommissioning racism.

RACIAL RECONCILIATION
AND INTERRACIAL JUSTICE

Perhaps the highest aspiration of racial dialogue is that it will lead to racial reconciliation and racial justice. Most dialogues will not achieve this. Reaching this goal would require commitment at the highest and deepest levels, and the power to implement restorative justice and make reparations. We will briefly consider the steps in this process here so readers can imagine what the process will look like when it does eventually occur.

Yamamoto (1999) has conceptualized this as a four-step process, which we will employ in our discussion. It refers to what has to happen on the institutional, discursive, and intergroup levels, as well as between individuals.

RECOGNITION

One of the most painful facets of racism in the United States is the denial and lack of awareness and acknowledgement by many white people. Racial reconciliation cannot begin until we recognize the historical and collective legacy of racism and acknowledge and validate the wounds and scars it has wrought and the terrible damage it has inflicted on generations of people of color. This acceptance precedes any formal apologies. White people will have to listen to the narratives of racism and its consequences as told by people of color, without denying, negating, or rejecting these stories. This is the foundation of racial rapprochement.

RESPONSIBILITY

Taking responsibility for colluding with racism follows the recognition of racism. This often is a difficult step, as many white people do not concede their racial privilege, and this is accompanied by common mechanisms of denial, such as slavery being a thing of the past, or distancing through statements such as, "My relatives never owned slaves."

Responsibility in the process of racial reconciliation goes beyond individual culpability. It refers to group exploitation and domination and the racial privileges that settlers and immigrants alike accepted as they were socially constructed as white. Taking responsibility means acknowledging the racial contract, the failure of Reconstruction, the litany of broken treaties with Native Americans, the exclusion of Chinese immigrants, the placing of innocent Japanese citizens in concentration camps, and the many other instances of racism. It also means taking responsibility for the web of racism today and committing to dismantling it.

RECONSTRUCTION

Only after the first two steps have been achieved can a person work on reconstructing the relationships torn asunder by racism. This is where formal apologies can be offered. Yamamoto, however, warns that apologies can be self-serving and a way of avoiding responsibility, and are susceptible to insincerity, misapprehension, poor timing, and inadequacy. Thus, apologies should be grounded in the first two steps, recognition and responsibility.

A sincere apology involves seeking forgiveness. Healing will not occur unless this forgiveness is requested and the apology is accepted in turn. This does not mean that there is absolution or a universal pardon. Rather, these are significant gestures by those who have benefited, as well as those who have suffered from racism to restore relationships and institute justice.

REPARATION

Apologies and forgiveness are important steps in the process of racial reconciliation and can lead to the final stage of reparations. The notion of reparations is complex and controversial. If material reparations were offered, who would receive them and where would the line of eligibility be drawn? What would be a fair amount of financial or economic reparations? These are complex questions, with no simple answers, yet they are not insurmountable barriers to having race-based reparations.

Reparations, as conceptualized by Yamamoto, include material reparations but also refer to attitudinal changes and shifts in interpersonal relationships and societal interactions. To respond only to the historical legacy of racism without dismantling the web of institutional racism, racist discourses, and racist attitudes is insufficient. Resources have to be redeployed.

Even if the government pledges itself to such actions, this does not ensure that the web of racism will dissolve. Local governments, institutions, organizations, policies, practices, intergroup relations and individual attitudes and behaviors are slow and resistant to change. Nevertheless, as we learned from the successes of the Great Society in the 1960s, however incomplete and transitory these may be, when the federal government makes a commitment of this nature, it can lead to profound social changes.

CONCLUSION

Talking about race and racism is challenging. Racial dialogue usually does not occur spontaneously and requires planning, resources, commitments, and skilled facilitation. Dialogue is an alternative to alienation and conflict. It is a tool that helping professionals can use to understand ourselves, the people we help, and the social world we all inhabit. Racial dialogues engage people in a process that renders visible what often is unseen, puts words to what is unsaid, and has the potential to connect people of all races to work together as allies to dismantle racism.

If local dialogues occur in communities, schools, religious organizations, and workplaces, they may generate momentum for larger-scale, society-wide conversations. Ultimately, the hope of having a genuine national process of racial reconciliation may be a dream deferred, but not a dream denied.

EXERCISE 8.1 PREPARING FOR DIALOGUE

1. Think of a topic pertaining to race and racism that you would like to discuss with others.
2. Who do you think should be part of this conversation? How will you ensure sufficient balance between people targeted and privileged by racism?
3. What dialogue norms or ground rules would you find helpful?
4. What preparatory reading would be useful for the dialogue? What concepts will be useful to introduce before the conversation? Are there historical or social narratives that should be shared early in the discussion?
5. What dialogue model would you like to use?
6. Who might facilitate this dialogue?
7. Are you concerned that the conversation might become "stuck"?
8. What mechanisms or interventions will be helpful if the conversation does stall?
9. What would you like to see come out of the dialogue? How might the conversation be followed up?

RESPONSES TO RACISM IN THE COMMUNITY

CHAPTER **9**

CHAPTER CONTENTS

This chapter begins with the fictional community of Millville, a composite community based on our research and activism. Throughout this chapter, Millville will be used to illustrate how racism is manifested in a community and how human service professionals can respond to it. Millville's fictional residents are based on people we have interviewed and worked with, but every community is unique and the dynamics of race and racism vary considerably in different communities and regions. We encourage you to plug your own community into this chapter and to explore how the dynamics of racism are manifested where you work and live.

This chapter will build on basic skills of macro and community-based practice and an analysis of the web of racism, described in Chapter 4. Community-based practice, as with work with individual, families, and groups, relies on a strong history and assessment, carefully planned strategy, and ongoing evaluation. As our description of Millville illustrates, racism in the community is manifested in many ways—in neighborhoods, schools, self-concepts, consciousness, and psyches. Racism shapes where people live, the educational opportunities, occupational options, and economic fortunes. Racism leads to intergroup tensions and conflicts, as well as clashes within groups. Combined with poverty and lack of economic opportunity, racism leads to unsafe streets, so people stay indoors, which makes the streets even more dangerous.

Racial and ethnic groups are blamed for the very urban decay and economic deterioration that plagues their lives and circumscribes their potential. Racism causes people to feel disrespected, unwanted, and wary of the motives of others. It can cause feelings of powerlessness. It can fuel anger and alienation. Places, events, and murals become hyper-charged symbols with meanings that validate or threaten social identity.

Those in the helping professions—social workers, community nurses, psychologists, guidance counselors, community organizers—work with systems, institutions, and programs, as well as with individuals, groups, and families. Workers use clinical and interpersonal skills coupled with their ability to work systemically. Their efforts to effect change must respond to local conditions, but with an eye toward national policies and global trends, which provide the context for inexorable historical patterns such as the deindustrialization that swept the United States and stranded many cities such as Millville with high social needs, lack of adequate jobs, and reductions in social and health services.

MILLVILLE

Millville is a mid-sized city, a deindustrialized mill town in the northeastern United States. Although the mills have closed, their hulking buildings remain. The city used to be mostly white, with people of predominantly Irish, French Canadian, and Polish descent, but now a growing population of Latinos, mostly Puerto Rican, constitutes a third of the city's population. Many of them live in the low-rent tenement housing abutting the abandoned mills and proximate to downtown. Millville has had a small African American community ever since the mills first opened in the late 19th century, currently constituting about 5% of the population. Most African Americans live in a low-rent area known as the Lincoln Square district, about a half-mile from downtown on the other side of an unused canal. A small number of middle-class African Americans live in a predominantly white, middle-class area.

Children of color constitute 80% of the public school population. The poverty rate in this community has escalated and now is one of the highest in the state. This is accompanied by high rates of unemployment, illiteracy, school drop-out, single-parent families, low-birthweight infants, teen pregnancy, HIV infection, and reports of child abuse and neglect. The Puerto Rican population tends to be younger and less educated than both black and white populations, with less capital, fewer resources, and less access to jobs and political power. There are no elected Puerto Rican officials and only one African American city councilor of the 14 at-large positions. Of a total of 90 city officials, there are three Puerto Rican and five African American city appointments. Gangs roam the city.

Millville has gone from being an industrial city to a social service city. The building that formerly housed its largest department store is now headquarters for the Department of Social Services. All residents agree that downtown Millville is not safe at night. The city's biggest cultural event is an annual St. Patrick's Day parade, which now marches through many predominantly Hispanic and African American neighborhoods.

SNAPSHOTS OF MILLVILLE RESIDENTS

MARTIN Martin, who is white and upper middle class, owns his own home and lives with his family in a mostly white neighborhood of stately homes on a hill. He is committed to remaining in Millville, where he grew up, but is concerned about the economic deterioration of the city and issues of safety. His children attend private school.

MIGUEL Miguel, a Puerto Rican man, owns a home in a lower-middle-class neighborhood, where neighbors are white and Puerto Rican. The neighborhood had been predominantly white but now is increasingly Latino. Miguel is a police officer in another city. He and his wife grew up in Millville after their parents migrated from Puerto Rico. He ran for city councilor and lost. During the campaign, when he entered white neighborhoods he had to wear a t-shirt with his campaign logo emblazoned on it so that residents did not continually call the police. He has battled the school department for trying to place his children in bilingual education classes, even though they were being reared in an English-speaking home. He is frustrated when he is followed in stores while shopping and is insulted that grocery stores label Hispanic food as "ethnic food" and put it next to the pet food.

SARAH   Sarah, who is white, divorced, and a mother of two, grew up downtown but now lives in a subdivision on the outskirts of the city in a completely white neighborhood of small, lower-middle-class homes. She works for the water department of Millville. Enraged by the deterioration of her old neighborhood, she blames this on the new, Hispanic residents, whom she believes do not care about their environment. She wanted to continue to reside within the city limits but is wary of living too close to downtown. One of her sons attends parochial school and the other, who has a learning disability, was transferred to the public school system.

YALDIRA   Yaldira is a 21-year-old Puerto Rican woman with three children. She was born in Puerto Rico and speaks English with difficulty. Her partner has found work in Puerto Rico and lives there while Yaldira remains in Millville, caring for her children and her parents, who give the appearance of being elderly although they are in their 40s. Her father used to work as a janitor but now is disabled and legally blind. Yaldira did obtain her high school diploma after being in mostly bilingual classes. She does not have a job outside of her home, and her lack of proficient English is problematic for many potential employers. Both she and her parents are wary of leaving their apartments during the day and rarely venture out at night, as they perceive the city as dangerous and unsafe.

HERBERT   Herbert, an African American man, grew up in Millville and presently is the director of a large anti-poverty/civil rights organization in the city. He was reared in what is now a mixed neighborhood of African Americans and Puerto Ricans but currently lives in the same, predominantly white neighborhood as Martin. He has been working with local business leaders to try to form a consortium that will improve the high school graduation rate and college acceptance rate. He graduated from a regional parochial high school, and his children are attending college.

RACISM IN MILLVILLE

Racism plays out in various ways in Millville, as shown in the following brief examples. A group of schoolchildren painted a public mural, attempting to display the joining of cultures and nationalities in Millville. The mural included both the American flag and the Puerto Rican flag. A white city councilor was offended that the Puerto Rican flag was higher than the U.S flag in the mural and threatened to paint over the whole thing. On their own, the children repainted the flags as the councilor preferred, before she could deface their artwork.

A white man who was running for mayor of Millville ran an advertisement on a billboard depicting a Hispanic-looking young man smoking a cigarette. The caption read, "The people who should read this can't. We have a problem. Our community isn't working together: In fact, a whole lot of us are not working at all."

THE DYNAMICS OF RACISM IN COMMUNITIES

In this chapter we will briefly review structural and institutional manifestations of racism in communities, considering the relationship between social identity and group membership, and the phenomenology of racism in the community—how it is experienced and what it means to people. Then we will consider the value of the concepts of social cohesion, community efficacy, and community integrity for helping professionals engaged in community-based work that confronts racism.

STRUCTURAL/INSTITUTIONAL RACISM

The Millville vignette describes a small city that is severely segregated residentially. Some neighborhoods, such as the one where Miguel lives, could be described as "transition zones" of racial integration, but even these neighborhoods have a tendency toward segregation. As more Puerto Ricans move in, more whites move out. New tract developments are carved out, such as the predominantly white enclaves where Sarah resides. Other whites move to outlying communities, spurring further ribbon development, where homes, malls, and highways are strung out increasingly farther from urban centers.

Many whites still living in the city remove their children from the public school system and place them in private and parochial schools, which diminishes community support for quality public education. Meanwhile, poor people of color find themselves stranded increasingly in high-poverty, mostly nonwhite neighborhoods, where the quality of public education is poor. They face obstacles to finding jobs, and many services that make up the infrastructure of a community (banks, stores, health providers, public transportation) and that generate community capital (wealth, knowledge, resources, recreation) are in short supply.

RESIDENTIAL SEGREGATION We will recap some relevant factors of the discussion of residential segregation in Chapter 4. Across the nation, the specific dynamics of residential segregation vary from community to community, although they have some trends in common. "Ghettoization" is increasing as the number of census tracts with 40% or more of the population living in poverty doubled between 1970 and 2000 and the population of people of color living in these neighborhoods increased accordingly (Polikoff, 2004).

High concentrations of poor people of color live in hypersegregated, impoverished neighborhoods, increasingly alienated and isolated from mainstream society, with upward mobility a receding tide and downward mobility pulling like a strong undertow (Massey & Denton, 1993; Wilson, 1996). Rusk (cited by Polikoff, 2004) describes it as if a crowd of people is trying to run up a descending escalator; a few make it to the top, but most are dragged downward.

Subcultures evolve, and informal economies and services develop to fill the economic and social vacuum. Those who are working or trying to buy homes have to rely on loan sharks and predatory mortgage dealers who charge exorbitant interest rates and set financial traps, depleting the fragile resources of families (Association of Community Organizations for Reform Now [ACORN], 2002; Calhoun & Bailey, 2005). As supermarkets move out, small grocery stores, with higher prices and sparse selections of healthy foods, take their place. Drug dealing increases and neighborhoods become more dangerous, which inhibits civic and community life.

George Galster of Wayne State University has articulated a vicious cycle that ensues (as cited in Polikoff, 2004). The spatial, economic, and social isolation leads to "behavioral adaptations" for residents, who are trying to survive under increasingly harsh conditions. The media then highlight these "deviant" lifestyles, fostering negative stereotypes and depicting poor people of color as different from mainstream Americans and culturally aberrant. This, in turn, validates preexisting white prejudice, such as that expressed by Sarah in the vignette, and fuels bigotry and social distancing, which promotes white discrimination and withdrawal from support of neighborhoods and public services, further deepening the plight of those stranded in the ghetto.

POLITICAL POWER

Residential and economic exclusion intersects with a lack of political power. Millville has no elected Hispanic city councilors and few African Americans or Latinos in appointed political positions. As we described in Chapter 4, at-large systems of voting can prevent minorities from gaining political power. Ward-style voting also can dilute political power, as people of color are confined to overcrowded, dense city wards, where they elect one or two local politicians but are unable to have any influence in the many other districts where they are underrepresented. The result is a city hall where people of color have diminished influence. The situation only worsens with state and national elections, as described in Chapter 4, in which people of color are even more severely underrepresented.

Lack of political power is a crucial dimension of community racism. Raskin (2005) has identified racism as an ongoing current in American political history. He and Wills (2003) argue that, from the beginning, Southern slaveholders were given disproportionate political power under the three-fifths rule. This rule allowed plantation owners to have an additional three-fifths vote for each of their slaves when calculating congressional apportionments. The South (and rural West) also benefited from the electoral college system used in presidential elections, with its winner-take-all policy, which has given disproportionate power to less populated states. This fact was evident in the 2000 election when the large, urbanized states predominantly voted for Al Gore, along with a plurality of the popular vote, while the Electoral College favored George Bush.

And the problems with electoral fairness go deeper than a flawed electoral system. People living in poor communities of color are much more likely to have outdated voting technology—with a greater likelihood of lost or miscounted votes. And there also have been outright attempts to intimidate voters of color and suppress their votes both before and during Election Day (Cohen, 2004; Fritz, 2001; Raskin, 2005; Waxman et al., 2001). This can be done by offering misinformation about where and when elections are being held, deceiving people about their voter eligibility, and intimidating voters with challenges as they attempt to vote (Overton, 2005).

Attempts to purge voter rolls of convicted felons also have been documented (Raskin, 2005), which presents two problems (Boyd, 2001; Overton, 2005; Raskin, 2005; Sengupta, 2000):

1. People often are falsely accused and are not allowed to vote.
2. With the disproportionate numbers of people of color who are incarcerated, and with the increasing trend in states to deny voting privileges for a convicted felon's lifetime, many people of color are *legally* being denied their right to vote.

CORPORATE EXECUTIVES Along with having less political power at all levels of government, people of color are dramatically underrepresented as high-level corporate executives, particularly as CEOs; and many groups of color—particularly African Americans, Native Americans, and various Hispanic groups—are poorly represented among small business owners. Corporate and business leaders work together with elected and appointed politicians to make decisions that strongly shape a community's destiny. Together they decide what programs are funded, where things get built, which social service agencies are worthy of capital campaigns, where hospitals and health care will be located, where highways will be constructed, and through which neighborhoods bus routes will pass. Local corporate elites also have influence over the direction of charitable funding, through mechanisms such as the United Way.

To be sure, politicians and the local business elite do not always have the same agenda, and how they exercise their power varies considerably in different communities. Some communities work vigorously to engage all citizens in civic life, while others actively exclude and marginalize people of color. And making assumptions or stereotyping the motives of the business and political elite can lead to excluding or alienating potential allies. For example, a white businessman may live in a highly segregated, predominantly white neighborhood or community but at the same time be dedicated to improving public education, strengthening local job-training programs, and making the streets safe for everyone. This may stem from the need for local businesses to have an educated and trained workforce, as well as a safe community for people to live, work, and shop in but also can reflect genuine compassion and concern for all community residents.

Other positions of power in communities may offer more access for people of color—including religious leaders, educators, social service agency directors, and local community activists. Herbert's stature and status as a community leader in Millville provides an example. Ethnic and racial minorities also can create their own newsletters and radio stations to contest the hegemony of a local newspaper or television station, in which their voices have been ignored or distorted. Communities are entities with many nodes of power and influence, some formal and others informal. Analyzing and understanding the unique mix of players and power in a given community is essential for workers in the helping professions who are hoping to have an impact.

SOCIAL IDENTITY AND GROUP MEMBERSHIP

Social identity and group allegiance emerge in relation to other people and groups. Communities are sites of competition between ethnic and racial groups for housing, jobs, cultural events and rituals, and political power. In Millville, people of color, particularly poor African Americans and recent Puerto Rican immigrants, face many barriers to achieving economic success—such as poor schools, lack of capital, inability to secure loans—yet they are blamed for living in poor, underserved neighborhoods. Residential segregation and the dystopic characterization of poor urban neighborhoods and their residents fuel a discourse of denigration and the creation of "other" (Miller & Schamess, 2000). Positive social identities are forged at the expense of those seen as less capable and worthy and whose cultures are viewed as supporting prosocial attitudes and behaviors.

In Chapter 6 we considered social identity formation and intergroup competition and conflict. Effective community interventions must take into account these dynamics, as they spawn a great deal of anger, alienation, and scapegoating. In Millville, as in many cities, deindustrialization and the accompanying loss of jobs, a declining city tax base, and ancient and inadequate infrastructures clearly are not the fault of any ethnic or racial group, let alone those who have arrived recently. Yet, as can be seen from Sarah's comments, the group becomes the symbol of the city's decline and the target of her sadness, rage, and discomfort. Apples are compared to oranges; the vibrant industrial city that Sarah recalls from her youth is contrasted with the decaying urban landscape in which Puerto Ricans are trapped, yet, in Sarah's view, blamed.

A trend in intergroup relations in the community is that whites and people of color frame the community narrative differently. People of color, particularly in poor neighborhoods, report consistent encounters with prejudice. They describe feeling stereotyped, excluded, and denied access to resources. They say they are followed in stores, are stereotyped by their children's teachers, and encounter police brutality, among other examples of overt and covert racism and bias (Miller, 1999). They are aware of the social and economic barriers they face daily. Miguel, the police officer, felt humiliated and stereotyped when the school department kept trying to place his children, born in the United States, in less academically oriented bilingual classes simply because they were Hispanic.

Whites, by comparison, frequently downplay or ignore the structural impediments to success and their own white privilege and focus more often on values. African Americans and Hispanics are seen as having an "alien culture," one that is antithetical to mainstream American values and behaviors (Miller, 1999). The storyline goes, "If only they would work harder ... if only they weren't so loud ... if only they weren't so messy ... if only they weren't so violent—this would be a better place to live."

This is not a new response to immigrants. Actually, the Irish had the same reaction to French Canadian immigrants in Millville in the 19th century, and this pattern has been replicated by ethnic groups across the nation. The view that recent arrivals are culturally deficient and responsible for urban decay has been around for a long time and was a driving force in the founding of professions such as social work (Gordon, 1988; Jansson, 2005). But when ethnic conflict arose in Millville and other American cities 50 or 100 years ago, sufficient blue-collar jobs were available so ethnic groups could move up the occupational and economic ladder and achieve social mobility.

This is less the case today. And, as we described in Chapter 3, white ethnic groups were quickly able to assume the mantle of white privilege, an option not available for African Americans and dark-skinned Latinos.

The Phenomenology of Community Racism

In addition to structural and intergroup racism, every community has a phenomenology of racism. A phenomenological approach considers the subjective meanings of history and experience (Seidman, 1991). What we mean by this for communities is a *historical* story of race and race relations in the community, the way residents currently *experience* race and racism, and the *meaning* of race and racism for residents.

Every community has historical narratives about how it was founded, what it represents and stands for, who lives there and how they arrived, and a story about the character of the community (Miller, 1997, 1999, 2001). Such collective group myths are part of a community's DNA, encoded in neighborhoods, inscribed on buildings, drawn on murals, written in books, and stamped on the psyches of its residents. For many communities the narrative is positive, validating, and self-affirming, but for others the narrative is one of deep poverty, unrelenting crime, and social isolation. It becomes a negative story about a community and its residents.

The larger community narrative contains specific group narratives and, within those, family narratives. Thus, stories are constructed *within* groups about how the Irish, African Americans, French Canadians, and Puerto Ricans came to live in a city such as Millville. Often cited are the hardships they left and initially encountered, and pride in the achievements and successes of the ethnic group gained over time. Other stories are spun *about* groups by other groups, which often are more critical and less charitable.

Within families, myths frequently are invoked about how a grandparent or great-grandparent, despite dismal conditions and severe hardships, was able to overcome adversity and create the conditions, often through self-sacrifice, for descendents to thrive. These myths and stories often are invoked to create invidious comparisons with recent immigrants, and they tend to ignore or minimize significant differences in social and economic opportunity.

The phenomenology of race and ethnicity in the community is articulated by public narratives, both formal and informal, about the citizens and the groups living there. These narratives guide news coverage, are expressed from the pulpits of churches, are printed in pamphlets and brochures, are woven into conversations with family and friends, and become part of the story that people tell themselves about who they are and where they live. The stories are reconstructed in public rituals—parades, holiday celebrations, civic events, community gatherings—as well as in micro interactions, such as when the police stop a car and search the passengers. The public narrative is affirmed and embodied in civic associations and their activities: Daughters of the American Revolution, Rotary Club, Shriners, Elks, discussion groups, salons, United Way campaigns, charity road races, school spelling bees.

All of these are part and parcel of community life, and vibrant communities have rich lattice works of associations, events, and installations—the capillary systems of the civic body. How these tie in with race and racism becomes clearer when we ask and explore certain questions.

Who is represented in a parade and who is ignored?

What neighborhoods does the parade move through?

What varying meanings does the parade have for different groups in the community?

Who is a member of the Chamber of Commerce and who is missing?

Which drivers are stopped and searched consistently and which continue unimpeded?

Who are the reporters on the local newspaper and what worldviews, assumptions, and values underlie their writing?

These and similar questions will guide our suggestions for ways by which people in the helping professions can strengthen community unity and inclusivity.

SOCIAL COHESION AND COMMUNITY INTEGRITY

As we consider how to respond to racism in the community, we must reflect on what contributes to healthy and vibrant communities. When conducting needs assessments and analyzing enduring inequalities and oppressions, we tend to focus on what is wrong and what is missing. Yet all communities have resources, assets, and sources of hope and inspiration (Kretzman & McKnight, 1996). Some communities with high poverty rates and residential and occupational racism are more cohesive than others with similar demographic characteristics (Miller, 2001). Why is this so?

From Wilson's (1995) research, he concluded that social cohesion results when residents are able to achieve communal objectives while maintaining effective social control. To achieve both of these goals, residents should have some efficacy to assert their agenda and supervise it, facilitated by richly cross-joined social networks (Sampson, Raudenbush, & Earls, 1997). An example of such an agenda is to have safe streets with no drug dealing. This must be articulated as a common goal, accompanied by the capacity to change and monitor the situation. It relies as well on adults working collectively to supervise the activities of children and other adults (Sampson, Morenoff, & Earls, 1999). It also requires resources—economic, financial, political, and social.

For example, the police force must be sufficient to be available to work with local residents, or after-school programs or sports leagues to engage children who otherwise may be congregating on the streets. Wealthier neighborhoods find it easier to develop collective efficacy because they have more social and economic capital. Sampson et al. (1999) identified five dimensions of social capital:

1. organizations and services (e.g., mental health services, crime-prevention programs, after-school programs),
2. kinship/friendship ties,
3. voluntary associations (e.g., local religious organizations, tenant associations, business and civic groups, ethnic/nationality clubs),
4. neighborhood activism, and
5. mutual trust.

Social networks are lubricated by mutual trust, and fostered by articulating common norms and goals and working together in pursuit of those goals (Putnam, 2000). When communities are divided by racism and intergroup conflict, the trust essential to these networks is difficult to generate. Multiple disadvantages, such as high concentrations of poverty and racism, compromise the ability to form such networks and take collective action (Sampson et al., 1999). With diminished trust, overwhelming social disorganization, and fewer collective resources, residents can readily feel disempowered and be less optimistic about their capacity to work together to improve the quality of their lives (Miller, 1994).

Social capital, community efficacy, and the integrity of families all interact with each other (Miller, 2001). *Family integrity* implies

> the ability of the family to consistently provide its members with the emotional, psychological, social, and economic foundations to support their engagement with the community. (p. 29)

Families are unable to achieve this when they have few economic opportunities, when danger is ubiquitous, and when hope is extinguished. Thus, family integrity depends on community integrity,

> the capacity of a community to provide for its families a safe, economically viable and meaningful place to live, with equal justice for all. (p. 29)

In examining how to confront racism in the community, we will articulate in greater detail what community integrity means and what workers in the helping professions can do to foster it.

RESPONDING TO RACISM IN THE COMMUNITY

We have considered four major dimensions of racism in the community: structural and institutional racism, intergroup conflict and its relation to social identity, the phenomenology of racism (how it is experienced, storied, and its different meanings), and the interaction of racism with social capital and community integrity. Meaningful interventions against racism in the community should address each of these dimensions. Consequently, our recommendations for action fall into four topical areas: (1) public dialogue, (2) re-storying the community, (3) structural interventions, and (4) generating social capital in the quest for community integrity.

PUBLIC DIALOGUE

In the previous chapter we considered public dialogue and racial conversations. Mechanisms should be in place to foster public dialogue and, in many instances, reconciliation between ethnic and racial groups in communities marked by tension or conflict. Intergroup misunderstanding and conflict contribute greatly to racism, as they lead to alienation and seeing the "other" as different and less-than, and foster stereotypes and scapegoating. These factors also cause white people to move out of cities to suburbs, exurbs, and gated communities, which create divided communities, bereft of resources.

Whites thus are less likely to support needed reforms and services and may even be moved to obstruct these efforts. Meanwhile, intergroup conflict between groups such as African Americans and Korean Americans drains and depletes groups and misdirects their anger and frustration towards one another rather than helping them to unite and work together for a more socially just community.

In Chapter 8 we described the benefits of creating structured opportunities to discuss race and racism. Community dialogue about race, ethnicity, and racism creates space for revisiting historical narratives, airing grievances, and going beyond frozen, dichotomized positions. Understanding can replace finger-pointing and blame. Myths and stereotypes can be interrogated.

Local leaders can support such conversations, formal and informal, and model their capacity to engage in them. Public discussions can be augmented by presentations, exhibits, and oral history projects (Miller, 1999).

As we described in Chapter 8, no single model of intergroup dialogue is applicable, as every community has its own unique history and current intergroup dynamics. Without dialogue, groups may be characterized by diatribe and conflict. Without a mechanism for being heard and recognized, people who are targeted are left with the options of acquiescing to their subordinate status or challenging it through confrontational tactics. Confrontation often is called for, and the Civil Rights Movement is a good example of what that can achieve. Whenever possible, though, constructive dialogue should be attempted to build bridges, heal wounds, repair broken relationships, and develop interracial coalitions.

RE-STORYING THE COMMUNITY

A positive outcome of dialogue is that new stories about the community emerge as old narratives are questioned. Community narratives are akin to individual narratives of self in that both rely on stories that explain who we are, and both reflect our experiences. Both also shape our actions and reactions by giving meaning to our reality. If our self-narrative is one of incompetence and failure, we are less likely to have the confidence to succeed when confronted by challenges. This also holds true for communities. If the public storyline accentuates the decline of community, dangers lurking in the streets, the antisocial behavior of targeted ethnic and racial groups, businesses will consider relocating, city government may neglect schools and parks, children will be kept inside, and the community will confirm the story of being a bad environment with little hope for improvement.

All communities go through demographic and economic changes, yet public narratives about the community often are slow to map these transformations and unable to translate the shifts into an adaptable community identity (Miller, 2001). Thus, the community identity can become a frozen, idealized, unattainable, air-brushed portrait of the past, with which current residents are saddled.

A community identity emerges from history, an economy, cultural traditions, and political leadership, and is formed in relation to surrounding communities. An identity can link a community to similar communities while also differentiating it, celebrating or decrying its uniqueness. Thus, terms are employed that resonate for residents as well as people who have never set foot in the community (Miller, 2001):

"thriving industrial city"
"decaying neighborhood"
"inner city"
"wealthy suburb"
"safe place"
"nice place to raise a family"
"college town"
"bedroom community"

Collective self-definitions like these give meaning to the lives of citizens and non-citizens.

When working with individual clients, helping professionals seek to uncover pathogenic beliefs such as, "I'm unworthy" or "It's my fault that this happened to me." Clients are helped to articulate a positive, affirming self-narrative—for example, "I'm competent" or "I have the strength to overcome adversity." In certain ways, this is what communities should be working toward, as well: to identify and desensitize negative and pessimistic public narratives while facilitating public discourses that foster an identity that is hopeful and inclusive of all citizens, one that is able to confront new challenges, so a community can validate its honorable past while also embracing its future (Miller, 2001). Helping professionals can work with a cross-section of residents and leaders to intentionally and collectively craft new visions of the community—a story of what the community would like to become.

Structural Interventions

In many ways, structural interventions are the most important initiative for community change, but they are unlikely to succeed without the groundwork being laid by the other two proposals. To put it simply and directly, none of the other dimensions of community intervention will have any meaningful impact without structural interventions to address racism and poverty in the community. The other suggestions may help to achieve a consensus for change and generate the narratives and networks to effect change, but ultimately the community must undergo concrete, material changes.

One of the most essential, unfinished tasks of the Civil Rights Movement at the community level is the need to desegregate communities. This entails many factors, including:

- the ability of people to move out of ghettos and into other neighborhoods;
- an end to residential redlining and restrictive covenants;
- the presence of banks, stores, and services in all neighborhoods;
- an end to the practice of predatory lending;
- the capacity for all people to generate sufficient capital to eventually own their homes and businesses, gain equity, and achieve social mobility.

THE GAUTREAUX PROGRAM   One of the most successful programs to break up ghettoes has been the Gautreaux program in Chicago (Polikoff, 2004). This was the result of a desegregation lawsuit that began in 1966, claiming that the Chicago Housing Authority had employed racially discriminatory policies (Rosenbaum, Popkin, Kaufman, & Rusin, 1991). This led to a U.S. Supreme Court consent decree in 1976 and a demonstration project known as the Gautreaux program (Rosenbaum, 1995; Rosenbaum et al., 1991; Keels, Duncan, Deluca, Mendenhall, & Rosenbaum, 2005). The program gave vouchers to low-income African Americans living in Chicago housing projects to enable them to live in private apartments. About half moved to predominantly black city neighborhoods and half to predominantly white suburbs.

This project has been one of the most studied desegregation efforts in the nation. Six to 22 years after being initially placed, the majority of program participants, most of whom have since moved, are living in neighborhoods that reflect the socioeconomic conditions of the neighborhood to which they had moved originally, rather than the housing projects from whence they came (Keels et al., 2005). Living in safer areas with better schools and more jobs has produced dramatic improvements in educational attainment, college attendance, employment status, and upward mobility, particularly for those who were moved to the suburbs (Rosenbaum, 1995; Keels et al., 2005). Upon their initial entry into their new neighborhoods, the residents did experience prejudice and harassment from white residents but, despite that, have made substantial socioeconomic progress after moving.

The program has served as a model for other cities, including Boston, Cincinnati, Dallas, and Hartford (Rosenbaum, 1995). It has led to recent calls for establishing a national Gautreaux program to break up high-density, inner-city neighborhoods of extreme segregation and poverty while also serving to integrate predominantly white areas (Polikoff, 2004). Such a program is unlikely to make much headway in the current conservative political environment, and the original program would not have been possible without the desegregation movement of the 1960s and a Supreme Court committed to furthering that agenda in the 1970s. These factors point to the importance of political activism at the local community level.

POLITICAL ACTIVISM   As long as people of color are denied political power, programs such as Gautreaux that reduce segregation will be difficult to enact. Political activism involves registering voters, an activity in which many health and human service agencies can actively engage as long as they remain nonpartisan. Working with voters' rights organizations, trade unions, and other groups concerned with a political voice for the disenfranchised is also necessary, as many registered voters do not vote. Also, human services professionals can help educate voters about candidates' positions and the relevance of various issues and initiatives.

The overt attempts to intimidate voters of color in the 2000 and 2004 Presidential elections underscore the importance of creating nonpartisan election commissions, which are found in most Western democracies (Overton, 2005). With the current system, the party in control of the state executive appoints a commissioner, often a political partisan actively working for a campaign, who may have a vested interest in curbing the votes of people of color. And challenges must be mounted to the odious practice of lifelong voter disenfranchisement because of a felony conviction. Coupled with the disproportionate numbers of African American men who are convicted of felonies, this has become a backdoor way to reintroduce a Jim Crow–like system of denying people of color the right to vote, which has had major local and national repercussions.

People of color must be represented on local city councils and school committees. As described, residents of color in far too many communities are not elected or meaningfully represented in appointed positions. Interethnic struggles over political power have been occurring ever since the first major waves of European immigrants arrived in the United States, and groups do not easily share or yield power once they have attained it. Among the many ways to work to achieve local representation are: registering voters; forming coalitions; and organizing, demonstrating, and mounting legal challenges to at-large systems of voting that end up stifling minority representation.

CREATING JOBS   Another structural area calling for ongoing activism is to create jobs, ensure adequate public transportation to take people to work, and strengthen public education. A community without sufficient jobs is simply not a viable community. Business leaders and politicians know this as well, and recognize the importance of public education in preparing a competent workforce. A related need is to advocate for more vocational, health, and human services. Without these, many families and individuals will be unable to take advantage of educational and occupational opportunities.

SAFETY   Safety is an essential ingredient for community integrity for all residents. Those who endure the least safe environments are poor people of color. They live farther from protection from crime and violence, coupled with the added risk of abuse by law enforcement authorities. One of the reasons the Gautreaux initiative has been so successful is that people moved to safe enough environments to be able to leave their houses, attend schools, and commute to work (Keels et al., 2005), which also allows social networks to evolve and public life to flourish. Adequate representation on police review boards, as well as citizen-driven efforts to maintain safe streets and neighborhoods, contributes to safer communities, and the process of participation in itself is empowering and offers hope.

GENERATING SOCIAL CAPITAL IN THE QUEST FOR COMMUNITY INTEGRITY

Engaging in interracial dialogue, producing new narratives, and implementing structural interventions help to generate social capital by encouraging social networks among people. The *process* of working and contributing together becomes another important achievement. The efficacy fostered by working together against racism and offering opportunities for all residents is a major accomplishment in itself. It results in what McKnight (1997) refers to as an "associational community," in which people with diverse backgrounds and identities work together to share capacities, skills, and resources to solve problems and spawn solutions as connected citizens rather than being isolated in the role of clients. This encourages collective efficacy as trust evolves between individuals and groups and as residents work collaboratively to solve pressing social needs (Sampson et al., 1997).

Kretzman and McKnight (1996) have developed a "community assets" map with three levels of resources:

1. local institutions (businesses, schools, parks, libraries, hospitals, community colleges);
2. citizen associations (churches, block clubs, cultural groups); and
3. gifts from individuals (people, income, art).

Every community has assets, or potential assets, but fears for safety, alienation, and inability to sustain oneself and family causes disruptions and ruptures in the social fabric, so assets are never mined and polished. Racism fosters community fissures, which is why dialogue and healing are so essential for creating the conditions for structural changes and development of assets.

Community integrity is boosted further by having civic associations and public institutions that "braid" families to the community and to one another (Miller, 2001). Community institutions such as schools and libraries can foster meaningful, inclusive public participation through parent associations, after-school programs, and public lectures, exhibitions, and concerts. Developing and securing public spaces, such as parks, playgrounds, community centers, and swimming pools, provide safe public places where children, families and other residents can gather. Public places offer sites where people are able to congregate and develop relationships and networks, which is essential for anti-racism activities.

Civic associations can contribute to dismantling racism when they include people from all ethnic and racial groups in the community. Organizations such as the Elks, Knights of Columbus, Rotary Club, and Junior League often have gender, class, and ethnic biases that deter people of color from even considering joining or participating in them. People need to feel welcomed, respected, and comfortable to join civic associations, and believe their participation is a meaningful way to contribute to the community.

Professionals in the helping professions can work with civic associations by offering anti-racism and cultural competence training, and by facilitating dialogue and public conversations to explore institutional white privilege and racism. These efforts may meet with resistance, but without becoming culturally diverse and opening doors to previously excluded groups, traditional civic organizations are unlikely to survive as vibrant organizations. If they do not become interracial, multicultural institutions, new civic associations that are inclusive will emerge to take their place.

Other important community resources that can promote exclusion or inclusion include public events and rituals—parades, celebrations, murals, and holiday decorations. These are part of a community's public narrative and can convey respect and appreciation for all cultures rather than privileging or marginalizing certain ethnic and racial groups. Traditions evolve over time but do not always keep up with demographic changes in the community. Thus, community leaders have to work actively to reconfigure public events and rituals to acknowledge the contributions of all of the community's ethnic and racial groups, prompting greater inclusivity (Etzioni, 1997).

Having presented a vision of a community with integrity, we now will consider concrete actions that people in the helping professions can take to make this a reality.

ANTI-RACISM WORK IN THE COMMUNITY

To challenge racism in the community, people in the helping professions are well positioned to work in any or all of the four areas just outlined and to make significant contributions. Social workers, nurses, psychologists, counselors, and other helping professionals are part of a community's social capital. They can sponsor and facilitate community dialogues about race and racism and contribute to the construction of inclusive, anti-racism community narratives. People in the helping professions working for agencies, associations, schools, and businesses can ensure that their organizations are anti-racism institutions (see Chapter 10) and act as partners in communitywide efforts to dismantle racism. We will briefly describe some general principles of community-based anti-racism work, all of which are appropriate for individuals and organizations pursuing an anti-racism agenda.

ASSESSMENT AND PRIORITIZATION

Assessment should be the starting point with any activism or change project. No community is the same. We described Millville to you to illustrate some issues of which you should be aware when examining racism in your community. Collecting demographic information is useful and often available from census reports, planning organizations, state agencies, the United Way, and the Chamber of Commerce.

What racial and ethnic groups live in the community?

Are patterns changing, or is the current population stable and enduring?

How does the demographic make-up of the community match the race and ethnicity of the children attending public schools?

How do the race and ethnicity of teachers and administrators correspond to those of the children attending the school?

Answering these questions provides simple statistical data for tracking local racial and ethnic patterns. Some of this information will be difficult to find, but a lot of data should be readily available without having to spend too much time searching for it. Areas of focus should include the racial dynamics of politics (who is elected and appointed), jobs and employment, residential patterns, transportation systems (particularly public), and social and health indicators. We should identify those community institutions that have power, as well as the source of their power. For example, in one community the power brokers may be the Democratic Party, the corporate elite, and the Catholic Church, and in another community a farmer's cooperative, county government, and a local extended family may wield considerable influence.

| BOX 9.1 | ANTI-RACISM COMMUNITY ASSESSMENT TOOL |

Demographic information: Track population changes, racial and ethnic make-up of the community, public school students, and teachers.
 Sources: Census data, state agencies, planning organizations, United Way, Chamber of Commerce

Political information: Research the race and the ethnicity of elected and appointed officials, voting patterns by party, and race and number of registered voters.
 Sources: City or county government, League of Women Voters

Transportation systems: Trace public transportation routes, highways, and local streets.
 Sources: Local department of transportation, maps

Residential patterns: Break down neighborhoods and towns by race and ethnicity.
 Sources: Planning departments of local government, census data

Religious patterns: Determine existing religious organizations and who attends them by race and ethnicity.
 Sources: Interfaith councils, Chamber of Commerce

Surrounding community: Compile similar information for county and nearby communities.

Key informants: Seek information from consumers, residents, commuters, politicians, health and human service workers, business leaders, shopkeepers, teachers and school administrators, college professors, community leaders, and local media. Key informants should be racially and ethnically diverse.

12 Questions to ask:
  1. What is it like to live (or work) in this community?
  2. What relationships do you detect between ethnic and racial groups? What do you surmise about race and racism?
  3. How would you describe the community?
  4. Who or what groups hold power in the community?
  5. What are the community's problems?
  6. What are its strengths and assets?
  7. What networks exist?
  8. What organizations are important in civic life?
  9. How do people get their local news?
 10. How safe is the community?
 11. What do various groups say about law enforcement in the community?
 12. What is the vision of what people would like the community to become?

Drawing a religious map of the community is another valuable tool in ascertaining whether ethnic and racial patterns coincide with religious affiliation and church participation. Also, we can place the community in a larger context: How does it compare with neighboring communities? What are the county, region, and state demographics? This should include an assessment of national and international developments, as well as historical trends. Piven and Cloward (1993) have argued that at some times in history there are seams where certain changes are possible, such as the era of civil rights and Great Society programs (Miller, 2002). These windows of opportunity do not last long, and when they close, so do the opportunities for large-scale changes. Therefore, we have to attempt the right strategy at the right time.

A statistical assessment is only part of the overall process. We can learn much from hearing from a variety of people about their experience of living in the community and what meaning it has for them. We can do this formally or informally, by talking with consumers, residents, local leaders, health and social service workers, religious leaders, politicians, and people from the media. At this stage, the goal is to gain a range of perceptions and opinions about race and the community, not to try to change anything or influence anyone. Mapping an array of experiences can help us to see which groups might work well together in coalitions and which issues are likely to be controversial or thorny.

As part of the assessment, priorities have to be established. Racism is ubiquitous, enduring, and complex, so it will not be possible to do everything at once. Based on the initial assessment, what are the most pressing community needs concerning racism? Which issues are likely to engage people, and which are likely to cause severe conflict and tension? Where are you and your organization positioned in all of this?

Helping professionals should evaluate the resources that they and their agencies can bring to the table, and should recognize their limits and liabilities. Working on racism in the community always will involve using assets and resources while also navigating and negotiating inevitable roadblocks and setbacks. We must be strategic, expect resistance, persist, and take a long-term view. We should work on issues that have a greater chance for success, at least initially, to generate the momentum that will allow for relationships and networks to develop and to achieve at least partial success that will motivate people to continue their efforts. The accompanying anti-racism assessment tool can help human service workers begin this process.

WORKING WITH EXISTING GROUPS AND ORGANIZATIONS

When engaging in anti-racism work, helping professionals understandably want to design their own change project. Usually, existing groups and organizations already are working on meaningful projects that they can join or affiliate with. Although anti-racism depends on individuals making their own contributions and engaging in self-reflection, community change efforts are more successful if they are driven by coalitions of organizations and people.

Sometimes meaningful change has not begun, and helping professionals can initiate change. Before taking this step, however, they should carefully review what is in place already. Starting a project when other change efforts are in motion already can become competitive and even elicit bad feelings from those who are engaged in anti-racism work already. This can dilute the effort and weaken the anti-racism actions.

A major exception is when existing change efforts are stalled and not gaining traction. Perhaps a coalition has been coopted and is being promoted for the sake of good public relations rather than confronting racism in the community in a meaningful way. When this is the case, creating a new structure or vehicle makes sense, to move the process forward. One should assess possible actions carefully, because establishing alternative change projects can generate problems, such as competition or dilution of effort. Even so, meaningful social actions capable of making progress and achieving results are equally important.

Whether working with an existing group or establishing a new one, helping professionals can expect to encounter resistance, differences, tensions, and conflicts. These dynamics are found in any organization or coalition, and when the topic is racism, feelings run high and these tendencies may become exacerbated. Just because people working together share a larger vision does not necessarily mean that their work together will be harmonious. Well-intentioned people bring their biases and interactional patterns to anti-racism work. Whatever the situation, we must remain in the fray and work through disagreements, possibly using some of the racial dialogue mechanisms discussed in Chapter 8.

WORKING IN COALITIONS

Coalitions offer advantages in anti-racism work. They bring together many individuals and organizations, multiplying the impact of any actions or initiatives. Coalitions provide legitimacy for a change project if they include a wide representation of stakeholders. An example is a coalition to improve the academic performance of children of color in the public school system, which could be reframed as improving the academic performance of schools serving children of color. Obvious core participants in this project are teachers, parents, and high school students. Civil rights and anti-racism organizations are other likely members.

If business leaders, the Chamber of Commerce, religious organizations, the United Way, colleges, community colleges, and universities become involved as well, the coalition gains more heft and political stature. Politicians also can be members of coalitions, but this carries the risk of alienating their political rivals, who may be helpful to the change efforts at some time. We should approach with caution the notion of including politicians directly in coalition efforts, as they might seek to hijack the coalition's work to support their own political agendas.

Coalitions increase the amount of resources available and are able to develop effective communication and action networks. Coalitions can lessen the load on any one person or organization by pooling resources and sharing organizational burdens. By working together, coalition members learn from one another and develop relationships that help to sustain change efforts. There is also a critical mass of effort, a center of gravity of momentum that coalitions can muster, keeping things moving even when some groups or people are feeling burned out and deenergized. Coalitions, too, can model interracial, cross-cultural collaboration for the community.

Working in coalitions can present both challenges and advantages. Having more people and players can entail more work to develop a consensus. They must devote more time to the process and work to achieve a consistent level of knowledge and commitment to the coalition's goals. Differences of opinion about outcomes and tactics may lead to conflicts.

If participants reach a consensus that is acceptable to all, it may dilute the capacity of the coalition to subvert the existing social order. This risk increases as more mainstream and conservative organizations join the coalition. Although their participation can enhance the credibility of the coalition's work, it carries the risk of slowing or even coopting the coalition's mission.

Multiracial coalitions are most effective when engaging in anti-racism work. This ensures a range of perspectives and validates the importance of racism being tackled by white people as along with people of color. As described in Chapter 8, talking and working together cross-racially and cross-culturally is rare, which may necessitate structured dialogues and confidence- and relationship-building exercises among group members. The coalition must strive not to re-create the racist imbalances of society at large but to ensure that people of color hold meaningful and influential leadership positions. If a coalition starts off predominantly white, chances are that it will remain that way.

DISRUPTIVE STRATEGIES

A collaborative approach such as a coalition usually is the strategy of choice. In many situations, however, this method simply will not be effective. A blatant example existed the Southern United States between the end of the Civil War and the legislation of the Great Society. In this entrenched, openly racist, essentially caste system, collaboration was not possible. The existing local and state political and civic power systems were not open to meaningful partnership and compromise. Confrontation was the only means available to further the cause of civil rights.

In some communities today, the efforts of progressive people to redress racial imbalances through collaborative efforts have not met with success. Their efforts are characterized by blatant segregation, along with racially targeted police harassment and school systems failing the needs of children of color. Thus, at times the tactics of nonviolent disruption are necessary. Piven and Cloward (1993) have argued that throughout history, the most significant social changes have resulted from disruption and social unrest, not from compromise and collaboration. Disruption is one of the most effective means available to those without power and privilege.

If a class action lawsuit had not been initiated in the 1960s in Chicago, the Gautreaux program described in this chapter would not have been initiated. Lawsuits and other legal actions often have paved the way for significant and large-scale efforts to dismantle racism. Another disruptive tactic initiates boycotts against employers with intransigent records of racist practices.

Protests and sit-ins are effective approaches for gaining public attention and putting pressure on leaders to respond to concerns and demands, but these methods also carry risks. Even peaceful demonstrators can get hurt and face the threat of arrest. Disruptive actions, too, can alienate potential supporters who are not comfortable with confrontational styles. And, though disruptive tactics can attract attention and garner publicity, the media might spin a negative narrative about the change project, which could alienate potential supporters and place those working for racial justice on the defensive. In short, disruptive strategies are important devices in the toolkit of anti-racism activists, but should be used judiciously.

PARTICIPATORY EFFORTS

Anti-racism activists can be involved directly in the community in many ways. Given the significance of political power, becoming involved politically is a vital facet of anti-racism activity in the community. A person can do this in many ways: run for office, join a political party and become an active participant, contribute to political organizations that support anti-racism, and hold meetings to brief and inform politicians about important issues. Running for office may seem daunting and takes time and resources, so it is not appropriate for everyone. Still, running for city council or the school committee is feasible for many people and can have a significant impact on local policy decisions. And running for higher office, such as mayor or congressperson, usually follows service in a local elected capacity.

People and organizations can identify viable candidates—those committed to an anti-racism platform—and work to get them elected. Anti-racism activists can volunteer for appointed political positions, such as serving on human rights commissions or local planning boards. Nonpartisan political organizations need volunteers to ensure fair and free elections and to help get out the vote at election time.

Among other ways of furthering an anti-racism agenda in the community are to be a poll-watcher or drive people to the polls. And people can serve on agency boards, commissions, and coalitions. It is imperative that consumers be represented on the boards of health and human service agencies. Professionals and other citizens can volunteer to work with people targeted by racism through mentoring, recreational, skill-building, and relationship-building programs. For those who will be working cross-culturally and cross-racially in this capacity, some of the principles are outlined in Chapter 11.

At times, people in the helping professions can take a direct leadership role in community efforts, and at other times they can more effectively identify someone else to take this role. For example, helping professionals may have formed a relationship with a volunteer on their agency's advisory board who is vice-president of a local bank and has indicated a strong commitment to anti-racism ideals and principles. Encouraging this board member to take a high-profile role in communitywide anti-racism efforts can be productive. Health and human service workers may be expected to advocate for progressive policies, but having a bank official take a leadership role in anti-racism projects offers legitimacy and credibility.

Anti-racism policies are not the only goal of direct community change efforts. As discussed earlier in this chapter, changing the way people think about racism and about the community represents a significant intervention. Art projects, such as murals or exhibits, can draw attention to issues of anti-racism. Writing workshops and poetry presentations serve this function as well. Even a well-placed letter to the editor of a local newspaper or an op-ed piece can create a ripple of reflection. Planning inclusive communitywide events and celebrations are other venues for anti-racism activists. Conferences and workshops can bring attention to issues of racism while serving as forums to generate creative ideas for addressing social inequities.

SELF-CARE

In any type of social activism, and with anti-racism work in the community in particular, self-care is essential. The scale of racism is daunting and the amount of anti-racism work to be done is huge. People who engage in anti-racism work often feel a great deal of passion and commitment, so they should monitor their own physical and emotional health and pace themselves during these activities.

Activists should be committed for the long haul so they will not burn out or take early retirement because of the stress involved in anti-racism activism. Also, they should develop ways to remain engaged and passionate about anti-racism work while maintaining time and energy for family and friends, and for pursuing restorative activities. Helping professionals should seek out colleagues they enjoy, trust, and are energizing. Relationships sustain anti-racism work.

Self-care can involve an extraordinary range of activities, of which we highlight two here.

1. Nurture your spiritual life if that is a meaningful part of your being. Participate in public organized religious activities or in personal, regular meditation. Having a larger philosophical and spiritual worldview can provide motivation for anti-racism activities, as well as to offer hope and help to deal with setbacks.
2. Engage in physical activity. Any kind of work or activism that involves strong commitments and deep passions can deplete the body or foster a build-up of unhealthy toxins. Some form of physical activity, however vigorous or gentle, can be restorative and offer balance and ballast to the life of an anti-racism activist.

Part of the motivation for anti-racism work is to improve the health and opportunities for people targeted by racism. How ironic it would be if activists were to physically compromise their own health in the process.

| SELF-CARE WHEN DOING ANTI-RACISM WORK

BOX 9.2

1. Do regular self-audits about stress and burnout. Monitor for preoccupation, difficulty sleeping, and not eating properly.
2. Set realistic goals. You can't do everything all of the time.
3. Seek regular supervision, consultation, peer consultation, support, and ally groups.
4. Seek balance between professional and personal lives. Set limits.
5. Pay attention to your physical health, and exercise.
6. Use meditation, mindfulness, and other techniques for self-awareness, self-relaxation, and self-healing.
7. Attend to your spiritual needs.
8. Don't lose contact with joy, beauty, humor, pleasure, and sources of enjoyment.
9. Stay connected with others.
10. Keep a journal about how your anti-racism work is going.

CONCLUSION

Millville is an example of how racism is manifested in a community. As with racism in other domains, this fictional town represents the concrete, institutional, and structural manifestation of racism in the community. Race and racism always intersect with identity at all levels—individual, family, group, and community.

Given the complexity of how racism is manifested in communities, we recommend four domains of intervention: engaging in public dialogue; reconstructing inclusive community narratives; intervening directly with the structural manifestations of racism; and working to generate and utilize community resources, assets, and capital. Helping professionals can engage in anti-racism work in the community in a number of ways, beginning with assessment and prioritization. This can be expanded to working with coalitions, political activities, and making direct social, interpersonal, and artistic contributions.

Anti-racism work at the community level involves understanding all facets of racism, past and present, and the ability to intervene with multiple systems at many levels. As daunting as this may seem, helping professionals can contribute in many ways to creating inclusive and equitable communities. Ultimately, when it comes to dismantling racism, we must have a national and international perspective even though most of our meaningful actions and activities will take place at the community level. Finally, whatever means and strategies we choose, we must take care of ourselves so we can remain energized for the long haul.

EXERCISE 9.1 MAPPING YOUR COMMUNITY

Consider these questions about the community where you are currently living or where you grew up.

1. When did different ethnic and racial groups arrive in the community, and what were their reasons for moving there?

2. What jobs were available in the community when specific ethnic and racial groups moved in?

3. Did ethnic and racial group members remain in the neighborhoods where they originally settled, or have they moved to new neighborhoods?

4. How would you characterize relationships among the different ethnic and racial groups in your community?

5. What ethnic and racial groups are represented in local city government, and which are not represented (e.g., mayor, selectmen, city councilors, school committee members, appointed officials)?

6. What major businesses are in your community, and what are their ethnic and racial staffing patterns? Are there differences between higher and lower status positions?

7. Who are considered the "civic elite" in your community, and what ethnic and racial groups do they represent?

8. What challenges in your community hinder anti-racism work and progress toward social justice?

9. What assets does your community have that further racial equity, justice, and reconciliation?

CONFRONTING RACISM IN AGENCIES AND ORGANIZATIONS

CHAPTER CONTENTS

Most helping professionals work for agencies and organizations. They represent the organizations for which they work, and their workplaces give meaning and direction to their professional efforts. Agencies, through their missions, charters, policies, and practices, define the parameters of what they can and cannot do, and by paying salaries and offering resources, they make possible the work of helping professionals.

Health and mental health clinics, family service agencies, counseling centers, and hospitals are the meeting places where clients, workers, and services coalesce. None of these locations is immune to the many forms of racism described in this book. Actually, health, human service, and educational facilities are likely to emulate the dynamics of racism in society at large. Thus, as important as it is for every human service professional to work individually to dismantle racism, equally important is to act to make our agencies anti-racism organizations. This is a strategy for pursuing social justice that will ultimately lead to greater organizational effectiveness and better services to consumers (Barak, 2000; Donner & Miller, 2005).

Clearly, racial segregation persists in our society. Many neighborhoods are racially segregated, which leads to segregated schools. This also reinforces social segregation, and many people in this country socialize with people primarily from their own racial group. Workplaces, however, tend to be more racially mixed (Donner & Miller, 2005). While this situation offers both opportunities for interracial cooperation and understanding, it also poses challenges of potential interracial conflict and miscommunication.

In this chapter, we will examine how people in the helping professions can work to make their agencies anti-racism institutions. We will consider what becoming an anti-racism institution means and reflect on the areas an organization should think about to make significant progress toward this target. The chapter also will present developmental conceptualizations of organizations seeking to become anti-racism entities and offer tools for tracking progress.

TERMINOLOGY

First we must define different types of organizations. A *multicultural organization* differs from an anti-racism organization. A multicultural organization values all consumers and employees while responding to the varying cultures that are part of the human mosaic. It respects all cultures and asserts that none should be privileged or marginalized. An *anti-racism organization* goes beyond this and acknowledges the destructive power of racism in society, which it attempts to ameliorate. An anti-racism organization certainly includes a commitment to multiculturalism but goes beyond this to examine power and inequities in privilege in addition to building cultural responsiveness and competency.

We use the term "anti-racism" rather than "anti-racist." The former implies a commitment to dismantling racism, which has dimensions that are institutional and social as well as attitudinal and behavioral. Using the term "anti-racist" carries the risk that change efforts will be directed toward trying to uncover or reform "racists," which can lead to severe conflict while leaving important areas for examination and change unattended (K. Basham, personal communication).

TYPES OF ORGANIZATIONS

There are two broad types of organizations. One is what we term a "mainstream" organization, which includes mental health clinics, hospitals, college counseling centers, and family service agencies—organizations that were established to offer social and health services, which may serve people of color but were not established for this purpose. These organizations tend to have mostly white boards and white executives and managers at the upper ends of the staffing pyramid, and a propensity to be Eurocentric in orientation. Most social and health service organizations in the country are of this type.

The second type of organization encompasses those that have been established specifically to serve communities of color by people of color, with boards, staffs, and executives of color. The mission statement of these ethnically focused organizations often emphasizes the population to be served as much as the types of services to be offered. These organizations may have a non-Eurocentric philosophy, such as an Africentric orientation, and emphasize sensitivity and cultural competence.

Anti-racism often is an assumed part of the agency's mission. Exemplifying such an organization is the Martin Luther King, Jr. Community Center in Springfield, Massachusetts, which serves families in a catchment area that is predominantly African American and Latino. Another is the Asian Counseling and Referral Service in the International District of Seattle. Both agencies were established to offer social, educational, vocational, health, and recreational services with specific populations in mind, using models of service provision that stress cultural responsiveness and a commitment to confronting oppression.

In a sense, these are social service organizations created in opposition to white European hegemony. This is not to say that they are not confronted with matters of diversity, including issues of class and immigration status, as well as prejudices and biases toward ethnic groups. In addition, funding sources stipulate the nature of service provision, which can put pressure on ethnically focused agencies to compromise their principles and values and emulate discriminatory practices found in mainstream agencies.

This chapter, however, is concerned primarily with mainstream organizations, because ethnically focused agencies, as a group, have done more thinking about issues of culture and oppression and have been working on the issues that we address from their very inception. They may work on other issues as well—homophobia, sexism, and conflicts over immigration status—but their existence, as well as their mission and practice, is already taking a step toward challenging racism. Another reason for concentrating on mainstream organizations is that most helping professionals work in these agencies.

HOW RACISM IS MANIFESTED IN SOCIAL SERVICE ORGANIZATIONS

As with any durable inequality (Tilly, 1998), racism is emulated in all mainstream agencies and can suffuse any part of that organization. Although some organizations overtly discriminate against people because of their race and ethnicity, this is comparatively rare in the United States today. Much more common are organizations that collude with racism by making choices, such as about what funding to pursue, which politicians to work with, which clients to serve, who is hired to serve them, and how services are delivered, as well as having unexamined, accepted policies and practices. We will look at some commonplace policies and practices that are problematic.

POLICIES

Most policies are covertly rather than overtly racist. Chapter 4 explored how transportation policies and housing policies, for example, may seem to be race-neutral yet promulgate programs and practices that serve to deepen racial divisions and inequalities. The same is true for health and human service agencies. Policies such as these may pertain to hiring and retention, as well as to services directed toward consumers. The questions to be considered are: Do the policies continue racial inequities, whether intentional or not, and do these policies do anything to dismantle racism? We will consider two examples: hiring and retention, as well as client policies.

HIRING AND RETENTION   As described in the previous chapters, people of color face many more hurdles and barriers in their efforts to become members of the helping professions. If hiring policies of a predominantly white agency consist merely of placing an advertisement in a local newspaper for an opening, will this result in more racial and ethnic diversity within the agency? The chances are that it will not. One issue to consider is who reads the local newspaper or has access to a computer to check its website. If the newspaper readership is weighted toward white readers, the chances of recruiting an applicant pool of people of color is lessened.

More often than not, people hear about jobs through friends and colleagues. If the staff is predominantly white, the people who learn about the opening most likely will be white as well. And it always helps to have someone inside of an agency advocating for a job applicant, so the default drift of a predominantly white organization will be to have white employees advocating for white applicants. It also helps to have people on the inside who can give an applicant the "inside scoop" about an agency, which can help the applicant prepare for interviews.

And who will conduct the interviews? Who will make the decisions? Unless this is considered carefully, the tendency will be to have a staff that re-creates itself racially and ethnically as well as culturally. Social groups are inclined toward feeling more comfortable and inclusive with people whom they perceive as similar.

What qualifications are being sought for the job, and will people of color have attained education and experience comparable to that of white people? This question can make some people feel uneasy, for it brings into the forefront the issue of qualifications and racism. One of the ways that white privilege works in society is to increase the social and educational capital of white people, so they are more likely to present as applicants with "better" qualifications. Nothing that was "race neutral" in society led to this. It is the cumulative result of social privileges favoring white people. To then approach hiring as a race-neutral enterprise favors people who have had race advantages all of their lives.

Now this, of course, raises other issues. For one, consumers must be served by skilled, competent people. We are not suggesting that agencies forego issues of competence in favor of a blanket policy of racial diversity. The choices are seldom either/or, yet the "competency" argument often is cited as a justification for not considering more applicants of color. If many clients are people of color and they are receiving services from predominantly white clinicians, would it not be in their interests to have more clinicians of color on staff who can empathize with their experiences of racism more readily, are more likely to understand them culturally, and also can serve as positive role models? Perhaps a person who can fulfill these expectations has had less actual job experience than a white candidate for the job. On paper, the white applicant might look better, but in practice, reality is more complex.

We have raised these questions and issues to illustrate how a "race-neutral" hiring policy actually can collude with a system of preferences that favors white people and may diminish the capacity of an agency to best serve its clients. This conundrum has no easy solutions, but even just considering the problem can lead to an agency re-thinking its overall recruitment strategy, which can make a difference in the long run. The agency can place advertisements in local neighborhood newspapers. Its employees can ask colleagues of color if they know any interested applicants. They can pay attention to the racial/ethnic composition of the search committees. The job qualifications can be expanded beyond the usual academic and work expectations to include intimate familiarity with cultural practices or the experiences of racial targeting and marginalization.

Staffing issues go well beyond hiring, as retention is just as important. Creating systems for mentoring younger and newer workers of color is essential. Because many workers of color are assigned to some of the agency's most challenging cases, the agency should monitor their caseloads to prevent burnout. Inservice training can help to increase the bank of social and professional capital that some workers lacked before joining the organization. The comfort level of co-workers and the atmosphere of the workplace make a difference as well. As we have described in previous chapters, bridging differences, embracing diverse cultural styles, and promoting an interracial and ethnic dialogue require a conscious effort, which many people have not experienced.

Agencies also must consider where staff members of color are placed within the organization. A common staffing pattern for mainstream agencies, which have made an effort to recruit a diverse staff, is to have many staff members of color clustered in lower-status jobs or working within teams that are more marginalized and less central to the agency's mission. With large agencies, patterns of segregation can emerge, replicating the segregation patterns of society. What is most challenging for mainstream agencies is to have significant racial and ethnic diversity among the supervisory and management team.

CLIENT POLICIES   Even the client policies that are considered race-neutral can cause difficulties in practice for people of color. Most organizations have policies about eligibility, expectations for client conduct, and protocols and methods for helping people. All should be examined for possible racial and cultural biases. Racism and cultural bias can manifest themselves in many ways. Pervasive racial and ethnic stereotypes can influence expectations for clients as well as their actual treatment. (We consider these dynamics in clinical settings in the next chapter.) This, in turn, can make clients feel as if they are misunderstood, invalidated, and even as if they are experiencing racial micro-aggressions. In response, clients become more guarded and defensive or even terminate their involvement with the agency, which will fulfill stereotypes that they indeed are "less motivated." Missing appointments and showing up late for appointments can be seen as indicators of client reactions to unexamined racism.

Theoretical biases can lead to misunderstanding clients of color or even pathologizing them. Eurocentric biases about human behavior and conduct can cause clients to feel unwelcome or unfairly judged. Attendance policies can contain biases. For instance, inadequate or unreliable public transportation can affect the ability of clients to make it to appointments on time. Some agencies give primacy to individuals, and confidentiality rules discourage seeing clients along with their relatives and friends. This might be consistent with many European cultural orientations but is less compatible with cultural orientations for people of color from Asia, Africa, and Latin America. As explored further in the next chapter, cultural biases can influence expectations about disclosing intimate information; expressing emotions; internal family roles, relationships, and hierarchy; and typical responses to authority.

Seemingly minor environmental factors can make clients feel welcome or unwelcome. The layout of waiting areas, where the receptionist sits, who the receptionist is and her or his demeanor all contribute to client comfort or discomfort. Are chairs clustered together to accommodate family groups, or are they all lined up against the wall? The type of artwork displayed, the magazines in the waiting room, what music is playing, or what TV channel is on—all serve as markers to clients, conveying information about the culture of the agency and who is being welcomed. In addition to these physical factors, the language spoken by the receptionist and clinicians has a big impact on client trust and comfort.

INTERPERSONAL RELATIONSHIPS

Within agencies that have made a commitment to diversity, interpersonal relationships often require attention. In our consultation work with agencies, we have found, not surprisingly, that people do not trust one another automatically and many misunderstandings and miscommunications arise. These disagreements can lead to open conflict or workers walking on eggshells, monitoring what they say or retreating from social interactions. This atmosphere is not conducive to effective teamwork and high staff morale.

Many people have not had a lot of practice working closely with people from different racial and ethnic backgrounds. Every staff member has his or her own social identity and, as discussed in Chapter 6, is in a different phase of this identity, which in turn is co-constructed by interactions with colleagues. The wider the range of social identities, the more complex the interpersonal relationships become. Some white staff members have thought a great deal about their white privilege or internalized stereotypes, which can lead to difficult and painful interactions for people of color. Some people of color are wary or mistrustful of white people and approach interactions guardedly. Microaggressions are likely to occur, further fueling tensions and more alienation. As a result, cliques and factions may form, widening divisions and inhibiting collaboration.

Therefore, organizations must actively and proactively initiate discussion and dialogue groups, along the lines recommended in Chapter 8. In the workplace, these dialogues should not be open-ended considerations of social identity, group membership, and intergroup relations but, instead, should be grounded in a consideration of the agency's mission, services to clients, working conditions, and ability of employees to effectively work together. Employees may be reluctant to share too much personally and emotionally in a work environment, and this should be respected. Despite this hesitation to disclose, dialogues still can include a myriad of issues connected to racial and ethnic differences and the pervasiveness of racism in society. Thus, we must consider the socioeconomic contexts that have an impact on clients and workers alike.

Exercises such as those suggested in many of the previous chapters can help staff members get in touch with their own experiences with people from different backgrounds, whether colleagues or clients, and reflect on their internalized attitudes, fears, biases, and stereotypes. Developing ground rules and norms for talking about these issues is crucial and may carry over from a discussion group to the agency as a whole.

ORGANIZATIONAL POWER

Organizational power probably is the most challenging issue for mainstream agencies. Although many organizations make well-intentioned efforts to diversify their staff and to offer training in cultural competency, the challenge of examining and shifting organizational power is exceedingly difficult. Power inequities are at the heart of racism. Therefore, it is not surprising to encounter great resistance to redistributing power, along with organizational inertia. Yet, without a good-faith effort to consider power and decision making within an organization, diversity efforts will fall short of true organizational transformation.

What does reordering power mean and how can it be achieved? In most mainstream agencies, power is manifested in many ways. Clients have the power to go elsewhere, file complaints, or not follow service plans. Receptionists can bend the rules and make it easier or more difficult for clients to access the program, and administrative assistants can rush or delay critical assignments. Line workers have the power to organize collectively, to work more slowly, and to censor what they share with their supervisors and management. Supervisors have the power to offer inducements or disincentives and to evaluate workers. Middle managers evaluate supervisors and make decisions about policies.

The highest levels of power involve program directors, executive directors, and boards of directors. They have the most authority for determining the organization's mission, ensuring its fiscal viability, setting the terms and conditions of employment, and hiring and firing staff members. In our experience, if the upper echelons exercise their power in a hierarchical and arbitrary fashion, it results in low morale and high staff turnover, or line staff will organize and resist in whatever ways are available to them. In any event, the organizational environment inevitably will suffer.

Thus, an organization committed to anti-racism should consider all of the ways by which power is exercised and where it resides, and be prepared to make changes and adjustments. This does not mean that the executive director necessarily has to step down, but it does imply reconsidering how decisions are made and working for power sharing among more of the agency's stakeholders. For example, in hiring, who makes the ultimate decision? If the executive director or board of directors makes the final decision, how much influence will the search committee or the middle managers have? When considering the office waiting room, who makes decisions about the décor and seating arrangements? Will the receptionist and line workers be part of this decision making? Will clients?

In our view, organizational anti-racism implies that those in the agency will take care in all decisions to include people of color in a meaningful way and recognize and avoid institutionalized racist patterns and unexamined racial biases and stereotypes influencing the outcome. Given the whitening of mainstream agencies at the higher ends of the organizational staffing pattern, power and decision making must be shared and decentralized wherever and whenever possible.

One direct way to achieve this is to empower work groups and committees. Another is to engage in open and honest discussions about power and decision making as part of an organization's anti-racism commitment. This way often meets with resistance and, in the short-term, white people may resent their diminished influence within the organization. Nevertheless, establishing clarity about who will make decisions, who will be consulted, and what criteria will be used is ultimately helpful to everyone because the agency will be a fairer, more just, and less oppressive place to work and clients will receive superior services.

Another pattern in many mainstream agencies is that more clients are people of color than are agency workers. Thus, seeking clients' ideas and forming client advisory groups is a way to ensure that people of color have input into the agency's decisions and policies. Also, having some clients serve on the agency's board of directors, whenever possible, is valuable. In this way, boards have more community representation as well as racial and ethnic diversity. Further, recruiting other community members, such as local business owners and professionals, promotes a spectrum of diverse community representation.

Setting numerical goals for boards eventually can result in more diversity. One author (Miller) worked with the board of a United Way organization that was virtually all white, despite serving a community with significant populations of people of color. This caused major community tensions and mistrust of the United Way by many people of color, as well as by progressive white people in the community. After a sometimes bitter discussion and power struggle, the white board of the organization eventually voted to ensure that at least a third of its members would be people of color.

This change at least set a goal of greater diversity, although there was still contention over how people of color would be nominated for the board: Would existing board members recommend them, or would they seek suggestions from organizations representing communities of color? Once this issue was resolved through a compromise, the board achieved its objective within one year. It gave the United Way more credibility in communities of color and also resulted in reallocating funding to more agencies serving people of color. This, of course, involved a struggle, at times highly politicized, and accompanying tensions with mainstream agencies that traditionally had received United Way funding without serving communities of color adequately. The United Way eventually hired its first African American president.

This example illustrates a power shift over time. Tensions between the organization and the community led to a vote to change the racial and ethnic representation of the board of directors. This resulted in hiring a person of color as the chief executive and reallocating funds. It also created a communitywide culture shift, as every agency receiving United Way funding was put on notice that serving communities of color was a priority. Every step of this process was marked by power struggles, yet the United Way achieved meaningful agency and communitywide change, set in motion by one vote of the board of directors.

RESOURCES DEVOTED TO ANTI-RACISM

A meaningful anti-racism change initiative by organizations requires resources. A commitment without sufficient resources is a Potemkin village—a shell of a commitment perhaps made more for good public relations than a meaningful pledge for change. This work requires many different kinds of resources, and all agencies have their limits, but a realistic discussion about what resources are necessary and what resources are available can yield commendable outcomes.

Staff time is one precious resource in this process. The time spent in meetings, planning initiatives, and engaging in dialogues and trainings requires a major agency commitment. If staff members are not given sufficient time to participate in these activities, they will not be invested in the outcome or will become disillusioned or burned out, or their anti-racism work could clash with their other agency responsibilities, including seeing clients. But middle and upper managers, as well as board members, must make the time to partake in anti-racism activities. This sends a strong message to the rest of staff that the organization makes this issue a high priority.

Agencies can demonstrate their commitment by providing training re-sources, such as books and videos, and hiring facilitators and consultants. Other resources are needed as well: funding for outreach for hiring; money for mentoring and other mechanisms designed for staff retention; and support for the continuing education of staff members, including pursing credit-bearing degrees. Scholarship and fellowship money targeted to support training for students and workers of color are other examples of how resources can be assembled to support anti-racism efforts.

Reallocating resources to support an anti-racism commitment entails complex decision making. Some programs may lose resources, and the staff members who operate them understandably will become uneasy as their assets are shifted and reprioritized. Board members who supported certain programs or who were comfortable with an agency culture may become perturbed. Supporters of the agency in the community (e.g., business leaders, politicians) also may become dismayed at the organization's shift in direction.

Funding bodies, including managed care organizations and insurance companies, may impose restraints that limit the amount of staff time available for anti-racism work. Whatever the obstacles, working with staff, board members, and community supporters to explain and negotiate these changes is essential. And anti-racism efforts must be linked to larger policy trends, by advocating and lobbying to change oppressive practices.

DEVELOPMENTAL MODELS OF ORGANIZATIONAL CHANGE

When embarking on the road to becoming an anti-racism organization, a map can be useful. The map will help to track what has been accomplished and offer a route for forward progress. We will suggest an audit tool for both of these purposes, after presenting developmental models of organizational movement toward becoming anti-racism institutions that will help in assessing what next steps will be realistic.

These models are similar to those of individual racial identity development, which we described in Chapter 6. They follow a linear, developmental sequence, in which attaining subsequent stages depends on having resolved prior stages. As with theories of individual racial development, these paradigms are too rigid, linear, and inflexible. An organization may not be involved entirely in one "stage" or another, and change does not necessarily follow a strict linear progression. Despite this caveat, though, these models can serve as helpful guideposts and are worth considering.

Many developmental models describe organizational pathways to becoming multicultural, diverse, or anti-oppression and anti-racism institutions (Golembiewski, 1995; Jackson & Hardiman, 1994; Jackson & Holvino, 1988; Minors, 1996; Sue et al., 1998; Valverde, in Valverde & Castenell, 1998). Some stress diversity and multiculturalism, and others challenge racism and strive to achieve social justice (Chesler, 1994). Sue et al. (1998) compared models of multicultural organizational development and extracted three metastages of development.

1. Overt (through outright hostility) or covert (through ignorance) dismissal or denial of diversity. These organizations are considered "monocultural": The centrality of whiteness and Eurocentric norms are so embedded and "normal" that they are invisible and unquestioned.
2. Overt commitment to diversity, yet with many unexamined, unconscious, white (Eurocentric) male biases and assumptions.
3. Embracing and valuing diversity. It has become part of the organization's DNA, with a de-centering of white race privilege and Eurocentric culture, metabolized by the organization and its staff.

Minors (1996) proposed a six-stage model of organizational development based on the work of Jackson and Holvino (1988) and Jackson and Hardiman (1994). Although Minors considers how a "Uni-versity" moves to "Poly-versity," his schema is applicable to health and human service organizations as well. This model is directed to anti-racism rather than multiculturalism, as summarized in Table 10.1. He has grouped the stages into a "continuum of growth," which has three phases: discrimination, nondiscrimination, and anti-discrimination. These phases work well with Sue et al.'s (1998) three stages, added to Table 10.1.

Thus, agencies that are monocultural often are discriminatory, both consciously and unconsciously. Those that are committed to diversity are commensurate with those that are nondiscriminatory. And an organization that is actively anti-racist is also likely to be a multicultural entity.

We recommend that organizations committed to becoming anti-racism institutions use a developmental model, such as that presented in Table 10.1, as a basis for assessment and strategic planning. One way to do this is to have important constituents (staff, board members, clients, etc.) meet or fill out a questionnaire, asking them to place the organization in one of the developmental phases. Breaking this down by considering separately the many dimensions listed on the organizational audit (Appendix 10-1) may help.

TABLE 10.1 | STAGES OF ORGANIZATIONAL DEVELOPMENT FROM DISCRIMINATORY TO ANTI-DISCRIMINATORY AND MONOCULTURAL TO MULTICULTURAL

Discriminatory / Monocultural

Excluding Organization

Organization is an inflexible structure designed to maintain the dominance of one group. Staff members are from the dominant group and provide services only to members of this group. Peer pressure often reinforces discriminatory practices. Such organizations will not acknowledge ineffective interventions; instead, they will label clients as "inappropriate." Strong belief in preserving established interests. Denial of existence of people with different beliefs, histories.

Passive Club

Organization does not explicitly advocate on behalf of white people but offers little support to people who are traditionally excluded. Small numbers of racial and ethnic "minorities" are hired, and only those who have the "correct" perspective. Provides services as always but with no attempt to adapt to or respond to client needs. Intent is to ensure that people assimilate. Minorities rarely participate in decision making process. Tends to hire people of color whose competence is in question. Goes through motions of embracing cultural diversity.

Nondiscriminatory

Token Acceptance

Organization begins to design procedures that will provide access to all qualified people at the bottom of the organization. Emphasizes preserving the merit principle by getting qualified people. Managers do little to change the management practices that support and maintain institutional racism. Staff members who are people of color are marginalized. Assumes that all people are the same, with little exploration of values and worldviews.

Symbolic Equity	Organizational changes come in the form of symbols rather than substance. Assumes equity will be achieved by removing barriers in employment practices. Ignores the impact of organizational culture on the extent to which people of color feel welcomed.
	Although organization actively recruits and promotes hiring of oppressed groups, it expects all members of the organization to conform to the norms and values of the dominant group. Organization begins to ask how it can respond to clients' needs. Its typical response is to reshape existing programs to fit the emerging needs of new clients. Problems are conceptualized as marketing problems; there is no attempt to change power dynamics within the organization.
Anti-discriminatory	
Substantial Equity	Organization has a flexible and responsive structure. Leaders review policies periodically and may revise the previously established mission. Structure ensures that people of color help to reshape organization's mission, systems, and modes of service delivery. Monitoring processes are instituted to ensure that services are delivered in ways that can be described as equitable. Makes use of multicultural teams at all levels to develop strategies and establish long- and short-term actions plans. Whiteness is decentered.
Including Organization	Organization reflects the contributions and interests of various groups in its mission and operations. Participation from the larger community at all levels is promoted. Organizational boundaries between staff, volunteers, and clients either disappear or shift in response to changing conditions. Attempts to maximize the knowledge, skills, and talents of staff, volunteers, and community members. Organization is equitable, responsive, and accessible at all levels. Truly multicultural.

Adapted from "From University to Poly-versity: Organizations in Transition to Antiracism," by H. Minors (1996), in *Perspectives on Racism in the Human Services Section*, edited by C.E. James (Toronto: University of Toronto Press, 1996), pp. 196–180); and *Multicultural Counseling Competencies: Individual and Organizational Development*, by D.W. Sue, R.T. Carter, J.M. Casas, N.A. Fouad, A.E. Ivey, M. Jensen, T. LaFromboise, J.E. Manese, J.G. Ponterotto, & E. Vazquez-Nutall (Thousand Oaks, CA: Sage Publications, 1998).

An agency may find itself at a higher level on one dimension, such as reconsidering theoretical models, than on another level, such as staffing. Engaging in this exercise helps to identify areas of progress and areas requiring more attention. Also, we can look at the overall picture by combining all agency variables to understand how far the organization has come and to determine the next steps. By applying a developmental model, organizations will not see the need to move from point A to point E all at once, which tends to be unrealistic. Rather, the agency can set its sights on moving to point B or C on the developmental continuum.

THE PROCESS OF BECOMING AN ANTI-RACISM ORGANIZATION

There is no one way to become an anti-racism organization, but some steps can be taken early, and certain activities are more likely to spell success. First, an organization should openly and honestly discuss whether it is willing to commit itself to this goal and consider what it will entail (Donner & Miller, 2005). Working to become an anti-racism organization requires commitment, and major organizational stakeholders must buy in to this mission. If an agency director is willing to make the commitment but the board and staff are not supportive, it is unlikely to be successful.

Organizational anti-racism work takes time and effort and involves overcoming hurdles and roadblocks. The effort is easily stalled or marginalized, with inevitable setbacks, disagreements over what constitutes meaningful change, and even conflict. After making a commitment, the organization must maintain dedication to this project for the long haul (Hyde, 2004).

Although this commitment is worth making, it is not without its risks, the biggest being that the organization will abandon its efforts without making substantive progress. This abandonment can prove to be demoralizing to all who have committed to the change process. Therefore, an organization should carefully consider why it wants to embark on this journey, what its goals are, what will serve as landmarks for success, what resources may be needed, and what potential turbulence it can anticipate and how it will respond.

If a consensus is not reached about moving to become an anti-racism organization, the next move is to work to create the conditions for making this commitment. An anti-racism change effort can originate with any level or sector of an organization and initially may face opposition from other parts of the agency. In the previous example of the United Way, the agency's leadership and many of its board members fiercely resisted the change at the start. Fortunately, significant numbers of people, some with power and influence, supported the change effort. Any organizational change project requires tactical and realistic thinking about how to move an anti-racism agenda forward and to enlist critical players as the project moves along. And any anti-racism commitment should be tied to providing superior services for clients (Hyde, 2004).

Ultimately, for the venture to succeed, people with formal power in an organization, such as the executive director and board, must support it (Hyde, 2004). Bringing all sectors of an organization on board is essential, yet complicated, and it will take time to educate people about the issues and discuss the importance of the commitment. Everyone will not be equally committed, but a critical mass of support is needed to maintain sufficient momentum.

MISSION STATEMENT

Codifying in writing the commitment to becoming an anti-racism institution is extremely helpful. Ideally, it should become part of the mission statement of an organization. This makes it fundamental to the raison d'être of an organization and means that it will be a central focus of activity. Other ways to enshrine the commitment are to include it as part of the agency's written policy and to have an anti-racism commitment statement that becomes part of all or most of the organization's literature and marketing materials, including websites.

Putting the commitment in writing serves to notify everyone who is inside the organization or comes in contact with it that this is a fundamental philosophy of the agency. This commitment, in itself, causes people to think about its meaning and their own positioning in the change effort. It also serves as a reminder of the commitment when setbacks are encountered and energy and motivation flags. It is a tool for holding the organization accountable.

PROJECT GROUP

The next step after making a commitment is to form a group that will be responsible for enacting the project and monitoring its progress. Ideally, this group will have diversity of composition, influence within the organization, access to agency leaders, and sufficient resources to operate. By "diverse composition" we mean that it should be racially and ethnically diverse but also organizationally diverse, drawing people from all sectors of the agency. It should include some people who have power and influence within the organization including access to the agency director and board. Placing board members and consumers on the committee can be helpful, too, as they can maintain links with people inside and outside of the system.

Needed resources for the group include a time to meet, a place to meet, and use of administrative services (copying, email, etc.). The project group also requires access to information—such as demographic information about clients and staff members, workloads, and funding—and must be able to interview the various organizational stakeholders. The project should not be tied down through usual organizational bureaucratic procedures. It must have a mandate to cut through organizational barriers. One group member should be responsible for convening meetings, ensuring follow-up, and reporting regularly to the entire organization.

ASSESSMENT AND PRIORITIZATION

One of the initial tasks for the group is to assess the organization (as suggested previously) for racism and anti-racism. This assessment may involve pulling together disparate views and opinions and will elicit value judgments that are likely to raise strong feelings, such as guilt, anger, and defensiveness. The project group should try to seek as wide a range of viewpoints as possible without discrediting or negating any perspectives, and try to balance subjective opinions with hard facts.

The data can be drawn from many of the documents mentioned in Chapter 9 (census reports, statistics from state agencies, etc.) as well as agency reports and statistics. We recommend using the audit developed by Donner and Miller (2005) (Appendix 10-1) to ensure that the assessment touches all of the bases and because using an audit can make the process more objective and less emotionally driven. But we do not want to minimize the likelihood or importance of feelings, as racism should arouse strong passions. Problem solving and dialogue mechanisms, such as those mentioned in earlier chapters, are helpful to respond to strong emotions, particularly if some issue is splitting the group or causing conflict.

As part of the assessment, prioritization is essential, as everything cannot be done at once. Setting short-term and long-term goals is useful. The group should consider each area separately but also think about how all of the pieces of the organization fit together when it comes to anti-racism. This is where a developmental model can be useful to put the organization's progress in perspective.

Recall that few, if any, mainstream agencies have achieved so much progress that they have become completely anti-racism organizations. More work always can be done. At the same time, measuring progress is essential so the organization can see that, as challenging as anti-racism work is, their efforts can produce forward movement. By reporting back to the larger organization regularly, the group can ensure that it does not move too far ahead of other employees. Part of its job is to engage people in the process, as well as to achieve certain goals and objectives. Last, written progress reports, at least annually, should be used to chart progress and to ensure that the anti-racism agenda is always on a front burner.

AN ANTI-RACISM AUDIT

Appendix 10-1 shows an anti-racism audit (Donner & Miller, 2005), which can be used to ensure that all critical areas are addressed as part of the agency's anti-racism effort. The audit can be reordered to fit the priorities of any organization, and specific areas or issues can be added as well. Although this chapter has highlighted the importance of many of the areas mentioned in the audit, all of the topics are worth consideration.

The audit has a rating system of *accomplished, in process,* and *unaddressed,* but these are broad and categorical. For each item that will be dealt with, more concrete goals and objectives can be set. For example, with staff hiring, establishing specific targets—such as a percentage goal of the staff as well as timeframes—can help to make the work more concrete and focused and less abstract. Or consider raising awareness about barriers to communication about race: What specific barriers are identified, and what strategies are suggested to overcome them? The audit is a starting point for gaining an overview of organizational tasks and progress and can be used as a tool for ongoing monitoring.

CONCLUSION

Agencies are a prime site for anti-racism work for human service professionals. If our organizations can move toward becoming anti-racism institutions, this will have a profound impact on workers, clients, communities, and society at large. The United Way example showed how anti-racism work can create a big ripple within a community.

We make a distinction between anti-racism and multiculturalism and encourage readers to work toward an anti-racism organizational commitment, which includes, but goes beyond, multiculturalism. We gear the analysis and recommendations in this chapter specifically toward mainstream health and human service agencies because they employ the majority of human service workers.

Seemingly benign and race-neutral policies in organizations often have significant implications for racism and social justice because of the racialized nature of U.S. society. Hiring policies and services toward clients can appear to be universal and equitable while reinforcing pervasive social inequities. It is important to directly confront issues of power when doing anti-racism work and securing sufficient resources to ensure success.

Anti-racism work in agencies depends on commitment, buy-in, and working to improve and deepen interpersonal and intergroup relationships. Disagreement, frustration, roadblocks, and setbacks will require structured processes to manage conflict and to help people to remain in alignment with the anti-racism commitment. Although a concerted and sustained effort is necessary to work toward anti-racism in agencies, progress is achievable and the contributions to client services and anti-racism work in society are significant.

EXERCISE 10.1 ANTI-RACISM AGENCY ASSESSMENT

1. Apply the Anti-Racism Audit (Appendix 10-1) to an organization in which you are currently involved (college, agency).
2. Using the stages of organizational development model in Table 10.1, where would you situate this organization? Does it fit neatly into one level, or do you see aspects of the organization in a number of levels?
3. If you were to initiate an anti-racism change project in this organization, who would you approach to work with you?
4. What would be your first steps?

CROSS-RACIAL CLINICAL WORK

CHAPTER CONTENTS

The last few chapters have covered racial dialogues, community responses to racism, and ways to confront racism in agencies and organizations. The focus now shifts to cross-racial clinical practice. This chapter assumes that readers have some foundational theory in clinical theory and practice. The emphasis is on how to engage in sensitive, competent, and responsive cross-cultural/ cross-racial clinical work, in which clinicians engage with clients who have racial and ethnic identities that differ from their own. Cross-cultural counseling involves working with people from different cultural backgrounds, and they may or may not be of the same race. For instance, an Anglo-American clinician from the Midwest working with an Italian American client from New York City involves two people who are "white" but who may have very different cultural orientations.

Working cross-racially usually (but not always) involves working cross-culturally but always implies potential differences in racial privilege, power and status, and social experiences. Thus, this chapter will consider all aspects of cross-racial work, including knowledge of cross-cultural practice.

Here, cross-racial clinical practice refers to counseling and therapy with individuals, couples and families, and small groups. The key dynamic is the importance of knowing oneself and willingness to examine one's social identity (see Chapters 2, 6, and 7). We believe in a relational, intersubjective, strengths-based approach to cross-cultural clinical practice. By *relational,* we mean that a helping professional is using her relationship with a client to help him; the interpersonal connection serves as a foundation for change and growth. *Intersubjective* refers to the intersecting inner worlds of clinician and client. Every person brings to the relationship his or her unique social identities, worldviews, thoughts, perspectives, values, and feelings. And a *strengths-based* approach is one in which workers seek to identify and work with a client's assets, resources, capacities, and strengths, much as was described for communities in Chapter 9.

Clinical relationships are intense and intimate. Intimacy brings into focus many issues of identity, relationship, and dialogue that were discussed in earlier chapters. How do workers negotiate cross-racial therapeutic relationships, in which social identity and race are so salient? There are challenges, to be sure, but this chapter offers some suggestions and encourages workers to be open to intersubjectivity. An intersubjective approach acknowledges ways by which our social identity shifts as it is co-constructed in the clinical encounter (Moffat & Miehls, 1999). So there are two intersecting social identities, and each person also is reconstructing his or her social identity in the presence of the other. This means that the workers as well as clients are potentially changed by the clinical encounter.

Each aspect of social identity is shaped by social contexts with differential power and privilege. Thus, Zuñiga & Nagda (2001) emphasize the importance of understanding history and the social world and how they differentially shape our experiences, leading to the development of a *critical social awareness.* Understanding our own social identity in relation to those around us is crucial for those engaged in cross-racial/cultural clinical work. Without knowing ourselves, we will have difficulty helping others, particularly when they have major differences in social identity. Knowledge of ourselves always is incomplete, and doing cross-racial/clinical work does not mean we will be mistake-free along the way—mistakes are inevitable and part of being a clinician—but, rather, that we try to minimize miscues, learn from our errors, and remain committed to learning more about how to respond effectively to clients.

In this chapter we will consider issues unique to those who identify as clinicians of color, clinicians who identify as multiracial, and those who identify as white. We will discuss the importance of worldviews, biases, and the meaning of culture as the therapeutic process unfolds, and the role of power in the clinical process. Strong emotions emerge in clinical relationships, and this chapter will explore some powerful feelings that might figure prominently in cross-racial work—especially anger, rage, guilt, and shame. We conclude with suggestions for practice and organizational interventions that enhance the effectiveness of cross-racial/cultural clinical work. Cross-racial clinical work is challenging but ultimately can be fulfilling for client and worker alike.

FIRST STEPS

When embarking on cross-cultural/racial clinical work, helping professionals should consider social identity; culture, values and worldviews; and power.

SOCIAL IDENTITY

Clinicians must recognize the ways by which social identity manifests itself in the clinical relationship. This understanding begins with the worker having insight and awareness of the salient parts of his or her own social identity. A worker who identifies as white and middle class and who is relatively new to the field, for instance, might not be aware of the impact and insensitivity of her words if she suggests to a poor, recently fired client with few marketable skills that he enroll in some classes to enhance his skills and thereby make himself more attractive to employers. As discussed, the web of racism presents multiple barriers, which the worker probably has not encountered and of which she is unaware. If she does not grasp this before intervening with her client, it could lead to an unrealistic service plan, and also to empathic failures that threaten the effectiveness of the clinical relationship. Other elements of social identity that can influence the strength of the clinical encounter include race, ethnicity, religious affiliation, sexual orientation, age, and level of ability.

Most workers, whatever their racial and ethnic identities, have good impulses in respecting clients' dignity and worth. Many workers, however, face challenges when conversations turn to race and ethnicity. Many in the United States, particularly those who identify as white, have been reared and socialized to believe that people are people and that we should not treat one another differently. A common refrain is, "To me, we're all just people. I don't see color. I don't care if you're black, brown, white, or purple; people are people, and talking about differences just drives us apart."

This notion is well-intentioned and ironically emerges from a person's desire to not discriminate by virtue of a person's race or ethnicity, but it can be hazardous to good cross-racial/cultural practice. As we have discussed throughout this book, we are not all "just people," as the aphorism would indicate. We all have complex social identities, including race and ethnicity. We come to the clinical encounter with rich but different cultures and heritages. We have an array of skin tones and body types. We *do* notice differences. Statements that seek to "equalize" us all by ignoring our differences, however well-meaning, minimize and devalue the experiences of many clients and the legacies of many groups in this country. Rather than denying our differences or either consciously or unconsciously negating them, we should find ways to value and acknowledge clients' varied traditions, histories, and experiences.

Thus, all clinicians engaging in cross-racial work should be aware of the impact of social identity on the clinical relationship. Those with race privilege are less likely to have thought about this aspect of their social identity daily. For many white workers in training or new to the field, this exploration is uncomfortable initially. As we discussed earlier, many white people in the United States do not consider the influence of their race and ethnicity on their own lives or the impact on people without race privilege. A worker's awareness of race and ethnicity, along with other aspects of social identity, both privileged and targeted, and his willingness to explore these issues in an open and nondefensive fashion, can have a positive influence on levels of trust that are generated and on a client's comfort level—both essential to the formation of a strong therapeutic alliance.

Clinicians of color and those who identify as multiracial must be aware of the effect of their own race and ethnicity on social identity and understand how this interacts in relationships with clients. Clinicians of color who work with clients of color must examine social identity to avoid overidentifying with clients of color and also to avoid falling prey to biases and judgments held about other groups of color, as well as white clients.

Issues of transference and counter-transference can become complex. Leary (1995), who is African American, describes a number of case vignettes in which she used transference and counter-transference with white and black clients to move the clinical work forward. She views therapy as a site where race and all of its attendant meanings and feelings can be explored in a grounded, socially situated fashion, rather than in an idealized or stereotypical fashion. For example, in a cross-racial therapeutic dyad, a white client discusses feeling unsure of herself because she believes she is surrounded by unqualified, incompetent people. The clinician of color in this dyad might discuss the meaning for the client of this feeling without directly confronting her fears that he is not competent enough to help her. Through this exploration, the client's ambivalence about having a clinician of color may emerge and become available for reflection.

CULTURE, VALUES, AND WORLDVIEW

Working cross-racially, as we mentioned, often involves working cross-culturally. The term "people of color" (African Americans, Native Americans,

‌

Latino/a Americans, and Asian Americans) encompasses a wide variety of nationalities, ethnic groups, and cultures. There are many differences in level of identification with mainstream Anglo-American culture and in cultural practices from other parts of the world and in North America before the arrival of Europeans. Also, many subcultures and hybrid cultures emerge from intermarriage, intergenerational adaptations, cross-cultural marriages, and other sources of cultural exposure, mixture, and reconfiguration. Within cultures, too, family values and orientations can vary considerably. Therefore, we must come to appreciate the many facets and nuances of culture that we will encounter as clinicians.

Sue and Sue (2003) have defined *culture* as the shared values, norms, traditions, customs, history, folklore, and institutions of a group of people. Essentially, culture is a learned perspective that is a central element of each person's social identity. Culture strongly influences a person's perceptions and behavior, as well as his or her interpretation of other people's behavior. *Values* and *worldviews* are subsumed under culture and embody the ways in which we are taught by our environments to be in the world. Values are the principles and standards by which individuals and groups guide their behavior. A preeminent value in the United States is individualism and the notion that hard work and individual strength prevail, as opposed to a more collectivist idea that emphasizes the importance and interdependence of groups and of people working collectively.

Some other prevalent mainstream U.S. values that influence how many North Americans see the world are (Katz, 1985)

- a belief in the equality of all individuals;
- a belief in the goodness of humanity;
- high regard for achievement, action, work, and materialism; and
- pride in styles of interaction that are direct, assertive, and action-oriented.

Appendix 11-1 summarizes some common Anglo-American values and sayings for reader reactions.

Although these values are dominant in U.S. culture, they are neither valid nor transferable to all racial and ethnic groups. Many people of color come from cultural backgrounds that place higher value on extended (as opposed to nuclear) family, show greater formality in social interactions, and have higher levels of respect for age and authority than in Anglo-American culture. People of color may have very different cultural norms about intimacy, making eye contact, shaking hands, disclosing emotion, parental discipline, and what children are and are not exposed to. For those who come from traditional societies in other parts of the world, cultural tensions can arise in the United States.

For example, a traditional Cambodian family may have to rely on the translation abilities of a 14-year-old son, who speaks better English than his parents. This may clash with expectations about respect when a worker addresses comments to the son rather than parents, as well as with beliefs about the propriety of disclosure, as the son hears about intimate matters involving his parents, leading to feelings of embarrassment or shame.

"Worldview" is an aspect of culture that refers to one's basic perceptions and understandings of the world, or how one makes sense of reality (Sue & Sue, 1990). Our worldview develops from our own experiences, and from interactions with members of our family and with those from similar or different cultural backgrounds. Worldviews greatly influence how we come to understand things such as time, space, work, play, and even the nature of families. They influence our sense of fairness, what we are and are not responsible for and able to control. Cross-racial clinical work has a greater likelihood of success when workers are aware of their own values and worldviews. To work effectively in this domain, careful attention must be paid, too, to areas such as the meaning of power and authority, as well as personal disclosure.

POWER

The intensity of the clinical relationship contrasts with the levels of intimacy in most other relationships. Personal disclosure, exploration of socially taboo topics, and even regression are common in clinical work. All relationships involve power, and those who hold greater power determine the nature of the relationship. Power in relationships is manifested by a hierarchy of spoken and unspoken rules (Carter, 1995). These rules are the assumptions about how people are supposed to be in relation to each other (e.g., in some traditional Orthodox Jewish families women are required to cover their heads in public and walk behind men).

The rules also dictate patterns of behavior, depending on one's context (e.g., the ways by which one might act at home with friends and family versus the way one acts at work with colleagues and clients). Carter (1995) explored the ways in which power is manifest in the clinical relationship, concluding that therapists who understand and use their own social identity will be better able to negotiate the therapeutic relationship to help clients effectively.

Ethnic and racial minorities often feel pressures to assimilate so they can achieve upward social mobility. When this pressure to assimilate is combined with respect for authority, group members may seem to be deferential toward people they perceive to be in authority, such as helping professionals. Clinicians, whatever their race, already have a great deal of power in the helping relationship by virtue of their training, status, professional role, authority over eligibility and appointment schedules, combined with the vulnerabilities implicit in being a client. This is compounded if the worker is white and has not examined white privilege thoroughly, which can be manifested in an overly authoritative stance. If not carefully monitored, the dynamics of internalized inferiority and internalized superiority can come to characterize the therapeutic relationship.

Thus, in cross-racial clinical encounters, clients might tell workers that they are finding the work together to be helpful and that they see improvements when there actually is little noticeable change or growth. Often in these situations, clients ultimately leave therapy prematurely, as they can have difficulty speaking out against, or even remotely criticizing, those whom they perceive to be authority figures. Therefore, clinicians should be mindful and sensitive to the nuances of power and respect in counseling relationships.

LEGACIES OF RACISM SEEN IN CLINICAL WORK

All clinical work engenders a range of complicated emotions for client and worker alike. Cross-racial work in particular can elicit powerful affective responses. Particularly in dyads involving a white clinician and a client of color, many elements of the client's everyday life can be reenacted in the clinical encounter. When the worker is a person of color, clients may question, overtly or covertly, the clinician's professional capabilities, which can evoke other experiences with racism. Workers, whatever their race, must be mindful of their own feelings, as well as of their own reactions and attitudes toward their client's expression of strong emotions. Otherwise they might offer unempathic responses to clients, leaving them feeling unheard and misunderstood.

Some common emotions and reactions that emerge in cross-racial work are anger, rage, guilt, shame, grief, and mourning. When expressions such as these do emerge, helpers must acknowledge, respond to, and be aware of how they can help or hinder therapy. We will briefly consider the sources of some common strong emotions, and later in the chapter examine ways to handle these emotions in counseling.

ANGER

We all feel anger, although some do not want to recognize, admit, or respond to this emotion. Here, "anger" is defined as an emotion that arises in the moment and generates an intensity that usually leads to an emotional release of some sort, which quickly reduces personal tension. Though anger is a common reaction to hurts or insults, feeling intense anger over a protracted period is not good for us and takes its toll. Frequent expressions of anger can be physically and emotionally taxing and can strain interpersonal and professional relationships.

RAGE

Rage is akin to anger, but is a more profound and worrisome emotion than anger (Hardy & Laszloffy, 1995). Rage speaks to incubated, suppressed anger. Rage simmers and lasts over time. It also hides a profound level of despair. It tends to develop gradually and has both functional and dysfunctional dimensions. Rage acts as a protective shield in many ways, because people tend to keep a distance from those who are enraged. This can buffer people from the effects of racism, as well as help a person retain a sense of self-respect.

Self-destructive behavior often ensues when rage is internalized and suppressed. Byproducts of rage are surges in substance abuse, prolonged sadness or depression, and suicidal gestures, ideations, or completions. Fighting can be an external expression of rage, and riots are a collective manifestation of rage. Hardy and Laszloffy (1995) described family therapy with an African-American family that was punctuated by the family members not talking to one another. For this family, not talking and suppressing anger were protective buffers against the trauma of oppression and the accompanying rage, but it also alienated them from one another and curtailed their capacity to be intimate and supportive.

The expression of rage sometimes releases the pain and humiliation associated with oppression. For people of color, particularly youth of color, these feelings may be attributed to a realization that they indeed are a member of a racial or ethnic group that is not fully valued or appreciated in our society, much like the second phase of targeted social identity described in Chapter 6.

Both anger and rage often lead to feelings of isolation and invalidation. Alvin Poussaint (2000) described the skyrocketing number of suicides in the black community as a direct example of rage taken to the extreme, in which people feel that they have no other options. Gripping, "uncontrollable" rage can affect people of color (bell hooks, 1995, p. 26):

> That rage is not pathological. It is an appropriate response to injustice. However, if not processed constructively, it can lead to pathological behavior.

She links this to counseling:

> Concurrently, without a more sophisticated understanding of those particularly extreme expressions of rage which indicate serious mental disorder, we will not be able to address the complexity and multidimensional nature of black rage. We will not be able to understand the psychological displacement of grief and pain into rage. And without that understanding the deeper dimensions of black rage cannot be acknowledged, nor the psychological wounds it masks attended to. (p. 27)

GUILT

Guilt arising from racism is a common emotion that can be manifested in clients, as well as workers, of any race. Clients of color may feel a sense of guilt over not having done more to challenge racism or to help family members. Guilt also can derive from feelings of doing better than one's family or community, perhaps because of having a lighter skin, or speaking English with an Anglo-American accent, or having achieved a higher level of education.

People of color also can experience guilt over their internalized racism or their feelings of prejudice toward other people of color or even those of their own race. White people may experience guilt about their privilege or because they have internalized racial stereotypes that conflict with their egalitarian values. People of any race may feel guilt over ways they have treated or responded to members of other racial and ethnic groups.

SHAME

Shame is to guilt as rage is to anger, but shame is a deeper emotion, the feelings of which often are attached to very early memories. Though guilt can lead to feeling bad about what happened to another person, shame is tied inextricably to feeling bad about oneself. The examples we gave about sources of guilt apply to shame as well, but the impact is more profound, self-negating, and immobilizing. Profound feelings of shame can be overwhelming and make it difficult for people to take the actions necessary to help themselves and others. Shame (and guilt) can lead to clinicians overreacting or underreacting to clients, which we will explore next.

STRESS AND TRAUMA

Stress is multifaceted, with many causes, types, and levels. Critical incidents (sudden, uncontrollable, overwhelming events) can cause acute stress disorders and even post-traumatic stress disorder (PTSD) (Perrin-Klinger, 2000). Long-term exposure to stressful situations can produce chronic stress disorder. All types of stress disorders have negative consequences—cognitive, emotional, behavioral, physical, interpersonal, and spiritual (Yassen, 1995). These include, but are not limited to, anxiety, irritability, difficulty concentrating, sleep disorders, hypervigilance, sadness and depression, and anger.

Racism and its consequences should not be reduced to, and labeled as, a medical disorder. Yet, when engaging in clinical work, the psychological and emotional effects of racism on people of color have to be recognized (Daniel, 2000). Poussaint (2000) has conceptualized racism as a source of chronic stress and trauma, with severe psychological consequences for African Americans. Trauma can be a function of sudden traumatogenic events or the result of repeated insults and injuries.

Clinicians, too, should be alert to intergenerational sources of trauma. African Americans, Native Americans, Japanese Americans, Jewish Americans, and other groups that have experienced extreme and overwhelming historical racism, such as genocide, ethnic cleansing, and slavery, have a collective memory that never completely goes away. The awareness that others could do this to one's ancestors (or you and your children, had you lived in that era) can foster a profound sense of sadness and dismay.

GRIEF AND MOURNING

When an awareness and acknowledgement of racism enters the clinical relationship, it involves getting in touch with something that is profoundly distressing. Such sadness is difficult to tolerate much of the time and thus is often repressed, displaced, or channeled elsewhere. Counseling and therapy create spaces where people can confront, and bring into conscious awareness, that which often has been unexamined. The depth of sadness that can be expressed is akin to the grief and mourning that follow when someone has died. Metaphorically and literally, racism is a process of truncating potential, limiting success, and causing pain, harm, wounds, and suffering.

Unexpressed grief usually finds an outlet, often one that is destabilizing or counterproductive. It can be the source of anger and rage or lead to chronic anxiety and depression. Thus, it is healthy and helpful to identify, name, and explore grief and to enter a process of mourning. Clients who have experienced racism can mourn the wounds that they and their loved ones have suffered. Those with race privilege can grieve their loss of innocence about the fairness of society or the losses that others have suffered. If it progresses through phases, mourning ultimately can be liberating, freeing people to empower themselves and to work on behalf of others.

THEORETICAL BIASES

In large measure, mental health work in the helping professions reflects dominant, Eurocentric cultural values. The foundation for counseling theory and practice methods developed out of the experience of white clinicians and researchers working almost exclusively with white clients' systems. The theoretical base for many of the helping professions is predicated on a certain worldview, a set of assumptions concerning human behavior, and set of values concerning mental health needs and interventions.

Our ability to be effective cross-racial workers is severely hampered if we do not recognize and act on these limitations. Theoretical biases are manifested in assumptions about human behavior, development, and expression, which we have discussed already. Even concepts that are basic and taken for granted in most clinical training programs can carry a great deal of cultural bias (Roland, 1996). For example, separation and individuation often are seen as healthy benchmarks of development. Yet these concepts are Westernized and presuppose that differentiating oneself from parents and siblings and attaining an independent sense of self is good and normal. Many cultures, however, emphasize interdependence and downplay an autonomous and freestanding self (Yeh & Hwang, 2000). Another example is a clinical emphasis on disclosure of affect and talking about feelings, which is a norm in Western cultures but not necessarily in others.

Theoretical biases are buttressed by their fit with assumptions and biases in the culture at large, which makes them appear "normal" while marginalizing other cultures and worldviews. They are replicated and promulgated because most clinicians have been trained in programs where these biases are centralized and privileged. Teachers in clinical programs often have internalized these assumptions from their own training and practice experience. Agencies also reflect theoretical biases through their models of practice and programmatic structure. Thus, interrogating and dislodging Eurocentric clinical assumptions is a difficult thing to do. This relates to our discussion about power, as theory gives clinicians the power to define and diagnose, which is difficult to give up.

One way to counter clinical biases is to identify them and offer alternative ways of conceptualizing human development and clinical services that are responsive to cultural diversity. Much has been written about this (Appendix 11-4 provides resources). Ultimately, although there are sound practice principles, which this chapter will discuss, there are no theoretical recipes to guide us in working with people of all races and cultures. There is not a one-size-fits-all approach to cross-racial work. Interventions that are effective with a Vietnamese-American adolescent female who is seeking autonomy from her family of origin may not be the same as those called for with an Orthodox Greek-American male struggling with similar issues of autonomy. Clinical case planning relies on an understanding of the client's cultural context, his or her experiences of power, privilege, and social oppression, and a thorough assessment of each person's unique situation (Gaw, 1993).

A final theoretical challenge for clinical cross-racial work, particularly when the client is a person of color or multiracial, is that many theories start with a premise of pathology. The emphasis is on problems, unfulfilled wishes and desires, developmental hitches, and interpersonal weaknesses. Certainly, most people do not seek, or are not referred for, therapy because they are feeling good. The impetus for therapy typically comes from dissatisfaction, dysfunction, and disaffection. But when working with anyone who has been subjected to sustained and ongoing pressure from social oppression, which surely stems from racism, we must try to understand how they have coped and survived! What sources of strength and resiliency have sustained people? A theoretical perspective that identifies and honors strengths instead of pathology is crucial to successful clinical work and essential to cross-racial clinical work.

BARRIERS TO EFFECTIVE CROSS-RACIAL CLINICAL WORK

This book has already presented many ways by which racism creates barriers between people in communities, schools, workplaces, and society at large, and also has discussed how people internalize racism. Therefore, it is no wonder that cross-racial clinical work faces significant barriers and relies on interpersonal relationships and the exploration of internal states. We have identified three major obstacles to successful cross-racial clinical work: internalized racism, inattention to power and privilege, and defensive racial dynamics.

INTERNALIZED RACISM

Internalized racism can mean either internalized feelings of superiority and privilege or feelings of being less worthy or responsible for one's own social oppression. Multiracial people may experience a mixture of both. As described in Chapter 6, social identity development involves uncovering internalized belief systems and trying to move beyond them. This is particularly important for clinicians, as any internalized racism potentially can be enacted with clients and could be damaging to the therapeutic process. Unexamined internalized racism also makes the therapist or counselor vulnerable to the client's internalized racism (Comas-Diaz & Jacobsen, 2001).

For clinicians of color and multiracial clinicians, the dynamics of internalized racism can play out in many ways. Working with clients of their own racial or ethnic background can evoke strong responses if a client is exploring an issue of low self-esteem. This could strike an empathic chord, resulting in overidentification, or, conversely, seem threatening to clinicians, causing them to erect an empathic wall with the client to avoid dealing with their *own* pain. Clients of color from ethnic or racial backgrounds different from the clinician's can stir up similar reactions or trigger the clinician's internalized biases toward that ethnic or racial group. If the client is perceived as having more privilege, it can foster feelings of resentment, and less empathy for the client (Ferguson & King, 1997). Many possible dynamics for clinicians of color working with white clients, including reenactment of agent-target roles or resistance to those roles, can become a form of counter-transference. These are but a few examples of the risks of carrying unprocessed internalized racism by clinicians of color.

For white clinicians working with clients of color, the greatest risk is that the clinician will enact unconscious feelings of privilege and superiority. With white clients there is the danger of colluding with racism by virtue of both client and worker carrying internalized racism. Another risk for white clinicians is that of carrying strong feelings of guilt and shame over racism and overreacting to clients of color or acting in ways that assuage the therapist's feelings but are not necessarily responsive to the client's needs. Unexamined internalized racism is a major dynamic in defensive racial dynamics.

INATTENTION TO POWER AND PRIVILEGE

As described above, unequal power and privilege are major elements of racism, and they carry over to clinical encounters. White clinicians working with clients of color all too readily exercise power in an unconscious way that reenacts the dynamics of societal racism. Clients may appear compliant, but this may be masking resentment, disaffection, and lack of investment in the therapeutic process with a clinician who appears to be insensitive and untrustworthy. Clinicians of color and multiracial clinicians, too, should be attentive to how issues of power and privilege have an impact on their relationship with clients, whatever the client's race or ethnicity.

DEFENSIVE RACIAL DYNAMICS

Ridley (1995) has argued that "defensive racial dynamics" pose a big threat to establishing a constructive therapeutic alliance and achieving positive treatment outcomes, particularly with white clinicians and clients of color. Examples include color-blindness, color-consciousness, cultural transference, cultural counter-transference, and cultural ambivalence.

COLOR-BLINDNESS Color-blindness is manifested when white clinicians do not recognize or acknowledge a client's race or ethnicity. As stated previously, this can be a consequence of a well-intentioned effort to treat all clients equally. In therapy, however, it can convey a strong lack of empathy about clients' race or ethnicity, unique cultural heritage, and social experiences that result from their racial or ethnic identity. It also closes off potential discussion of the client's reactions to the therapist's race or ethnicity, which can truncate the relation-ship and create prohibited zones of discourse.

Although Ridley was addressing white clinicians working with people of color, color-blindness can be problematic for clinicians of color and multiracial clinicians as well. If clinicians of color do not recognize the meaning of a client's race/ethnicity, or the impact that their own race may have on a client's reactions and transference, the same problems identified with white clinicians can emerge.

COLOR-CONSCIOUSNESS   At the other end of the spectrum from color-blindness is color-consciousness, in which clinicians overly emphasize race and ethnicity. Although race and ethnicity are important, they are not always central to the therapeutic process or the critical area of focus for clinician and client. Race and ethnicity can be overemphasized, or brought up at the wrong time, which changes the agenda and direction to reflect the clinician's ideology more than the client's needs. The result can be to amplify differences and underplay commonalities and areas for potential joining and collaboration, which weakens the therapeutic alliance.

CULTURAL TRANSFERENCE AND COUNTER-TRANSFERENCE   We use the terms "transfer-ence" and "counter-transference" broadly here. Transference denotes the client's feelings and reactions toward a clinician, shaped and influenced by earlier experiences and relationships. Thus, the clinician might remind the client of someone else—often a significant person in the client's life—or the clinician–client relationship unconsciously evokes other relationships.

Counter-transference refers to clinicians' projections onto the client, as well as clinicians' reactions to clients' interactions and transference toward clinicians. Although Ridley uses the term "cultural," transference and counter-transference can be attached to race, as well as to ethnicity and culture. Race and culture add to the dimensions of transference and counter-transference, potentially heightening and deepening their interaction. This is true particularly if strong feelings or reactions (negative or positive) are attached to the thera-pist's or client's race, or if either party has had limited exposure to the racial or ethnic group that the other represents. In such situations, stereotypes or symbols gain importance and can become the grist of the mutual process of transference.

In our view, transference and counter-transference are metaphors for the intersubjective dance of clinical work. When working cross-racially/culturally, the subjective worlds of both parties influence and are influenced by the other person. With families or groups, this dynamic is magnified and becomes even more complex.

CULTURAL AMBIVALENCE   What Ridley means by "cultural ambivalence" is that clinicians are conflicted about their reactions, including transference and counter-transference, toward the client. An example is a white clinician who feels threatened by a client of color and holds tightly to the reins of power, and at the same time he wants to be seen by the client as empathic and not racially preju-diced. For a clinician of color, it could mean that she rigidly maintains her professional authority while fending off racially based (and possibly gender-based) challenges from a white male client. Multiracial clinicians, while having the advantage of being able to connect with more than one race and culture, are also subject to ambivalence about identifying with clients who consider them-selves to be exclusively white or of exclusively of color. In all these examples, the clinicians are expressing their own needs and reactions at the possible expense of clients' progress and well-being.

GUIDELINES FOR EFFECTIVE CROSS-RACIAL CLINICAL WORK

As mentioned earlier in this chapter, the many nuances and complexities of working cross-racially/cross-culturally depend on many factors, including the client's and clinician's race and ethnicity, as well as the meaning that race and ethnicity has for their social identity. (Appendix 11-4 provides sources of further reading about these factors and recommendations for more culturally responsive clinical practice.) We will identify basic principles of cross-racial/cultural work for multiracial clinicians, clinicians of color, and white clinicians. These principles include working with social identity, developing listening and observation skills, using racial transference and counter-transference, working with strong emotions, viewing clients in their historical and social context, and providing mirroring and empathy. It also will address when to bring up race and culture and how to deal with bias.

WORKING WITH SOCIAL IDENTITY

To put this as simply as possible, working with social identity means knowing one's own social identity and learning about clients' social identifies. An honest appraisal of one's own social identity entails looking at all of the dimensions mentioned in Chapter 6, as well as evaluating what phase(s) one is in, par-ticularly with respect to race and ethnicity. The exercises provided in Chapter 6 facilitate this process. The more aware clinicians are of their social identities, the less likely they will be to act on their own needs and impulses. Awareness of social identity also strengthens a clinician's capacity to tolerate challenges and strong emotions from clients.

Working with social identity involves trying to understand the client's identity and the meaning it has for him or her. It is an exercise in inter-subjectivity, as both client and worker learn about themselves and one another together (Greene, Jensen, & Jones, 1996). Each person brings his or her own experiences and meanings, as shaped and constructed by family, community, and society, which then are reconfigured in the consulting room. Ultimately, working with social identity means that clinicians are in touch with and able to access the full range of their social identities and to create space for clients' social identities to emerge and find recognition and validation. (See Exercise 11.1 for an example of the interaction of client and worker social identities, as well as Appendix 11-2 to explore culturally influenced behaviors.)

FOCUSING ON STRENGTHS

Every clinician must come to understand and apply his or her own worldview and biases in all types of clinical work, but particularly in cross-racial clinical practice. A strengths-based perspective (Woods & Hollis, 2000; Saleebey, 2002) allows the clinician to frame clients' struggles in a way that highlights their supports, assets, and resourcefulness rather than their pathology, or to fall into a pattern of placing blame. Helping clients to identify personal, family, and community resources is a powerful way to include them in the clinical process, offering them the opportunity to have a meaningful stake in their own treatment. Many ethnic groups in the United States, particularly people of color, see reliance on family and community as a great strength, rather than a liability.

If clinicians fail to heed clients' values about help-seeking behavior and assume that clients should solve their problems on their own, clinicians might inadvertently isolate clients by encouraging them to fend for themselves rather than helping them to flourish in an available community of support. Conversely, if clinicians come from a culture with a collective orientation, they may not appreciate the importance for some clients to achieve autonomy. Whatever a clinician's values and biases about the relative virtues of autonomy and collective support, he or she must not impose them on clients and, instead, empower clients by validating their strengths.

LISTENING AND OBSERVING

All clinical work involves trying to understand another person from that person's perspective. This holds true for psychodynamic and cognitive-behavioral approaches, as well as many other subgroups of therapeutic orientations that rely on the clinician–client relationship. When working across race and culture, clinicians are asked to take their clients' perspective empathically when clinician and client have significant differences in social identity and accompanying power and privilege (Dyche & Zayas, 2001). Even when clients and clinicians have many similarities in personality, feelings, and values, important parts of a client's experience will diverge from those of the clinician. Thus, the therapist must develop keen listening and observation skills.

What clinicians see and hear from clients present access points to the clients' experience. Clinicians may use their own feelings to try to gauge the clients' feelings—wondering if they are experiencing their own inner maps and libraries of experiences. And when working across race and culture, experiences or consciousness may differ so significantly from that of clients that clinicians take a wrong fork in the road. Internalized stereotypes and biases lurking beneath the radar screen of consciousness further cloud clinical acumen (Perez-Foster, 1998). This is why we stress anchoring perceptions, hypotheses, and interventions with the observable, as much as possible. By letting clients know what we see and hear, we convey attentiveness while opening up channels to pursue as the client helps us to understand the meaning of what we detect.

WORKING WITH RACIAL TRANSFERENCE AND COUNTER-TRANSFERENCE

As Ridley (1995) has argued, the cultural dimension of transference and counter-transference is always present, and we extrapolate that to include racial transference and counter-transference. Many therapists, particularly those using psychodynamic methods, discuss transference and counter-transference as a means for using the clinical relationship to further client insight, growth, and change. Working cross-racially requires space for consideration of this dimension—how it feels and what it means to both client and worker. It should not be treated as the proverbial "elephant in the room."

Although the clinician does not have to raise the issue immediately, it certainly should be discussed at some point. For the clinician, this means being able to access and track one's own transference and counter-transference, as well as develop the capacity to share reflections and explore meanings with clients. Leary (1995, 1997, 2000) has written about the use of racial transference and counter-transference.

One of the authors of this text (Garran) encountered this dynamic in a family session with a white, Italian-American, upper-middle-class family. The parents clearly were distressed that their son was in psychotherapy, and they wanted him to be discharged from receiving services. During a particularly volatile family meeting, the mother repeatedly maligned the worker, a woman of color, questioning her credentials and her ability to offer help to the family. The worker endured several tacit references to her "lack of adequate preparation" and to the allegation that she held her position only "because of affirmative action." At one point in the session, after the therapist's listening and gentle challenging, the parents revealed that they were fearful they had been summoned to participate in their son's psychotherapy because the worker was questioning their competence as parents and shaming them for their son's difficulties.

With this issue in the open, the work moved forward. The worker assured the parents that that was not her intent, and they were able to relax and relate to the therapist in a more appropriate and less inflammatory manner. This session was pivotal in the son's psychotherapy. Communication within the family improved as each recognized the assumptive styles of interaction that often impeded open dialogue with one another. (See Appendix 11-3 for a self-inventory about experiences with people from different cultures.)

ABILITY TO TOLERATE AND RESPOND TO STRONG AFFECT

We have described many of the strong feelings that racism can evoke in clients—anger, rage, guilt, shame, stress and trauma, and grief and mourning. When clients express these feelings, counselors and therapists may have difficulty tolerating these emotions, and this in turn can elicit strong affective reactions from clinicians. Although therapy often is enhanced by the expression and processing of strong affect, when it comes to race and racism, the magnitude of the reaction can feel overwhelming.

Many people are uncomfortable with direct and powerful manifestations of feelings such as rage and shame, and others are uneasy with candid confrontations about race and racism. Combining these emotions creates a potent combination. But if experiences of racism and attendant emotions cannot be expressed in counseling and therapy, where can they be processed?

Whatever affect a clinician is unable to handle becomes forbidden territory for clients. This reinforces the social unacceptability of both the feeling and its expression. The wider the range of feelings about racism that a clinician can accept, the more space is granted for clients to use these feelings as therapeutic levers. So how can clinicians increase their affective capacities? One way is through experience. The more they encounter powerful affect, the better they are able to manage reactions. Another way is to explore one's own experience with these emotions and to use self-reflection and insight to better understand their powerful hold. Clinicians can use exercises to explore their reactions to feelings, as well as try to desensitize themselves to feeling overwhelmed. (See Exercise 11:2, which helps clinicians to explore their reactions to anger and rage, and Exercise 1:2, Inventory of Triggers, in Chapter 1.)

A final way to work toward increasing affective capacity is through supervision. Supervisors and clinicians should be vigilant about bringing these issues out in the open to further the clinical work. With both cross-racial and racially homogeneous supervisory dyads, supervision can be challenging when it involves processing the powerful affect that tends to arise in cross-racial work. Workers and supervisors must be creative and open to finding ways to negotiate any discomfort or powerful affect that might arise from discussing these cases, or that might surface between them as the discussions unfold (Peterson, 1991).

Once therapists have expanded their affective tolerance, they can use a range of interventions. A helpful one is to connect the emotion with the client's presenting problems (Hardy & Laszloffy, 1995). A discussion of possible transference is another avenue to pursue. Tying emotions with historical and social conditions, such as webs of oppression, helps to externalize the source of unpleasant feelings, and it is a means to validate them as well. Clients can be assisted in sorting out what they are responsible for and what they have no control over. Hardy and Laszloffy also suggest that seeking underlying feelings, such as the grief and mourning beneath anger, is of value to clients. Clinicians should try to help clients find more socially constructive expression of feelings that are less likely to be personally harmful or counterproductive. A summary of these important factors is illustrated in Box 11.1.

| GUIDELINES FOR EFFECTIVE CROSS-CULTURAL/ CROSS-RACIAL WORK

- Know yourself. Assess your own racial and social identities, assumptions, worldviews, cultural values, privilege.
- Know your clients. Learn from them how they view themselves, the world, and you.
- Learn about your clients' culture to establish context.
- Learn about how webs of racism and oppression or passports of unearned privilege have affected your clients socially and have been internalized.
- Be self-reflective and introspective about the process between yourself and your clients, particularly cultural and racial transference and counter-transference.
- Be aware of blind spots, stereotypes, biases, internal tapes, and fears.
- Enhance your ability to tolerate pain, rage, and client mistrust.
- Seek supervision and consultation.
- Examine theories for biases and assumptions, and learn about alternative theories (e.g., empowerment and resiliency-oriented).
- Seek organizational support for multiculturalism and anti-racism.

SITUATING CLIENTS IN THEIR HISTORICAL AND SOCIAL CONTEXT

Clients may or may not know about the historical and social conditions of racism that have contributed to psychic scars and wounds, and discussing these directly may or may not be clinically appropriate. What is important, in any case, is that clinicians have a good understanding of these conditions and of the ways by which webs of racism affect their clients. This helps to avoid unfair pathologizing and problematizing of what often are normal reactions to exceedingly stressful circumstances. It also helps clinicians to better understand the social conditions to which their clients return upon leaving the consulting room and to enact realistic interventions and follow-up. For example, a client who has relocated to the United States recently from war-torn Rwanda might not be comfortable speaking of the atrocities witnessed, because of a continuing fear of retribution that the client has internalized. Clinicians should be aware of these nuances so they do not rush clients to tell their stories before they are ready.

MIRRORING AND EMPATHY

We have described at length the lack of validation and mirroring for many people of color in society. Mirroring is the process whereby a person receives a reflection of himself or herself from others that is positive, affirming, and validating. The concept of mirroring is derived from Heinz Kohut's theory of *self-psychology*, which refers to the reflections that people receive from family members and other significant others (Eagle, 1984). Hertzberg (1990) expanded this theory to include cultural and social markers.

Social mirroring occurs when viewing beauty advertisements, reading greeting cards, or seeing national politicians or CEOs, which frequently reflect positive images of white people and either an absence of or negative images of people of color. Hertzberg employs additional concepts from self-psychology, such as "idealizing," which involves internalizing another person as a self-ideal. She argues further that this happens on a public and social level, where fewer affirmative role models are available for people of color.

Therapists can employ mirroring effectively with their clients using a technique similar to Rogers's (1951) client-centered therapy. Here, the clinician makes a sustained effort to maintain an empathic connection with a client, whatever material is being brought up, and to mirror the client's value and worth by communicating empathic understanding. In this process, clients do not feel judged or humiliated and are better able to explore feelings or self-concepts that are unpleasant, damaged, or stigmatized. Given the feelings considered in the previous section, mirroring is an effective stance from which to develop a therapeutic alliance and to help repair self-concepts damaged as a consequence of racism.

Mirroring also is consistent with a strengths-based approach, in which clinicians help clients identify and access their strengths, assets, and coping mechanisms. Clinicians must review with clients how they have survived and endured oppression through their resiliency, which can be difficult to retrieve in times of duress. Consider an adolescent of color from an urban area and her need for role models of color as she travels to a majority white community to attend boarding school. What are the mirroring needs of this young woman and how can they be met? What are her strengths, and how might she draw upon them? Mirroring is particularly important for people whose self-concept has been injured by racism and those who suddenly find themselves in a new situation, where they have difficulty seeing themselves in those around them.

Bringing up Issues of Race and Racism

One of the questions that students most commonly ask is when and how to bring up issues of race and racism. Unfortunately, this question has no simple answer. From experiences of grappling with these issues (Carter, 1995; Ridley, 1995), there is no set rule. Clinicians should be willing and able to broach the topic, but they should understand that there is no formula about when and how to do this effectively.

Talk about race and racism should occur within the overall context of counseling and therapy, which includes the client's presenting problems, the organizational context of treatment, treatment goals, the bond between client and worker and the dynamics of that relationship. We caution against rigid admonitions such as telling clinicians to always bring up race or ethnicity, but at the same time are wary when clinicians seldom or never bring it up.

Certain situations lend themselves to inquiries about this topic, such as when a client of color relates examples of racism with a white clinician or a white client working with a clinician of color brings up racial stereotypes or expresses negativity or ambivalence about people of color. Both instances present an opening for the clinician to invite reflection and discussion about the salience of these issues in the clinical relationship. At times, indirect yet probing questions can invite clients to talk about race and racism if they choose. Clients must have agency with this process and the clinician should neither close it off nor force it open.

Clinicians should be self-reflective and mindful of their own inclinations to want to bring up or avoid talking about race (Cook, 1994). Writing process recordings and reviewing them allow clinicians to track themes that are either present but unnamed or avoidant maneuvers by the therapist. Supervision, case conferences, and discussions with trusted colleagues are other avenues for exploring and monitoring these themes. Audio and visual recording sessions can assist with tracking the clinical process and highlighting verbal and bodily reactions.

Ultimately, both client and worker are aware of race and ethnicity on some level (Leary, 1997, 2000). Their relevance and importance vary considerably for each client and therapeutic dyad. As in making most clinical decisions, counselors and therapists should follow the lead of their clients and also use their own judgment, in consultation with others, about the relevance of this topic for treatment, the timing of discussing it, and the best way to frame it.

RESPONDING TO BIAS

Racial biases and stereotypes will inevitably surface in clinical work. Although workers should not collude with bias, they should consider how best to respond in a clinical context. Maintaining the clinical relationship is essential and necessary for helping the client. Rupturing the relationship in response to client bias will not help clients with either their presenting problems or their prejudices.

Clients may express intolerance in the consulting room in two ways:

1. by describing their views and feelings toward people outside of the therapeutic dyad, or
2. by expressing them directly toward the therapist.

The latter is more challenging because of its potential to trigger strong reactions in the clinician, but it also provides opportunities for counselors to explore these views, and the implicit transference, directly with the client. When bias is directed outside of the consulting room, it also may stir up strong reactions in the therapist. A risk for some clinicians is that they will not perceive or acknowledge client bias and will signal approval either actively or passively through acquiescence.

Clinicians can use several strategies in these situations. One strategy is to continue to work on one's own triggers and to increase the capacity to tolerate feelings of outrage, anger, pain, and disgust engendered by the client's statements. Ideally, clients should not have to consult with clinicians who are so overwhelmed in the moment by such strong emotions. Also fruitful is to question clients' prejudicial attitudes, much as counselors help clients explore other pathogenic or irrational belief systems. This is much more likely to be effective if it can be done in a nonjudgmental, nonaggressive fashion.

Another strategy is to make overt the covert, if the client is raising bias in a coded or indirect manner. Clinicians, too, can make their own values known, as long as they do this in a way that does not attack the client or make him or her feel less worthy or honorable. If this seems too delicate and raises concerns that such a challenge might influence the therapeutic alliance adversely, clinicians can discuss the views and values of others, such as public figures and social scientists, to offer an opposing narrative. Then both client and worker can interrogate the contrast between nonracist viewpoints and the perspective the client expresses.

All of these interventions should be linked to the client's presenting problems and the themes and issues of treatment. Also, clinicians must seek supervision and consultation to process their feelings and reactions and to ensure that their responses are crafted to achieve maximum effectiveness.

Issues for Clinicians Who Identify as White

White clinicians must continually monitor and work through any internalized feelings of white privilege, as well as stereotypes and biases, some of which remain unrecognized. It is hard for people to see their own unconscious prejudices, which is why supervision, consultation, and the use of process and video recordings are so useful. As discussed, all clinicians should be mindful of their power, and this is particularly relevant for white clinicians working with clients of color.

Clinicians who identify as white also should be mindful of impulses to please clients of color or to be seen as a "good guy." This can produce situations of colluding with clients or backing away from situations in which confronting or challenging clients is called for.

All clinicians, and certainly white clinicians, benefit from regularly assessing and doing an inventory of their own social identities and understanding how this influences clients who have different identities. White clinicians whose social identity includes a lot of privilege will benefit from learning about the webs of oppression that their clients encounter, webs they have not experienced personally.

Consulting with people of color can assist this process, as long as the burden of education is not shifted overly to colleagues of color. All clinicians should question their theoretical orientations for culturally biased assumptions and principles. White clinicians in particular should be cautious about accepting theoretical assumptions because they potentially are consistent with the clinician's own worldview and value system and thus are more difficult to detect.

ISSUES FOR CLINICIANS WHO IDENTIFY AS PEOPLE OF COLOR OR MULTIRACIAL

As with white clinicians, clinicians of color, and those who identity as biracial or multiracial should complete regular social-identity inventories and consider ways in which their own social identities may interact with those of clients. The same is true for conducting inventories of triggers, issues that clients can stir up, assumptions, and worldviews, as well as internalized biases and stereotypes. Clinicians have to be mindful of the potential for over-identification, particularly with clients who have similar backgrounds and experiences, as well as the potential to under-identify, which is more likely with clients who have led significantly more or less privileged lives.

One of the biggest challenges for clinicians of color and multiracial clinicians is the potential for being the target of direct racist comments by clients, or hearing clients talk in biased ways against others. Hearing biased comments, including those directed toward one's own race or culture, is particularly common for multiracial clinicians who look white. Clients also may test the clinician's authority and expertise. Clinicians of color often have to work harder than their white counterparts to establish their credentials. This may necessitate confronting clients more frequently, which has to be balanced with establishing and maintaining therapeutic alliances.

Clinicians of color and multiracial clinicians also may identify agency policies and procedures that are detrimental to their clients. This places the clinician in the position of advocating within his or her own organization or trying to protect clients from destructive practices. This takes extra energy and can put the clinician in a more confrontational, and even vulnerable, position with the agency administration. Clinicians who are bicultural and bilingual often find themselves managing heavy and demanding caseloads and without adequate time for translation, advocacy, and other necessary activities.

All of these factors are indicative of the importance of clinicians of color having support systems inside and outside of agencies. Clinicians of color and multiracial workers have to contend with the issues already discussed and also with bias, exclusion, and other forms of racism among their colleagues, and systemically within the organization. Confronting these problems is time-consuming and emotionally draining. Organizations themselves must be aware of these dynamics and take steps to protect and support workers of color.

SUPERVISION AND CONSULTATION

Clearly, cross-racial/cultural work requires honest self-awareness, the ability to manage strong emotions and reactions, and the capacity to empathize with people who have very different experiences, worldviews, and access to resources. Supervision and consultation always are important in clinical work and certainly are necessary in cross-racial/cultural work. Clinical supervision is a relational and developmental process and, thus, many of the issues that have been identified with clients must be negotiated—in a process that often parallels the helping relationship itself. Supervision involves teaching as well as ensuring professional accountability, which includes the capacity to work cross-racially/cross-culturally.

Supervisors and supervisees alike have to be able to track and analyze the clinical work being done with clients and to collaboratively explore issues of race and culture. Supervisors, too, must be able to tolerate not only the strong affect originating from clients but also their own feelings, as well as reactions stirred up in themselves.

The supervisory relationship is a space where both worker and supervisor will have to process issues that arise between them, as well as issues between worker and client. To this end, supervisors must be skilled in recognizing the dynamics that emerge in cross-racial work, and also how they may play out in supervision (Cashwell, Looby, & Housley, 1997). Thus, supervisors should be able to raise issues of difference or sameness in the supervisory relationship in a way that does not intimidate or shut down a supervisee. A supervisor of color should be able to discuss with a white worker, as well as a multiracial worker or a worker of color, the implications of race and ethnicity on the clinical material as it unfolds. The same is true of a white supervisor. Supervisors of any racial or ethnic identity have to be able to track the complex levels of transference and counter-transference that involve client, worker, supervisor, and other agency personnel.

Supervisors often are the ones who have to broach the subject of race and ethnicity in cross-racial work. Workers (student interns and professional workers) are often uncomfortable doing so or feel unsure about how their comments, observations, or questions might be received. If a supervisor is comfortable discussing the racial dynamics of clinical work, this confidence and comfort will be evident to most supervisees. Supervisors should be aware, though, that mentioning race and ethnicity just once is not sufficient. These issues and concerns must be revisited so the supervisee will feel permission to discuss them and also to convey a message of acceptance on the part of the supervisor (Black, Maki, & Nunn, 1997).

At times, supervisors and supervisees will benefit from additional consultation. Consultation can be about the work with the client, the supervisory relationship itself, the clash between agency policies and client well-being, or a combination of these. Consultants may help to clarify roles and expectations, as well as give specific feedback about cultural misunderstandings and unacknowledged racial dynamics. Depending on the racial or cultural mix of client, worker, and supervisor, there are times when even more perspectives will be valuable and clinical work will benefit from multiple consultants. Adding more people to the clinical process presents a greater potential for role confusion, conflicting advice, or splitting and triangulation of relationships. This is particularly true with issues of race and culture, which carry strong affect, as well as questions of identity and ideology.

Thus, all professional players must work together to minimize rifts and covert dynamics that undermine colleagues and, ultimately, services to clients. Direct, open, above-board communication is necessary, along with a willingness to process and negotiate conflicts and differences of opinion.

STRUCTURAL AND ENVIRONMENTAL ISSUES

In Chapter 10 we explored how helping professionals can work to transform their agencies into anti-racism organizations. This section will briefly consider some issues that particularly apply to those health and human service organizations that offer counseling and therapy.

ENVIRONMENT

The agency environment encompasses the physical building, waiting room, consulting rooms, and accessories such as artwork and magazines. It also includes the climate and culture conveyed to consumers. Is this a place where all people, whatever their social identities, feel welcomed and comfortable? Many agencies take the overall environment for granted, yet it sends distinct messages to clients seeking services. Small details, such as outdated reading materials or magazines and signs only in English in an agency that serves many people who speak Spanish only, influence whether consumers will feel comfortable. The condition and appearance of waiting rooms, office spaces, even restrooms send unspoken yet potent messages to clients about how much they are valued and respected.

Clients also notice if the spaces for workers are in much better condition than those for consumers. The clinical environment should reflect, respect, and respond to various cultures and be one where all consumers feel included.

ACCESS

To take advantage of clinical services, clients must have adequate access to care. As described in previous chapters, people of color are more likely to rely on public transportation and less likely to have sufficient health insurance or the ability to pay for services. Thus, clinical service agencies must be located near adequate public transportation. Extended clinic hours will accommodate consumers who are working early or late shifts and those who have to transfer buses several times to get to work. Safety, too, is important, both in the area surrounding the agency and inside the agency itself.

For financial or cultural reasons, some consumers do not use daycare for their preschool children or after-school care for older children. Providing adequate play spaces for children, or even supervised crèches, enables clients to utilize these services and concentrate better while they are attending sessions.

Cutbacks in public funding for counseling and mental health programs, as well as tightened eligibility requirements and restrictions by insurance and managed-care companies, have made it more difficult for agencies to serve all of the clients who would benefit from their services, as well as to offer enough sessions. Although this is a difficult issue for financially strapped agencies, it is significant nonetheless. As described many times in this book, as an overall group, people of color have less economic and social assets and resources, so they are affected disproportionately by cuts in public services. Even if an agency has done a good job in training the staff to be culturally responsive, it will go for naught if clients cannot access the services. This has to be an ongoing priority for clinical agencies working on their own and in concert with one another.

STAFFING AND BOARD REPRESENTATION

This topic was covered in Chapter 10 and is reiterated here only briefly. To effectively serve a multiracial, multicultural population, an organization must have multiracial/cultural staff represented at all levels. If clients speak languages other than English, the organization should have bilingual staff members as well. Advisory and policy-making boards should reflect the diversity of the clients (including consumer representation on boards) and of the community being served.

CONCLUSION

Working across race and culture can be a positive and beneficial experience for workers, and ultimately of value to consumers as well as the agency providing the services. Cross-racial/cross-cultural work is found in the worker–client relationship and also is manifested in supervisory, consultative, and collegial associations. Because clinical services explore intimate, personal issues, they represent an avenue for countering internalized racism for those with race privilege as well as those who are targeted.

Clinical work demands that workers be aware of their own complex social identities, learn about their clients' social identities, and develop skills for bridging differences in experience, culture, and meaning. Power is a dynamic in any clinical situation—particularly when working cross-racially/culturally—and it must be managed with sensitivity and respect because strong feelings and reactions are ever present in the mix.

Despite the many obstacles to cross-racial/cross-cultural clinical work, staffs of many counseling and mental health services across the country have responded to the challenges and developed the capacity to provide quality clinical services for consumers having a range of ethnic and racial backgrounds. Becoming culturally responsive workers, who confront oppression in themselves as well as others, must be ongoing, but the investments are well worth the gains.

EXERCISE 11.1 CROSSED RACIAL IDENTITY
BETWEEN WORKER AND CLIENT

A second-generation Chilean American sophomore attending a state university is seeking counseling about her test anxiety. Upon arriving at the university, she did not view herself as a person of color, but with encouragement from her friends recently joined the Council for Students of Color. She has been rethinking events and relationships from high school in light of her new awareness of being a Latina in the United States.

The counselor at the college counseling service is white and has not thought a lot about his own racial or ethnic identity. When the student tries to talk about her newfound awareness of her racial and ethnic identities, the counselor tries to redirect her to examine her parents' expectations for her when she was younger and whether she has any cognitive or neurological learning disabilities.

The student accuses the counselor of turning her identity into a pathology and says that a number of students in the Council for Students of Color have had this experience at the college counseling center. The therapist feels defensive and believes the student is using her identity as a way to avoid examining important and painful issues.

QUESTIONS:

1. Using the social identity models presented in Chapter 6, how might you describe both the student's and the counselor's racial and ethnic identity development?
2. How are their respective levels of racial and ethnic identity interacting in this vignette?
3. Can you think of ways the counselor can respond more helpfully?
4. What kind of work or training might be helpful to the counselor to better prepare him for working cross-culturally and cross-racially?
5. How can the counselor's supervisor be helpful?

EXERCISE 11.2   EXPLORING EMOTIONS

The following questions will help you explore your reactions to anger and rage. The same questions can be asked about other emotions, such as guilt, shame, and grief.

QUESTIONS ABOUT ANGER AND RAGE:

What are your values about expressing rage and anger?
What are your thoughts and reactions to rage when a client is expressing rage?
How can you identify rage?
How do you validate the client's rage?
What are some constructive ways for clients to channel rage and anger?

12 CHAPTER | TEACHING ABOUT RACISM

CHAPTER CONTENTS

To include a chapter on teaching in a book whose readers are primarily students may seem odd. Why bring up teaching with prospective helping professionals who are still learning about racism?

We talk about teaching because learning about racism is an ongoing endeavor, even for teachers—who often learn from their students. Viewing students as teachers is consistent with the model of relational, interactive learning articulated by educator and philosopher Paulo Freire (1970, 1994). Teaching and learning can be similar. For instance, studying about anti-racism necessitates self-reflection, understanding and respecting others, and working collaboratively with other people—as does teaching.

Freire made an important distinction between a "banking mode" of education and a dialogic or problem-posing approach (Adams, 1997; Freire, 1970, 1994). The former assumes that teachers are repositories of knowledge that they can transfer or deposit into the vault of a student's mind. A dialogic approach is a collaborative method of posing questions and seeking answers without knowing them in advance. Teaching, then, is not only about obtaining information from an expert. It is also an interactive process in which teachers and students approach education in an open and inquisitive fashion and learn from one another. Social learning does not occur by itself; it requires other people (Wasserman & Doran, 1999). As instructors, we have learned about racism and our own relationship to racism every time we have been in a teaching situation, whether in the classroom or in agencies.

This chapter assumes a broad definition of teaching. Teaching helping professionals takes place in classrooms as well as in internships, workshops, conferences, and continuing education programs. It also occurs in "unlearning racism" support groups and in organizations that support and advocate on behalf of students of color. Teaching, too, takes place in relationships, whether intimate or casual, with family, friends, colleagues. Learning moments happen in encounters with strangers. Although this chapter is devoted to teaching in classrooms and workshops, the ideas presented also apply to micro-interactions. Teaching and learning about racism constitute an ongoing enterprise.

A good place to start is to think about what has helped and hindered your learning about racism.

> What have been your most important and significant learning experiences?
>
> What teaching techniques reached you, and which ones did you not respond to?
>
> Have you had experiences with learning about racism in which you shut down or felt overwhelmed by feelings of anger, guilt, or shame?
>
> If you could replay the tape, what would you do differently or hope that others would do differently with you?
>
> Have you been in discussions in which you struggled to say what you believe or lacked the information or confidence to present your case effectively?

As teachers and learners, we all carry reservoirs of experiences upon which we can draw as we pursue anti-racism education. Each of us has our own unique mix of learning styles and strengths and weaknesses as communicators. Many, if not most people, learn in multiple ways and integrate knowledge from various sources.

Learning about racism requires knowledge about facts and concepts, history and social patterns, but also requires introspection, self-awareness, and empathy. Conceptual understanding helps us to discern patterns of communication and intergroup relations. Because of the levels of racism, learning about it requires a combination of cognitive understandings and personal insights. Thus, a variety of teaching strategies, both inside and outside of the classroom, leads to a deeper and wider grasp of racism and anti-racism.

Teaching about any topic in a group setting necessitates responding to many different learning styles. When teaching about racism, several factors make the enterprise even more complex. One is the *emotional resonance* of the topic, which invariably activates strong feelings and, at times, defensive maneuvers. Another major dynamic is that students and instructors have all had different experiences of racism and are at different phases of racial and social identity development. Thus, we end up with diverse needs, divergent reactions to material, varying political stances, and different levels of awareness. Powerful cross-currents, tides, and undertows of interpersonal interactions elevate the importance of good group facilitation and management skills, as people or subgroups can easily become hurt, alienated, angry, and withdrawn.

Another risk is that instructors will meet the needs of some students at the expense of others. Because whites and people of color have had dissimilar experiences of racism, their learning goals often are different. For example, a primary learning task for many white students is to learn about white privilege and internalized stereotypes and racist attitudes and beliefs, while for students of color, the task can be to excise internalized racism and feel validated and empowered. Responding to all of these needs at once in a racially mixed class is difficult.

This dilemma frequently is resolved by instructors' spending a great deal of time helping white students work through resistance or paralyzing emotions such as guilt and shame. Although this is essential work, it can occur at the expense of the learning needs of students of color in the class. It can be inspiring to witness people with privilege working to dismantle it but also painful for people of color to observe white people, perhaps their friends, struggling with their lack of awareness of racism.

A dynamic frequently encountered in classrooms is that white students seek "safety" as they explore racism, which often means that they will not be "attacked" for harboring racist stereotypes or lack of awareness of white privilege. Often, students of color respond that they have never had the privilege of being "safe" from the wounds of racism. Yet white people do need space to explore the complexities of racism and white privilege before "unlearning" it. These are examples of the complex interactions and group dynamics that have to be considered when teaching about race and racism.

EXAMPLES

Despite the complexities, we do not believe that a person has to wait until he or she feels like a "race expert" to teach about racism. The following are examples of students being teachers.

REGINA

A social work student in our experience, whom we will call Regina, grew up white in a predominantly black community. Initially she took the stance of knowing a great deal about racism because of her extensive experience with people of color, but she soon opened up to exploring the white privileges that she had, which most of her childhood friends were not accorded.

After taking the anti-racism course, Regina entered her field placement, where she, like all students, was expected to conduct a small anti-racism project. She decided to offer a mini-version of the anti-racism course that she had taken as a brown-bag lunch seminar meeting for the staff in her agency. The group that met was racially and ethnically mixed and numbered about 10 to 15 people.

Regina realized that she did not have extensive teaching skills, nor did she consider herself to be an expert on racism. But she did have a strong commitment to doing meaningful anti-racism work and knew that she could draw on her life experiences, knowledge, and self-awareness, having been a student in an anti-racism course. She proceeded cautiously and with humility, using articles and handouts from her anti-racism course, consulting with her former professors, and working closely with her supervisor, who was a white woman also strongly committed to anti-racism work. Regina was open and transparent about her lack of teaching experience and her limited perspective about racism as a white person. And she modeled a willingness to explore her own biases and blindspots.

She first worked with the group to clarify expectations and establish norms—a topic we will consider in greater detail later. Her pedagogical approach was to ask staff members to read one or two articles addressing an important aspect of racism and then to facilitate a discussion. Some difficulties and tensions between staff members surfaced in the seminar, but the overall feedback—formally solicited through anonymous questionnaires—indicated that all staff members had found this to be a productive endeavor. It was a good learning experience about racism in a human service workplace and put anti-racism front and center as an organizational undertaking. The seminar opened up a difficult topic of conversation and demonstrated that it could be discussed and considered without huge emotional explosions.

Some staff members became more introspective and began considering issues that often were sidestepped or ignored. The seminar provided a space for people to listen and reflect while forming potential anti-racism alliances with one another. It also was a good experience for Regina, who learned more about herself and racism, strengthening her commitment to continue work as an anti-racism activist and educator.

The project involved some risks as well: The process could have become ensnared if staff conflicts had erupted. But the staff also had simmering feelings about the failure to explore this issue, and Regina's willingness to pursue it diligently, with caution and the support of allies, led to a meaningful experience and success.

ALICIA

Another real-life example of a student teaching others comes from a classroom experience in the graduate social work program where we teach. An advanced institutional racism course was being co-taught by a professor of color and a white professor. On more than one occasion, one white student attempted to find explanations *other* than racism when people of color in the class were describing incidents of racism that they had experienced, including one example given by the professor of color. The white professor confronted the white student strongly, which caused her to shut down and withdraw from class discussion.

A student of color in the classroom, Alicia, was disturbed by this. She e-mailed the professors, then raised her concerns in a subsequent class. Her major point was that students should be able to make mistakes, and that when the professor confronted a student too strongly, it inhibited learning and personal growth. This prompted class discussion that processed the interactions leading up to the confrontation by the professor, as well as the professor's response, including a fishbowl discussion (see Chapter 8).

Alicia then encouraged the white professor and the student who had been confronted to continue their conversation outside of the class, which they did. By the end of the course, many students reported that Alicia's intervention and the subsequent introspection, reflection, dialogue, and reparation of relationships was the most significant "learning moment" of the course.

MICHAEL

A final example of a student also being a teacher is Michael. When he was a junior in high school, he was the only teenager participating in a Study Circle group (see Chapter 8) to discuss race and racism. He lived in a town where people of color constituted only 12% of the population but were 25% of the public school population. Michael, who is white, was so affected by his Study Circle dialogue experience that he decided to do an anti-racism project as an independent study project while he was a senior. His project was ambitious: to prepare a curriculum to be distributed to all elementary and middle school teachers, in which teachers would learn how to discuss race and racism in their classes in a developmentally appropriate fashion, including explorations of white privilege.

After research, as well as consulting with anti-racism teachers and activists, he produced a 15-page booklet, which he then presented to the town's human rights commission, to an anti-racism activist group, to the local school committee, and at a meeting of all of the town's school principals. The *Anti-Racism Handbook* covered many relevant topics: teaching in a diverse classroom, definitions and concepts, breaking down personal prejudices, creating inclusive learning communities, examples of anti-racism class projects, dealing with resistance, and how to frame diversity issues. It also included an extensive bibliography and a survey for teachers to complete about their reactions to the handbook.

In his introduction, Michael used self-disclosure to open up the discussion:

> When I passed through the public elementary and middle schools in this town, I know that I often picked up on who teachers prioritized and encouraged most in the classroom, and it had an impact on my own personal prejudices that I wish didn't exist. I also internalized a sense that I was more deserving of attention than my classmates of color. It is so necessary for the classroom to create an anti-racism culture of resistance, by prioritizing traditionally marginalized groups and challenging racist language, values, assumptions, and behavior.

We do not want to minimize the challenges of teaching about racism or the importance of carefully preparing to engage in this enterprise. These examples illustrate some of the many ways to teach and how people with the status of "student" are able to work effectively as teachers. We now will discuss ways to enhance the effectiveness of teaching about race and racism: developing an effective course and class structure, co-creating a positive classroom climate, understanding ourselves as teachers and knowing our students, and employing specific teaching strategies and techniques. We also will consider what to do when conflict erupts or teachers feel stuck. The appendices include some exercises that teachers can use in helping students explore racism.

COURSE AND CLASS STRUCTURE

The starting point for teaching about race and racism is to have a framework and format for the course and each class, to maximize the chances for success. Like all teaching, this implies thinking carefully about an applicable course description, course goals and objectives, and developing a syllabus that supports attaining these targets. Every course, whether it lasts 14 weeks or is a 1-hour workshop, should have a map that allows students and teachers alike to follow where it is heading.

When creating a structure for a course or class on racism, the sequencing of both content and activities has to be considered. Bell and Griffin (1997) recommend moving from lower to higher risk as a course or class progresses. If participants feel too uncomfortable or unsafe in the early going, they are less likely to invest and take risks as the course progresses. Attendees need a foundation, trust, and a modicum of security to expend the personal energy necessary for deep learning.

Thus, sequencing has to take into account the importance of establishing confidence and creating a group environment in which norms are established and people are committed to working together. Bell and Griffin also recommend moving from the more concrete to the abstract and from the personal to the institutional. They also have found that beginning with less threatening concepts, such as diversity, is helpful, and then moving on to more challenging and emotionally laden notions, such as power and privilege.

We have found such sequencing to be helpful, with some modifications. Before considering concepts, attendees should be encouraged to first situate themselves, thereby focusing on social identity by exploring the many different identities they carry. Conversations about difference always are easier to initiate than those about privilege, dominance, and exploitation. But examining personal issues of racism, along with social and historical subjects on a parallel track, is also fruitful. For example, a class may look at the history and sociology of the interaction of race and immigration while also leaving space to explore how students have internalized beliefs, narratives, and myths that stem from the immigration experiences of their ancestors. All areas of content should be linked continually with an ongoing awareness and focus on students' social identities.

Early in the course it is useful to introduce concepts that act as a lens through which to view material. These concepts provide ways to explain strong reactions and emotions, linking the personal with the social and political. An example is "racial identity," a concept that encapsulates history, sociology, the construction of meaning, relationships, loyalty and affiliation, interpersonal preferences and interactions, self-concept, and one's innermost psychological and emotional life.

Another useful concept is to develop a "critical consciousness" (Adams, 1997; Zuniga & Nagda, 2001). This establishes an expectation that students will interrogate their assumptions, learn about important historical and social contexts, and engage in introspection. It allows for questioning and challenging and asks students to dig deeper without being critical or putting down anyone. As we mentioned in Chapter 8, concepts such as triggers, comfort zone, and learning edge (Griffin, 1997) or the three aspects of a difficult conversation (content, emotions, identity) (Stone, Patton, & Heen, 1999), help to interpret unsettling or confusing feelings and interactions.

Course structure and meaningful concepts establish a framework for teaching about racism and help to create a holding environment for the class. Inevitably, unanticipated issues will come up, such as confrontations between students or between students and teachers, or distracting class undercurrents. At times, it is prudent to let go of a class plan and respond to the circumstance that presents itself in the classroom or workshop. Some of the deepest learning moments can occur at these times.

But we must not let process become an end in itself and lose the thread of the syllabus or agenda. A class is not a dialogue group, and though dialogue should be part of an anti-racism curriculum, it is not the entire program. At times a teacher has to acknowledge strong feelings and unresolved conflicts and suggest other places where conversations can be continued, such as after class or through an online chat room, and refocus the class on the course content. The teacher should maintain a balance between adhering to the class structure and taking advantage of learning moments embedded in unforeseen hurdles.

Maintaining clear boundaries with time management is essential to any teaching situation, and this is certainly the case when teaching about race and racism. Classes or workshops should begin and end on time. The temptation may be to extend time periods, particularly when misunderstandings, tensions, or conflicts crop up, but this can be counter-productive. Sometimes during an intense discussion, people lock into rigid or redundant patterns of thinking and interacting, so taking a break and providing time for reflection and to regain perspective can be helpful. If racism classes do not end on time, people may feel emotionally overwhelmed and depleted. Running over time also can take time away from other classes, commitments, and activities, which can fuel pressure or resentment.

At the same time, provisions should be made for the spillover of feelings or leftover dynamics that are not resolved during actual class time. Conversations can (and often will) continue outside of the classroom in pairs or small groups. Encouraging students to use journals to write down perplexing questions, confused thoughts, and powerful feelings offers a space for processing, reflection, and capturing important moments or reactions. If participants are able to write about their conflicts or painful emotions, they can let go of them at least temporarily, return to them later, mull them over, and perhaps share them in class later. Establishing websites as a forum for students to exchange reactions, either with instructors or with the entire class, also can extend learning outside of the classroom.

Whenever any of these alternative venues are used, the issues raised should be brought back into the actual classroom eventually. This can be done with a summary at the beginning of the next class or a check-in time during which students share thoughts or feelings that have stayed with them or that they are still working on. Even an acknowledgement that there have been further conversations or unresolved feelings can be a form of validation and allow for the group to tolerate ambiguity and complexity and move forward.

CLASSROOM CLIMATE

The primary factor affecting classroom climate is student motivation, and the ability of teachers to kindle and fan motivation, at whatever level. People have various reasons for taking courses or workshops about racism. In some instances they are required to do so—perhaps to meet a curricular requirement or because a worksite supervisor or boss strongly encourages it. In these situations, motivation may be low and resistance high, with students feeling ambivalent about being in the class. Nevertheless, many students study racism because they are genuinely interested in it. Even those in this group have many different motivations: wanting to explore their own experiences or identity, trying to learn about how institutional racism is manifested, attempting to intellectually grasp the causes and reasons for racism, seeking to develop better intervention skills, or desiring to explore one's internalized biases. In most learning situations, students have mixed motivations for being there.

Given this, as well as helping students to explore their social identities, it is useful to conduct a survey about why students are attending and what they think about taking the course or workshop. To enable the discussion, teachers or facilitators must convey and model a nonjudgmental, tolerant stance, creating a space for people to be open and honest. If participants are concerned about politically correct responses, they will self-monitor, hesitate to share, and may withdraw or have their guard up. One way to confront this dynamic is by asking students about their hopes and fears for the course. This normalizes talking about concerns and reservations while also asking people to identify and articulate goals.

Teachers can gain information about who is in their class and why they are there, allowing instructors to respond empathically and to validate what students are feeling and thinking. Teachers also can clarify what the class is supposed to cover, including what is likely to be addressed and what is not within the purview of the course. Instructors can share their own goals for the course, which also can serve as a bridge to discussing classroom climate and determine how everyone can work together to create a positive learning environment. Instructors should emphasize that the purpose of the course goes beyond gaining an intellectual and theoretical understanding of racism, to attendees' learning about themselves and gaining the skills and knowledge they need to engage in anti-racism activities (Miller, Hyde, & Ruth, 2004).

Ideally, in any class, a culture is established that is characterized by a community of inquisitive, self-aware, and self-directed learners. For this to happen, students have to feel motivated and inspired to work hard and take risks, moving beyond their "comfort zone." The basis for this is a foundation of trust. How is trust established in the classroom?

CLASSROOM SAFETY

Perhaps the biggest fear that students express in racism classes is that they do not trust that they will be "safe." What do they mean by this? Certainly, racism itself creates an unsafe environment for people of color. They may encounter discrimination, prejudice, biases, micro-aggressions, or aversive racism, be asked to represent their group, encounter outright hostility, or endure social exclusion. One aspect of safety that students of color seek is that this will not occur in the classroom.

And many students of color wonder if white students will be authentic and honest about their attitudes, beliefs, and experiences. Students of color often are wary of white students who will say what they think instructors and other students want to hear, without sincere self-reflection or disclosure. A related concern is that white students will talk the talk in the classroom but not walk the walk after the class ends. This impinges upon the safety of students of color who may have taken the risk of sharing their experiences with racism without knowing how white students will use this.

For white students, safety often means that they will not be called a racist or if they accidentally "make a mistake," they will not encounter severe criticism or hostility. They may be concerned about unresolved stereotypes or that if they say the "wrong" thing, they will offend or hurt someone. They also may be concerned that teachers and other students will not misunderstand or misjudge them. White students also may be concerned that if they have ideas and values that seem at odds with the instructors or many fellow students, they will suffer academic consequences or group censorship.

All students, regardless of their race, are wary of others' labeling or misinterpreting them. Fears for their safety undermine trust. These concerns work against establishing a learning environment that embraces difficult questions, deep listening, complexity, paradox, and subtlety. People who are feeling vulnerable, wary, or unsafe tend to cling to the familiar or they shut down, closing themselves off to new ideas and material. They are less prone to speak honestly and take risks, leading to predictable discourses and "soapbox speeches," with fixed and ritualistic classroom roles.

Classroom Norms

To establish a classroom environment with sufficient trust to enable fruitful discourse and inquiry, the dynamic of safety must be addressed. One way to approach this is to ask students about their concerns and what might help them to feel less fearful. This can lead to a discussion about classroom norms of conduct, which may include, but is not limited to, expecting confidentiality, listening to one another, appreciating differences, speaking for oneself and not having to represent one's group or others, being honest, owning one's feelings, and challenging and criticizing ideas and assumptions while still respecting the person.

Establishing norms often works best when done with the group, as it then can form the basis of a learning contract to which everyone has contributed. Instructors can suggest additional norms that do not emerge in the group discussion (Miller, Donner, & Fraser, 2004). Some useful norms that should be included are: trying to be fully present, taking responsibility for oneself (including challenging oneself), accepting that another person's frame of reference has meaning for them, and the importance of working through conflict and "leaning into discomfort" (Wasserman & Doran, 1999). It also is helpful to write out the norms and distribute them to all students. The act of generating norms and discussing them in itself begins the conversation about race and racism and explores why talking about this subject is so challenging. Ultimately, no discussion about race and racism is entirely "safe"—if safety refers to possible misunderstanding, hearing biased and prejudiced comments, or having painful realizations and hurt feelings—but norms can create "safer" learning environments.

When establishing norms, one of the thorniest issues is that while people are encouraged to take risks, they also will reveal biases. For example, if a white student has stereotypes about African Americans, which he learned from his parents, and honestly shares them in a class with African American students, what he is saying can be painful and offensive to hear. This interaction may be compounded by relationships outside of the class.

If the discussion is taking place in an agency, people are expected to continue to work together. At this point, it is helpful to introduce the concept of racial identity formation and to acknowledge how students have had different experiences of racism and are at different phases in their racial identity development. This serves to frame the notion that people taking the course are at different places, with different experiences of racial oppression and privilege, and have a range of ideas, views, feelings, needs, and aspirations. Facilitators can share examples of when they have made remarks that they later regretted or how they felt hurt by others' statements. This models how instructors as well as students are still engaged in the process of learning and are capable of being wounded or hurting others. A delicate balance is required between honest sharing and wounding or offending others.

We have managed this balance by reminding people that what they are about to say will have a potential impact on other people. Sometimes it is better to note an idea, thought or feeling, but to work on it in a different environment. At the same time, students should be gentle with themselves and others when they make missteps and painful revelations, as this is part of the learning process. It can help to look at *intentions*, which often are well meaning, and to acknowledge them. At the same time, it is important to examine the *impact* of well-meaning but painful interactions, which also is critical to learning about racism.

CAUCUS GROUPS

In our experience, students of any racial/ethnic background can express biased statements and hurt others or be hurt by what others say; however, most students of color contend with racism outside of the classroom, which white students do not. As we described in earlier chapters, even if white students are targeted by other social oppressions (e.g., homophobia, sexism, anti-semitism), they do not experience systemic racism. Thus, even though each individual has unique learning needs, generally speaking, there are differences in learning expectations for students of color and white students in a racism class. Any student in the class should be able to explore internalized biases or prejudices as part of unlearning racism, but attempts should be made to protect those who are already exposed to racism from further insults or injuries.

So how can a class on racism open up space for all students to explore internalized racism without students of color having to witness or be the target of racist ideas, feelings, or actions? To respond to this dilemma, the facilitator might try to create spaces in classes in which people can explore their prejudices, beliefs, attitudes, and experiences, without placing students of color in unnecessarily vulnerable positions. This can be accomplished in a number of ways. We have already mentioned the value of keeping journals in helping students explore stereotypes and biases without the people who are the targets of such prejudices having to hear them. Another useful strategy is to break up classes into caucus groups in which people who identify as white can examine white privilege and racism and where people of color can explore internalized racism and reactions to white racism with less vulnerability and risk of causing harm.

Caucus groups can focus on the varied learning needs of different groups of students. Dividing the group may meet with resistance initially, particularly from white students who want to hear what people of color have to say about racism. This division is a temporary realignment, as it always is important to reconvene as a large group and to share themes (although not always the details) that emerged from the caucuses in a larger discussion. A great deal of learning can take place in both the small group and in the class as a whole. Caucus groups create a structure that encourages honesty as well as self-awareness about the impact of one's statements on others.

If using caucus groups in a classroom or workshop, we must remain mindful that some students, who identify as being multiracial and multiethnic, may feel as if dividing into caucus groups pressures them to have to choose one part of their identity over the other. There is no simple way to respond to this tension, but it can help to encourage people to choose whichever group they wish to participate in or if there are sufficient numbers, to establish a separate caucus group for those who have a more mixed, complex, or ambivalent racial identity.

When using any of these techniques, instructors should be as transparent as possible about their reasoning. The discussion about *why* and *how* to break up into caucus groups is part of an important conversation about the differential impact of racism on people and their consequent learning needs in a class on racism. If students are merely told to do something without adequate discussion and preparation, an important learning moment may be lost and the community of problem solvers that we seek to create will not evolve. But we as instructors have found that it also is important to confront the inevitable resistance about breaking into caucus groups because students often do not appreciate the potential gains and benefits until they try it.

INSTRUCTOR SELF-AWARENESS

Knowing who we are, our strengths and weaknesses, our vulnerabilities and assets, and our trigger points and hot spots is essential for teaching about racism (Bell, Washington, Weinstein, & Love, 1997; Miller, Hyde, & Ruth, 2004). Racism courses certainly are going to challenge students and will test teachers as well. Preparing for this task minimizes the risks and increases effectiveness. Bell et al. have identified a number of areas about which all instructors who teach social justice courses should be mindful while preparing for and actually teaching courses. These include

- awareness of one's social identity,
- confronting one's own biases,
- taking an inventory of one's triggers,
- preparing for how to respond to biased comments by students,
- confronting one's own doubts and anxiety about competency, and
- being aware of one's need for student approval.

They also suggest that teachers prepare for difficult situations in the classroom and fears of losing control of the process, which raises issues about authority and how to exercise it.

Drawing on our own experiences to use as examples can be helpful to students, including sharing times we made mistakes or felt inadequate—as long as we are cautious about not telling too many "war stories," which shifts the spotlight to us and away from our students. Instructors may use their own feelings, reactions, and internal processes effectively as points of discussion and reflection, if this is done selectively and strategically. When teaching by example, instructors should consider what level of self-disclosure is comfortable and use caution. Some personal examples can stir up a lot of feelings within the instructor.

In general, a teacher's being able to tolerate strong affect in a group requires practice, whether it is being expressed by someone else or experienced internally. Expanding this capacity and desensitizing trigger points without sacrificing empathy and compassion builds confidence in one's capacity to handle most situations.

RESISTANCE

Resistance is common in anti-racism courses (Goodman, 2001; Mildred & Zuniga, 2004). People with race privilege often resist examining racism, and people targeted by racism may hesitate to re-live or re-experience painful situations. Students who are ambivalent about their racial identities also may experience resistance. When people feel threatened, they understandably respond with resistance (Goodman, 2001).

Whatever the sources of resistance, it is often directed at those teaching the course. It can manifest itself as denial, anger, withdrawal, sabotage, or as a direct challenge to the credibility of teachers. When presented with new and disturbing material or insights, participants frequently question the teacher's expertise or the validity of his or her experience. Thus, anti-racism teachers should expect to have their integrity contested. Goodman recommends that educators recall a time when they felt resistant themselves so they can connect empathically with the students' experiences.

People of color and white teachers have reported variations on how this theme affects their teaching experience. Students, particularly white male students, are more likely to challenge the authority and credibility of teachers of color (Goodman, 2001). Whenever professors or facilitators are teaching about a form of oppression they directly experience, students who have unearned and unexamined privileges are likely to be resistant and may try to discredit the teacher's legitimacy and accuse them of being self-serving by advocating for their own cause (Bell et al., 1997). As we considered in Chapters 6 and 7, the interactions of social identity may magnify students' resistance, so women of color face devaluation by white men by virtue of both their race and their gender.

White teachers and facilitators also face certain types of resistance when teaching about racism. Miller, Hyde, and Ruth (2004) identified three challenges for white educators teaching about racism:

1. questions about their legitimacy when talking about racism;
2. negotiating their own privileges, including biases;
3. being viewed with hostility as "race traitors" by resistant white students.

A fourth hurdle, which has an impact on all teachers, whatever their race and ethnicity, is the lack of institutional support for teaching such demanding and potentially volatile courses. Racism courses can be marginalized within an undergraduate or graduate program and viewed as an "add-on," rather than being central to the curriculum. When racism courses are required, many students enter them with low motivation and high levels of skepticism. The volatility of the topic itself presents the possibility of difficult class experiences, potentially resulting in negative course evaluations or even student protests (Miller, Hyde, & Ruth, 2004). This has happened to the most experienced anti-racism teachers. The risks raise concerns about the professional wisdom of taking on this sort of teaching.

SUPPORTING ANTI-RACISM TEACHING

Fortunately, the teaching risks can be minimalized, both institutionally and within the classroom. Institutions of higher education and human service organizations can make explicit commitments toward anti-racism, creating a context in which courses are offered. Part of the commitment should ensure that the courses receive adequate support and resources and that the potential risks and burdens of teaching these courses are recognized and acknowledged administratively.

MULTIRACIAL / CO-TEACHING TEAMS   One way of providing institutional support to anti-racism classes is to offer multiracial teaching teams. This is a pedagogically sound intervention and has many advantages over solo teaching. Co-teaching teams offer a wider range of perspectives, experiences, and models of anti-racism professionals (Miller, Hyde, & Ruth, 2004). These teams allow for greater support and consultation inside and outside of the classroom, because co-teachers are able to back up one another and step in if their colleague becomes triggered or the target of strong student resistance. Co-teachers can plan classes together and serve as advisors to each other, providing feedback about the other's blindspots and prejudices. Co-teaching also allows greater flexibility and creativity about how material is presented and who presents it. If the class breaks up into caucus groups, the teachers are available to split up as well.

Solomon (2000) conducted a 3-year study of cross-racial teaching dyads. The finding that emerged was that this partnership helped to break down racial barriers between instructors; teachers learned from one another; and when prejudice was directed toward one of the teaching partners, they were able to back each other up and serve as a buffer.

Co-teaching has its own risks and demands. Racial patterns can be reenacted if white professors take a dominating leadership role. Power must be negotiated (Anti-Defamation League [ADL], 1998). Teachers like to teach and can trip over one another or have difficulty operating within a more circum-scribed, shared teaching space. The danger of splitting is always present, with one teacher becoming idealized and the other disparaged. This dynamic also may follow typical patterns of racism. In many situations, white students feel more comfortable sharing things with the white professor, thereby minimizing or marginalizing the role of the professor of color. Co-teachers, too, may have disagreements over topics or teaching strategies, and these can spill over into classes. And they can trigger one another.

If the teaching team becomes stuck and unable to work out tensions between themselves, there should be a fall-back mechanism for conflict reso-lution, involving a third party or a group of peers. This should be set up in advance of any actual tensions or conflict.

Thus, co-teaching should be approached thoughtfully and carefully. Co-teachers need to get to know one another, develop trust, and become familiar with their partner's style. Sufficient time must be allocated for planning classes and debriefing afterward. A game plan should be drawn up for each class, including timeframes, roles, and techniques. Co-teachers should plan how they will present themselves to the class: Will they stand up together, or will one sit down while the other is taking the lead role (ADL, 1998)? Both professors should read and comment on all written work. In our experience, co-teaching takes up to twice as much time as teaching solo, but the benefits far outweigh the potential risks, and the time invested in co-teaching is well spent.

STRONG SUPPORT NETWORKS   Whether teaching alone or with a partner, all anti-racism educators benefit from strong support networks. These might include fellow teachers, supervisors, and other colleagues. Everyone needs space to process difficult emotions and reactions, and teachers should create these places for themselves outside of the classroom.

Weekly group meetings of all anti-racism teachers are useful, allowing them to share experiences and provide mutual support and consultation. Newer anti-racism educators, in particular, benefit from access to support systems, including teaching mentors, who can help with teaching strategies as well as course content.

UNDERSTANDING STUDENTS

Understanding who our students are and where they are coming from is essential for anti-racism educators (Adams, Jones, & Tatum 1997). Planning and thinking about this can begin before a course starts.

What do we know about the organizational culture and context for the course?

Is the course required, or have students chosen to take this class?

What classes or experiences in this field have student already had?

Are there any incidents or ongoing dynamics within the organization that may affect the course?

What are the likely ethnic and racial identities of participants?

What other aspects of social identity may be particularly salient for this course?

These are a few examples of questions instructors can ask themselves before classes even start.

Once the course begins, as we mentioned, it is useful to have students situate themselves and to introduce exercises that illuminate the complexities of their social identities and that summarize critical experiences, worldviews, and perspectives relevant to this learning project (see exercises and appendices in chapters 1, 5, 6, and 11, as well as the exercise at the end of this chapter). Assessing this information and applying concepts such as social identity formation can help instructors anticipate likely learning needs, potential sources of resistance, and interpersonal and group dynamics. We can attempt to match curricular goals with who is actually in the class (Adams et al., 1997). As a caveat, we can only imagine potential scenarios and have to be open to surprises and prepared for the unexpected as the class progresses.

In any class, instructors should track who talks a lot and who is silent. Do any racial or ethnic patterns become apparent in who speaks up and who listens? Are there expectations about who should respond to certain material? Usually, roles emerge after a couple of classes, and it is helpful to map them out along with their impact on group dynamics. Inevitably, when some students talk too much and others too little, what intervention strategy, if any, should the instructor use? Additional questions include:

What kinds of body language does the teacher notice?

What kinds of responses do different teaching techniques elicit?

How does what is happening in the classroom correspond to what a teacher is reading in student journals?

Who does an instructor feel triggered by or drawn to?

By getting to know the students, instructors are creating pathways for feedback as the course moves along, allowing instructors to adapt and adjust teaching strategies (Adams et al., 1997).

As with all teaching, letting students know that the instructor regards them as individuals is helpful. Simple things, such as learning their names, go a long way. Unfortunately, racism courses sometimes are offered in a large lecture format, which cuts down on the possibilities for experiential learning and makes it more difficult for instructors to develop a textured understanding of who their students are and how to respond them differentially.

TEACHING STRATEGIES AND TECHNIQUES

In addition to the recommendations presented for structuring anti-racism classes, creating a positive learning environment, being aware of ourselves as instructors, and knowing our students, some specific teaching strategies and techniques are more likely to result in positive and meaningful classes for students. Much of what is discussed here pertains to all effective teaching but has been tailored to anti-racism courses.

The actual choice and mix of techniques should be influenced by what instructors are trying to convey, their assessment of students' learning needs and styles, and their own skills and strengths as teachers. If the goal is to convey information, such as the history of racism or statistics about the web of institutional racism, a lecture format works well. Slides and handouts can augment learning, as can readings. Materials of this nature, however, are likely to engender student reactions. Small discussion groups and journals can deepen students' personal connection to the content, as can class exercises that highlight patterns of racism or its consequences. Videos, too, can be used to respond to the learning needs of some students and illustrate abstract or dry material with visual images, human faces, and personal narratives. And reading personal accounts humanizes theoretical and historical approaches.

When the learning goals are geared more toward personal exploration and growth, lecture usually is not the pedagogical strategy of choice. Focused small-group discussions, exercises, and simulations stimulate reflection and introspection. Journals and Web-based discussion groups also further dialogue and self-awareness. Watching a video such as *The Color of Fear* (Wah, 1994) and then breaking into small discussion groups can introduce important themes in a powerful and dramatic way. This allows students to witness intense racial conflict (and reconciliation) without engaging directly in it. Structured racial dialogues or temporarily breaking into racial or ethnic caucus groups can create spaces where students can learn to talk about race and racism while also exploring assumptions and stereotypes and their consequences.

If the topic is white privilege or the types of activities in which anti-racism activists can engage, brainstorming and other large-group activities can generate a variety of ideas. Small groups can refine or react to what is generated and deepen understanding. Simulations and exercises can illustrate concepts such as privilege in graphic and visual ways.

EXERCISES

For example, Adams et al. (1997) describe an activity called "Common Ground" in which students are asked to line up on one side of a room and listen to a series of statements. If a statement applies, such as "I am a woman," the student steps to the other side of the room. This begins to illustrate the different social identities that students bring to the course. If no one crosses the room in response to a statement such as "I am bisexual," it visualizes that the class has no student with that social identity or that students do not feel comfortable disclosing this aspect of their identity publicly. This exercise usually is followed by a class discussion.

A variation on this exercise is to have participants take a step forward in response to questions that ask about privilege, or take a step backward if the question is about lack of privilege and applies to them. This visually illustrates the differential privileges of students in the class, which can prompt illumi-nating discussions and deep self-realizations. It also can be painful to see these differences, and this exercise can elicit strong emotions. But this is an effective way to break through resistance if many students in the class are unaware of their unearned privileges. This type of exercise can be done with any aspect of social identity or a combination of social identity axes.

Interviewing in Pairs

A more gentle and private way to engage in similar explorations is to pair the participants and have them interview each another about aspects of their social identity (see the exercise in Chapter 1). This is more intimate and less threat-ening than some exercises and also builds relationships between classmates and deepens empathy. When pairs report back themes to the larger class, it can lead to a discussion or lecture about relevant concepts and theories. Exercises should always have a "pass rule," so if students do not feel comfortable saying something or even participating, they can opt out without explanation.

Maintaining Balance

Most anti-racism teachers have found it helpful to mix and vary the types of learning strategies used in any given class. Two hours of lecture by a professor can be counterproductive. Conversely, too many exercises and small-group discussions may represent a lack of focus and clarity, at the expense of the students' learning important concepts and ideas. Exploring racism in society and the world, as well as racism that is internalized or expressed interperson-ally, requires balance and a variety of teaching approaches.

The use of self as an instructor is another way of achieving balance. As we mentioned, self-disclosure can be valuable as long as it does not unduly trigger a professor or direct too much class attention toward the teacher and away from the students. A teacher's ability to convey passion and optimism without sacrificing realism is a powerful stimulant to learning. Students are seeking role models and looking for ways to be helpful and make a difference. If only the negative consequences of racism are presented, the students can easily feel overwhelmed, hopeless, and despondent.

The other side of the coin is that if the teacher overstates hope and under-states the dismal reality of racism, people of color in the class can feel devalued and white students may gloss over the destructiveness of racism and not honestly explore their own white privileges. A balance must be struck. The class has to move and progress toward taking action and feeling empowered. Yet, if the course moves too quickly toward action, students may not adequately grasp the depth of racism or genuinely reflect about how racism has affected them. Without introspection, students may engage in actions that detract from feelings, such as guilt and shame, and reenact prejudices and stereotypes.

Another pedagogical balance is that of validating and supporting while also challenging and confronting. Moving to either end of the spectrum compromises learning. Students have to be confirmed and encouraged, for without these, pessimism or resentment can seep in. Yet all learners can and will get stuck and usually are capable of digging deeper. Effective anti-racism teaching inevitably involves some confrontation, but delivering it in a way that will be meaningfully received is an art that takes practice. A direct confrontation that makes a student feel humiliated or put down is not an effective intervention.

Instructors can ask questions about something a student said or invite them to reflect on it. They can solicit reactions from other students in a structured fashion—asking what people agreed with and disagreed with. Another way to confront students is through self-revelation, perhaps by teachers sharing a story about a time when they said or did something they regretted and how they came to understand this.

Yet another balancing act in anti-racism teaching is between process and content. The content about racism is seemingly endless. Most instructors fret over all they think must be covered and the inadequacy of the time to do this. Yet significant learning takes place through the class process, and this will not occur if the process is rushed and does not allow sufficient time for reflection. If teachers do not attend to potholes and grimly drive on, rushing to present content, the class may be in for a rough ride. On the one hand, few anti-racism teachers think, in retrospect, that they covered every topic they had hoped to, in as much depth as they wished! On the other hand, too much attention to process can be seductive, and every class has some students who would like to concentrate exclusively on group dynamics, to the detriment of learning important factual and conceptual material.

Another challenge to teaching about race and racism is to set a tone in class that is respectful and dignified while also allowing for participants to relax and even express humor. Because nothing is light or funny about racism, we must be serious and sober about its terrible consequences. Study of this topic often calls for a solemn and somber atmosphere, which is understandable and appropriate. Yet, taken to an extreme, it can feel so heavy and burdensome that students feel deflated by the sheer weight of the subject. In any group situation, humor and self-deprecation can be a helpful lubricant, as long as it is not manifested gratuitously or inappropriately. Again, a balance is called for.

AVAILABILITY OF TEACHERS

Last, teachers should be available to students outside of actual class time, within reasonable limits. Whether this is through office hours, by moderating Web-based discussion groups, or by checking informally with students during breaks, teachers must be accessible to their students. Racism courses stir up a great deal of feelings, and at times students need some space outside of class to consult with teachers or process their reactions so they can gain sufficient perspective to return to class as fully engaged learners.

We also recommend copious feedback by instructors on student logs and papers. This engages students in a more personal and intimate dialogue with professors, which is validating and spurs motivation. Ample written feedback is one of the most effective ways of encouraging engagement and working through resistance. (The exercise and appendix to this chapter offer examples of assignments that can support the course objectives, in addition to those already presented as exercises and appendices in previous chapters.)

FEELING STUCK

Everyone who teaches about race and racism will encounter situations that are unanticipated, challenging, and stump us as educators. Anticipating "stuckness" is important, because it will be less frightening when it occurs if teachers are able to remind themselves that this is normal. The next step is to take a deep breath—maybe a few deep breaths—and let the feeling of panic pass. When we feel stuck, we may not know what to do immediately, but we will think of something eventually, and we and the class will learn from the experience.

What are some typical situations that teachers find challenging? These vary but some rise to the top of the list:

- intense and unanticipated conflict between students;
- overt hostility directed toward other students or the instructor;
- direct challenges to the teacher's authority and credibility;
- severe emotional reactions, including leaving the room;
- profoundly racist statements and comments;
- behind-the-scenes provocations, including orchestrating group rebellions in class.

The power and valence of these scenarios will vary from teacher to teacher and according to the context in which they occur. What makes any of them particularly hard to deal with is the element of surprise, when we fail to see what is coming.

We can prepare in many ways for the unexpected and respond effectively once it happens. As an anti-racism educator, a key intervention is to predict teacher mistakes and invite criticism from the class. This immediately takes away the sting when missteps do occur or if students are challenging or critical. It normalizes and models openness and nondefensiveness. No intervention works in all situations and for all people, and this intervention is not effective if some students are committed to undermining the instructor's credibility or if his or her social identity becomes an issue. In these situations a direct confrontation sometimes is needed, including marshaling administrative resources as back-up. But usually it is better to try to avoid unnecessary showdowns with students.

Another way to deal with the unexpected is to call a time-out. This comes in handy if the need arises near the time for a break anyway. Even if it does not, there is nothing wrong with giving the class (and teacher) 5 minutes to reflect on what happened before responding to it. This can break a negative chain of interactions, interrupt ritualized conflict, and give the teacher and everyone else a few moments to become more centered and to think of effective ways to respond in the moment. The time-out option is successful when teaching with others or alone.

A variation is to ask students to write down the answers to some questions before further discussion. Examples of questions are:

What do you think just happened?

What did you observe and hear?

What was your immediate reaction?

What other reactions do you think people in the class might be having?

What would be a helpful way to follow up?

What did you learn from this incident?

Questions like these offer structure and direction to student reactions. It usually is helpful to pose at least one question in which students are asked to speculate on what other students might be feeling. Although this may seem to be at odds with the classroom norm of speaking for oneself, it can be helpful for students to engage in understanding others' perspectives and explore valid reactions that differ from their own. It is useful to explain to the class the rationale for asking the question.

Breaking up into caucus groups or several small groups is another helpful strategy in a time of stress and uncertainty. The teacher should give small groups specific guidelines about what to cover, and to be clear on time limits. This allows clusters of people to explore a difficult situation in small groups where they are more likely to take risks while also having their perspectives expanded, modified, and challenged by discussing the situation with others. When the small groups report back to the larger class, students are exposed to an even wider range of narratives generated about the original incident, which adds another layer of reflection about the event and its meaning.

The fishbowl (see Chapter 8) is a variation on breaking up into small groups. Fishbowls allow for smaller, more intimate conversations, but in front of the entire class. The filtering system allows people to enter and leave the fishbowl. Some students find it easier to observe than to participate, and this gives them the opportunity to benefit from a discussion that they think would be threatening if they were mandated to participate.

Still another strategy is to address class issues in a homework assignment, such as having students respond in their journals to questions similar to those we suggested previously for exploring reactions in class. Or students can be asked to link their discussions to some of the concepts and theories that have been presented in the course. This depersonalizes and connects micro-events with macro-processes and helpful concepts. A related strategy is to punt—to acknowledge that a difficult incident arose in class and that at some point it should be revisited, but to acknowledge that the teacher needs some time to think about the best way to do that.

When we are stuck, we often feel triggered, stirred up, overwhelmed, numb, at a loss for words, angry, and treated unfairly. Feelings of shame can bring to the surface a narrative of inadequacy, and failure begins to take shape in our mind. These are normal reactions, and the more we are able to be gentle with ourselves and give ourselves time to regain our footing, the more we can turn these situations into learning moments. Deep breathing and meditative techniques can be helpful. Listening to others, rather than talking, can give us space to calm down, but this is not appropriate if an out-of-control, escalating conflict is raging in the class. In these circumstances, a time-out is preferable.

We must remember that we are all learners, teachers, and human beings, with warts, blemishes, and moments of uncertainty. It is not the end of the world if students see that we are upset or flustered. We frequently have received feedback from students that this made us seem more accessible and real, and our willingness to be vulnerable was something that students admired. It does not feel good at the time, and being open and exposed is in conflict with traditional images of teachers and facilitators.

Those teaching about anti-racism should expect such moments, and they can lead to unexpected insights. The more we can relax and accept these moments, the better we become at dealing with them. What is important is that we stay in the process when we are feeling beleaguered, and that we encourage our students to do the same. Most anti-racism courses and workshops will benefit participants, even when there are painful or disturbing moments, as long as the participants remain authentic and engaged.

CONCLUSION

Students should think of themselves as potential teachers, and teachers always as students. The potential risks and pitfalls of teaching anti-racism courses should not be minimized, but a variety of ideas can be applied to designing and facilitating meaningful learning environments.

This work can be immensely rewarding, but both teaching and learning about race and racism require a great deal of commitment and time. Personal experiences and professional experiences alike serve as important learning tools. Ultimately, working together toward a fuller understanding of the history of race and racism in the United States, as well as the implications for helping professionals, can lead to enhanced service delivery for all populations and to greater job satisfaction for all involved. Teaching and learning about race and racism offer important opportunities for helping professionals. They contribute to the larger project of anti-racism work, which will be covered in the final chapter.

EXERCISE 12.1

This homework assignment can help students identify examples of cultural racism and cultural sensitivity and empowerment.

* * *

Take a field trip and observe the world around you. The trip can be any place where there are cultural markers (public signs and symbols that convey cultural norms, assumptions, values, and expectations)—downtown, around campus, the dorms and dining rooms, the library, the media, and so on.

Do a cultural audit and find *five* examples of cultural, ethnic, or racial bias and *five* examples of racial or ethnic sensitivity or empowerment.

Referring to your audit, what generalizations would you make about how cultural markers can be constructed in an empowering and respectful fashion? Did you notice any stereotypes or hidden assumptions? What was visible and invisible? Did you encounter anything surprising?

Write up your findings in a *two-page* paper.

Source: This exercise was suggested by Andrea Ayvazian and Norma Akamatsu.

DISMANTLING RACISM: CREATING THE WEB OF RESISTANCE

CHAPTER CONTENTS

The persistence of racism relies on collusion of the majority of white people in the United States, a form of bystanding that allows existing racial privileges for whites and the web of racism for people of color to remain unchallenged. Although this inactivity may stem in part from an unwillingness to give up group advantages based on race, it also may be a result of white people either being unaware of race privilege or not knowing what to do about it. Racism is complex and intractable. It is not easily remedied by a few reforms, and it migrates, shifts, and reconfigures when confronted (Massey, 2005), much like a virus or bacteria that has altered in response to antibiotics.

Despite the persistence of racism, progress has been forthcoming. As described in previous chapters, the most egregious forms of racism now are considered wrong and abhorrent in the United States. Even the manifestations of racism as recently as the mid-1950s are unacceptable today. The values of racial equity, nondiscrimination, and integration now are part of a national consensus, a marked shift in the past half-century (Bobo, 2001).

In the wake of the Great Society, affirmative action led to breaking down longstanding racial barriers and dislodged the embedded "affirmative action" of white privilege in many sectors of the economy. The African American middle class has grown markedly. Although much of this book has described the persistence of racism and what remains to be achieved, we must acknowledge what has been accomplished.

Before moving to create a web of resistance to racism, however, we must acknowledge some of the biggest challenges. A major one is the feeling of inevitability and hopelessness instilled by such a profound, multifaceted, adaptable, and durable form of oppression and social inequality. Racism is pervasive and suffuses all of American society, to the extent that it seems to be a normal state of affairs. By bestowing privileges and granting social and economic passports for white people while creating webs of oppression for people of color, racism has divided us. The greatest risks are that people targeted by racism will despair or be so consumed with survival that they have little energy left to confront the sources of their oppression, while people with privilege have an impaired capacity to see racism or become apathetic and indifferent to its injustices. We must not underestimate the enormity of the anti-racism project.

Perhaps the biggest challenge to dismantling racism is that it is inside of us as well as outside of us. The social structure of racism is predicated on generalizations and stereotypes based on the appearance of our bodies, but its poisonous fumes actually invade our bodies. The vapors of racism sap our spirit, damage the psyche, and cloud the mind. It distorts how we see ourselves and others. So we must repair the damage to our thoughts, feelings, and self-concepts and reconnect with our capacity for empathy.

Apathy leads to acquiescence with racism and hopelessness begets apathy. By contrast, resisting racism is an act of liberation and engenders hope. Every steel thread in the web of racism can be dissolved in nonviolent ways, replacing the web with a tapestry of resistance. Racism relies on isolation, division, dehumanization—turning sisters and brothers into "others." A web of resistance to racism starts with humanizing everyone, including humanizing ourselves.

Humanizing ourselves implies being compassionate and gentle toward our flaws while also having the courage to move beyond our comfort zones, extending that compassion to others through our actions. Racism alienates us from ourselves, divides and isolates us from others. By contrast, forming groups of allies unites us so we can provide support, encouragement, and assistance to one another. The dams of racism block opportunity while ripples of actions create waves of liberation.

Helping professionals work to engender hope in their clients. Social and psychological challenges and problems deflate individuals' belief in themselves and in the beneficence of others. Every human service worker has encountered situations in which their clients' inability to feel optimistic and to envision a better future hinders their progress as much as the presenting problems that led to their demoralization. Empowerment comes from acknowledging real barriers and limitations and recognizing our inability to control everything, while also believing in our capacity to have some influence over the course of our lives.

As discussed in the Preface, helping professionals must abide by mandates in codes of ethics about social justice, respect for diverse cultures, and the worth and dignity of all people. Spurred by professional mandates and buoyed by a belief in their ability to make a difference, helping professionals are positioned to take a leadership role in the move to dismantle racism, empowering ourselves and seeking to inspire our clients.

CREATING THE WEB OF RESISTANCE

Our colleague Lisa Werkmeister Rozas once said to us, "If there's a web of racism, there also must be a web of resistance." We have developed this idea with her, and Figure 13.1 diagrams a web of resistance to racism, showing a set of core values and six realms of activities. We will examine these core values and what takes place in each of the anti-racism realms.

CORE VALUES

Four major values underpin any form of anti-racism activity:

1. being aware of racism,
2. staying connected with others,
3. maintaining compassion for ourselves and others, and
4. remaining engaged in some form of activism.

AWARENESS   Anti-racism work requires an awareness of racism and all of its forms. If we do not see or hear racism, it is difficult to confront. Harro (2000b) calls this "waking up." Although most people of color are acutely aware of racism, most white people are not attuned to its vicissitudes. One way of thinking about this is that many white people have severe vision problems when it comes to seeing racism. Therefore, a precise lens can bring into view things

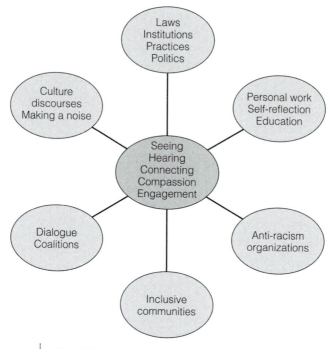

FIGURE 13.1 | THE WEB OF RESISTANCE

previously undetected. The brain then has to have concepts to make sense of the new information being observed. And if the lens is removed too quickly, we will revert to visual impairment.

Those who do not encounter racism have difficulty seeing it and understanding what they are viewing. Anti-racism work is ongoing, as the obfuscating fog of racism is always in the air.

CONNECTION   We are not alone in this fight, and yet racism can cause us to feel isolated and divided. Anti-racism work is more effective when we do it with others. All of us, people of color and white people both, need other people to form coalitions, transform organizations, change communities, and have a political impact. Being connected with others who are confronting racism enhances our power and increases our effectiveness, and the actual process of resisting with others is empowering as well.

COMPASSION   Anti-racism calls for having compassion for everyone and dissolving artificial boundaries that cause us to extend compassion to some but not others. This means having compassion for ourselves as well as for people who are similar to and different from us. In our view, it also extends to people who are perpetrating racism consciously or unconsciously. We condemn racism while trying to maintain compassion for those it damages, including those with race privilege.

ENGAGEMENT   The positive changes to date have resulted from the sustained engagement of dedicated people. Monumental transformations take place at seams in history, but even these moments of profound change depend on concerted efforts leading up to them and collective vigilance afterward. The dissolution of racism requires a major effort and commitment from a multitude of individuals, groups, and organizations who are willing to remain engaged for the long haul.

THE INTRAPERSONAL REALM: INTROSPECTION AND EDUCATION

Introspection and self-reflection are instrumental to anti-racism work at all times. A great deal of this book considers how racism is internalized and can distort our view of ourselves and others. Introspection can take many forms. Keeping a journal allows us to express ourselves and explore what we are thinking and feeling. The act of writing is illuminating in itself. When we share our narratives with trusted others, we receive feedback and learn from what others see and hear. Structured exercises, such as those described in the appendices to previous chapters, are useful ways to explore what is inside of us. These can be done alone or in the presence of others, such as discussion groups or pairs.

Other acts of introspection include participating in support groups that focus on unlearning racism or on how to be a better ally, reading and reflecting about others' experiences and mapping out goals for ourselves that move us out of our comfort zone and engage us in action. Talking with partners, children, friends, and colleagues is another vehicle for learning about ourselves and others.

Introspection will take different forms for different people. One influential factor is our experience with racism. For those who have encountered racism and have developed strengths, resiliency, and effective coping strategies, a task of introspection can be to build on these capacities and become even stronger. Or perhaps a coping strategy has mixed results, such as dealing with racism in the moment but leaving a lingering sense of pain or self-doubt. Exposing our vulnerabilities can be difficult, even to ourselves, yet by doing so, we can become even more adaptive and effective in advocating for ourselves and the rights and needs of others.

For people who have experienced race privilege, or have not had experiences of racism, introspection can help to uncover blindspots or stereotypes. Introspection also involves taking risks and exploring painful and unpleasant internalizations. Yet, without insight and awareness, we are vulnerable to the power of unexamined prejudice. People with race privilege also should have a plan of education, to learn about the history, manifestations, and consequences of racism.

Although we have described different tasks for people with different racial identities, we are not suggesting that some tasks are exclusively for either people of color or white people. For example, people of color also internalize prejudices or stereotypes and can learn more about the history of racism and how to conceptualize it, while whites benefit from reflecting on how best to respond to racism in the moment. We recommend a personal plan of education and reflection for all anti-racism activists and offer an anti-racism activist audit in Exercise 13.1.

THE INTERPERSONAL REALM: ENGAGING IN DIALOGUE/WORKING IN COALITIONS

Chapter 6 addressed the topic of social identity formation and group membership, and Chapter 8 considered how we can talk about race and racism. It is human nature to identify with groups and for identity to be influenced by our group affiliations. This can be a positive source of norms, values, mutual support, and validation. Groups can buffer people from social assaults and violations. Feeling positive about one's group need not lead to fearing, disliking, exploiting. or oppressing members of another group (Brewer, 2001). Yet racism is an extreme example of in-group validation and social privileges for white people, at the expense of people of color. Thus, a major task for anti-racism work is to repair and reconstruct intergroup relationships.

This concept is important because less intergroup hostility, particularly from whites toward people of color, diminishes collusion with racist practices. Greater intergroup cooperation fosters mutual respect and compassion extending beyond one's own ethnic or racial group. It also is important because interracial coalitions are effective mechanisms in confronting racism. Coalitions offer more resources, generate a wider range of ideas, have greater access to a variety of people and systems, and can establish more credibility than disparate clusters of individuals. Coalitions have clout! Anti-racism coalitions that bring in a wide range of people and organizations increase the number of stakeholders actively committed and working together toward common goals.

Anti-racism activists can choose from many existing coalitions to join. Some are national organizations, such as the National Association for the Advancement of Colored People (NAACP) and the Urban League, which have local chapters in many communities. Other groups are local and address specific community issues. For example, in Portland, Maine, a coalition is working to ensure that Somali refugees living in the city, who have experienced the barriers of racism and the upheavals of immigration, have access to adequate health and mental health services. And in Northampton, Massachusetts, a local Study Circle met for 6 weeks, culminating in the formation of an ongoing communitywide coalition working against racism in the community. The group's mission is to transform the public school system into a nonracist institution.

When no local coalition is addressing pressing issues pertaining to racism, human service professionals can link with other concerned groups and individuals to form one. Communities usually have a critical mass of helping professionals, clergy, activists, local political leaders, educators and students, progressive business leaders, and residents who are concerned about racism and are willing to work on it. To draw attention to critical issues, coalitions can arrange press conferences, teach-ins, and demonstrations.

Any work with groups and coalitions takes patience and willingness to share and compromise. Coalitions working against racism must be particularly cognizant of who is and is not represented in their ranks and who ends up in positions of leadership. White members must not dominate the coalition or assume power. Successful coalitions usually have democratic mechanisms to resolve disputes and foster dialogue and understanding among members. And, as discussed in Chapter 8, structured conversations about race and racism increase the ability of people to work together, as well as respect and understand one another.

THE ORGANIZATIONAL REALM: CREATING ANTI-RACISM ORGANIZATIONS

Helping professionals can challenge institutional racism programs and agencies, as outlined in Chapter 10, as well as in funding entities and professional associations. We also can challenge racist practices that are built into systems that serve clients and lobby for changes and reforms. Most of us work for agencies, and all of us are members, or potential members, of professional associations. As we work with others to dismantle racism, we must ensure that our own houses are in order.

THE COMMUNITY REALM: CREATING INCLUSIVE COMMUNITIES

Helping professionals can work to foster communities that are inclusive and in which people of all races and ethnicities are treated fairly and equitably and have equal access to resources. All human service professionals live and work in communities and can engage in this work as residents as well as professionals. Chapter 9 covers how helping professionals can work toward this goal.

BEING HEARD: THE REALM OF DISCOURSE AND CULTURE

The web of racism explored in Chapter 4 explains how this culture privileges Western, Eurocentric worldviews and values and how other cultures are marginalized or subjected to negative stereotypes. It also considers how public discourses reinforce cultural patterns and serve to normalize white race privilege while also denigrating and blaming people of color for their social exclusion. Therefore, anti-racism work by human professionals should seek to address public discourses and narratives about racism and to expand and diversify the vision of American culture to value and include nonwhite, non-Western groups.

Although this task initially may appear abstract and daunting, helping professionals can participate in anti-racism discourses in many ways. This book already has mentioned how coalitions can do this through demonstrations, teach-ins, press releases, and many other activities for individuals and groups. Helping professionals have access to clients' stories. We can help them tell their stories by publishing letters and submitting journal articles, and arranging events to give them access to the media.

We can write our own stories, too, along with letters to the editor and op-ed pieces. We can call radio comment lines to highlight issues of race and racism. We can conduct research about the impact of racism on the lives of clients and publish the results in journals, magazines, and newspapers. Human service professionals can prepare leaflets and brochures that inform the public about racism and ways to confront it. We can discuss racism on-line in chat rooms. These are examples of ways that helping professionals can contribute to the public discourse about race and racism using our unique position of working directly with clients, as well as with the social service systems that affect them.

Further, we can make a noise through our conversations with colleagues, friends, and family. We can show videos and sponsor discussion groups. We can challenge racist assumptions that come up in staff meetings. Just as micro-aggressions of racism take their cumulative toll, we can offer micro-acts of anti-racism that contribute to a discourse of liberation.

THE POLITICAL AND SOCIAL REALM: LAWS, INSTITUTIONS, AND PRACTICES

The web of institutional racism described in Chapter 4 is the level of pervasive, societal racism that eventually must be transformed to ensure that the United States lives up to its ideals of equality, justice, and freedom.

When we consider the Spectrum of Racism (Figure 2.1), and look at the lefthand side of the diagram, we can see the most egregious, extreme forms of state-supported racism: genocide, apartheid, slavery, and ethnic cleansing. All of these have occurred in the past in this country, and we still witness with horror their presence in other parts of the world today.

State-supported racism includes racist codes and laws, legal segregation and exclusion, and Jim Crow laws. These were part of our nation's more recent history, extending well into the 1960s in some parts of the country. Although there are remnants of state-supported racism—such as the disenfranchisement of significant numbers of African American men by virtue of criminal convictions in certain states—the national consensus is that these practices are wrong, unlawful, and un-American (Bobo, 2001).

Institutional racism is the most entrenched, destructive, and enduring form of racism on the spectrum of racism in the United States today. Because it is so omnipresent and complex, confronting it feels daunting. Yet, just as with the extreme forms of racism that no longer are acceptable in this nation, institutional racism can be dismantled.

What sustains this web? Many things, including ignorance and lack of awareness by white people, cultural discourses legitimizing it, the economic inequalities and advantages that accrue for whites, intergroup competition, political manipulation, and the persistence of both intentional and unintentional segregation. Many of the strategies already mentioned work to undermine some of these forces. But more is needed.

In Chapter 4 we considered the web of institutional racism. The default setting for all institutions and organizations is to reflect the structure and practices of racism in society. Active efforts are required to negate and transform this dynamic. One of the most insidious facets of the web of racism is how the steel threads connect: For example, residential racism leads to educational and transportation racism, which contribute to a lack of employment opportunities as well as the capacity to accumulate wealth.

The web is so huge and linked that working to dismantle all of it at once would be a Herculean task. Still, because it is so connected, if progress can be made in one part of the web, it starts to pull on the other strands, creating fissures and tensions that eventually can lead to collapse of the web. For example, if political racism is confronted successfully, more lawmakers are likely to understand the importance of equal access to health care, and of protecting poor people of color from environmental hazards, which will give rise to challenges to health-care and environmental racism. If communities become truly racially integrated, a foundation will be laid from which to confront educational and occupational racism. The success of the Gautreaux program, mentioned in Chapter 9, is encouraging in this regard.

Helping professionals can become engaged in a number of anti-racism strategies that will erode the web of institutional racism. These involve making legal challenges to racism, supporting laws that foster equality, and backing affirmative action and some form of reparations. At some point, a social movement will have the power of the Civil Rights Movement of the past, but until the relevant factors coalesce, helping professionals have other options.

Part of the challenge to the persistence of racism is to articulate a vision of a society without racism. In such a world, people would live wherever they want and there would be much greater racial integration. The homes owned by people of color and the neighborhoods where they reside would be as valuable as those of white people. These neighborhoods would be served by banks rather than by predatory lenders. Educational achievement at all levels would not reflect racial gaps. All occupations and professions would have a range of racial representation consistent with the demographics of the country. Health, infant mortality, access to health care, and life expectancy would not reflect racial patterns. Fewer people would be in jail, and jails would not be grossly over-populated by African Americans and other people of color. Broken treaties with Native American tribes would be revisited and repaired. Salaries and wealth would not reflect racial inequities. There would be cultural pluralism. Everyone would have a right to vote, and their votes would be counted. And politicians, particularly at state and national levels, would not be over-whelmingly white. Every office of government, including the Presidency, would be open to anyone, regardless of race. Social opportunity and access would be available to people of all races, and everyone could make choices about their occupations, neighborhoods, and lifestyles as *individuals*, not as representatives of their race.

Granted, this is only a partial vision, but it illustrates the types of activities in which helping professionals can engage. Wherever we work (and live), we can challenge practices by real estate firms, banks, and local municipalities that continue segregation. For those of us who work in or with public schools, ending the racial achievement gap can be our highest priority. We can join coalitions, Parent–Teacher Organizations, run for school committee positions, and exert our influence as professionals and parents. We can ensure that our own professions do not have racial patterns of staffing, promotion, and leadership. We all have interactions with the health system, and we can work with health care providers and systems to serve all people equally, regardless of race. We can help to form task forces and coalitions to lower infant mortality rates in all communities.

All of these local actions are significant. Also, we can advocate for state and national priorities—universal health care coverage, adequate minimum wages, an end to racial profiling, and policies geared to ensure that people of color attend college and have access to jobs in industries that still are predominantly white. Everyone in the United States has the right to vote, and we can advocate for that right. These are huge national issues in the struggle for racial equality.

An inescapable conclusion is that helping professionals must be politically active. The conservative trend in this country has been a regression in the struggle for civil rights. Without leadership from presidents, senators, members of Congress, governors, and state lawmakers, the agenda we are calling for will be blocked, stalled, derailed. Helping professionals are a large group, a growing sector of the U.S. economy. We need to exercise our political muscle through our own efforts and those of our professional organizations. Helping professionals can join national organizations, form local chapters, and work with politicians to advocate for these issues. National organizations such as the National Association of Social Workers (NASW) are already lobbying for these and similar policies and should be encouraged to do even more. Registering clients and consumers to vote also is empowering, as they then can advocate for their own interests. We urge helping professionals to work for two other platforms: affirmative action and reparations.

AFFIRMATIVE ACTION   Affirmative action has been grossly distorted in the public discourse and by conservative politicians appealing to economic and social insecurities of white voters. Affirmative action does not take away college positions and jobs from whites. It opens up semi-closed systems to people of all races.

The real affirmative action in the United States has been the knapsack of privileges carried by all white citizens. What has been called "affirmative action" since the Great Society in the 1960s finally has penetrated virtually all-white niches and enclaves. Without it, college campuses doubtless would not be as integrated as they are and police and fire departments would not have more than a token representation of people of color. If affirmative action continues to come under attack and be diluted, we likely will regress to pre-affirmative action racial patterns.

REPARATIONS   The notion of reparations is exceedingly complex and controversial. We support a national dialogue about reparations because, as we have tried to illustrate, the historical legacies of racism have created profound structural imbalances that disadvantage many people of color. The U.S. government is highly unlikely to return in full the land appropriated from Native Americans or Mexican Americans. There is no way to restore the many resources lost by African Americans. But, as a nation, we can examine the economic and social consequences of these and other historical heritages and consider policies that will acknowledge their impact, seek to repair the social and psychological damage, and reverse economic inequalities. An example of the attempt to do this were the reparations finally granted to Japanese Americans who were interned during World War II.

Some readers will support all of these priorities, while others may support only some or envision other initiatives crucial to dismantling institutional racism. What is most important is that helping professionals work to intervene with laws, policies, and institutions and not sit on the sidelines. Policy formation involves setting agendas and lobbying by various interest groups. If human service professionals are hesitant or opt out of full participation, the vacuum created by inaction will be filled by other interest groups, including those committed to maintaining white privilege and dominance.

MAINTAINING MOTIVATION

Engaging in anti-racism activism can be enlivening and liberating, but it also involves commitment and dedication. Taking a stand against injustice and working for racial equality impart a sense of empowerment. As a person becomes more actively engaged in this work, the investment in dismantling racism deepens. High motivation and passion fuel the level of energy that this work takes. As with any strong commitments, frustration can set in when progress is slow or there are setbacks.

Tensions between fellow activists can arise over differences in opinion about priorities and tactics. Misunderstandings crop up because of cultural differences and unexamined stereotypes, as well as reflexive patterns of group conflict. Struggles over power and leadership increase the frustration and pressure. The anti-racism movement needs all of the help it can muster and, thus, we must consider strategies that can encourage activists to stay involved and be effective in their work.

Self-Care

All activism requires taking care of oneself. Many helping professionals are already struggling with self-care, as they are endowed with deep reservoirs of compassion and are working with clients who have pressing needs. Engaging in anti-racism work usually increases concern for the well-being of consumers and fires up fervor for fairness and social justice. Under these circumstances, self-care may be viewed as a luxury or as a failure of will. But without self-care, burnout becomes a distinct risk.

Self-care may take many different forms, ranging from vigorous physical exercise to reading, meditating, or socializing with friends. Although individuals must identify what works best for them, helping professionals should build in activities and time that allow for a break from the intensity of anti-racism work. We all function with greater strength and acuity if we can nurture ourselves periodically *before* becoming fried and frazzled.

SELF-COMPASSION

Anti-racism helping professionals know how racism damages people and are aware of its capacity to distort perceptions of self and others. So it can be particularly frustrating and discouraging to be reminded of one's own unfinished personal business when an ethnic or racial stereotype bubbles up or a wound of racism is reopened. Helping professionals who are people of color have related how painful and dispiriting it can be to be engaged continually in talking about racism and trying to "educate" white people, even if the cause is just. Helping professionals who are white at times feel appalled at their unresolved biases or a sense of shame when they inadvertently engage in micro-aggressions with colleagues of color. To retreat from activism when criticized by others can be tempting.

We urge anti-racism activists to be compassionate and gentle with themselves. While we are working for a fair and just society, we are all "works in progress" and imperfect people. Of course, our own personal work is an important part of the struggle against racism, but mistakes and unresolved issues are inevitable, and becoming overly self-critical can diminish our energy and motivation. If we are feeling tired or burdened by anti-racism work, or upset with our own internalized stereotypes and racism, we may take out these feelings on other people, criticizing or even verbally attacking them, which alienates potential allies. Sometimes anti-racism activists should take a deep breath or even take a break from the intensity of the work. Self-compassion is an important stance to develop.

AVOIDING HUMILIATING OTHERS

The same compassion that we apply to ourselves should be applied to others as well. All people are potential anti-racism allies and, like ourselves, have flaws. No one likes to feel humiliated or shamed. Sometimes our own anger or passion results in our strongly confronting others. We must always challenge racism, but we have to learn to do it in a way that does not shut down other people. How can we help other people to think about or reflect on their beliefs, motivations, or behaviors without pushing them into a defensive or regressive posture?

Again, respect and compassion can go a long way, and if we can convey this while also persisting in our willingness to challenge racism, we achieve better results. Confronting others should be a two-way street. Nobody appreciates being lectured by someone who is not willing to listen in return. We are more likely to help a person self-reflect if we are genuinely willing to hear what they have to say to us.

We also are tempted to dismiss someone if we think he or she is just "not getting it" and never will "get it." This response is typical, and understandable Sometimes we do need to disengage from a person because we are so frustrated or estranged from him or her. This should be a temporary response, and we will be able to reestablish our compassion for that person and engage in authentic and productive dialogue at some point. The scenarios in Exercise 13.2, taken from conversations with students, illustrate the tension between confronting racism and not humiliating others.

Working Together

Helping professionals who choose to become anti-racism activists are not alone, as many people are engaged in this work in a variety of ways. Anti-racism work requires a great deal of energy, a willingness to confront racism consistently, and a commitment to stay active for the long haul. At times this can feel isolating and lonely.

This chapter already has described the many advantages of working in coalitions. Also helpful is to develop personal support systems and anti-racism allies—people to whom we can turn when things become complicated or overwhelming and who can also turn to us. Groups that help people of color feel buffered from the effects of racism and groups that support white people committed to unlearning racism offer validation and support.

Taking the Long View

Kivel (1996) has urged anti-racism activists not to confuse the battle with the war. Anti-racism work involves many losses and setbacks, as well as achievements. Progress toward social justice has not moved forward consistently. Therefore, we must see anti-racism work as part of a chain of resistance and liberation that has taken place over thousands of years. We have witnessed in our own nation how the most extreme manifestations of racism now are morally, socially, and politically unacceptable.

Taking the long view involves a Janus-like perspective, looking both backward and ahead, noting progress and at the same time identifying what work remains to be done. We should celebrate successes and not become overly discouraged when encountering roadblocks. Dismantling racism is a massive historical project, and many acts of activism are necessary for it to happen. Placing our work on a larger historical canvass can connect us with our predecessors while illuminating the path for our successors.

Valuing the Process as Well as the Product

We value working together to confront racism to change racist policies and practices. We also seek to overcome the group divisions and conflict that racism fosters, as well as the schisms that develop between individuals. Working together to overcome racism, particularly in multiracial teams, illustrates how the process becomes part of the product. As DeMott (1995) has argued, focusing on just becoming "friends" can obscure the social and economic consequences of racism by making it seem as if the problem is solely one of our "just getting along."

Clearly, we are committed to far more than merely getting along, but being able to break down the interpersonal barriers of racism is vital to creating a racially just society. To take just one example: Interpersonal connections have a great deal to do with who does and does not get certain jobs or other opportunities (Steinberg, 2001). When interpersonal preferences are based on the construction of race, structural racism is buttressed and reified. Working together against racism helps us to dissolve the divisive and negative intergroup comparisons that are central to maintaining racism, and leads to greater equity of opportunity.

GROWING AS ACTIVISTS

All of us can continue to develop and hone our skills as anti-racism activists. What are our strengths, and what challenges us? What can we learn more about racism or anti-racism? How can people of color remain engaged with anti-racism work without getting hurt or becoming drained? For white people in particular, what will help to sharpen and deepen the critical consciousness needed to observe and apprehend racism? Exercise 13.1 presents a self-audit for anti-racism activists to use. Working with others and seeking and soliciting feedback offers opportunities for growth. Keeping a journal is another useful tool for self-reflection and processing complex and difficult reactions.

ETERNAL VIGILANCE

The sociologist Stanley Liberson (1985) warned that when a group is used to having power and is pressured or required to cede some of its advantages, it will seek to regain its favored position either by changing the rules or by moving the playing field. Ever since the high-water mark of the Great Society in the mid-1960s, we have witnessed the veracity of Liberson's analysis, through consistent attempts to dismantle affirmative action rather than racism by reframing diversity on campus to increase the numbers of conservative white male professors, and defunding and privatizing public services that offered a safety net to people of color.

Enforcement of discrimination laws and policies has become more lax, and many school districts have abandoned attempts at desegregation, supported by an increasingly conservative judiciary. And while the public discourse accompanying this backlash heralds the achievement of racial equality in the nation, civil rights struggles are relegated to history.

Massey (2005) concluded that Liberson's prediction is at work with housing discrimination as well. Now people of color have an easier time getting housing loans than they did in the past (which is progress), but they disproportionately receive their loans from predatory lenders rather than banks, the former of which charge exorbitant interest rates and carry severe default penalties. Further, the loans are for properties that are less valuable than those in predominantly white neighborhoods. So, even when one hurdle is cleared, other obstacles appear.

All of us engaged in anti-racism work must forge ahead, breaking new ground while securing what has been achieved and guarding against an inevitable backlash. We do this not only for ourselves but for our neighbors and for those who have the right to be our neighbors; not only for *our* children but for *all* children; not only for the present generation but for generations to come. We are not alone. We are all connected and part of a chain that predates us and will continue with our nieces and nephews, children and grandchildren, long after we no longer can walk or raise our voices. They, in particular, need to see us lighting the torch so they know how to do it, as the flame of hope is passed on, match by match, person by person.

As Massey (2005) said:

> Whenever one social group derives systematic benefits from an institutionalized system of subordination, its members can be expected to resist efforts to dismantle the system despite its injustice. Instead, as old forms of discrimination are curtailed, new mechanisms will be invented. The struggle to achieve civil rights may thus be expected to be a long, drawn-out affair. As with liberty, the price of racial justice is eternal vigilance.

EXERCISE 13.1 ANTI-RACISM ACTIVIST SELF-AUDIT

This audit can be responded to alone, in pairs, or in small groups.

1. Strengths
2. Resources
3. Support systems
4. Triggers
5. Areas I need to learn more about
6. Concerns I have about my role as an anti-racism ally (After listing concerns, develop a strategy to respond to each one.)
7. Goals for myself

EXERCISE 13.2 CONFRONTING RACISM WITHOUT HUMILIATING OTHERS

The following situations raise questions about how to confront racism without humiliating others. Responses to the questions can be done alone, in pairs, or in small groups.

SITUATION ONE:
A professor of color is teaching a human behavior class. After presenting a lecture about race and identity development, three or four white students ask challenging questions that seem to you to be a cross-examination of the

professor. One student suggests that the professor may not adequately understand identity theory. You notice that that the professor is becoming tense. What are some ways in which you can intervene? What might you be concerned about saying? What would be your goal in this situation, and what would be a productive outcome?

SITUATION TWO:

A white professor makes a remark in the classroom about how racism is not central to a consideration of housing segregation, which makes you feel that he is insensitive to people of color and the profound influence of racism in this country. After his statement, the room becomes noticeably silent, and some students fidget and look uncomfortable. How might you bring up the content of what the professor said? Would you address the group dynamic you perceive? If yes, how would you do this?

SITUATION THREE:

After you return home for a holiday, a close relative (or friend) with whom you have a good relationship starts making jokes that disparage a racial or ethnic group. You used to listen to these jokes, but now, after studying about racism, you have a strong negative reaction. You care about the person but think you must speak up. How might you raise this issue? What would be your fears or concerns? What positive outcome might come from your confrontation?

SITUATION FOUR:

You overhear a conversation in the dining room between three people, two of whom you know and one of whom you do not. The person you do not know is making stereotypical and offensive remarks about a colleague, generalizing about that colleague's racial or ethnic group. What might you be feeling at this time? Would it be appropriate to say something in the moment and if so, what might you say? If you did not intervene, can you envision any kind of follow-up that would be helpful?

STUDY CIRCLES DIALOGUES

Study Circles Resource Center is a nonprofit organization, sponsored by the Topsfield Foundation, that trains local people to facilitate racial dialogues in communities, schools, and workplaces. Multiracial groups of 8 to 12 people are formed, facilitated by two people, one a person of color and the other white. Meetings take place every week or every 2 weeks and last for 2 hours. The goals of the discussions are to

- listen respectfully to the experiences of others;
- consider a variety of viewpoints about complex issues, exploring disagreements and searching for common ground;
- address racism by devising practical actions and strategies that local communities can implement.

Five scheduled sessions address the following topics:

1. Race relations and racism: Experiences, perceptions, and beliefs
2. Dealing with race: What is the nature of the problem?
3. What should we do to make progress on race relations?
4. What kinds of public policies will help us deal with race relations?
5. How can we move from words to action in our community?

Each topical area includes suggestions for specific questions, examples, and scenarios to present, and ideas for further discussion. The fifth session asks people to consider what they can do as individuals, how they can work with their communities, and how they can keep the dialogue going. Usually, a large-group action forum, which includes members of all of the Study Circles, moves from the phase of discussion to one of taking action.

For further information contact www.studycircles.org.

Source: Study Circles Resource Center, Pomfret, CT.

8-2 APPENDIX | STEPS TO SUCCESSFUL INTERGROUP CONVERSATION: A CRITICAL-DIALOGIC MODEL

This model is used for small groups of 12 to 16 students, who meet for 7 to 12 weeks in 2-hour sessions. They are co-led by facilitators who represent target and agent identities in the area being considered.

Step One: Group beginnings—forming and building relationships
- Establishes an environment conducive to honest and meaningful dialogue
- Includes identity work (Who am I? Who are you? How will we talk as a group?)

Step Two: Exploring differences and commonalities of experience
- Builds on the identity work of the first step
- Challenges individuals to examine the advantages and disadvantages of social group membership and status as members of privileged and targeted social groups
- Allows group-building activities with increased opportunities for talking and listening to each other's experiences and perspectives

Step Three: Exploring and talking about *Hot Topics*
- Encourages individuals to explore questions and issues from various perspectives
- Examines personal, interpersonal, cultural, institutional, and historical factors that cause tensions or estrangement between social identity groups

Step Four: Action planning and alliance building
- Shifts the focus from dialogue and conflict exploration to action planning and alliance building
- Individuals identify necessary steps to address injustices and to bridge differences

Source: Based on a model developed by X. Zúñiga, B.A. Nagda, and T.D. Sevig, 2002, "Intergroup Dialogues: An Educational Model for Cultivating Engagement Across Differences," *Equity and Excellence in Education*, 35(1), 7–17.

9-I APPENDIX | ISSUES TO CONSIDER WHEN CONFRONTING INSTITUTIONAL RACISM

- Have a vision with both a long-term and a short-term plan.
- Map out steps toward achieving the long-term goal.
- Determine what level of institutions, organizations, laws, or policies you will concentrate on influencing and changing.
- Decide who will constitute the group working on this strategy. For example, will you work with a few people who think like you, or a larger, more diverse group?
- Understand what is feasible within the current historical, social, economic, and political contexts.
- Come up with strategies for resolving conflict.
- Review previous efforts and their strengths and areas for improvement.
- Define what role clients and consumers will play.
- Analyze formal and informal power.
- Anticipate unintended consequences.
- Determine ways to sustain momentum and monitor progress, and have an idea of what constitutes success.
- If collaboration is ineffective, explore other available options.
- Consider the risks to you and others, and understand your limitations.

ACTIVITIES TOWARD BECOMING AN ANTI-RACISM ORGANIZATION

APPENDIX 10-1

Following each statement, indicate the level of activity for your organization as:

(A) Accomplished   (IP) In Process   (U) Unaddressed

	Kinds of Activities	Progress
	Writing a mission statement that includes anti-racism goals	
	Hiring more faculty and/or staff of color	
	Making a commitment to become an anti-racism organization in almost all organizational literature	
	Reviewing curricula and policy relevant to anti-racism practices and diversity content	
	Increasing financial resources allocated toward anti-racism initiatives	
	Holding ongoing discussions on racism and race for staff	
	Increasing training for staff on culturally informed service delivery	
	Sponsoring regular seminars for faculty or staff about racism and diversity	

Continued

	Kinds of Activities	Progress
	Engaging in public dialogues on race and racism open to all organizational constituencies, including volunteers, boards, and trustees	
	Giving continued attention to outreach recruitment	
	Creating and facilitating alliances among individuals, groups, and organizations to challenge policies and practices that perpetuate systemic discrimination, prejudice, and ill treatment of people of color	
	Supporting practices, policies, and attitudes necessary to create an inclusive environment and culture	
	Redistributing decision-making power to reflect the organizational diversity of people, communities, ideas, and interests	
	Designing an appropriate and voluntary mentoring system to assist recent hires in learning the ropes	
	Attending to interpersonal and intergroup relations	
	Creating opportunities and structures for addressing and resolving inequitable or discriminatory behavior, policies, or practices related to race	
	Including models of practice or service delivery that address the needs of diverse clients, students, or consumers	
	Supporting caucus groups or identity groups as they grapple with issues unique to them in their organization	
	Raising awareness about the barriers to communication about race	
	Providing space and appropriate context for the expression of fears, hopes, anxieties, understandings, and misunderstandings that people experience in the process of anti-racism work	
	Exploring worldviews, biases, and assumptions of staff	
	Examining cultural assumptions of service delivery programs	

Source: Adapted from "The Road to Becoming an Anti-Racism Organization," by S. Donner and J. Miller, in *Community Based Clinical Practice*, edited by A. Lightburn and P. Sessions (New York: Oxford University Press, 2005).

CULTURAL VALUES AND WORLDVIEWS

VALUES

Some areas in which cultures have different values:

- Privacy versus being part of a group
- Well-being of the individual versus well-being of the group
- Independence versus interdependence
- Seeking help versus managing one's own problems
- Encouraging children to express themselves versus "children should be seen but not heard"
- What to do when a child is sick
- The roles of men and women in the family
- How to express respect
- Whether authority is to be trusted and respected or challenged
- Time and punctuality

QUESTIONS

1. What are your values in these areas?
2. Where have you noticed differences between your values and those of your clients?
3. How have these differences in values caused conflicts between you and your clients?
4. How have you tried to bridge these differences? What has worked and what has not worked?

SAYINGS

In most of our families, we grew up hearing sayings or expressions that reflected the family's values. Here are some common North American sayings:

- Pull yourself up by your own bootstraps.
- Don't beat around the bush.
- Time is money.
- A man's home is his castle.
- He's all talk and no action.
- A stitch in time saves nine.
- Stand on your own two feet.
- God helps those who help themselves.
- You've made your bed. Now lie in it.

QUESTIONS

1. Did you ever hear these expressions while you were growing up?
2. If yes, what did they mean and what did you think of them?
3. What values and worldviews are implicit in these sayings?
4. Did you grow up with other expressions, and what values did they reflect?

CULTURALLY INFLUENCED BEHAVIORS

Examine your own values and the origin of these values in the sections below. Discuss with colleagues and compare.

Help-seeking behavior

Medical care and illness

Gender roles

Role of family

Behavior toward authority

Time and punctuality

Source: Includes ideas from *Developing Cross-Cultural Competence*, by E.W. Lynch and M.J. Hanson (Baltimore: Paul H. Brookes Publishing, 1992).

II-3 APPENDIX | QUESTIONS ABOUT CROSS-CULTURAL CONTACTS

1. Describe your first contacts with members of other racial and ethnic groups.

2. What was your most positive encounter with a person from another ethnic or racial group?

3. What is your most negative encounter with a person from another ethnic or racial group? If you could replay the tape of what happened, what do you wish you could do differently?

4. Which clients have you found to be most challenging? Why?

5. Which ethnic, religious, or cultural groups would you like to learn most about?

6. What is the best way for you to learn about other cultures? (e.g., discussion groups, dialogue groups, classes, reading, visiting different neighborhoods, attending films, listening to music)

FURTHER READING ABOUT CROSS-RACIAL/ CULTURAL CLINICAL PRACTICE

Carter, R.T. (1995). *The influence of race and racial identity in psychotherapy: Toward a racially inclusive model.* New York: Wiley.

Comas-Diaz, L., & Greene, B. (Eds.) (1994). *Women of color: Integrating ethnic and gender identities in psychotherapy.* New York: Guilford Press.

Comas-Diaz, L., & Jacobsen, F.M. (1995). The therapist of color and the white patient dyad: Contradictions and recognitions. *Cultural Diversity and Mental Health, 1*(2), 93–106.

Ferguson, S.A., & King, T.C. (1997). There but for the grace of God: Two Black women therapists explore privilege. *Women & Therapy, 20*(1), 5–14.

Fuertes, J.N. (1999). Asian Americans' and African Americans' initial perceptions of Hispanic counselors. *Journal of Multicultural Counseling and Development, 27,* 122–135.

Hawkins, C.E. (Ed.) (1997). *Handbook of psychotherapy supervision* (pp. 570–588). New York: John Wiley & Sons.

Helms, J.A., & Cook, D.A. (1999). *Using race and culture in counseling and psychotherapy: Theory and process.* Needham Heights, MA: Allyn & Bacon.

Leary, K. (2000). Racial enactments in dynamic treatment. *Psychoanalytic Dialogues, 10*(4), 639–653.

Leary, K. (1997). Race, self-disclosure, and "forbidden talk": Race and ethnicity in contemporary clinical practice. *Psychoanalytic Quarterly, 66*(2), 163–189.

Lijtmaer, R.M. (2001). Countertransference and ethnicity: The analyst's psychic changes. *Journal of the American Academy of Psychoanalysis, 29*(1), 73–83.

Lum, D. (2000). *Social work practice and people of color: A process stage approach* (4th ed.). Belmont, CA: Brooks/Cole.

McGoldrick, M., Giordano, J., & Garcia-Preto, N. (2005). *Ethnicity and family therapy* (3rd ed.). New York: Guilford Press.

Perez Foster, R.M., Moskowitz, M., and Javier, M.A. (Eds). *Reaching across boundaries of culture and class: Widening the scope of psychotherapy.* Northvale, NJ: Jason Aronson.

Perez Foster, R.M. (1998). The clinician's cultural countertransference: The psychodynamics of culturally competent practice. *Clinical Social Work Journal,* 26(3), 253–270.

Ridley, C.R. (1995). *Overcoming unintentional racism in counseling and therapy.* Thousand Oaks, CA: Sage Publishing.

Sue, D.W., & Sue, D. (2003). *Counseling the culturally diverse: Theory and practice* (4th ed.). New York: Wiley.

Tang, N., & Gardner, J. (1999). Race, culture, and psychotherapy: Transference to minority therapists. *The Psychoanalytic Quarterly,* 68(1), 1–20. *[Especially relevant for clinicians of color]*

Vontress, C.E., & Epp, L.R. (1997). Historical hostility in the African American client: Implications for counseling. *Journal of Multicultural Counseling and Development,* 25(3), 170–184.

Weaver, H.N. (2005). *Explorations in cultural competence: Journeys to the four directions.* Belmont, CA: Brooks/Cole.

IMAGINARY LETTER

This assignment can help students to empathize with a person who may be racially or ethnically different from them. It involves perspective taking and searching for strengths as well as struggles.

Read one of the assigned narratives or stories. Write a *two-page* imaginary letter reacting to the narrative to either a character in the narrative or the narrator, with particular attention to the importance or unimportance of race and ethnicity. How is the character's or the narrator's culture and worldview similar to or different from your own? Do you have any concerns about their vulnerabilities or encouragement about their strengths that you would like to share with them? Please ask any questions about them and share what you learned about them and yourself.

Examples of narratives:

Beatty, P. (1996, Spring). Taken out of context. *Granta, 53,* 167–194.

Cose, E. (1993). *The rage of a privileged class.* New York: HarperCollins [either Chapter 2, Tiptoeing around the truth, pp. 27–52, **or** Chapter 7, Young people, old ideas, pp. 135–152].

Exchange with a national socialist. (1996). *Race Traitor, 5,* 17–48.

Finnegan, W. (1996, March 25). A reporter at large: The new Americans. *New Yorker,* pp. 52–71.

Gilmore, M. (1991, Autumn). Family album. *Granta, 37,* 11–52.

Hale, J.C. (1993). *Bloodlines: Odyssey of a Native daughter.* New York: Random House, pp. 25–87 [Daughter of Winter].

Hassenback, I. (1996, Jan. 8). How Nazis are made. *New Yorker,* pp. 36–56.

Kingston, M.H. (1991). No name woman. In *Braided lives.* St. Paul: Minnesota Humanities Commission.

Kozol, J. (1991). *Savage inequalities* (pp. 7–39). New York: Crown.

Kotlowitz, A. (1991). *There are no children here* (pp. 43–56). New York: Anchor.

McMillan, T. (1990). Ma'Dear. In T. McMillan (Ed.), *Breaking ice: An anthology of contemporary African-American fiction* (pp. 457–465). New York: Penguin.

Piper, A. (1993). Passing for white, passing for black. *Transition, 58,* 4–33.

Rodriguez, A. (1992). No more war games (pp. 31–44). In A. Rodriguez, Jr., *The boy without a flag: Tales of the South Bronx.* Minneapolis: Milkweed Editions.

Wilson, K., Wilson, M., & Hall, R. (1992). *The color complex: The politics of skin color among African Americans.* New York: Anchor. [Chapter 3, Embracing whiteness, pp. 41–61 **or** Chapter 9, The media: Images in Black and light, pp. 135–160]

REFERENCES

Abramovitz, M. (1988). *Regulating the lives of women. Social policy from colonial times to the present*. Boston: South End Press.

Acevedo-Garcia, D., & Osypuk, T.L. (2004, July/August). Racial disparities in housing and health. *Poverty and Race, 13*(4), 1–2, 11–13.

Adams, M. (1997). Pedagogical frameworks for social justice education. In M. Adams, L.A. Bell, & P. Griffin (Eds.), *Teaching for diversity and social justice: A sourcebook* (pp. 30–43). New York: Routledge.

Adams, M., Jones, J., & Tatum, B. (1997). Knowing our students. In M. Adams, L.A. Bell, & P. Griffin (Eds.), *Teaching for diversity and social justice: A sourcebook* (pp. 311–325). New York: Routledge.

Adelman, L. (Producer), and Smith, L. (Director). (2003). *Race: The power of an illusion, part 3: The house we live in*. [Videorecording]. (Available from California Newsreel, San Francisco.)

Adorno, T.W., Frenkel-Brunswick, E., Levinson, D.J., & Sanford, R.N. (1950). *The authoritarian personality*. New York: Harper.

Aldarondo, F. (2001). Racial and ethnic identity models and their application: Counseling biracial individuals. *Journal of Mental Health Counseling, 23*(3), 233–255.

Allen, T.W. (1994). *The invention of the white race*. New York: Verso.

Allport, G.W. (1948). *The ABC's of scapegoating*. Chicago: B'nai B'rith Press.

Allport, G.W. (1954). *The nature of prejudice*. New York: Addison Wesley.

Altimari, D., Budoff, C., & Davis, T. (2001, July 15). Suburbs more diverse, but not town halls. *Hartford Courant*, A1, A6.

American Psychological Association. (2002). Ethical principles of psychologists and code of conduct. Washington, DC: APA.

American School Counselor Association. (2004). *Ethical standards for school counselors*. Alexandria, VA: ASCA.

Angier, N. (2000, August 22). Do races differ? Not really, DNA shows. *New York Times*, F1.

Anti-Defamation League. (1998). *A classroom of difference trainer's manual*. New York: Author.

Arnove, A., & Zinn, H. (2004). *Voices of a people's history of the United States*. New York: Seven Stories Press.

Arredondo, P. (1999). Multicultural counseling competencies as tools to address oppression and racism. *Journal of Counseling and Development, 77*, 102–108.

Associated Press. (2000, June 26). Mass. congressmen lag in number of minority hires. *Daily Hampshire Gazette*, B1.

Association of Community Organizations for Reform Now. (2002). *Separate and unequal: Predatory lending in America*. Washington, DC: Author.

Atkinson, D., Morten, G., & Sue, D. (1993). *Counseling American minorities* (4th ed.). Dubuque, IA: W.C. Brown.

Axinn, J., & Levin, H. (1992). *Social welfare: A history of the American response to social need* (3rd ed.). New York: Longman.

Balsam, K.F., Huang, B., Fieldand, K.C., Simoni, J.M., & Walters, K.L. (2004). Culture, trauma, and wellness: A comparison of heterosexual and lesbian, gay, bisexual and Two-Spirit Native Americans. *Cultural Diversity and Mental Health, 10*(3), 287–301.

Barak, M. (2000). Beyond affirmative action: Toward a model of diversity and organizational inclusion. *Administration in Social Work, 23*(3/4), 47–68.

Bargal, D., & Bar, H. (1994). The encounter of social selves: Intergroup workshops for Arab and Jewish youth. *Social Work with Groups, 17*(3), 39–59.

Bashi, V. (1998). Racial categories matter because racial hierarchies matter: A commentary. *Racial and Ethnic Studies, 21*(5), 959–968.

Bayor, R.H. (1988). *Neighbors in conflict: The Irish, Germans, Jews and Italians of New York City, 1929–1941*. Urbana: University of Illinois Press.

Becker, C., Chasin, L., Chasin, R., Herzig, M., & Roth, S. (1995). From stuck debate to new conversation on controversial issues: A report from the public conversations project. *Journal of Feminist Family Therapy, 7*(1/2), 143–161.

Begley, S. (1995, Feb. 13). Three is not enough: Surprising new lessons from the controversial science of race. *Newsweek*, 67–69.

Bell, L.A., & Griffin, P. (1997). Pedagogical frameworks for social justice education. In M. Adams, L.A. Bell, & P. Griffin (Eds.), *Teaching for diversity and social justice: A sourcebook* (pp. 44–58). New York: Routledge.

Bell, L.A., Washington, S., Weinstein, G., & Love, B. (1997). Knowing ourselves as instructors. In M. Adams, L.A. Bell, & P. Griffin (Eds.), *Teaching for diversity and social justice: A sourcebook* (pp. 299–310). New York: Routledge.

Berman-Rossi, T., & Miller, I. (1994). African-Americans and the settlements during the late 19th and early 20th centuries. *Social Work with Groups, 17*(3), 77–92.

Berry, B. (1958). *Race and ethnic relations*. Boston: Riverside Press.

Black, J., Maki, M., & Nunn, J. (1997) Does race affect the social work student–field instructor relationship? *Clinical Supervisor, 16*(1): 39–54.

Blair, I.V., Ma, J.E., & Lenton, A.P. (2001). Imagining stereotypes away: The moderation of implicit stereotypes through mental imagery. *Journal of Personality and Social Psychology, 81*(5), 838–841.

Blank, R.M. (2001). An overview of trends in social and economic well-being, by race. In N.J. Smelser, W.J. Wilson, & F. Mitchell (Eds.), *America becoming: Racial trends and their consequences* (Vol. I, pp. 21–39). Washington, DC: National Academy Press.

Blauner, R. (1969). Internal colonialism and ghetto revolt. *Social Problems, 16*, 393–408.

Blaylock, H.M., Jr. (1967). *Towards a theory of minority-group relations*. New York: John Wiley & Sons.

Blumenfeld, W.J. (2000). How homophobia hurts everyone. In M. Adams, W.J. Blumenfeld, R. Castaneda, H.W. Hackman, M.L. Peters, & X. Zuniga. (Eds.), *Readings for diversity and social justice: An anthology on racism, anti-Semitism, sexism, heterosexism, ableism, and classism* (pp. 267–275). New York: Routledge.

Bobo, L.D. (2001). Racial attitudes and relations at the close of the twentieth century. In N.J. Smelser, W.J. Wilson, & F. Mitchell (Eds.), *America becoming: Racial trends and their consequences* (Vol. I, pp. 265–301). Washington, DC: National Academy Press.

Bourgois, P. (1995). *In search of respect*. New York: Cambridge.

Boyd, G. (2001, July 31). *The drug war is the new Jim Crow*. New York: American Civil Liberties Union.

Brewer, M.B. (2001). Ingroup identification and intergroup conflict: When does ingroup love become outgroup hate? In R.D. Ashmore, L. Jussim, & D. Wilder (Eds.), *Social identity, intergroup conflict, and conflict resolution* (pp. 17–41). New York: Oxford University Press.

Bronner, E. (1998, April 1). Black and Hispanic Admissions Off Sharply at U. of California. *New York Times*, A1.

Brown, E.R., Ojeda, V.D., Wyn, R., & Levan, R. (2000). *Racial and ethnic disparities in access to health insurance and health care*. Los Angeles: UCLA Center for Health Policy Research.

Brown, M.K., Carnoy, M., Currie, E., Duster, T., Oppenheimer, D.B., Shultz, M.M., & Wellman, D. (2003). *Whitewashing race: The myth of a colorblind society.* Berkeley: University of California Press.

Brown, R. (1995). *Prejudice.* Cambridge, MA: Blackwell.

Bruner, J. (1990). *Acts of meaning.* Cambridge, MA: Harvard University Press.

Building Blocks for Youth. (2001). *Drugs and disparity: The racial impact of Illinois' practice of transferring young drug offenders to adult court.* Washington, DC: Author.

Calhoun, M., & Bailey, N. (2005). Predatory lending: Undermining economic progress in communities of color. *Poverty & Race, 14*(1), 17–19.

Carlton-LaNey, I. (1999). African American social work pioneer's response to need. *Social Work, 44*(4), 311–321.

Carnes, J. (1995). *Us and them: A history of intolerance in America.* Montgomery, AL: Southern Poverty Law Center.

Carnevale, A.P., & Rose, S.J. (2003). *Socioeconomic status, race/ethnicity, and selective college admissions.* New York: Century Foundation.

Carson, M. (1990). *Settlement folk: Social thought and the American settlement movement, 1885–1930.* Chicago: University of Chicago Press.

Carter, R.T. (1995). Race and psychotherapy: Clinical applications in a sociocultural context. Chapter 13 in *The influence of race and racial identity in psychotherapy: Toward a racially inclusive model* (pp. 225–241). New York: Wiley.

Cartmill, M. (1999). The status of the race concept in physical anthropology. *American Anthropologist, 100*(3), 651–660.

Cashwell, C., Looby, E.J., & Housley, W. (1997). Appreciating cultural diversity through clinical supervision. *Clinical Supervisor, 15*(1), 75–85.

Charles, C.Z (2000). Neighborhood racial-composition preferences: Evidence from a multiethnic metropolis. *Social Problems, 47*(3), 379–407.

Charles, C.Z. (2001). Processes of racial residential segregation. In A. O'Connor, C. Tilly, & L.D. Bobo (Eds.), *Urban inequality: Evidence from four cities* (pp. 217–271). New York: Russell Sage Foundation.

Chasin, R., Herzig, M., Roth, S., Chasin, L., Becker, C., & Stains, R.R., Jr. (1996). From diatribe to dialogue on divisive public issues: Approaches drawn from family therapy. *Mediation Quarterly, 13*(4), 323–345.

Chesler, M. A. (1994). Organizational development is not the same as multicultural organizational development. In E.Y. Cross, J.H. Katz, F.A. Miller, & E.W. Seashore (Eds.), *The promise of diversity* (pp. 240–251). Burr Ridge, IL: Irwin.

Cloward, R.A., & Ohlin, L.E. (1960). *Delinquency and opportunity.* New York: Free Press.

Cohen, A. (2004, June 21). Indians face obstacles between the reservation and the ballot box. *New York Times.* A18.

Cokley, K.O. (2002). Testing Cross's revised racial identity model: An examination of the relationship between racial identity and internalized racism. *Journal of Counseling Psychology, 49*(4), 476–483.

Collins, P.H. (1990). *Black feminist thought: Knowledge, consciousness and the politics of empowerment.* New York: Routledge.

Coltrane, S., & Messineo, M. (2000). The perpetuation of subtle prejudice: Race and gender imagery in 1990s television advertising. *Sex Roles, 42*(5/6), 363–389.

Comas-Diaz, L., & Jacobsen, F.M. (2001). Ethnocultural allodynia. *Journal of Psychotherapy Practice and Research, 10*, 246–252.

Consolacion, T.B., Russell, S.T., & Sue, S. (2004). Sex, race/ethnicity, and romantic attractions: Multiple minority status adolescents and mental health. *Cultural Diversity and Ethnic Minority Psychology, 10*(3), 200–214.

Cook, D.A. (1994). Racial identity in supervision. *Counselor Education and Supervision, 34*(2), 132–141.

Cooley, C.H. (1922). *Human nature and the social order.* New York: Scribner.

Cose, E. (1993). *The rage of a privileged class.* New York: HarperCollins.

Cose, E. (1995, June 5). Black men, black women. *Newsweek*, 66–69.

Cotter, D.A., Hermsen, J.M., & Vanneman, R. (1999). Systems of gender, race, and class inequality: Multilevel analyses. *Social Forces, 78*(2), 433–460.

Council of Economic Advisors. (1998). *Changing America: Indicators of social and economic well-being by race and Hispanic origin.* Washington, DC: Author.

Cox, O.C. (1948). *Caste, class and race: A study in social dynamics.* New York: Doubleday & Co.

Crocker, J., & Luhtanen, R. (1990). Collective self-esteem and ingroup bias. *Journal of Personality and Social Psychology, 58*(1), 60–67.

Cross, W. (1978). The Thomas and Cross models of psychological nigrescence. *Journal of Black Psychology, 4*, 13–31.

Cross, W. (1991). *Shades of black: Diversity in African-American identity.* Philadelphia: Temple University Press.

Croteau, J.M., Talbot, D.M., Lance, T.S., & Evans, N.J. (2002). A qualitative study of the interplay between privilege and oppression. *Journal of Multicultural Counseling and Development, 30*, 239–258.

Damasio, A. (2000). *The feeling of what happens: Body, emotions and the making of consciousness.* London: Vintage.

Daniel, J.H. (2000). The courage to hear: African American women's memories of racial trauma. In L.C. Jackson and B. Greene (Eds.), *Psychotherapy with African American women: Innovations in psychodynamic perspectives and practice.* New York: Guilford.

Davis, D.B. (1997). A big business. *New York Review of Books, XLV*(10), 50–52.

Davis, D.B. (2001). Slavery—White, Black, Muslim, Christian. *New York Review of Books, XLVIII* (11), 51–55.

Davis, K. (1997). Managed care, mental illness and African Americans: A prospective analysis of managed care policy in the United States. *Smith College Studies in Social Work, 67*(3), 623–641.

Davis, L.E., & Proctor, E.K. (1989). *Race, gender and class for practice with individuals, families, and groups.* Englewood Cliffs, NJ: Prentice Hall.

Davis, N.J. (1992). Teaching about inequality: Student resistance, paralysis, and rage. *Teaching Sociology, 20*, 232–238.

Davis, S. (2004, November 22). Deported from America; Under U.S. laws passed in the mid-1990s and now being strictly enforced, minor and long-forgotten offences can lead to jail and eventual exile. *New Statesman.* Available at http://www.newstatesman.com/200411220005

Delgado, R., & Stefanic, J. (1997). Introduction. In R. Delgado & J. Stefanic (Eds.), *Critical white studies: Looking behind the mirror* (pp. xvii–xviii). Philadelphia: Temple University Press.

DeMott, B. (1995). *The trouble with friendship: Why Americans can't think straight about race.* New York: Atlantic Monthly Press.

Diamond, J. (1997). *Guns, germs and steel: The fates of human societies.* New York: W.W. Norton.

Diamond, L.M. (2003). Special section: Integrating research on sexual-minority and heterosexual development: Theoretical and clinical implications. *Journal of Clinical Child and Adolescent Psychology, 32*(4), 490–498.

Dinnerstein, L. (1994). *Anti-Semitism in America.* New York: Oxford University Press.

Dion, K.L. (2002). The social psychology of perceived prejudice and discrimination. *Canadian Psychology, 43*(1), 1–10.

Dobbins, J.E., & Skillings, J.H. (2000). Racism as a clinical syndrome. *American Journal of Orthopsychiatry 70*(1), 14–27.

Donner, S., & Miller, J. (2005). The road to becoming an anti-racism organization. In A. Lightburn & P. Sessions (Eds.), *Community based clinical practice.* New York: Oxford University Press.

Donner, S., & Miller, J. (2007). The complexity of multidimensional social identity development. In S. Borrmann, M. Klassen, & C. Spatscheck (Eds.), *International Social Work: Social problems, cultural issues and social work education* (pp. 75–94). Opladen, Germany: Barbara Budrich Publishers.

Douglas, T. (1995). *Scapegoats: Transferring blame.* New York: Routledge.

Dovidio, J.F., Gaertner, S.L., Kawakami, K., & Hodson, G. (2002). Why can't we all just get along? Interpersonal biases and interracial distrust. *Cultural Diversity and Ethnic Minority Psychology, 8*(2), 88–102.

Dovidio, J.F., Gaertner, S.L., Niemann, Y.F., & Snider, K. (2001). Racial, ethnic and cultural differences in responding to distinctiveness and discrimination on campus: Stigma and common group identity. *Journal of Social Issues, 57*(1), 167–188.

Dyche, L., & Zayas, L.H. (2001). Cross-cultural empathy and training the contemporary psychotherapist. *Clinical Social Work Journal, 29*(3), 245–258.

Eagle, M.N. (1984). *Recent developments in psychoanalysis: A critical evaluation.* Cambridge, MA: Harvard University Press.

Edsall, T.B., & Edsall, M.D. (1991). *Chain reaction: The impact of race, rights and taxes on American politics.* New York: W.W. Norton.

Elmelech, Y., & Lu, H. (2004). Race, ethnicity and the gender poverty gap. *Social Science Research, 33*, 158–182.

Epps, E.G. (1973). *Race relations: Current perspectives*. Cambridge, MA: Winthrop Publishers.

Eriksen, T.H. (2001). Ethnic identity, national identity and intergroup conflict: The significance of personal experience. In R.D. Ashmore, L. Jussim, & D. Wilder (Eds.), *Social identity, intergroup conflict, and conflict resolution* (pp. 42–68). New York: Oxford University Press.

Eriksen, T.H. (1996). Ethnicity, race, class and nation. In J. Hutchinson & A.D. Smith (Eds.), *Ethnicity* (pp. 28–31). New York: Oxford University Press.

Erikson, E.H. (1963). *Childhood and society* (2nd ed.). New York: W.W. Norton.

Erikson, E.H. (1968). *Identity, youth and crisis*. New York: W.W. Norton.

Espenshade, T.J., Fix, M., Zimmerman, W., & Corbett, T. (1996–97, Fall/Winter). Immigration and social policy: New interest in an old issue. *Focus, 18*(2), 1–10.

Esposito, L., & Murphy, J.W. (2000). Another step in the study of race relations. *Sociological Quarterly, 41*(2), 171–187.

Etzioni, A. (1997). A new fourth: A national unity day? *Responsive Community, 7,* 6–8.

Faber, D.R., & Krieg, E.J. (2001). *Unequal exposure to ecological hazards: Environmental injustices in the Commonwealth of Massachusetts*. Boston: Northeastern University, Philanthropy and Environmental Justice Research Project.

Feagin, J.R. (1999). Excluding blacks and others from housing. *Cityscape: A Journal of Policy Development and Research, 4*(3), 79–91.

Feagin, J.R., & Feagin, C.B. (1994). Theoretical perspectives in race and ethnic relations. In F.L. Pincus & H.J. Ehrlich (Eds.), *Contending views on prejudice, discrimination, and ethnoviolence* (pp. 29–47). Boulder, CO: Westview Press.

Feagin, J.R., & Feagin, C.B. (1999). *Racial and ethnic relations* (6th ed.). Upper Saddle River, NJ: Prentice Hall.

Fenton, S. (1999). *Ethnicity, racism, class and culture*. Lanham, MD: Rowman & Littlefield Publishers.

Ferguson, S.A., & King, T.C. (1997). There but for the grace of God: Two Black women therapists explore privilege. *Women & Therapy, 20*(1), 5–14.

Fisher, R.J. (1990). *The social psychology of intergroup and international conflict resolution*. New York: Springer-Verlag.

Foner, P. (1975). *History of Black Americans* (Vol 1). Westport, CT: Greenwood Press.

Frankenberg, E., Lee, C., & Orfield, G. (2003). *A multiracial society with segregated schools: Are we losing the dream?* Cambridge, MA: Harvard University Civil Rights Project.

Fredrickson, G. (1981). *White supremacy: A comparative study in American and South African history*. New York: Oxford University Press.

Fredrickson, G. (1988). *The arrogance of race: historical perspectives on slavery, racism, and social inequality*. Middletown, CT: Wesleyan University Press.

Fredrickson, G. (2002). *Racism: A short history*. Princeton, NJ: Princeton University Press.

Freire, P. (1970). *Pedagogy of the oppressed*. New York: Seabury Press.

Freire, P. (1994). *Pedagogy of hope: Reliving pedagogy of the oppressed*. New York: Continuum.

Fritz, N. (2001, March). Electoral debacle: Our response. *Civil Liberties,* 2–6.

Furstenberg, F. (2001). The fading dream: Prospects for marriage in the inner city. In E. Anderson & D.S. Massey (Eds.), *Problem of the century: Racial stratification in the United States* (pp. 224–246). New York: Russell Sage Foundation.

Galinsky, A., & Moskwitz, G.B. (2000). Perspective-taking: Decreasing stereotype expression, stereotype accessibility, and in-group favoritism. *Journal of Personality and Social Psychology, 78*(4), 708–724.

Gardner, R., & Blackburn, R. (1996). *People who move: New reproductive health focus*. (Population Reports, Series J, 45). Baltimore: Johns Hopkins School of Public Health.

Gaw, A. C. (Ed.) (1993). *Culture, ethnicity, and mental illness*. Washington, DC: American Psychiatric Publishing.

Geis, K.J., & Ross, C.E. (1998). A new look at urban alienation: The effect of neighborhood disorder on perceived powerlessness. *Social Psychology Quarterly, 61*(3), 232–245.

Gillens, M. (1999). *Why Americans hate welfare*. Chicago: University of Chicago Press.

Gilligan, C. (1977). In a different voice: Women's conceptions of self and morality. *Harvard Educational Review, 47,* 481–517.

Gilligan, C. (1982). *In a different voice: Psychological theory and women's development*. Cambridge, MA: Harvard University Press.

Gipson, L.M. (2002). Poverty, race and LGBT youth. *Poverty and Race, 11*(2), 1–6, 11.

Glazer, N., & Moynihan, D.P. (1963). *Beyond the melting pot: The Negroes, Puerto Ricans, Jews, Italians and Irish of New York City*. Cambridge, MA: M.I.T. Press.

Goffman, E. (1959). *The presentation of self in everyday life*. New York: Anchor.

Goldsborough, J. (2000). Out-of-control immigration. *Foreign Affairs, 79*(5), 89–101.

Goleman, D. (1992, April 21). Black scientists study the "pose" of the inner city. *New York Times,* C1.

Golembiewski, R.T. (1995). *Managing diversity in organizations.* Tuscaloosa, AL: University of Alabama Press.

Goodman, D. (2001). *Promoting diversity and social justice: Educating people from privileged groups.* Thousand Oaks, CA: Sage Publishing.

Gordon, L. (1988). *Heroes in their own lives: The history and politics of family violence, Boston, 1880–1960.* New York: Viking.

Gordon, L. (1991). Black and white visions of welfare: Women's welfare activism, 1890–1945. *Journal of American History, 85*(3), 559–590.

Greene, B., & Boyd-Franklin, N. (1996). African American lesbians: Issues in couples therapy. In J. Laird & R.J. Green (Eds.), *Lesbians and gays in couples and families: A handbook for therapists* (pp. 251–271). New York: Jossey-Bass.

Greene, G. J., Jensen, C., & Jones, D.H. (1996). A constructivist perspective on clinical social work practice with ethnically diverse clients. *Social Work, 41*(2), 172–180.

Griffin, P. (1997). Introductory module for single issue courses. In M. Adams, L.A. Bell, & P. Griffin (Eds.), *Teaching for diversity and social justice: A sourcebook* (pp. 61–81). New York: Routledge.

Griffin, P., & Harro, B. (1997). Heterosexism curriculum design. In M. Adams, L.A. Bell, & P. Griffin (Eds.), *Teaching for diversity and social justice: A sourcebook* (pp.141–169). New York: Routledge.

Groot, M., & Marcus, P. (1998). Digging out of the white trap. *Poverty and Race, 7*(2), 1–2, 5.

Group for the Advancement of Psychiatry [GAP]. (1987). *Us and them: The psychology of ethnonationalism.* New York: Brunner/Mazel.

Guglielmo, J., & Salerno, S. (Eds.) (2003). *Are Italians white? How race is made in America.* New York: Routledge.

Guglielmo, T.A. (2003). "No color barrier": Italians, race and power in the United States. In J. Guglielmo & S. Salerno (Eds.), *Are Italians white? How race is made in America* (pp. 29–43). New York: Routledge.

Haney-Lopez, I.F. (1998). The social construction of race: Some observations on illusion, fabrication, and choice. *Harvard Civil Rights–Civil Liberties Law Review, 29*(1), 1–62.

Hardiman, R. (1982). *White identity development: A process-oriented model for describing the racial consciousness of White Americans.* Unpublished doctoral dissertation, University of Massachusetts, Amherst.

Hardiman, R. (1994). White racial identity development in the United States. In E.P. Sallett & D.R. Koslow (Eds.), *Identity in multicultural perspective* (pp. 117–140). Washington, DC: National Multicultural Institute.

Hardiman, R., & Jackson, B.W. (1997). Conceptual foundations for social justice courses. In M. Adams, L.A. Bell, & P. Griffin (Eds.), *Teaching for diversity and social justice: A sourcebook* (pp. 16–29). New York: Routledge.

Hardy, K.V., & Laszloffy, T.A. (1995). Therapy with African Americans and the phenomenon of rage. *In session: psychotherapy in practice, 1*(4), 57–70.

Hardy, M.A., & Hazelrigg, L. (1995). Gender, race/ethnicity, and poverty in later life. *Journal of Aging Studies, 9*(1), 43–63.

Harmon, A. (1998, April 17). Racial divide found on internet highway. *New York Times,* A1.

Harper, G.W., Jernewall, N., & Zea, M.C. (2004). Giving voice to emerging science and theory for lesbian, gay and bisexual people of color. *Cultural Diversity and Mental Health, 10*(3), 187–199.

Harro, B. (2000a). The cycle of socialization. In M. Adams, W.J. Blumenfeld, R. Casteneda, H.W. Hackman, M.L. Peters, & X. Zuniga (Eds.), *Readings for diversity and social justice: An anthology on racism, anti-semitism, Sexism, heterosexism, ableism, and classism* (pp. 15–21). New York: Routledge.

Harro, B. (2000b). The cycle of liberation. In M. Adams, W.J. Blumenfeld, R. Casteneda, H.W. Hackman, M.L. Peters, & X. Zuniga (Eds.), *Readings for diversity and social justice: An anthology on racism, anti-Semitism, sexism, heterosexism, ableism, and classism* (pp. 463–469). New York: Routledge.

Hawkins, D.F. (2001). Commentary on Randall Kennedy's overview of the justice system. In N.J. Smelser, W.J. Wilson, & F. Mitchell (Eds.), *America becoming: Racial trends and their consequences* (Vol. II). Washington, DC: National Academy Press.

Healey, J.F.C. (1995). *Race, ethnicity, gender and class: The sociology of group conflict and change.* Thousand Oaks, CA: Pine Forge Press.

Helms, J. (1990). *Black and white racial identity: Theory, research and practice.* New York: Greenwood Press.

Helms, J.E., & Cook, D.A. (1999). *Using race and culture in counseling and psychotherapy.* Boston: Allyn & Bacon.

Henriksen, R.C., Jr., & Trusty, J. (2004). Understanding and assisting black/white biracial women in their identity development. *Women & Therapy, 27*(1/2), 65–83.

Herek, G.M. (2000). Internalized homophobia among gay men, lesbians, and bisexuals. In M. Adams, W.J. Blumenfeld, R. Castaneda, H.W. Hackman, M.L. Peters, & X. Zuniga (Eds.), *Readings for diversity and social justice: An anthology on racism, anti-Semitism, sexism, heterosexism, ableism, and classism* (pp. 281–283). New York: Routledge.

Hernstein, R., & Murray, C. (1994). *The bell curve: Intelligence and class structure in American life.* New York: Free Press.

Hertzberg, J.F. (1990). Feminist psychotherapy and diversity: Treatment considerations from a self-psychology perspective. In L.S. Brown & M.P.P. Root (Eds.), *Diversity and complexity in feminist therapy* (pp. 275–297). Binghamton, NY: Haworth.

Hill, J. (1999). Language, race and white public space. *American Anthropologist, 100*(3), 680–689.

Hoare, C.H. (2003). Psychosocial identity development in United States society: Its role in fostering exclusion of cultural others. In E.P. Salett & D.R. Koslow (Eds.), *Race, ethnicity and self: Identity in multicultural perspective* (2nd ed., pp. 17–35). Washington, DC: National Multicultural Institute.

hooks, bell. (1995). *Killing rage: Ending racism.* New York: Henry Holt & Co.

hooks, bell. (2000). Homophobia in black communities. In M. Adams, W.J. Blumenfeld, R. Castaneda, H.W. Hackman, M.L. Peters, & X. Zuniga (Eds.), *Readings for diversity and social justice: An anthology on racism, anti-Semitism, sexism, heterosexism, ableism, and classism* (pp. 283–287). New York: Routledge.

Human Rights Watch. (2000). *United States—Punishment and prejudice: Racial disparities in the war on drugs.* New York: Author.

Hyde, C. (2004). Multicultural development in human service agencies: Challenges and solutions. *Social Work, 49*(1), 7–16.

Iglehart, A.P., & Becera, R.M. (1995). *Social services and the ethnic community.* Boston: Allyn & Bacon.

Ignatiev, N. (1995). *How the Irish became white.* New York: Routledge.

Jackson, B., & Hardiman, R. (1994). Multicultural organizational development. In E.Y. Cross, J.H. Katz, F.A. Miller, & E.W. Seashore (Eds.), *The promise of diversity* (pp. 231–239). Burr Ridge, IL: Irwin.

Jackson, B., & Holvino, E. (1988). Developing multicultural organizations. *Creative change: The Journal of Religion and the Applied Behavioral Sciences, 9*(2), 14–19.

Jansson, B. (2005). *The reluctant welfare state: American social welfare policies: Past, present and future* (5th ed.). Belmont, CA: Brooks/Cole.

Johnson, C., & Smith, P. (1998). *Africans in America: America's journey through slavery.* New York: Harcourt Brace.

Johnson, J.H., & Oliver, M.L. (1994). Interethnic minority conflict in urban America: The effects of economic and social dislocations. In. F.L. Pincus & H.J. Ehrlich (Eds.), *Race and ethnic conflict: Contending views on prejudice, discrimination, and ethnoviolence* (pp. 194–205). Boulder, CO: Westview Press.

Joiner, L.L. (2004, November/December). The state of black health. *The Crisis, 111*(6), 17–27.

Jones, J. (1985). *Labor of love, labor of sorrow: Black women, work and the family, from slavery to the present.* New York: Basic Books.

Katz, J.H. (1985). The sociopolitical nature of counseling. *Counseling Psychologist, 13*(4), 615–624.

Katz, M.B. (1986). *In the shadow of the poor house: A social history of welfare in America.* New York: Basic Books.

Katz, M.B. (1989). *The undeserving poor: From the war on poverty to the war on welfare.* New York: Pantheon.

Kaufman, C. (2001). A user's guide to white privilege. *Radical Philosophy Review,* (1/2), 30–38.

Kawakami, K., Moll, J., Hermsen, S., Dovidio, J.F., & Russin, A. (2000). Just say no (to stereotyping): Effects of training in the negation of stereotypic associations on stereotype activation. *Journal of Personality and Social Psychology 78*(5): 871–888.

Keels, M., Duncan, G.J., Deluca, S., Mendenhall, R., & Rosenbaum, J. (2005). Fifteen years later: Can residential mobility programs provide a long-term escape from neighborhood segregation, crime, and poverty? *Demography, 42*(1), 51–73.

Kelman, H.C. (2001). The role of national identity in conflict resolution: Experiences from Israeli–Palestinian problem solving workshops. In R.D. Ashmore, L. Jussim, & D.Wilder (Eds.), *Social identity, intergroup conflict, and conflict resolution* (pp. 187–212). New York: Oxford University Press.

Kennedy, R. (2001). Racial trends in the administration of criminal justice. In N.J. Smelser, W.J. Wilson, & F. Mitchell (Eds.), *American becoming: Racial trends and their consequences* (Vol. 2, pp. 1–20). Washington, DC: National Academy Press.

Kibria, N. (1998). Multiracial America and the new immigration. *Society, 35*(6), 84–88.

Killen, M., Stangor, C., Horn, S., & Sechrist, G.B. (2004). Social reasoning about racial exclusion in intimate and nonintimate relationships. *Youth & Society, 35*(3), 293–322.

Kingston, R.S., & Nickens, H.W. (2001). Racial and ethnic differences in health: Recent trends, current patterns, future directions. In N.J. Smelser, W.J. Wilson, & F. Mitchell (Eds.), *America becoming: Racial trends and their consequences* (Vol. 2, pp. 253–310). Washington, DC: National Academy Press.

Kinloch, G.C. (1974). *The dynamics of race relations: A sociological analysis.* New York: McGraw Hill.

Kinloch, G.C. (1979). *The sociology of minority group relations.* Englewood Cliffs, NJ: Prentice Hall.

Kivel, P. (1996). *Uprooting racism: How white people can work for racial justice.* Philadelphia: New Society Publishers.

Klinkenborg, V. (2002, July/Aug.). Liverpool's heart of darkness. *Mother Jones,* 64–67.

Komar, B. (2003, Jan./Feb.). Race, poverty and the digital divide. *Poverty & Race, 12*(1), 1–2, 5.

Kovel, J. (1970/2001). White racism: A psychohistory. In E. Cashmore & J. Jennings (Eds.), *Racism: Essential readings* (pp. 136–140). Thousand Oaks, CA: Sage.

Kozol, J. (1991). *Savage inequalities: Children in American schools.* New York: Crown Publishers.

Kretzman, J., & McKnight, J.P. (1996). Assets-based community development. *National Civic Review, 85*(4), 23–29.

Kwan, K.K., & Sodowsky, G.R. (1997). Internal and external ethnic identity and their correlates: A study of Chinese ethnic immigrants. *Journal of Multicultural Counseling and Development, 25*(1), 51–68.

Laub, J. (2000). Crime over the life course. *Poverty Research News, 4*(3), 4–7.

Lawson, K., Koman, B., & Rose, A. (1998). *Building one nation.* Washington, DC: Leadership Conference Education Fund.

Leary, K. (1995). "Interpreting in the dark": Race and ethnicity in psychoanalytic psychotherapy. *Psychoanalytic Psychology, 12*(1), 127–140.

Leary, K. (1997). Race, self-disclosure, and "forbidden talk": Race and ethnicity in contemporary clinical practice. *Psychoanalytic Quarterly, LXVI,* 163–189.

Leary, K. (1999). Passing, posing and "keeping it real." *Constellations, 6*(1), 85–96.

Leary, K. (2000). Racial enactments in dynamic treatment. *Psychoanalytic Dialogues, 10*(4): 639–653.

Leman, N. (1991). *The promised land.* New York: Knopf.

Lewis, A. (2004, October). The road to Abu Ghraib; How the United States played a role in creating international human rights—and then abandoning them. *American Prospect, 15*(10), 3.

Liberson, S. (1985). *Making it count: The improvement of social research and theory.* Berkeley: University of California Press.

Lieberman, R.C. (1998). *Shifting the color line: Race and the American welfare state.* Cambridge, MA: Harvard University Press.

Lim-Hing, S. (2000). Dragon ladies, snow queens, and Asian–American dykes: Reflections on race and sexuality. In M. Adams, W.J. Blumenfeld, R. Castaneda, H.W. Hackman, M.L. Peters, & X. Zuniga (Eds.), *Readings for diversity and social justice: An anthology on racism, anti-Semitism, sexism, heterosexism, ableism, and classism* (pp. 296–299). New York: Routledge.

Logan, J.R., Oakley, D., & Stowell, J. (2003, September 1). *Segregation in neighborhoods and schools: Impacts on minority children in the Boston region.* Unpublished paper presented at Harvard Colorlines Conference, Boston.

Lopez, I.F.H. (1994). The social construction of race: Some observations on illusion, fabrication, and choice. *Harvard Civil Rights–Civil Liberties Law Review, 29*(1), 1–62.

Lopez, I.F.H. (1996). *White by law: The legal construction of race.* New York: NYU Press.

Loury, G. (2001). *The anatomy of racial inequality.* Cambridge. MA: Harvard University Press.

Lu, Y.E., Landsverk, J., Ellis-Macleod, E., Newton, R., Ganger, W., & Johnson, I. (2004). Race, ethnicity and case outcomes in child protective services. *Children and Youth Services Review, 26,* 447–461.

Lum, D. (2000). *Social work practice and people of color: A process-stage approach* (4th ed.) Belmont, CA: Brooks/Cole.

Lynch, E.W., & Hanson, M.J. (1992). *Developing cross-cultural competence.* Baltimore: Paul H. Brookes Publishing.

Manning, R.D. (1999). Poverty, race, and the two-tiered financial services system. *Poverty & Race, 8*(4), 1–2, 11.

Marcia, J.E. (1980). Identity in adolescence. In J. Adelson (Ed.), *Handbook of adolescent psychology* (pp. 159–187). New York: Wiley.

Marcia, J., Waterman, A., Matteson, D., Archer, S., & Orlofsky, J. (1994). *Ego identity: Handbook of psychosocial research.* New York: Springer–Verlag.

Massey, D.S. (2001). Segregation and violent crime in urban America. In E. Anderson & D. Massey (Eds.), *Problem of the century: Racial stratification in the United States* (pp. 317–344). New York: Russell Sage Foundation.

Massey, D.S. (2005). Racial discrimination and housing: A moving target. *Social Problems, 52*(2), 149–151.

Massey, D.S., & Denton, N.A. (1993). *American apartheid: Segregation and the making of the underclass.* Cambridge, MA: Harvard.

Mayer, J. (2005, Feb. 14). Outsourcing torture: The secret history of America's "extraordinary rendition" program. *New Yorker,* 106.

McCoy, M.L., & Sherman, R.F. (1994). Bridging the divides of race and ethnicity. *National Civic Review, 83*(2), 111–119.

McDonagh, E.C., & Richards, E.S. (1953). *Ethnic relations in the United States.* New York: Appleton-Century-Crofts.

McDowell, T., & Jeris, L. (2004). Talking about race using critical race theory: Recent trends. *Journal of Marital and Family Therapy, 30*(1), 81–94.

McIntosh, P. (1989, July/Aug.). White privilege: unpacking the invisible knapsack. *Peace and Freedom,* 10–12.

McIntosh, P. (1992). White privilege and male privilege: A personal account of coming to see correspondences through work in women's studies. In M. Anderson & P.H.Collins (Eds.), *Race, class and gender: An anthology* (pp. 70–81). Belmont, CA: Wadsworth.

McKnight, J.L. (1997). A 21st-century map for healthy communities and families. *Families in Society, 78*(2), 117–127.

McLoyd, V.C., & Lozoff, B. (2001). Racial and ethnic trends in children's and adolescents' behavior and development. In N.J. Smelser, W.J. Wilson, & F. Mitchell (Eds.), *America becoming: Racial trends and their consequences* (Vol. 2, pp. 311–350). Washington, DC: National Academy Press.

Memmi, A. (2000). *Racism.* Minneapolis: University of Minnesota Press.

Merghi, J.R., and Grimes, M.D. (2000). Coming out to families in a multicultural context. *Families in Society, 81*(1), 32–41.

Mildred, J., & Zuniga, X. (2004). Working with resistance to diversity issues in the classroom: Lessons from teacher training and multicultural education. *Smith College Studies in Social Work, 74*(2), 359–375.

Miller, J. (1994). A family's sense of power in their community: Theoretical and research issues. *Smith College Studies in Social Work, 64*(3), 221–241.

Miller, J. (1997). *How families construct their relationship to their community: A reflective research approach.* Unpublished doctoral dissertation, University of Connecticut, Storrs.

Miller, J. (1999). *Holyoke at the crossroads: Family, ethnicity and community in a de-industrialized small city* (Proceedings of the 13th conference on the small city and regional community) (pp. 277–286). Stevens Point, WI: Center for the Small City.

Miller, J. (2001). Family and community integrity. *Journal of Sociology and Social Welfare, 28*(4), 23–44.

Miller, J. (2002). "I do what I write about and I write about what I do": A narrative interview with Richard A. Cloward. *Reflections, 8*(1), 44–64.

Miller, J. (2003). Create a crisis and pray: A narrative interview with Richard Cloward. *Journal of Community Practice, 11*(1), 11–37.

Miller, J., & Donner, S. (2000). More than just talk: The use of racial dialogue to combat racism. *Social Work with Groups, 23*(1), 31–53.

Miller, J., Donner, S., & Fraser, E. (2004). Talking when talking is tough: Taking on conversations about race, sexual orientation, gender, class, and other aspects of social identity. *Smith College Studies in Social Work, 74*(2), 377–392.

Miller, J., Hyde, C., & Ruth, B.J. (2004). Teaching about race and racism in social work: Challenges for white educators. *Smith College Studies in Social Work, 74*(2), 409–426.

Miller, J., & Schamess, G. (2000). The discourse of denigration and the creation of other. *Journal of Sociology and Social Welfare, 27*(3), 39–62.

Miller, R.L., & Rotheram-Borus, M.J. (1994). Growing up biracial in the United States. In E.P. Salett & D.R. Koslow (Eds.), *Race, ethnicity and self: Identity in multicultural perspective* (pp. 143–169). Washington, DC: National Multicultural Institute.

Miller, S.M., & Ferroggiaro, M. (1996). Respect. *Poverty & Race, 5*(1), 1–4, 14.

Mills, C.W. (1997). *The racial contract*. Ithaca, NY: Cornell.

Minors, A. (1996). From university to poly-versity: Organizations in transition to anti-racism. In C. E.James (Ed.), *Perspectives on racism and the human service sector: A case for change* (pp. 196–208). Toronto: University of Toronto Press.

Moffat, K., & Miehls, D. (1999). Development of student identity: Evolution from neutrality to subjectivity. *Journal of Teaching in Social Work, 19*(1/2), 65–76.

Montagu, A. (1965/2001). Man's most dangerous myth: The fallacy of race. In E. Cashmore & J. Jennings (Eds.), *Racism: Essential readings* (pp. 98–110). Thousand Oaks, CA: Sage.

Monteith, M. (1993). Self-regulation of prejudiced responses: Implications for progress in prejudice-reduction efforts. *Journal of Personality and Social Psychology, 65*(3), 469–485.

Monteith, M.J., Sherman, J.W., & Devine, P.G. (1998). Suppression as a stereotype control strategy. *Personality and Social Psychology Review, 2*(1), 63–82.

Montgomery, D. (1993). *Citizen worker: The experience of workers with democracy and the free market during the nineteenth century*. New York: Cambridge University Press.

Moraga, R., Silnutzer, R., Tincknell, R., & Tolles, K. (1985). *From true stories to nonsense rhymes: Oral traditions of Holyoke*. Holyoke, MA: Holyoke Public Schools.

Morales, E.S. (1990). Ethnic minority families and minority gays and lesbians. *Marriage and Family Review, 14* (3/4). 212–239.

Morales, E.S. (1996). Gender roles among Latino gay and bisexual men. In J. Laird and Robert-Jay Green (Eds.), *Lesbians and gays in couples and families: A handbook for therapists* (pp. 272–297). San Francisco: Jossey-Bass.

Morawska, E. (2001). Immigrant-black dissensions in American cities: An argument for multiple explanations. In E. Anderson & D.S. Massey (Eds.), *Problem of the century: Racial stratification in the United States* (pp. 47–96). New York: Russell Sage Foundation.

Morgan, M.C. (1962). *Skid road: An informal portrait of Seattle*. New York: Viking.

Moskowitz, G.B., Gollwitzer, P.M., Wasel, W., & Schaal, B. (1999). Preconscious control of stereotype activation through chronic egalitarian goals. *Journal of Personality and Social Psychology 77*(1), 167–184.

Muhammad, D., Davis, A., Lui, M., & Leondar-Wright, B. (2004). *The state of the dream 2004: Enduring disparities in black and white*. Boston: United for a Fair Economy.

Muldoon, B. (1997, March). Deep listening resolves conflict. *Personal Transformations*, pp. 34–37.

Myers, L.J., Speight, S.L., Highlen, P.A., Cox, C.I., Reynolds, A.L., Adams, E.M., & Hanley, P. (1991). Identity development and worldview: Toward an optimal conceptualization. *Journal of Counseling and Development, 70*, 54–63.

National Academy of Sciences. (2002). *Unequal treatment: Confronting racial and ethnic disparities in health care*. Washington, DC: Author.

National Association of Social Workers. (1999). National Association of Social Workers code of ethics. Washington, DC: Author.

Norman, A.J. (1994). Black–Korean relations: From desperation to dialogue, or from shouting and shooting to sitting and talking. *Journal of Multicultural Social Work, 3*(2), 87–99.

O'Connor, A. (2001). Understanding inequality in the late twentieth-century metropolis: New perspectives on the enduring racial divide. In A. O'Connor, C. Tilly, & L.D. Bobo (Eds.), *Urban inequality: Evidence from four cities* (pp. 1–33). New York: Russell Sage Foundation.

O'Donoghue, M. (2004). Racial and ethnic identity development in white mothers of biracial, black–white chidren. *Affilia, 19*(1), 68–84.

Ojito, M. (2000, June 5). Best of friends, worlds apart. *New York Times*, A1.

Oliver, M.L., & Shapiro, T.M. (2000). A sociology of wealth and racial inequality. In M. Adams, W.J. Blumenfeld, R. Casteneda, H.W. Hackman, M.L. Peters, & X. Zuniga (Eds.), *Readings for diversity and social justice: An anthology on racism, anti-Semitism, sexism, heteorsexism, ableism, and classism* (pp. 402–406). New York: Routledge.

Oliver, P.E. (2001). Racial disparities in imprisonment: Some basic information. *Focus, 21*(3), 28–31.

Omatsu, G. (2000). Racism or solidarity? Unions and Asian immigrant workers. In M. Adams, W.J. Blumenfeld, R. Casteneda, H.W. Hackman, M.L. Peters, & X. Zuniga (Eds.), *Readings for diversity and social justice: An anthology on racism, anti-Semitism, sexism, heterosexism, ableism, and classism* (pp. 407–412). New York: Routledge.

Omi, M. (2001). The changing meaning of race. In N. Smelser, W.J. Wilson, & F. Mitchell (Eds.), *America becoming: Racial trends and their consequences* (Vol. 1, pp. 243–263). Washington, DC: National Academy Press.

Omi, M., & Winant, H. (1994). *Racial formation in the U.S.: From the 1960s to the 1990s* (2nd ed.). New York: Routledge.

Ong Hing, B. (1998). Don't give me your tired, your poor: Conflicted immigrant stories and welfare reform. *Harvard Civil Rights–Civil Liberties Law Review, 33*(1), 159–182.

Overton, S.A. (2005). Stealing liberty. *The Crisis, 112*(1), 15–18.

Oshinsky, D.M. (1996). *"Worse than slavery": Parchman Farm and the ordeal of Jim Crow justice.* New York: Free Press.

Paden, J.N., & Singer, P.W. (2003, May/June). America slams its door (on its foot): Washington's destructive new visa policies. *Foreign Affairs*, p. 8.

Padilla, Y.C. (1997). Immigrant policy: Issues for social work practice. *Social Work, 42*(6), 595–606.

Parillo, V.N. (1996). *Diversity in America.* Thousand Oaks, CA: Pine Forge Press.

Park, Y., & Miller, J. (2006). The social ecology of Hurricane Katrina: Rewriting the discourse of natural disasters. *Smith Studies in Social Work, 76*(3), 9–24.

Parks, C.A., Hughes, T.L., & Matthews, A.K. (2004). Race/ethnicity and sexual orientation: Intersecting identities. *Cultural diversity and ethnic minority psychology, 10*(3), 241–254.

Patrick, J.J., Pious, R.M., & Ritchie, D.A. (2001). *The Oxford guide to the United States government.* New York: Oxford University Press.

Pelletiere, D. (2005, May/June). House of cards: The state of black housing. *The Crisis, 112*(3), 16–19.

Perez Foster, R.M. (1998). The clinician's cultural countertransference: The psychodynamics of culturally competent practice. *Clinical Social Work Journal, 26*(3), 253–270.

Perrin-Klinger, G. (2000). The integration of traumatic experiences: Culture and resources. In J.M. Violanti, D. Patton, & C. Dunning (Eds.), *Posttraumatic stress intervention* (pp. 43–64). Springfield, IL: Charles Thomas Pub.

Peterson, F.K. (1991). Issues of race and ethnicity in supervision: Emphasizing who you are, not what you know. *Clinical Supervisor, 9*(1), 15–31.

Pfuetze, P.E. (1954). *Self, society and existence.* New York: Harper Torch Books.

Phillips, K., (1990). *The politics of rich and poor: Wealth and the American electorate in the Reagan aftermath.* NY: Random House.

Phinney, J. (1989). Stages of ethnic identity development in minority group adolescents. *Journal of Early Adolescence, 9*, 34–49.

Phinney, J. (1992). The multigroup ethnic identity measure: A new scale for use with diverse groups. *Journal of Adolescent Research, 7*(2), 156–176.

Phinney, J. (1993). A three-stage model of ethnic identity development. In M.E. Bernal & G.P. Knight (Eds.), *Ethnic identity: Formation and transmission among Hispanics and other minorities* (pp. 61–79). Albany: State University of New York Press.

Phinney, J., & Kohatsu, E.L. (1999). Ethnic and racial identity development and mental health. In J. Schulenberg, J.L. Maggs, & K. Hurelmann (Eds.), *Health risks and developmental transitions during adolescence* (pp. 420–443). New York: Cambridge University Press.

Pierce, C., Carew, J., Pierce-Gonzalez, D., & Wills, D. (1978). An experiment in racism: T.V. commercials. In C. Pierce (Ed.), *Television and education* (pp. 62–88). Beverly Hills, CA: Sage.

Pinderhughes, E. (1989). *Understanding race, ethnicity, and power: The key to efficacy in clinical practice.* New York: Free Press.

Piven, F.F., & Cloward, R.A. (1993). *Regulating the poor: The functions of public welfare* (updated edition). New York: Vintage.

Poe-Yamagata, E., & Jones, M.A. (2000). *And justice for some.* Washington, DC: Building Blocks for Youth.

Polikoff, A. (2004). Racial inequality and the black ghetto. *Poverty & Race, 13*(6), 1–2, 8–12.

Ponterotto, J.G. (1988). Racial consciousness development among white counselor trainees: A stage model. *Journal of Multicultural Counseling and Development, 16*, 146–156.

Poussaint, A. (2000). *Lay my burden down: Unraveling suicide and the mental health burden of African Americans.* Boston: Beacon Press.

Poston, W.S.C. (1990). The bi-racial identity development model: A needed addition. *Journal of Counseling and Development, 69,* 152–155.

Powell, J.A. (1999). Achieving racial justice: What's sprawl got to do with it? *Poverty & Race, 8*(5), 3–5.

Price, H. (1999, Dec. 18). Speech to the National Urban League [online]. ftp://ftp.nul.org/pub/bigotry.txt

Putnam, R.D. (2000). *Bowling alone: The collapse and revival of American community.* New York: Simon and Schuster.

Quadagno, J. (1994). *The color of welfare: How racism undermined the war on poverty.* New York: Oxford University Press.

Quintero-Somaini, A., & Quirindongo, M. (2004). *Hidden ranger: Environmental health threats and the Latino community.* New York: National Resources Defense Council.

Ransford, E. (2000). Two hierarchies. In M. Adams, W.J. Blumenfeld, R. Castaneda, H.W. Hackman, M.L. Peters, & X. Zuniga (Eds.), *Readings for diversity and social justice: An anthology on racism, anti-Semitism, sexism, heterosexism, ableism, and classism* (pp. 412–418). New York: Routledge.

Raskin, J. (2004). From slave republic to constitutional democracy: The continuing struggle for the right to vote. *Poverty & Race, 13*(6), 3–4, 13–18.

Reid, P.T., & Comas-Diaz, L. (1990). Gender and ethnicity: Perspectives on dual status. *Sex Roles, 22*(7/8), 397–408.

Reiss, D. (1981). *The family's construction of reality.* Cambridge, MA: Harvard University Press.

Renner, K.E., & Moore, T. (2004). The more things change, the more they stay the same: the elusive search for racial equity in higher education. *Analyses of Social Issues and Public Policy, 4*(1), 227–241.

Reynolds, A.L., & Pope, R.L. (1991). The complexities of diversity: Exploring multiple oppressions. *Journal of Counseling and Development, 70,* 174–180.

Ridley, C.R. (1995). *Overcoming unintentional racism in counseling and therapy.* Thousand Oaks, CA: Sage.

Roberts, D. (2002, Fall). Racial harm. *Colorlines,* pp. 19–20.

Roberts, S. (1995, June 18). The greening of America's black middle class. *New York Times,* Sec. 4, pp. 1, 4.

Rockquemore, K.A., & Brunsma, D.L. (2004). Negotiating racial identity: Biracial women and interactional validation. *Women & Therapy, 27*(1/2), 85–102.

Rogers, C. (1951). *Client-centered therapy: Its current implications, practice and theory.* Boston: Houghton Mifflin.

Roland, A. (1996). *Cultural pluralism and psychoanalysis: The Asian and North American experience.* New York: Routledge

Roland, A. (2003). Identity, self, and individualism in multicultural perspective. In E.P. Salett & D.R. Koslow (Eds.), *Race, ethnicity and self: Identity in Multicultural Perspective* (2nd ed., pp. 3–15). Washington, DC: National Multicultural Institute.

Rollock, D., & Gordon, E.W. (2000). Racism and mental health in the 21st century: Perspectives and parameters. *American Journal of Orthopsychiatry, 70*(1), 5–13.

Rosenbaum, J.E. (1995). Changing the geography of opportunity by expanding residential choice: Lessons from the Gautreaux program. *Housing Policy Debate, 6*(1), 231–269.

Rosenbaum, J.E., Popkin, S.J., Kaufman, J.E., & Rusin, J. (1991). Social integration of low-income black adults in middle-class white suburbs. *Social Problems, 38*(4), 448–461.

Ruiz, V.L. (2000). Color coded. *National Forum, 80*(2), 16–20.

Sabnani, H.B., Ponterotto, J.G., & Borodovsky, L.G. (1991). White racial identity development and cross-cultural counselor training: A stage model. *Counseling Psychologist, 19,* 76–102.

Sabol, W.J., & Lynch, J.P. (1997). *Crime policy report: Did getting tough on crime pay?* Washington, DC: Urban Institute.

Sacks, K.B. (1996). How did Jews become white folks? In S. Gregory & R.Sanjek (Eds.), *Race* (pp. 78–102). New Brunswick, NJ: Rutgers.

Saleebey, D. (2002). *The strengths perspective in social work practice* (3rd ed.). Boston: Allyn & Bacon.

Sampson, R.J., Morenoff, J.D., & Earls, F. (1999). Beyond social capital: Spatial dynamics of collective efficacy for children. *American Sociological Review, 64,* 633–660.

Sampson, R.J., Raudenbush, S., & Earls, F. (1997). Neighborhoods and violent crime: A multilevel study of collective efficacy. *Science, 277,* 918–924.

Schiller, B.R. (1998). *The economics of poverty and discrimination* (7th ed.). Upper Saddle River, NJ: Prentice Hall.

Schmader, T., Major, B., & Gramzow, R.H. (2001). Coping with ethnic stereotypes in the academic domain: Perceived injustice and psychological disengagement. *Journal of Social Issues, 57*(1), 93–111.

Segal, B.S. (Ed.) (1966). *Racial and ethnic relations: Selected readings.* New York: Thomas W. Crowell.

Seidman, I.E. (1991). *Interviewing for qualitative research.* New York: Teachers College Press.

Sellers, R.M., & Shelton, J.N. (2003). The role of racial identity in perceived racial discrimination. *Journal of Personality and Social Psychology, 84*(5), 1079–1092.

Sellers, R.M., Smith, M.A., Shelton, N., Rowley, S.A.J., & Chavous, T.M. (1998). Multidimensional model of racial identity: A reconceptualization of African American racial identity. *Personality and Social Psychology Review, 2*(1), 18–39.

Sengupta, S. (2000, Nov. 3). Felony costs voting rights for a lifetime in 9 states. *New York Times,* A18.

Sennett, R., & Cobb, J. (1972). *The hidden injuries of class.* New York: Knopf.

Sentencing Project. (2004, May). *New prison figures demonstrate need for comprehensive reform.* Washington, DC: Author.

Shapiro, T.M. (2004). *The hidden cost of being African American: How wealth perpetuates inequality.* New York: Oxford.

Shelton, J.N., & Richeson, J.A. (2005). Intergroup contact and pluralistic ignorance. *Journal of personality and social psychology, 88*(1), 91–107.

Shipler, D. (1997). *A country of strangers: Blacks and whites in America.* New York: Knopf.

Shorris, E. (1992). *Latinos: A biography of the people.* New York: W.W. Norton & Co.

Simpson, G.E., & Yinger, J.M. (1953). *Racial and cultural minorities: An analysis of prejudice and discrimination.* New York: Harper & Brothers.

Simson, E. (2002). *Justice denied: How felony disenfranchisement laws undermine American democracy.* Washington, DC: Americans for Democratic Action Education Fund.

Skillings, J.H., & Dobbins, J.E. (1991). Racism as a disease: Etiology and treatment implications. *Journal of Counseling and Development. 70*(1), 206–212.

Smith, E.J. (1991). Ethnic identity development: Toward the development of a theory within the context of majority/minority status. *Journal of Counseling and Development, 70,* 181–188.

Solomon, R.P. (2000). Exploring cross-race dyad partnerships in learning to teach. *Teachers College Record, 102*(6), 953–979.

Solorzano, D., Ceja, M., & Yosso, T. (2000). Critical race theory, racial microaggressions, and campus racial climate: The experiences of African American college students. *Journal of Negro Education, 69*(1/2), 60–73.

Squires, G.D. (1999, Jan./Feb.). The indelible color line. *American Prospect, 42,* 67–70.

Stannard, D.E. (1992). *American holocaust: The conquest of the New World.* New York: Oxford.

Staples, B. (1999, Dec. 19). Unearthing a riot. *New York Times Magazine,* 64–69.

Staub, E. (2001). Individual and group identities in genocide and mass killing. In R.D. Ashmore, L. Jussim, & D. Wilder (Eds.), *Social identity, intergroup conflict, and conflict resolution* (pp. 159–184). New York: Oxford University Press.

Steakley, L., Rubin, D.K., & Reina, P. (2004, Dec. 6). After 9/11, overseas find foreigners need not apply; Visa application hurdles start to ease but long-term impacts loom. *Engineering News-Record, 253*(22), 28.

Steinberg, S. (2001). *The ethnic myth: race, ethnicity and class in America* (3rd ed.) Boston: Beacon Press.

Steinhorn, L., & Diggs-Brown, B. (1999, Nov./Dec.). By the color of our skin: The illusion of integration and the reality of race. *Poverty & Race, 8*(6), 1–5.

Stephan, W.G., & Finlay, K. (1999). The role of empathy in improving intergroup relations. *Journal of Social Issues, 55*(4), 729–743.

Stets, J.E., & Burke, P.J. (2000). Identity theory and social identity theory. *Social Psychology Quarterly, 63*(3), 224–237.

Stoll, M.A. (2004). *African Americans and the color line.* New York: Russell Sage Foundation.

Stone, D., Patton, B., & Heen, S. (1999). *Difficult conversations: How to discuss what matters most.* New York: Viking.

Study Circles Resource Center. (1997). *Facing the challenge of racism and race relations: Democratic dialogue and action for stronger communities* (3rd ed.). Pomfret, CT: Author.

Study Circles Resource Center. (1998). Year 1—1997. *A report on the focus groups.* Pomfret, CT: Author.

Sue, D.W., Carter, R.T., Casas, J.M., Fouad, N.A., Ivey, A.E., Jensen, M., LaFromboise, T., Manese, J.E., Ponterotto, J.G., & Vazquez-Nutall, E. (1998). *Multicultural counseling competencies: Individual and organizational development.* Thousand Oaks, CA: Sage Publications.

Sue, D.W., & Sue, D. (1990). *Counseling the culturally different: Theory and practice* (2nd ed.). New York: Wiley and Sons.

Sue, D.W., & Sue, D. (2003). *Counseling the culturally diverse: Theory and practice* (4th ed.). New York: Wiley.

Sullivan, M. (1989). *Getting paid: Youth, crime and work in the inner city.* Ithaca, NY: Cornell University Press.

Tajfel, H. (1981). *Social identity and intergroup relations.* London: Cambridge University Press.

Takaki, R. (1987). The metaphysics of civilization: Indians and the Age of Jackson. In R. Takaki (Ed.), *From different shores: Perspectives on race and ethnicity in America* (pp. 54–68). New York: Oxford.

Takaki, R. (1993). *A different mirror: A history of multi-cultural America.* Boston: Little, Brown.

Tatum, B. (1997). *"Why are all the black kids sitting together in the cafeteria?" and other conversations about race.* New York: Basic Books.

Taylor, M.C. (1998). How white attitudes vary with the racial composition of local populations: Numbers count. *American Sociological Review, 63,* 512–535.

Taylor, R. (1997). The changing meaning of race in the social sciences: Implications for social work practice. *Smith Studies in Social Work, 67*(3), 277–298.

Taylor, S. H. (1995). *The sweeter the juice: A family memoir in black and white.* New York: Touchstone.

Templegrove Action Research Limited. (1996). *Public discussions on aspects of sectarian division in Derry Londonderry.* Derry Londonderry, Northern Ireland: Author.

Tervalon, M., & Murray-Garcia, J. (1997). Cultural humility versus cultural competence: A critical distinction in defining physician training outcomes in multicultural education. *Journal of Health Care for the Poor and Underserved, 9*(2), 117–125.

Thomas, L. (1994). Group autonomy and narrative identity: Blacks and Jews. In P. Berman (Ed.), *Blacks and Jews: Alliances and arguments.* New York: Delacorte Press.

Thompson, M., & Sekaquaptewa, D. (2002). When being different is detrimental: Solo status and the performance or women and racial minorities. *Analysis of Social Issues and Public Policy, 2*(1), 183–203.

Tilly, C. (1998). *Durable inequality.* Berkeley: University of California Press.

Trattner, W.I. (1999). *From poor law to welfare state: A history of social welfare in America* (6th ed.). New York: Free Press.

Triandafyllidou, A. (1998). National identity and the 'other'. *Ethnic and Racial Studies, 21*(4), 593–612.

True Colors (video recording) (1991), Northbrook, IL: MTI Film and Video.

Urban League. (2002). *The state of Black America, 2002. New York: Author.*

Urban League. (2004). *The state of Black America, 2004. New York: Author.*

U.S. Census Bureau. (2000). *Statistical abstract of the United States.* Washington, DC: U.S. Government Printing Office.

Valverde, L.A. (1998). Future strategies and actions. Creating multicultural higher education campuses. In L.A. Valverde & L.A. Castenell (Eds.), *The multicultural campus* (pp. 19–29). Walnut Creek, CA: Altamira Press.

Vander Zanden, J.W. (1963). *American minority relations: The sociology of race and ethnic groups.* New York: Ronald Press.

van Dijk, T.A. (1995). Elite discourse and the reproduction of racism. In R.K. Whillock & D. Slayden (Eds.), *Hate speech* (pp. 1–27). Thousand Oaks, CA: Sage Publications.

Volkan, V.D. (1988). *The need to have enemies and allies: From clinical practice to international relationships.* Northvale, NJ: Jason Aronson.

Wade, J.C. (1993). Institutional racism: An analysis of the mental health system. *American Journal of Orthopsychiatry, 63*(4), 536–544.

Wah, L.M. (1994). *The color of fear: A film.* Berkeley, CA: Stir-Fry Productions.

Walsh, M.W. (2000, Sept. 3). Where G.E. falls short: Diversity at the top. *New York Times,* Sec. 3, p. 1.

Wasserman, I.C., & Doran, R.F. (1999). Creating inclusive learning communities. In A.L. Cooke, M. Brazzel, A.S. Craig, & B. Greig (Eds), *Reading book for human relations training* (8th ed.) (pp. 307–310). Alexandria, VA: NTL Institute for Applied Behavioral Science.

Waxman, H., et al. (2001, July 9). *Income and racial disparities in the undercount in the 2000 Presidential election.* Washington, DC: U.S. House of Representatives.

Weitzer, R., & Tuch, S.A. (2004). Race and perceptions of police misconduct. *Social Problems, 51*(3), 305–325.

Wellman, D. (2000). From evil to illness: Medicalizing racism. *American Journal of Orthopsychiatry, 70*(1), 28–32.

Western, B. (2001). Incarceration, unemployment and inequality. *Focus, 21*(3), 32–36.

Westin, A. (2001). The color of ratings. *Brill's Content, 4*(3), 82–85, 129–131.

Whillock, R.K. (1995). The use of hate as a stratagem for achieving political and social goals. In R.K. Whillock & D. Slayden (Eds.), *Hate speech* (pp. 28–54). Thousand Oaks, CA: Sage Publications.

Wilkinson, D.Y. (1995). Gender and social inequality: The prevailing significance of race. *Daedalus, 124*(1), 167–178.

Williams, D.R. (2001). Racial variations in adult health status: Patterns, paradoxes, and prospects. In N.J. Smelser, W.J. Wilson, & F. Mitchell (Eds.), *America becoming: Racial trends and their consequences* (Vol. 2, pp. 371–410). Washington, DC: National Academy Press.

Wills, G. (2003, Nov. 6). The Negro President. *New York Review of Books, 50*(17).

Wilson, J. (1998). *The earth shall weep: A history of Native America.* New York: Grove.

Wilson, W.J. (1973). *Power, racism and privilege: Race relations in theoretical and sociohistorical perspectives* (pp. 47–67). New York: Free Press.

Wilson, W.J. (1987). *The truly disadvantaged: The inner-city, the underclass and public policy.* Chicago: University of Chicago.

Wilson, W.J. (1995). *When work disappears: The world of the new urban poor.* New York: Knopf.

Winant, H. (1997). Racial dualism at century's end. In W. Lubiano (Ed.), *The House that Race Built: Black Americans, U.S. Terrain* (pp. 87–115). New York: Pantheon.

Winant, H. (1998). Racism today: Continuity and change in the post-civil rights era. *Ethnic and Racial Studies, 21*(4), 755–766.

Wolff, E.N. (2001). *Public policy brief 66: Racial wealth disparities; Is the gap closing?* Annandale-on-Hudson, NY: Levy Economics Institute of Bard College.

Woods, M.E., & Hollis, F. (2000). *Casework: A psychosocial therapy.* Boston: McGraw Hill.

Woody, D.J., & Green, R. (2001). The influence of race/ethnicity and gender on psychological well-being. *Journal of Ethnic and Cultural Diversity in Social Work, 9*(3/4), 151–166.

Yamamoto, E. (1999). *Interracial justice: Conflict and reconciliation in post-civil rights America.* New York: NYU Press.

Yassen, J. (1995). Preventing secondary traumatic stress disorder. In C.R. Figley (Ed.), *Compassion fatigue: Coping with secondary traumatic stress disorder in those who treat the traumatized* (pp. 178–208). New York: Brunner/Mazel.

Yeh, C.J., & Hwang, M.Y. (2000). Interdependence in ethnic identity and self: Implications for theory and practice. *Journal of Counseling and Development, 78*, 420–429.

Yeskel, F., & Leonard-Wright, B. (1997). Classism curriculum design. In M. Adams, L.A. Bell, & P. Griffin (Eds.), *Teaching for diversity and social justice: A sourcebook* (pp. 231–260). New York: Routledge.

Yinger, J. (2001). Housing discrimination and residential segregation as causes of poverty. *Focus, 21*(2), 51–55.

Zhou, M. (2001). Contemporary immigration and the dynamics of race and ethnicity. In N. Smelser, W.J. Wilson, & F. Mitchell (Eds.), *America becoming: Racial trends and their consequences* (Vol. 1, pp. 200–242). Washington, DC: National Academy Press.

Zinn, H. (1980). *A people's history of the United States.* New York: Harper & Row.

Zuniga, X., & Nagda, B.A. (2001). Design considerations in intergroup dialogue. In D. Schoem &. S. Hurtado (Eds.), *Intergroup dialogue: Deliberative democracy in school, college, community and workplace* (pp. 306–327). Ann Arbor: University of Michigan Press.

Zuniga, X., Nagda, B.A., & Sevig, T.D. (2002). Intergroup dialogues: An educational model for cultivating engagement across differences. *Equity and Excellence in Education, 35*(1), 7–17.

Zwerdling, D. (2005, March 2). Electronic anklets track asylum seekers in U.S. *Morning Edition.* Washington, DC: National Public Radio.

INDEX